WHO'S
RUNNING AMERICA?

FIFTH EDITION

WHO'S RUNNING AMERICA?
THE BUSH ERA

Thomas R. Dye
Florida State University

PRENTICE HALL
Englewood Cliffs, New Jersey 07632

Library of Congress Cataloging-in-Publication Data

Dye. Thomas R.
  Who's running America? : the Bush era / Thomas R. Dye.—5th ed.
    p.   cm.
  Includes bibliographical references.
  ISBN 0-13-958224-X
  1. Elite (Social sciences)—United States. 2. United States—
Politics and government—1989– 3. Power (Social sciences)
4. Leadership.   I. Title.
HN90.E4D93 1990
305.5'52'0973—dc20

89-37333
CIP

Editorial/production supervision
  and interior design: Virginia L. McCarthy
Cover design: Wanda Lubelska Design
Manufacturing buyer: Robert Anderson

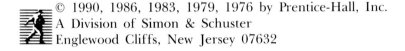

Printed in the United States of America
10 9 8 7 6 5 4 3 2 1

ISBN 0-13-958224-X

Prentice-Hall International (UK) Limited, *London*
Prentice-Hall of Australia Pty. Limited, *Sydney*
Prentice-Hall Canada Inc., *Toronto*
Prentice-Hall Hispanoamericana, S.A., *Mexico*
Prentice-Hall of India Private Limited, *New Delhi*
Prentice-Hall of Japan, Inc., *Tokyo*
Simon & Schuster Asia Pte. Ltd., *Singapore*
Editora Prentice-Hall do Brasil, Ltda., *Rio de Janeiro*

CONTENTS

CHAPTER THREE
THE GOVERNING CIRCLES   64

CHAPTER FOUR
THE NEWSMAKERS   116

CHAPTER FIVE
THE CIVIC ESTABLISHMENT   138

PREFACE

Who's Running America? has *not* been supported by any grant or contract from any institution, public or private. It grew out of a graduate seminar "Research on Power and Elites" at Florida State University in the spring of 1972. Biographical data for over 5,000 members of various institutional elites was painstakingly collected and coded by students. These computerized biographies constituted the original data base for the continuing project *Who's Running America?* The data base was revised in 1980–81 by students at Florida State University, and data on over 7,000 new institutional elites was collected and coded.

Two articles based on this data from the early 1970s were published in social science journals:

> Thomas R. Dye, Eugene R. DeClercq, and John W. Pickering, "Concentration, Specialization, and Interlocking among Institutional Elites," *Social Science Quarterly* (June 1973), pp. 8–28.
> Thomas R. Dye and John W. Pickering, "Governmental and Corporate Elites: Convergence and Specialization," *Journal of Politics* (November 1974), pp. 900–25.

We are indebted to a number of commentators who wrote to us before and after publication of these articles, including scholars G. William Domhoff, Suzanne Keller, John Walton, Robert Lineberry, Harmon Zeigler, and Charles Bonjean. Professor Gordon Bowen, Mary Baldwin

College, and Professor Kenneth W. Grundy, Case Western Reserve University, reviewed the manuscript for this Fifth Edition.

The First Edition of this book was published in 1976 and described national leadership in the Nixon-Ford years. The First Edition was subtitled *Institutional Leadership in the United States.*

The Second Edition of this volume, *The Carter Years*, reflected changes in national leadership which occurred with the election of Jimmy Carter to the presidency and the advent of a new Democratic administration.

The Third Edition of this book, *The Reagan Years*, involved the collection of an entire new data base for national leaders in 1980–81. Special topics were addressed in several articles in professional journals, including:

> Thomas R. Dye, "Obligarchic Tendencies in National Policy-Making: The Role of the Private Policy-Planning Organization," *Journal of Politics*, 40 (May 1978), 309–31.
>
> Thomas R. Dye and Julie Strickland, "Women at the Top," *Social Science Quarterly*, 63 (March 1982).

The Fourth Edition, *The Conservative Years*, discussed changes in national leadership during the 1980s. Additional research on corporate ownership was examined in professional journals:

> Thomas R. Dye, "Who Owns America?" *Social Science Quarterly*, 64 (December 1983), 862–70.
>
> Thomas R. Dye, "Strategic Ownership Positions in U.S. Industry and Banking," *American Journal of Economics and Sociology*, 44 (January 1985), 9–22.

The Fifth Edition, *The Bush Years*, updates both corporate and governmental leadership in 1990 and incorporates much of the new research literature on American elites. Additional detailed analysis of institutional power can be found in:

> Thomas R. Dye, "Organizing Power for Policy Planning," in *Power Elites and Organizations*, eds. G. William Domhoff and Thomas R. Dye (Beverly Hills: Sage, 1987).

This volume is divided into three parts. Part I, Power in American Society, sets forth our questions for research, defines terms and concepts, and explains our method of identifying the nation's institutional elite. Part II, Institutional Leadership in America, describes concentration of power in industry, banking, insurance, utilities, government, the news media, the law, investment finance, foundations, civic and cultural organizations, and universities. It also describes the type of persons who occupy top institutional leadership positions in these various sectors of society; it "names names," and in so doing, makes use of brief biographical sketches. These sketches are designed to give us a general introduction to the characteristics of elites: the schools they attend, their early careers, their records of achievement, and the multiple positions of leadership they occupy. These sketches are updated with each new edition of the book. These sketches are derived from a wide variety of sources: *Who's Who in America, Current Biography, Forbes, Fortune, Congressional Quarterly*, and individual articles and books.[1] The sketches in Part II are designed to pave the way for more systematic analysis of biographical data, which follows in Part III.

Part III, The Structure of Institutional Elites, is a systematic investigation of interlocking and specialization among elites, overlapping elite membership, recruitment paths, socioeconomic backgrounds, previous experience, racial and sexual bias, club memberships and life styles, attitudes and opinions, competition and consensus, factionalism, and patterns of interaction in policy-making. Part III relies heavily on the computerized biographical files which we compiled at Florida State University on thousands of top institutional elites in 1970–71 and in 1980–81. What is suggested in a general way about characteristics of America's elites in Part II is subject to more careful systematic analysis in Part III.

The decision to "name names" was carefully considered. We know that occupants of top institutional positions change over time, and that some of our informaiton will be out of date by the time of publicaiton. And with thousands of names, some mistakes are inevitable. However, the biographical sketches provide "flesh and bones" to the statistical analysis; they "personalize" the numbers and percentages in our research. The people who run America *are* real people, and we know of no better way to impress this fact upon our readers.

THOMAS R. DYE
Tallahassee, Florida

---

[1]*Who's Who in America*, published biannually by Marquis Who's Who, Inc., Chicago; *Current Biography*, published monthly and annually by H.L. Wilson Co., New York; *Forbes*, published biweekly by Malcom S. Forbes, New York; *Fortune*, published monthly by Time-Life, Inc., New York; *Congressional Quarterly Weekly Report*, published weekly by Congressional Quarterly, Inc., Washington, D.C.

CHAPTER ONE
ELITISM IN A DEMOCRACY

Great power in America is concentrated in a handful of people. A few thousand individuals out of 240 million Americans decide about war and peace, wages and prices, consumption and investment, employment and production, law and justice, taxes and benefits, education and learning, health and welfare, advertising and communication, life and leisure. In all societies—primitive and advanced, totalitarian and democratic, capitalist and socialist—only a few people exercise great power. This is true whether or not such power is exercised in the name of "the people."

Who's Running America? is about those at the top of the institutional structure in America—who they are, how much power they wield, how they came to power, and what they do with it. In a modern, complex industrial society, power is concentrated in large institutions: corporations, banks, utilities, insurance companies, broadcasting networks, the White House, Congress and the Washington bureaucracy, the military establishment, the prestigious law firms, the large investment houses, the foundations, the universities, and the private policy-planning organizations. The people at the top of these institutions—the presidents and principal officers and directors, the senior partners, the governing trustees, the congressional committee chairpersons, the Cabinet and senior

1

presidential advisers, the Supreme Court Justices, the four-star generals and admirals—are the objects of our study in this book.

We want to ask: Who occupies the top positions of authority in America? How concentrated or dispersed is power in this nation? How do these institutional leaders attain their positions? What are their backgrounds, attitudes, and goals? What relationships exist among these people of power? How much cohesion or competition characterizes their relationships? Do they agree or disagree on crucial issues confronting the nation? How do they go about making important decisions or undertaking new programs or policies?

We also want to ask about stability and change: Is America's leadership changing over time? Is there a true "changing of the guard" occurring at the top of the nation's institutional structure, or do top leaders today resemble those of a decade or more ago in terms of social origins, education, attitudes, and experiences? Is power gradually dispersing over time to larger and more diverse leadership groups, or do we find even greater concentrations of power today than years ago? Are women and blacks making significant inroads into top positions in America, or are "the higher circles" still nearly all male and all white?

THE INEVITABILITY OF ELITES

The *elite* are the few who have power in society; the *masses* are the many who do not. We shall call our national leaders "elites" because they possess formal authority over large institutions that shape the lives of all Americans.

America is by no means unique in its concentration of great power in the hands of a few. The universality of elites has been a prominent theme in the works of scholars throughout the ages. The Italian sociologist Vilfredo Pareto put it succinctly: "Every people is governed by an elite, by a chosen element of the population."[1]

Traditional social theorizing about elites views them as essential, functional components of social organization. The necessity of elites derives from the general need for *order* in society. Whenever human beings find themselves living together, they establish a set of ordered relationships so that they can know how others around them will behave. Without ordered behavior, the concept of society itself would be impossible. Among these ordered relationships is the expectation that a few people will make decisions on behalf of the group. Even in primitive

[1]Vilfredo Pareto, *Mind and Society* (New York: Harcourt Brace Jovanovich, 1935), p. 246.

societies someone has to decide when the hunt will begin, how it will proceed, and what will be done with the catch.

Nearly two centuries ago Alexander Hamilton defended the existence of the elite by writing:

> All communities divide themselves into the few and the many. The first are the rich and well-born, the other the masses of people. The voice of the people has been said to be the voice of God; and however generally this maxim has been quoted and believed, it is not true in fact. The people are turbulent and changing, they seldom judge or determine right.[2]

The Italian political scientist Gaetano Mosca agreed:

> In all societies—from societies that are very underdeveloped and have largely attained the dawnings of civilization, down to the most advanced and powerful societies—two classes of people appear—a class that rules and a class that is ruled. The first class, always the less numerous, performs all of the political functions, monopolizes power, and enjoys the advantages that power brings, whereas the second, the more numerous class, is directed and controlled by the first, in a manner that is now more or less legal, now more or less arbitrary and violent.[3]

Contemporary social scientists have echoed the same theme. Sociologist Robert Lynd writes:

> It is the necessity in each society—if it is to be a society, not a rabble—to order the relations of men and their institutional ways of achieving needed ends. . . . Organized power exists—always and everywhere, in societies large or small, primitive or modern—because it performs the necessary function of establishing and maintaining the version of order by which a given society in a given time and place lives.[4]

Political scientists Harold Lasswell and Daniel Lerner are even more explicit: "The discovery that in all large-scale societies the decisions at any given time are typically in the hands of a small number of people confirms a basic fact: Government is always government by the few, whether in the name of the few, the one, or the many."[5]

Elitism is *not* a result of inadequate education of the masses or of poverty or of a "military-industrial complex" or of capitalist control of

[2]Alexander Hamilton, *Records of the Federal Convention* of 1787.

[3]Gaetano Mosca, *The Ruling Class* (New York: McGraw-Hill, 1939), p. 50.

[4]Robert Lynd, "Power in American Society," in *Problems of Power in American Society*, ed. Arthur Kornhauser (Detroit: Wayne State University Press, 1957), pp. 3–4.

[5]Harold Lasswell and Daniel Lerner, *The Comparative Study of Elites* (Stanford, Calif.: Stanford University Press, 1952), p. 7.

the mass media or of any special problem in society. The necessity for leadership in social organizations applies universally. Robert Michels, who as a student was active in socialist politics in Europe in the early 1900s, concluded reluctantly that elitism was *not* a product of capitalism. *All* large organizations—political parties, labor unions, governments— are oligarchies, even radical *socialist* parties. In Michels' words, "He who says organization says oligarchy." Michels explains his famous "iron law of oligarchy" as a characteristic of *any* social system.[6]

Thus, the elitist character of American society is not a product of political conspiracy, capitalist exploitation, or any specific malfunction of democracy. *All* societies are elitist. There cannot be large institutions without great power being concentrated within the hands of the few at the top of these institutions.

THE INSTITUTIONAL BASIS OF POWER

Power is not an attribute of individuals, but of social organizations. Power is the potential for control in society that accompanies certain roles in the social system. This notion reflects Max Weber's classic formulation of the definition of power:

> In general, we understand by "power" the *chance* of a number of men to realize their own will in a communal act even against the resistance of others who are participating in the action.[7]

"Chance" in this context means the opportunity or capacity for effecting one's will. Viewed in this fashion, power is not so much the *act* of control as the *potential to act*—the social *expectation* that such control is possible and legitimate—that defines power.

Power is simply the capacity or potential of persons in certain roles to make decisions that affect the conduct of others in the social system. Sociologist Robert O. Schultze puts it in these words:

> . . . a few have emphasized that *act as such* rather than the *potential to act* is the crucial aspect of power. It seems far more sociologically sound to accept a Weberian definition which stresses the potential to act. Power may thus be conceived as an inherently group-linked property, an attribute of social statuses rather than of individual persons. . . . Accordingly, power will denote the *capacity* or *potential* of persons *in certain statuses* to set

---

[6]Robert Michels, *Political Parties: A Sociological Study of the Oligarchical Tendencies of Modern Democracy* (1915) (New York: Free Press, 1962), p. 70.

[7]Hans Gerth and C. Wright Mill, eds., *From Max Weber* (New York: Oxford University Press, 1946), p. 180.

conditions, make decisions, and/or take actions which are determinative for the existence of others within a given social system.[8]

Thus, elites are people who occupy power roles in society. In a modern, complex society, these roles are institutionalized; the elite are the individuals who occupy positions of authority in large institutions. Authority is the expected and legitimate capacity to direct, manage, and guide programs, policies, and activities of the major institutions of society.

It is true, of course, that not all power is institutionalized. Power can be exercised in transitory and informal groups and in interpersonal interactions. Power is exercised, for example, when a mugger stops a pedestrian on the street and forces him to give up his wallet, or when a political assassin murders a President. But great power is found only in institutional roles. C. Wright Mills, a socialist critic of the structure of power in American society, observed:

> No one . . . can be truly powerful unless he has access to the command of major institutions, for it is over these institutional means of power that the truly powerful are, in the first instance, powerful.[9]

Adolf A. Berle, who spent a lifetime studying private property and the American corporation, was equally impressed with the institutional basis of power:

> Power is invariably organized and transmitted through institutions. Top power holders must work through existing institutions, perhaps extending or modifying them, or must at once create new institutions. There is no other way of exercising power—unless it is limited to the range of the power holder's fist or his gun.[10]

Individuals do not become powerful simply because they have particular qualities, valuable skills, burning ambitions, or sparkling personalities. These assets may be helpful in gaining positions of power, but it is the position itself that gives an individual control over the activities of other individuals. This relationship between power and institutional authority in modern society is described by Mills:

> If we took the one hundred most powerful men in America, the one hundred wealthiest, and the one hundred most celebrated away from the

[8]Robert O. Schultze, "The Bifurcation of Power in a Satellite City," in *Community Political Systems*, ed. Morris Janowitz (Glencoe: Free Press, 1961), p. 20.

[9]C. Wright Mills, *The Power Elite* (New York: Oxford University Press, 1956), p. 9.

[10]Adolph A. Berle, *Power* (New York: Harcourt Brace Jovanovich, 1967), p. 92.

institutional positions they now occupy, away from their resources of men and women and money, away from the media of mass communication . . . then they would be powerless and poor and uncelebrated. For power is not of a man. Wealth does not center in the person of the wealthy. Celebrity is not inherent in any personality. To be celebrated, to be wealthy, to have power, requires access to major institutions, for the institutional positions men occupy determine in large part their chances to have and to hold these valued experiences.[11]

Power, then, is an attribute of *roles* in a social system, not an attribute of individuals. People are powerful when they occupy positions of authority and control in social organizations. Once they occupy these positions, their power is felt as a result not only in their actions but in their failures to act as well. Both have great impact on the behaviors of others. Elites "are in positions to make decisions having major consequences. Whether they do or do not make such decisions is less important than the fact that they do occupy such pivotal positions: Their failure to act, their failure to make a decision, is itself an act that is often of greater consequence than the decisions they do make."[12]

People in top institutional positions exercise power whether they act overtly to influence particular decisions or not.[13] When the social, economic, and political values of elite groups, or, more importantly, the structures of the institutions themselves, limit the scope of decision-making to only those issues which do not threaten top elites, then power is being exercised. Political scientists Peter Bachrach and Morton S. Baratz refer to this phenomenon as *"non–decision-making."* A has power over B when he or she succeeds in suppressing issues that might in their resolution be detrimental to A's preferences. In short, the institutional structure of our society, and the people at the top of that structure, encourage the development of some kinds of public issues, but prevent other kinds of issues from ever being considered by the American public. Such "non–decision-making" provides still another reason for studying institutional leadership.

POWER AS DECISION-MAKING: AN ALTERNATIVE VIEW

It is our contention, then, that great power is institutionalized—that it derives from roles in social organizations and that individuals who occupy top institutional positions possess power whether they act directly

---

[11]Mills, *The Power Elite*, p. 9.

[12]Ibid., p. 4.

[13]Peter Bachrach and Morton S. Baratz, "Decisions and Non-Decisions," *American Political Science Review*, 57 (September 1963), 632–42.

to influence particular decisions or not. But these views—often labeled as "elitist"—are not universally shared among social scientists. We are aware that our institutional approach to power conflicts with the approach of many scholars who believe that power can be viewed only in a decision-making context.

This alternative approach to power—often labeled as "pluralist"—defines power as *active participation in decision-making.* Persons are said to have power *only* when they participate directly in particular decisions. Pluralist scholars would object to our presumption that people who occupy institutional positions and who have formal authority over economic, governmental, or social affairs necessarily have power. Pluralists differentiate between the "potential" for power (which is generally associated with top institutional positions) and "actual" power (which assumes active participation in decision-making). Political scientist Robert A. Dahl writes:

> Suppose a set of individuals in a political system has the following property: there is a high probability that if they agree on a key political alternative, and if they all act in some specified way, then that alternative will be chosen. We may say of such a group that it has a high *potential* for control. . . . But a *potential* for control is not, except in a peculiarly Hobbesian world, equivalent to *actual* control.[14]

Pluralists contend that the potential for power is not power itself. Power occurs in individual interactions: "A has power over B to the extent that he can get B to do something that B would not otherwise do."[15] We should not simply assume that power attaches to high office. Top institutional officeholders may or may not exercise power—their "power" depends upon their active participation in particular decisions. They may choose not to participate in certain decisions; their influence may be limited to specific kinds of decisions; they may be constrained by formal and informal checks on their discretion; they may be forced to respond to the demands of individuals or groups within or outside the institutions they lead; they may have little real discretion in their choice among alternative courses of action.

Pluralists would argue that research into institutional leadership can describe at best only the *potential* for control that exists within American society. They would insist that research on national leadership should proceed by careful examination of a series of important national decisions—that the individuals who took an active part in these decisions be identified and a full account of their decision-making behavior be

---

[14]Robert A. Dahl, "Critique of the Ruling Elite Model," *American Political Science Review,* 52 (June 1958), 66 [italics mine].

[15]Robert A. Dahl, "The Concept of Power," *Behavioral Science,* 2 (1957), 202.

obtained. Political scientist Nelson Polsby, a former student of Robert A. Dahl at Yale, reflects the interests of pluralists in observing specific decisions:

> How can one tell, after all, whether or not an actor is powerful unless some sequence of events, competently observed, attests to his power? If these events take place, then the power of the actor is not "potential" but actual. If these events do not occur, then what grounds have we to suppose that the actor is powerful?[16]

And, indeed, much of the best research and writing in political science has proceeded by studying specific cases in the uses of power.

Pluralism, of course, is more than a definition of power and a method of study—it is an integrated body of theory that seeks to reaffirm the fundamental democratic character of American society. Pluralism arose in response to criticisms of the American political system to the effect that individual participation in a large, complex, bureaucratic society was increasingly difficult. Traditional notions of democracy had stressed individual participation of all citizens in the decisions that shape their own lives. But it was clear to scholars of all persuasions that relatively few individuals in America have any *direct* impact on national decision-making.

Pluralism developed as an ideology designed to reconcile the *ideals* of democracy with the *realities* of a large-scale, industrial, technocratic society. Jack L. Walker writes that the "principal aim" of the pluralists "has been to make the theory of democracy more realistic, to bring it into closer correspondence with empirical reality. They are convinced that the classical theory does not account for 'much of the real machinery' by which the system operates."[17]

Pluralists recognize that an elite few, rather than the masses, rule America and that "it is difficult—nay impossible—to see how it could be otherwise in large political systems."[18] However, they reassert the essentially democratic character of America by arguing that competition between leadership groups protects the individual—that is, countervailing centers of power check each other and guard against abuse of power. Leadership groups are not closed; new groups can be formed and gain access to the political system. The existence of multiple leadership groups in society gives rise to a "polyarchy"—leaders who exercise power over some kinds of decisions do not necessarily exercise power

---

[16]Nelson Polsby, *Community Power and Political Theory* (New Haven: Yale University Press, 1963), p. 60.

[17]Jack L. Walker, "A Critique of the Elitist Theory of Democracy," *American Political Science Review,* 60 (June 1966), 286.

[18]Robert A. Dahl, "Power, Pluralism and Democracy," paper delivered at the Annual Meeting of the American Political Science Association, 1966, p. 3.

over other kinds of decisions. Finally, pluralists acknowledge that public policy may not be majority preference, but they claim it is the rough equilibrium of group influence and therefore a reasonable approximation of society's preferences.

IDENTIFYING POSITIONS OF POWER

We are committed in this volume to the study of institutional power. It is *not* our purpose to assert the superiority of our approach to power in America over the approaches recommended by others. We do *not* intend to debate the merits of pluralism or elitism as political philosophies. Abstract arguments over conceptualizations, definitions, and method of study already abound in the literature on power. Rather, working within an *institutional* paradigm, we intend to present systematic evidence about the concentration of resources in the nation's largest institutions, to find out who occupies top positions in these institutions, to explore interlocking and convergence among these top position-holders, to learn how they rose to their positions, to investigate the extent of their consensus or disagreement over the major issues confronting the nation, to explore the extent of competition and factionalism among various segments of the nation's institutional leadership, and to learn how institutional leadership interacts in national policy-making.

We hope to avoid elaborate theorizing about power, pluralism, and elitism. We propose to present what we believe to be interesting data on national institutional elites and to permit our readers to relate it to their own theories of power.

A great deal has been said about "the power elite," "the ruling class," "the liberal establishment," "the military-industrial complex," "the powers that be," and so on. But even though many of these notions are interesting and insightful, we never really encounter a systematic definition of precisely *who* these people are, how we can identify them, how they came to power, and what they do with their power.

Admittedly, the systematic study of power and elites is a frustrating task. Political scientists Herbert Kaufman and Victor Jones once observed:

> There is an elusiveness about power that endows it with an almost ghostly quality. It seems to be all around us, yet this is "sensed" with some sixth means of reception rather than with the five ordinary senses. We "know" what it is, yet we encounter endless difficulties in trying to define it. We can "tell" whether one person or group is more powerful than another, yet we cannot measure power. It is as abstract as time yet as real as a firing squad.[19]

[19]Herbert Kaufman and Victor Jones, "The Mystery of Power," *Public Administration Review*, 14 (Summer 1954), 205.

We agree that power is elusive and that elites are not easy to identify. Scholars have encountered great difficulty in finding a specific working definition of a national elite—a definition that can be used to actually identify powerful people. However, this is the necessary starting place for any serious inquiry into power in America.

Our first task, therefore, is to develop an operational *definition* of a national elite. We must formulate a definition that is consistent with our theoretical notions about the institutional basis of power and that will enable us to identify, by name and position, those individuals who possess great power in America.

Our institutional elites will be individuals who occupy *the top positions in the institutional structure of American society.* These are the individuals who possess the formal authority to formulate, direct, and manage programs, policies, and activities of the major corporate, governmental, legal, educational, civic, and cultural institutions in the nation. Our definition of a national elite, then, is consistent with the notion that great power in America resides in large institutions.

For purposes of analysis, we have divided American society into twelve sectors: (1) industrial corporations, (2) utilities and communications, (3) banking, (4) insurance, (5) investments, (6) mass media, (7) law, (8) education, (9) foundations, (10) civic and cultural organizations, (11) government, and (12) the military.

In the corporate sectors, our operational definition of the elite is *those individuals who occupy formal positions of authority in institutions which control more than half of the nation's total corporate assets.* Our procedure in identifying the largest institutions was to rank corporations by the size of their assets, and to cumulate these assets, moving from the top of the rankings down, until at least 50 percent of the nation's total assets in each sector are included (see Tables 2–1, 2–2, 2–3, and 2–4 in the next chapter). We also identified the nation's fifteen largest Wall Street investment firms (see Table 2–5). Then we identified by name the presidents, officer-directors, and directors of these corporations.

We also included in our definition of the elite *those individuals who occupy formal positions of authority in the mass media, the large prestigious New York and Washington law firms, the well-endowed private universities, the major philanthropic foundations, and the most influential civic and cultural organizations.* The identification of these institutions involved some subjective judgments. These judgments can be defended, but we recognize that other judgments could be made. In the *mass media,* we include the three television networks (CBS, ABC, and NBC); the *New York Times;* Time, Inc.; *Washington Post–Newsweek;* and fifteen newspaper empires which account for over one half of the nation's daily newspaper circulation. Because of the rapidly growing influence of the news media in America's elite structure, we have devoted a special chapter to "The Newsmakers."

Leadership in a variety of sectors is considered under the general heading of "The Civic Establishment." In *education,* we identify the twenty-five colleges and universities with the largest private endowment funds; we exclude public universities. Our twenty-five universities control two-thirds of all private endowment funds in higher education, and they are consistently ranked among the nation's most "prestigious" private colleges and universities. Our leadership group includes their presidents and trustees. Our selection of foundations is based on *The Foundation Directory's* data on the nation's fifty largest foundations. These foundations, and their trustees/directors, control over 40 percent of all foundation assets. Identifying top positions in the *law* was an even more subjective task. Our definition of positions of authority in the law includes the senior partners of twenty-five large and influential New York and Washington law firms. Top positions in *civic and cultural affairs* were identified by qualitative evaluations of the prestige and influence of various well-known organizations. The civic organizations are the Council on Foreign Relations, the Business Roundtable, the Brookings Institution, the Committee for Economic Development. The cultural organizations are the Metropolitan Museum of Art, the Museum of Modern Art, the Smithsonian Institution, Lincoln Center for the Performing Arts, and the John F. Kennedy Center for the Performing Arts. The members of the governing boards of trustees or directors were included in our definition of institutional leadership.

In the governmental sectors, the operational definition of the elite is *those individuals who occupy formal positions of authority in the major civilian and military bureaucracies of the national government.* Positions of authority in government were defined as the President and Vice-President; secretaries, undersecretaries, and assistant secretaries of all executive departments; senior White House presidential advisers and ambassadors-at-large; congressional committee chairpersons and ranking minority committee members in the House and Senate; House and Senate majority and minority party leaders and whips; Supreme Court Justices; and members of the Federal Reserve Board and the Council of Economic Advisers. Positions of authority in *the military* include both civilian offices and top military commands: secretaries, undersecretaries, and assistant secretaries of the Departments of the Army, Navy, and Air Force; all four-star generals and admirals in the Army, Navy, Air Force, and Marine Corps, including the chairman of the Joint Chiefs of Staff; and the chiefs of staff and vice-chiefs of staff of the Army and Air Force, the chief and vice-chief of Naval Operations, and the commanding officers of the major military commands.

Any effort to operationalize a concept as broad as a national institutional elite is bound to generate discussion over the inclusion or exclusion of specific sectors, institutions, or positions. (Why law, but not medicine? Why not law firms in Chicago, Houston, or Atlanta? Why not religious institutions or labor unions? Why not governors or mayors of big cities?) *Systematic* research on national elites is still in the exploratory stage, and there are no explicit guidelines. Our choices involve many subjective judgments. Let us see, however, what we can learn about concentration, specialization, and interlocking using the definitions above; perhaps other researchers can improve upon our attempt to operationalize this elusive notion of a national institutional elite. In the analysis to follow, we will present findings for our aggregate elites, and for specific sectors of these elites. Clearly, findings for specific sectors will be free of whatever bias might exist in the aggregate elite as a result of our inclusion or exclusion of specific sectors.

DIMENSIONS OF AMERICA'S ELITE

Our definition of a national institutional elite results in the identification of 7,314 elite positions:

CORPORATE SECTORS	NUMBER OF LEADERSHIP POSITIONS
1. Industrial corporations (100)	1,475
2. Utilities, communications, transportation (50)	668
3. Banks (50)	1,092
4. Insurance (50)	611
5. Investments (15)	479
Total	4,325
PUBLIC INTEREST SECTORS	
6. Mass media (18)	220
7. Education (25)	892
8. Foundations (50)	402
9. Law (25)	758
10. Civic and cultural organizations (12)	433
Total	2,705
GOVERNMENTAL SECTORS	
11. Legislative, executive, judicial	236
12. Military	48
Total	284
Total	7,314

These top positions, taken collectively, control over one half of the nation's industrial assets; one half of all assets in communication and utilities; over one half of all U.S. banking assets; over three quarters of all insurance assets; and they direct Wall Street' s largest investment firms. They control the television networks, the influential news agencies, and the major newspaper chains. They control nearly 40 percent of all the assets of private foundations and two thirds of all private university endowments. They direct the nation's largest and best-known New York and Washington law firms as well as the nation's major civic and cultural organizations. They occupy key federal governmental positions in the executive, legislative, and judicial branches. And they occupy all the top command positions in the Army, Navy, Air Force, and Marines.

These aggregate figures—roughly 7,300 positions—are themselves important indicators of the concentration of authority and control in American society. Of course, these figures are the direct product of our specific definition of top institutional positions.[20] Yet these aggregate statistics provide us with an explicit definition and quantitative estimate of the size of the national elite in America.

SOME QUESTIONS FOR RESEARCH

Our definition of America's institutional elite provides a starting place for exploring some of the central questions confronting students of power. How concentrated are institutional resources in America? How much concentration exists in industry and finance, in government, in the mass media, in education, in the law, in the foundations, and in civic and cultural affairs? Who are the people at the top of the nation's institutional structure? How did they get there? Did they inherit their positions or work their way up through the ranks of the institutional hierarchy? What are their general attitudes, beliefs, and goals? Do elites in America generally agree about major national goals and the general directions of foreign and domestic policy, and limit their disagreements to the *means* of achieving their goals and the details of policy implementation? Or do leaders disagree over fundamental *ends* and values and the future character of American society?

Are institutional elites in America "interlocked" or "specialized"? That is, is there convergence at the "top" of the institutional structure in America, with the same group of people dominating decision-making in industry, finance, education, government, the mass media, foundations, law, investments, and civic and cultural affairs? Or is there a separate elite in each sector of society with little or no overlap in authority? Are there opportunities to rise to the top of the leadership structure for

[20]In earlier editions of this volume, using data from 1970–71, we included only 5,416 positions. In recent editions, using data from 1980–81, we added the investment firms and expanded the number of utilities, insurance companies, universities, and foundations. This produced 7,314 positions. Thus, even minor changes in the definition of an elite can produce substantial differences in the overall size of the elite.

individuals from both sexes, all classes, races, religions, and ethnic groups, through multiple career paths in different sectors of society? Or are opportunities to acquire key leadership roles generally limited to white, Anglo-Saxon, Protestant, upper-class and upper-middle-class males whose careers are based primarily in industry and finance? Is the nation's institutional leadership recruited primarily from private "name" prep schools and "Ivy League" universities? Do leaders join the same clubs, intermarry, and enjoy the same life styles? Or is there diversity in educational backgrounds, social ties, club memberships, and life styles among the elite?

How much competition and conflict take place among America's institutional elite? Are there clear-cut factions within the nation's leadership struggling for preeminence and power, and if so, what are the underlying sources of this factionalism? Do different segments of the nation's institutional elite accommodate each other in a system of bargaining, negotiation, and compromising based on a widely shared consensus of values?

How do institutional elites make national policy? Are there established institutions and procedures for elite interaction, communication, and consensus building on national policy questions? Or are such questions decided in a relatively unstructured process of competition, bargaining, and compromise among a large number of diverse individuals and interest groups? Do the "proximate policy-makers"—the President, Congress, the courts—respond to mass opinions, or do they respond primarily to initiatives originating from the elite policy-planning organizations?

Is America's leadership changing over time, and if so, how? Is power becoming more or less concentrated or dispersed over time? Is there more or less "interlocking" today than a decade ago? Do the same types of people occupy top leadership positions today as compared to a decade ago? Have blacks and women gained significant representation among top positions over the last ten years?

These are the questions that we will tackle in the pages to follow. In Part II, Institutional Leadership in America, we will describe the concentration of power in a limited number of institutions in various sectors of society. We will also describe in general terms the type of individuals who occupy top positions in these institutions; we will provide a number of brief biographical sketches suggestive of the characteristics of these elites—who they are and how they got there. These sketches are designed to "personalize" the statistical analysis that follows. In Part III, The Structure of Institutional Elites, we will examine the questions posed above in a more systematic fashion, employing computerized data files on our top 7,314 elites.

CHAPTER TWO
THE CORPORATE
DIRECTORS

A great deal of power is organized into large economic institutions—industrial corporations, banks, utilities, insurance companies, and investment firms. Control of economic resources provides a continuous and important base of power in any society. Economic organizations decide what will be produced, how much it will cost, how many people will be employed, and what their wages will be. They determine how goods and services will be distributed, what technology will be developed, what profits will be made and how they will be distributed, how much money will be available for capital investment, what interest rates will be charged, and many similarly important questions.

ECONOMIC POWER IN AMERICA

Decisions made in corporate boardrooms affect our lives as much as, or perhaps even more than, those typically made by governments. In communist and socialist societies, economic leaders *are* government officials, and decisions about economic affairs *are* governmental decisions. While it is true that in private-enterprise societies, corporate leaders are considered private citizens, nonetheless, their decisions still carry great *public consequences*. Charles E. Lindblom writes:

> Public affairs in market-oriented systems are in the hands of two groups
> of leaders, government and business, who must collaborate to make the
> system work.
> ... The duality of leadership is reminiscent of the medieval dualism
> between church and state. . . .[1]

Traditionally, pluralism has portrayed business as just another interest group, competing with all the other interest groups to influence
public policy. Corporate power, according to the pluralists, depended on
the political skills and resources of particular individuals, groups, and
industries within the corporate world; the performance of the economy;
the climate of public opinion; and the relative strength of competing
groups.

In contrast, we view economic elites as distinctively powerful, not
only in shaping government policy but also more importantly in making
decisions themselves which directly influence the lives of all of us. Even
some of the leading pluralist scholars have revised their views about
corporate power in America. Robert A. Dahl and Charles E. Lindblom
publicly confessed their "error":

> ... in our discussion of pluralism we made another error—and it is a
> continuing error in social science—in regarding business and business
> groups as playing the same interest-group role as other groups in polyar-
> chal systems, though more powerful. Businessmen play a distinctive role
> in polyarchal politics that is qualitatively different from that of any inter-
> est group. It is also much more powerful than an interest-group role.[2]

Today these scholars lament that the private corporation is "hierarchical" and not governed democratically by its employees. Of course,
this is true. But what these pluralists still do not understand is that *all
organizations are hierarchical.* Corporate governance is not unique. "Virtually all nongovernment institutions can be described in similar terms.
Universities, foundations, labor unions, many professional and trade
associations, religious institutions and organizations, charitable
organizations—even public-interest groups—all exercise political power,
and yet none is governed according to democratic principles or pre-
cepts. In its internal system of authority, the corporation is actually quite
typical of the social structures that characterize democratic societies."[3]
Business and financial leaders make decisions about "who gets

[1]Charles E. Lindblom, *Politics and Markets* (New York: Basic Books, 1977), p. 175.

[2]Robert A. Dahl and Charles E. Lindblom, *Politics Economic and Welfare,* 2nd ed.
(New York: Harper, 1976), preface.

[3]David Vogel, "The New Political Science of Corporate Power," *The Public Interest,* 87
(Spring 1987), 63–79.

what when and how."[4] Studies of power in society must include economic power.

THE CONCENTRATION OF ECONOMIC POWER

Economic power in America is highly concentrated. Indeed, only about 4,300 individuals—two one-thousandths of 1 percent of the population—exercise formal authority over more than one half of the nation's industrial assets; two thirds of all banking assets; one half of all assets in communications and utilities; and more than two thirds of all insurance assets. These individuals are the presidents, officer-directors, and directors of the largest corporations in these fields. The reason for this concentration of power in the hands of so few people is found in the concentration of industrial and financial assets in a small number of giant corporations. The following statistics can only suggest the scale and concentration of modern corporate enterprise in America.

There are about 200,000 *industrial corporations* in the United States with total assets in 1986 of about over $2 trillion. The 100 corporations listed in Table 2–1 control 61.1 percent ($1.2 trillion) of all industrial assets. The five largest industrial corporations—General Motors, Exxon, IBM, Ford Motor, and Mobil—control 15 percent of all industrial assets.

TABLE 2–1   The Largest Industrial Corporations (Ranked by Assets)

RANK	COMPANY	ASSETS ($ BILLIONS)	CUMULATIVE PERCENT*
1	General Motors	87.4	4.3
2	Exxon	74.0	8.0
3	IBM	63.7	11.1
4	Ford Motor	45.0	13.4
5	Mobil	41.1	15.4
6	General Electric	38.9	17.3
7	American Telephone & Telegraph	38.4	19.2
8	Chevron	34.5	20.9
9	Texaco	34.0	22.6
10	du Pont de Nemours	28.2	24.0
11	Shell Oil	26.9	25.3
12	Amoco	24.8	26.6
13	BP America	23.3	27.7
14	Atlantic Richfield	22.7	28.8

(Continued)

[4]Which, of course is Harold Lasswell's very definition of *politics*. See Harold D. Lasswell, *Politics: Who Gets What When and How* (New York: McGraw-Hill, 1936).

TABLE 2–1 *(Continued)*

RANK	COMPANY	ASSETS ($ BILLIONS)	CUMULATIVE PERCENT*
15	Chrysler	19.9	29.8
16	USX	19.6	30.8
17	Philip Morris	19.1	31.7
18	Tenneco	18.5	32.6
19	RJR Nabisco	16.9	33.5
20	Occidental Petroleum	16.7	34.3
21	Eastman Kodak	14.5	35.0
22	Dow Chemical	14.4	35.7
23	Procter & Gamble	13.7	36.4
24	ITT	13.4	37.1
25	Sun	12.6	37.7
26	Boeing	12.6	38.3
27	Phillips Peroleum	12.1	38.9
28	United Technologies	11.9	39.5
29	Xerox	11.6	40.1
30	Allied-Signal	10.2	40.6
31	Unocal	10.1	41.1
32	Unisys	10.0	41.6
33	Westinghouse Electric	10.0	42.1
34	Aluminum Co. of America	9.9	42.6
35	Pepsico	9.0	43.0
36	Rockwell International	8.7	43.4
37	International Paper	8.7	43.9
38	McDonnell Douglas	8.5	44.3
39	Monsanto	8.5	44.7
40	Digital Equipment	8.4	45.1
41	Goodyear Tire & Rubber	8.4	45.5
42	Coca-Cola	8.4	45.9
43	Hewlett-Packard	8.1	46.4
44	Minnesota Mining & Manufacturing	8.0	46.7
45	Coastal	8.0	47.1
46	Beatrice	7.9	47.5
47	Union Carbide	7.9	47.9
48	Baxter Travenol Lab	7.6	48.3
49	American Brands	7.3	48.7
50	Weyerhaeuser	7.2	49.0
51	Pfizer	6.9	49.4
52	Caterpillar	6.9	49.7
53	Johnson & Johnson	6.5	50.0
54	Anheuser-Busch	6.5	50.3
55	Joseph E. Seagram & Sons	6.3	50.7
56	Lockheed	6.3	51.0
57	Champion International	6.1	51.3
58	Georgia-Pacific	5.9	51.6
59	LTV	5.7	51.8
60	Merck	5.7	52.1
61	Kraft	5.5	52.4

TABLE 2–1 *(Continued)*

RANK	COMPANY	ASSETS ($ BILLIONS)	CUMULATIVE PERCENT*
62	Hoechst Celanese	5.4	52.7
63	Textron	5.3	52.9
64	Motorola	5.3	53.2
65	Amerada Hess	5.3	53.5
66	Eli Lilly	5.3	53.7
67	Honeywell	5.2	54.0
68	General Dynamics	5.0	54.2
69	PPG Industries	5.0	54.5
70	Borg-Warner	5.0	54.7
71	Litton Industries	4.9	55.0
72	IC Industries	4.9	55.2
73	Emerson Electric	4.9	55.4
74	Bethlehem Steel	4.8	55.7
75	Deere	4.8	55.9
76	Bristol-Myers	4.7	56.1
77	American Home Products	4.6	56.4
78	Scott Paper	4.5	56.6
79	W.R. Grace	4.5	56.8
80	SmithKline Beckman	4.4	57.0
81	Time Inc.	4.4	57.3
82	Abbott Laboratories	4.4	57.5
83	TRW	4.4	57.7
84	Reynolds Metals	4.3	57.9
85	Texas Instruments	4.3	58.1
86	Coca-Cola Enterprises	4.3	58.3
87	James River Corp. of Virginia	4.2	58.5
88	Sara Lee	4.2	58.7
89	NCR	4.2	58.9
90	Borden	4.2	59.1
91	American Cyanamid	4.1	59.4
92	Raytheon	4.1	59.6
93	Ashland Oil	4.1	59.8
94	Amax	4.0	59.9
95	Kimberly-Clark	3.9	60.1
96	Ralston Purina	3.9	60.3
97	Archer Daniels Midland	3.9	60.5
98	Pillsbury	3.9	60.7
99	Cooper Industries	3.8	60.9
100	Triangle Industries	3.8	61.1
	Total Industrial Assets: $2,022 billion		
	Total Number of Industrial Corporations:	202,000	

*In this table, and in Tables 2–3 and 2–4, cumulative percent refers to the total percentage of the nation's assets in, for example, industrial enterprise at a specific ranking. Thus, the first ten corporations (through du Pont) account for 24.0 percent of the nation's industrial assets. Company figures are for 1987; total asset figures are for 1986.

Sources: Derived from data found in *Fortune*, April 25, 1988, p. 311; *Statistical Abstract of United States*, 1988, p 513.

The concentration of resources among a relatively few industrial corporations is slowly increasing over time. In a 37-year period, the proportion of all industrial assets controlled by the top 100 corporations grew as follows:

1950	1960	1970	1980	1983	1986
39.8%	46.4%	52.3%	55.0%	58.2%	61.1%

Concentration in *communications* and *utilities* is even greater than in industry. For many decades, this sector of the nation's economy was dominated by the American Telephone and Telegraph Company (AT&T)—the single largest private corporation in the world, prior to 1984. Following the federal court-ordered divestiture of its telephone operating companies, AT&T itself has become the nation's seventh largest industrial corporation; its communications companies now occupy six of the top ten positions on Table 2–2. (See Chapter 6, AT&T: Evidence of Convergence.)

TABLE 2–2 The 50 Largest Utilities and Communications Companies (Ranked by Assets)

RANK	COMPANY	ASSETS ($ BILLIONS)
1	GTE	28.7
2	Bell South*	27.4
3	NYNEX*	22.8
4	Pacific Gas & Electric	21.7
5	Southwestern Bell*	21.5
6	Bell Atlantic*	21.2
7	Pacific Telesis Group*	21.1
8	Southern	19.2
9	U.S. West*	19.1
10	American Information Technologies*	18.8
11	Commonwealth Edison	18.2
12	Middle South Utilities	15.2
13	Southern California Edison	14.2
14	American Electric Power	14.0
15	Texas Utilities	14.0
16	Centerior Energy	11.3
17	Philadelphia Electric	11.2
18	Detroit Edison	11.2
19	Public Service Enterprise Group	10.9
20	FPL Group	10.0
21	Houston Industries	9.7
22	Dominion Resources	9.7
23	Consolidated Edison of New York	9.4
24	MCS Energy	9.4
25	Long Island Lighting	9.3
26	Duke Power	8.5

TABLE 2–2   *(Continued)*

RANK	COMPANY	ASSETS ($ BILLIONS)
27	Ohio Edison	7.9
28	Enron	7.7
29	Carolina Light and Power	7.6
30	Central & West	7.6
31	Pennsylvania Power and Light	7.2
32	Niagara Mohawk Power	6.8
33	Pinnacle West Capital	6.7
34	Gulf States Utilities	6.7
35	Northeast Utilities	6.7
36	United Telecommunications	6.6
37	General Public Utilities	6.3
38	Union Electric	6.0
39	Illinois Power	5.9
40	Pacificorp	5.7
41	Contel	5.5
42	Columbia Gas System	5.4
43	MCI Communications	5.4
44	Texas Eastern	5.1
45	Pacific Enterprises	5.0
46	Baltimore Gas & Electric	4.5
47	New York State Electric and Gas	4.5
48	Northern States Power	4.4
49	Allegheny Power System	4.3
50	Transco Energy	4.3

*Formerly parts of AT&T.

Source: Derived from data found in *Fortune*, June 6, 1988 p. D33.

The financial world is equally concentrated. The 50 largest *banks* (see Table 2–3), out of 14,236 banks serving the nation, control 66 percent of all banking assets. Three banks (Citicorp, Chase Manhattan and BankAmerica) control 15 percent of all banking assets.

In the *insurance* field, 50 companies (see Table 2–4), out of 2,321, control over 80 percent of all insurance assets. Three companies (Prudential, Metropolitan, and Equitable) control 26 percent of all insurance assets.

Finally, in the field of *investment* banking, we have identified fifteen major Wall Street firms (see Table 2–5). These firms are in a central strategic position in the American economy. They decide whether, when, and under what terms American corporations (and state and local governments) can sell stocks, bonds, and other securities. These firms "underwrite" the sale of new securities, usually joining together in a large syndicate to do so. Then they sell these stocks, bonds, and securities to their own individual and institutional client-investors.

TABLE 2–3   The Fifty Largest Commercial Banking Companies (Ranked by Assets)

RANK	COMPANY	ASSETS ($ BILLIONS)	CUMULATIVE PERCENT
1	Citicorp (New York)	203.6	7.9
2	Chase Manhattan Corp. (New York)	99.1	11.8
3	BankAmerica Corp. (San Francisco)	92.8	15.4
4	Chemical New York Corp. (New York)	78.2	18.4
5	J.P. Morgan & Co. (New York)	75.4	21.3
6	Security Pacific Corp. (Los Angeles)	73.4	24.2
7	Manufacturers Hanover Corp. (New York)	73.3	27.0
8	Bankers Trust New York Corp. (New York)	56.5	29.2
9	First Interstate Bancorp. (Los Angeles)	50.9	31.2
10	First Chicago Corp. (Chicago)	44.2	32.9
11	Wells Fargo & Co. (San Francisco)	44.1	34.6
12	Bank of Boston Corp. (Boston)	34.1	36.0
13	First RepublicBank Corp. (Dallas)	33.2	37.3
14	Continental Illinois Corp. (Chicago)	32.4	38.5
15	PNC Financial Corp. (Pittsburgh)	31.4	39.7
16	Mellon Bank Corp. (Pittsburgh)	30.5	40.9
17	Bank of New England Corp. (Boston)	29.5	42.1
18	NCNB Corp. (Charlotte, N.C.)	28.9	43.2
19	First Fidelity Bancorp. (Newark)	28.9	44.3
20	First Union Corp. (Charlotte, N.C.)	27.6	45.4
21	Suntrust Banks (Atlanta)	27.2	46.4
22	First Bank Systems (Minneapolis)	26.9	47.5
23	Shawmut National Corp. (Boston)	26.5	48.5
24	Marine Midland Banks (Buffalo and New York)	25.5	49.5
25	Irving Bank Corp. (New York)	23.5	50.4
26	Barnett Banks of Florida (Jacksonville)	23.5	51.3
27	NBD Bancorp. (Detroit)	23.3	52.2
28	Bank of New York Co. (New York)	23.1	53.1
29	Republic New York Corp. (New York)	22.4	54.0
30	Sovran Financial Corp. (Norfolk)	21.2	54.8
31	Norwest Corp. (Minneapolis)	20.7	55.6
32	Citizens and Southern (Atlanta)	20.4	56.4
33	MCORP (Dallas)	20.2	57.2
34	First Wachovia Corp. (Winston-Salem)	19.3	58.0
35	Banc One Corp. (Columbus)	18.7	58.7
36	Midlantic Banks (Edison, N.J.)	17.8	59.4
37	MNC Financial (Baltimore)	16.7	60.0
38	CoreStates Financial Corp. (Philadelphia)	15.0	60.6
39	National City Corp. (Cleveland)	14.9	61.2
40	U.S. Bancorp. (Portland)	13.4	61.7
41	Southeast Banking Corp. (Miami)	12.8	62.2
42	Union Bankcorp. (Los Angeles)	11.9	62.7
43	Keycorp. (Albany, N.Y.)	11.6	63.1
44	National Westminster Bank USA (New York)	11.5	63.6
45	Valley National Corp. (Phoenix)	11.3	64.0
46	First City Bancorp. of Texas (Houston)	11.2	64.5
47	Signet Banking Corp. (Richmond)	10.7	64.9
48	Harris Bankcorp. (Chicago)	10.6	65.3

TABLE 2–3   *(Continued)*

RANK	COMPANY	ASSETS ($ BILLIONS)	CUMULATIVE PERCENT
49	Ameritrust Corp. (Cleveland)	10.3	65.7
50	United Jersey Banks (Princeton)	10.1	66.1
	Total Commercial Banking Assets: $2,573 billion		
	Total Number of Commercial Banks: 14,236		

Sources: Derived from data found in *Fortune*, June 6, 1988, p. D13, for largest banks; *Statistical Abstract of United States*, 1988, p. 472, for total bank assets.

TABLE 2–4   The 50 Largest Life Insurance Companies (Ranked by Assets)

RANK	COMPANY	ASSETS ($ BILLIONS)	CUMULATIVE PERCENT
1	Prudential of America (Newark)	108.8	11.6
2	Metropolitan Life (New York)	88.1	21.0
3	Equitable Life Assurance (New York)	49.3	26.3
4	Aetna Life (New York)	45.7	31.1
5	Teachers Insurance & Annuity (New York)	33.2	34.7
6	New York Life (New York)	31.8	38.1
7	Travelers (Hartford)	28.6	41.1
8	John Hancock Mutual Life (Boston)	27.4	44.0
9	Connecticut General Life (Bloomfield)	26.8	46.9
10	Northwestern Mutual Life (Milwaukee)	22.6	49.3
11	Massachusetts Mutual Life (Springfield)	19.9	51.4
12	Principal Mutual Life (Des Moines)	19.0	53.5
13	Mutual of New York (New York)	14.8	55.0
14	New England Mutual Life (Boston)	14.2	56.5
15	Executive Life (Los Angeles)	11.4	57.8
16	Mutual Benefit Life (Newark)	10.1	58.8
17	Connecticut Mutual Life (Hartford)	9.9	59.9
18	IDS Life (Minneapolis)	9.0	60.9
19	State Farm Life (Bloomington, Ill.)	8.5	61.8
20	Variable Annuity Life (Houston)	7.8	62.6
21	Nationwide Life (Columbus, Ohio)	7.3	63.4
22	New York Life & Annuity (Wilmington, Del.)	7.1	64.1
23	Pacific Mutual Life (Newport Beach, Calif.)	7.0	64.9
24	Aetna Life & Annuity (Hartford)	6.6	65.6
25	Equitable Variable Life (New York)	6.6	66.3
26	Lincoln National Pension (Fort Wayne)	6.3	67.0
27	Continental Assurance (Chicago)	6.1	67.6
28	Allstate Life (Northbrook, Ill.)	6.0	68.2
29	Southwestern Life (Dallas)	5.8	68.9
30	Transamerica Life & Annuity (Los Angeles)	5.5	69.5
31	Provident National Assurance (Chattanooga)	5.2	70.0
32	Phoenix Mutual Life (Hartford)	5.2	70.6

(Continued)

TABLE 2–4 *(Continued)*

RANK	COMPANY	ASSETS ($ BILLIONS)	CUMULATIVE PERCENT
33	Transamerica Occidental Life (Los Angeles)	5.0	71.1
34	Lincoln National Life (Fort Wayne)	4.9	71.6
35	Northwestern National Life (Minneapolis)	4.7	72.1
36	State Mutual of America (Worcester, Mass.)	4.4	72.6
37	General American Life (St. Louis)	4.4	73.1
38	Guardian of America (New York)	4.2	73.5
39	Mutual of America Life (New York)	4.2	74.0
40	Unum Life (Portland, Me.)	4.1	74.4
41	Penn Mutual Life (Philadelphia)	4.1	74.8
42	Minnesota Mutual Life (St. Paul)	4.0	75.3
43	Franklin Life (Springfield, Ill.)	4.0	75.7
44	Kemper Investors Life (Chicago)	3.9	76.1
45	Western & Southern Life (Cincinnati)	3.9	76.5
46	Keystone Provident Life (Providence, R.I.)	3.8	76.9
47	Provident Life & Accident (Chattanooga)	3.6	77.3
48	National Life (Montpelier, Vt.)	3.6	77.7
49	Home Life (New York)	3.5	78.1
50	American General Life (Nashville)	3.5	78.4
	Total Life Insurance Assets: $938 billion		
	Total Number of Companies: 2,321		

Sources: Derived from data found in *Fortune*, June 6, 1988, p. 25 for largest companies; *Statistical Abstract of United States*, 1988, p. 488, for total assets and number of companies.

TABLE 2–5   The Investment Firms

Brown Brothers, Harriman & Co.
Dean Witter Reynolds Inc.
Dillon, Read & Company, Inc.
Drexal Burnham Lambert, Inc.
First Boston Corporation
Goldman, Sachs and Company
E.F. Hutton & Company, Inc.*
Kidder, Peabody and Company, Inc.
Lehman Brothers Kuhn Loeb, Inc.
Merrill Lynch, Pierce, Fenner and Smith, Inc.
Morgan Stanley and Company, Inc.
Paine Webber Inc.
Bache Halsey Stuart Shields, Inc.**
Shearson Lehman/American Express, Inc.*
Lazard Frères and Company

*Subsequently merged into Shearson, Lehman, Hutton.
**Subsequently merged into Prudential Bache.

THE MULTINATIONALS: WORLDWIDE BIG BUSINESS

The concentration of industrial power in a relatively few large institutions is not an exclusively American phenomenon. On the contrary, since World War II the growth of world trade, increasing overseas investments, and international corporate mergers all have combined to create giant multinational corporations whose operations span the globe. The trend toward corporate concentration of resources is worldwide. It is not only large American corporations which have expanded their markets throughout the world, invested in overseas plants and banks, and merged with foreign countries. Large European and Japanese firms compete very effectively for world business. Just as American companies have greatly expanded investments abroad, so too have foreign companies sharply increased their business in the United States. The result is the emergence of truly supranational corporations, which not only trade worldwide but also build and operate plants in many nations.

The *world's* largest corporations in six different industries are listed in Table 2–6. Note that most giant multinational corporations are *not* American. General Motors and Exxon, the largest industrial corporations in the United States, and the giant British-Dutch firm, Royal Dutch Shell, annually compete for the top spot as the world's largest industrial corporation. In world banking, Citicorp is followed by the giant Tokyo and Paris banks.

Foreign corporations sell their products in the United States (steel, automobiles, chemicals, electrical products) and also buy American corporations, which become subsidiaries of the foreign multinationals. For example, Royal Dutch Shell (Netherlands) owns Shell Oil; British Petroleum (UK) owns Standard Oil of Ohio, Tengelmann (Germany) owns A&P supermarkets; Nestlé (Switzerland) owns the Libby, Stouffer, and Beech-Nut corporations; Unilever (UK) owns the Lever Brothers and Lipton companies; Bayer (Germany) owns Miles and Cutter Laboratories (Bayer aspirin); and so on.

While a great deal has been written about the "dangers" of multinationalism in subverting the national interest, in most cases the opposite is true. The multinational corporation is in a very exposed position vis-à-vis its investments overseas. These investments may be confiscated by revolutionary governments without notice; may be subject to discriminatory taxes, duties, or quotas; or may be forced to be sold or transferred to new foreign owners. The multinational corporation is at the mercy of the host government. Multinationals must conform to the conflicting laws of many nations. On the other hand, the legal maze in which multinationals operate leaves cracks in which clever managers can walk: shifting resources or profits to the lowest tax countries in which they operate; avoiding antitrust laws with international mergers; obscur-

TABLE 2–6   The Multinationals: Top Five Corporations in the World

CORPORATION	COUNTRY	ASSETS ($ BILLIONS)
OIL		
Royal Dutch Shell	Netherlands	75
Exxon	USA	74
British Petroleum	UK	44
Mobil	USA	41
Pemex	Mexico	37
BANKING		
Citicorp	USA	204
Dai-ichi Kangyo	Japan	131
Fuji Bank	Japan	130
Credit Agricole	France	126
Banque Nationale de Paris	France	124
AUTOMOBILES		
General Motors	USA	87
Ford Motors	USA	45
Chrysler	USA	20
Toyota Motor	Japan	17
Nissan Motor	Japan	14
CHEMICALS		
E.I. du Pont	USA	28
B.A.S.F.	Germany	16
Bayer	Germany	16
Hoechst	Germany	14
DOW	USA	14
STEEL		
USX	USA	20
Siderbras	Brazil	17
Nippon Steel	Japan	15
Nippon Kokan	Japan	10
Sumitomo	Japan	9
FOOD		
RJR Nabisco	USA	17
Unilever	Netherlands	13
Nestlé	Switzerland	12
Taiyo Fisheries	Japan	3
Associated British Foods	UK	2

Source: *Forbes,* July 28, 1986.

ing corporate reporting through foreign subsidiaries; shifting cash revenues from one currency to another; and so on.

In brief, the central feature of the American economy is the concentration of resources in relatively few large corporations. Most of this concentration occurred many years ago. "The long-established norm of market structure and behavior is that of oligopoly, that is, the constrained rivalry of a few interdependent sellers who compete mainly by means of product differentiation."[5] In recent years concentration has continued to increase, although at a slower rate than early in the twentieth century. It is clear that society is *not* going to return to a small, romanticized, perhaps mythical, world of individual enterprise.

WHO CONTROLS THE CORPORATION

In the formal, legal sense, the board of directors "controls" the modern corporation. The average number of board members in the 100 largest industrial corporations is 15. However, "inside" directors—those who are also top management officers in the corporation—usually dominate board decision-making and even the process of choosing directors. Inside directors usually include the president and the top senior vice-presidents. About 44 percent of corporate directors are inside directors. Outside directors—persons who serve on the board but who take no direct part in managing the corporation—usually defer to the judgment of the inside officer-directors. About 56 percent of all directors are "outside" directors. However, *all* directors have a legal responsibility to the owners (stockholders) of the corporation to protect their investment. All directors are formally elected by the stockholders, who cast their votes on the basis of one share equals one vote.

The millions of middle-class Americans who own corporate stock have virtually no influence over the decisions of directors. When confronted with mismanagement, these stockholders simply sell their stock, rather than try to challenge the powers of the directors. Indeed, most stockholders sign over "proxies" to top management so that top management may cast these proxy votes at the annual meetings of stockholders. Management itself usually selects its own "slate" for the board of directors and easily elects them with the help of proxies.

While a majority of large corporations are controlled by their own top management, some corporations are dominated by a small "control bloc" of stock owners in cooperation with top management. The stock of large corporations is widely distributed among the stock-owning public. This sometimes enables small "control blocs" of only 1 or 2 percent of the total stock of the corporation to hold a strategic positon—electing its own directors and influencing corporate decisions. Thus, some outside directors may represent the interest of "control blocs" of stock on the board.

---

[5]Edward S. Herman, *Corporate Control, Corporate Power* (Cambridge, Mass.: Cambridge University Press, 1981), p. 1.

Another type of outside corporate director is one representing financial interests (banks, insurance companies, investment firms). These financial interests wish to oversee the use of their funds by the corporation. Sometimes part of the price of a large loan from a major bank or insurance company to an industrial corporation will include a seat on the board of directors of that corporation. Outside directors representing financial interests do not usually take a direct role in decision-making; they perform a general watch-dog role over their investment.

A few outside directors of large corporations represent public relations efforts by top management to improve the image of the corporation. For example, a few corporations have selected civil rights activists, blacks, women, and consumer activists for their boards. (When the Chrysler Corporation faced the prospect of bankruptcy, it ceded a seat on its board to the president of the United Automobile Workers, Douglas Fraser, in exchange for union acceptance of a less costly contract.) It may be true that these corporations really want the counsel of these people; however, one suspects that they also want to promote an image of social responsibility. It is doubtful that these particular people are influential in corporate decision-making.

Finally, there are the corporate directors—whether inside officers or outsiders—who represent family owners. Family ownership and domination of large corporations has not yet disappeared in America despite marked decline in family control of corporations over the last several decades.

Thus, corporate board members can be divided into types. The following percentage approximations of various types of corporate directors are estimated for the 1,475 members of the 100 largest industrial corporations:[6]

INSIDERS	
Manager-directors	44%
OUTSIDERS	
Former managers	6
Financial representatives	8
Ownership representatives	13
Substantial business with corporation	11
Charitable, civic, or educational representatives	5
Other	13
OUTSIDER TOTAL	56%

Managers usually triumph in the boardroom. The "managerial revolution"—the displacement of owners as corporate decision-makers

---

[6]Estimates from materials presented in Herman, *Corporate Control, Corporate Power*, chap. 2.

by professional managers—has become part of our conventional wisdom, accepted by liberals and conservatives alike.[7] The inside directors, although only a minority of most boards, usually vote as a solid, unified block under the direction of the president. Their block voting strength on the board is augmented by their greater depth of knowledge of the organization, its technology, and its business problems. Insiders work full time on corporate affairs, continuously communicating with each other. Outsiders have no such information or communication base.

Outside directors, with some exceptions, are "invited" to serve on boards by the managers. They are "guests" in the boardroom. They usually have a sense of loyalty to the president who put them on the board. They are passive on most management decisions. "No one likes to be the skunk at the garden party."[8] They may advise on special areas of competence; they may help coordinate decision-making with major suppliers or buyers; and by their presence on the board they may help assure the outside world that the organization is in good hands. The only important exceptions to these usually passive outside managers are those who still represent large stockholder interests.

The rising tide of litigation in corporate America and the fear of liability has tarnished the attractiveness of outside directorships. It is true that corporations usually purchase liability insurance for their directors, but legal hassles and time demands still weigh heavily on board members. As a result, in recent years there has been a shifting away from outside directors and a trend toward smaller boards, fewer meetings, and more inside directors. An outside director who walked away from a seat on the Control Data Corp. board was quoted as saying: "I didn't want to risk my personal net worth for the $50,000 a year I'd get from the board."[9]

While some executives may shy away from outside directorships, there are a few "professional outside directors"—people who sit on multiple boards. Among the most popular women outside corporate directors is Juanita M. Kreps, former secretary of commerce who sits on ten separate boards, including Citicorp and AT&T. Among the most popular black outside corporate directors are Andrew F. Brimmer and Vernon E. Jordon, Jr., both with eight directorships including Bank-

[7]For some Marxists and others on the left, managerialism is still denied, because it complicates the theory of class struggle in a capitalist society. They still argue that great families, or banking empires, have retained latent power—power to be exercised when something goes seriously wrong. Some Marxists, however, have accepted the managerial thesis and simply focus on managers as "the leading echelon of the capitalist class." See Paul A. Baran and Paul M. Sweezy, *Monopoly Capital* (Newark: Monthly Review Press, 1966).

[8]*Business Week*, September 8, 1986, p. 60.

[9]Ibid., p. 56.

America, American Express, and Xerox. Former President Gerald R. Ford is another favorite outside director with ten board seats. Thus, corporations seek prestige and name recognition, as well as the representation of women and blacks in selecting outside directors.

Adolf A. Berle, Jr. summarizes the dominance of managers in corporate America:

> Management control is a phrase meaning merely that no large concentrated stockholding exists which maintains a close working relationship with the management or is capable of challenging it, so that the board of directors may regularly expect a majority, composed of small and scattered holdings, to follow their lead. Thus, they need not consult with anyone when making up their slate of directors, and may simply request their stockholders to sign and send in a ceremonial proxy. They select their own successors. . . . Nominal power still resides in the stockholders; actual power in the board of directors.[10]

THE CORPORATE DIRECTORS

Who are the people at the top of the nation's corporate structure? Let us begin with some brief sketches of a few selected corporate leaders. Later in this volume we will examine recruitment patterns, interlocking and specialization, social backgrounds, attitudes and opinions, cohesion and competition, and patterns of interaction. Let us first, however, give a general notion of who the people at the top are.

Roger B. Smith.   Chairman and chief executive officer, General Motors Corporation. The son of a banker and auto parts supply company owner. Following service in the U.S. Navy in World War II, he earned B.A. and M.B.A. degrees from the University of Michigan. He began his corporate climb in the accounting department of GM, rising over the years to treasurer, vice-president for finance, and corporate director. He supervised the expansion of General Motors Acceptance Corporation into a major consumer finance company, underwriting the sale of millions of GM cars. He became CEO in 1981 only to confront Japanese competition, which was rapidly eroding GM markets and profits. He laid off thousands of white-collar and blue-collar workers, forced union concessions on wage scales, and negotiated the import of Japanese cars with Chevrolet nameplates. He imported Japanese expertise to introduce computerized robotics in GM factories and to establish a plant with Japanese management style. He reorganized GM, purchased Ross Perot's Electronic Data Systems Corporation as well as Hughes Aircraft Company. But so far GM has failed to regain its mar-

[10]Adolf A. Berle, Jr., *Power Without Property* (New York: Harcourt Brace Jovanovich, 1959).

ket share against Japanese automakers. Smith is a director of Citicorp and Johnson & Johnson, as well as of the Detroit Economic Growth Corporation and Detroit Renaissance. He is a trustee of the Cranbrook School, the Graduate School of Business of Stanford University, the California Institute of Technology, the John F. Kennedy Center for the Performing Arts, and the Business Roundtable.

John F. Akers. Chairman and chief executive officer of IBM. Attended Yale University, majoring in engineering, and served four years as a U.S. Navy pilot. Began with IBM in 1960 as a sales representative, climbing corporate ladder to corporate vice-president in 1982. Tough competition from Japan, AT&T, and Digital Equipment caused trouble for IBM's senior officers, and the relatively youthful Akers was made president in 1983. Although IBM accounts for almost three quarters of all of the profits earned by U.S. computer companies, "Big Blue" remained under siege from Japanese products throughout the 1980s. The survival of the U.S. computer industry rests in large measure in John F. Akers. He is a director of the New York Times Company, the Metropolitan Museum of Art, the California Institute of Technology, the United Way of America; and co-chairman of the Business Roundtable.

Alden W. Clausen. Chairman and chief executive officer, BankAmerica. Former chairman of the World Bank. Attended tiny Carthage College in Illinois and received a law degree from the University of Minnesota in 1949. He immediately went to work with the Bank of America in San Francisco, under its founder and long-term president, A.P. Gianini, working his way up the corporate ladder to president and chief executive officer in 1970. He served as CEO during the 1970s, a decade in which the bank made heavy investments in Mexico, Brazil, Argentina, and oil-producing nations. In 1981 Clausen accepted appointment as chairman of the World Bank, an international lending agency with a mission of Third World development. Clausen's successor at BankAmerica, Samuel H. Armacost, was faced with extensive uncollectable foreign loans; the bank lost its U.S. leadership to Citicorp. In 1986 the directors called Clausen back to the chairman's post, even though he had been initially responsible for its international exposure to debt. Resolution of the world debt crisis rests largely on Clausen's shoulders. He is past chairman of the United Way of America, and a trustee of the Brookings Institution, the San Francisco Opera, the Stanford Research Institute, and the Harvard Business School.

David Rockefeller. Former chairman of the board of Chase Manhattan Bank. Youngest of five sons of John D. Rockefeller, Jr.; heir of the Standard Oil Co. (Exxon) fortune; grandson of John D. Rockefeller, Sr., who founded the company that made the Rockefeller family one of the richest families in the world. Attended Lincoln School in New York, Harvard, The London School of Economics, and the University of Chicago (Ph.D. degree in economics). He has been a member of the board of directors of the BF Goodrich Co., Rockefeller Bros., Inc., and Equitable Life Assurance Co. He is a trustee of the Rockefeller Institute of Medical Research, the Museum of Modern Art, Rockefeller University, the Downtown Lower Manhattan Association, Rockefeller Center, and Harvard College. He is former Chairman of the Council on Foreign Relations and former chairman of the Trilateral Commission. He has gradually relinquished his institutional positions in recent years. (See Chapter 6.)

Clifton C. Garvin.   Former chairman of the board of Exxon Corporation. Attended public school and received a B.S. degree in chemical engineering from Virginia Polytechnic Institute. He began work as an engineer for Standard Oil Co. (now Exxon) in Baton Rouge, Louisiana, in 1947. He climbed the executive ranks of Standard Oil and its subsidiaries for twenty-eight years, becoming chairman of the board in 1975. He is also a director of Citicorp, Pepsico, and Sperry Rand, and is a member of the National Petroleum Council. He is a former chairman of the Business Roundtable. He is a trustee of the Committee on Economic Development, the Business Council, and the American Petroleum Institute, Memorial Sloan-Kettering Cancer Center, Alfred P. Sloan Foundation, Vanderbilt University, and the Council on Foreign Relations.

Robert V. Roosa.   Senior partner of Brown Brothers, Harriman & Co. (Wall Street investment firm). Former chairman of the board of trustees of the Brookings Institution, Washington, D.C. He earned a Ph.D. (economics) from the University of Michigan and is a Rhodes Scholar. A director of American Express Co., Owens-Corning Fiberglas, and Texaco. Former Undersecretary of the Treasury. A director of the Council on Foreign Relations and a trustee of the Rockefeller Foundation and Memorial Sloan-Kettering Cancer Center.

Theodore F. Brophy.   Chairman of the Board of General Telephone and Electric (GTE). Yale undergraduate and Harvard Law School degrees. Joined the prestigious New York law firm of Dewey, Ballantine, Bushby, Palmer & Wood. Named general counsel to GTE and later executive vice-president, president, and chairman. A director of Continental Oil, Charter New York Corp., Procter & Gamble, *Reader's Digest*, and Irving Trust Co. Various official posts in the Boy Scouts of America, the Boys Clubs of America, the International Chamber of Commerce, the Business Council, the Business Roundtable, and the Brookings Institution.

Frank T. Cary.   Former chairman of the executive committee of IBM. Attended UCLA and Stanford, where he earned an M.B.A. Began climbing the ladder at IBM in 1948, became president in 1971, and later chairman. A director of IBM, Morgan Guaranty Trust, American Broadcasting Company (ABC), Merck & Co. (drugs), Hospital Corporation of America, Pepsico, Texaco, and the New York Stock Exchange. A trustee of the Brookings Institution, the Museum of Modern Art, Rockefeller University, and M.I.T. He is a member of the Business Council, the Business Roundtable, and the Committee for Economic Development.

It is clear from these brief sketches that some individuals gain corporate power through inheritance, but most come up through the ranks of corporate management. People such as Rockefeller and Ford inherited their position and power. Others, such as Smith, Akers, Clausen, Garvin, and Iacocca, rose to power through the ranks of management. In fact, we will see that a surprising percentage of top corporate leaders have achieved their power that way.

THE MANAGERS: CLIMBING THE CORPORATE LADDER

The top echelons of American corporate life are occupied primarily by people who have climbed the corporate ladder from relatively obscure and powerless bottom rungs. It is our rough estimate that less than 10 percent of the 1,475 presidents and directors of the top 100 corporations are heirs of wealthy families. The rest—the "managers"—owe their rise to power not to family connections, but to their own success in organizational life. Of course, these managers are overwhelmingly upper middle class and upper class in social origin, and most attended Ivy League colleges and universities. (The social origin and background of top elites are discussed in Chapter 7.) The rise of the manager is a recent phenomenon. As recently as 1950, we estimate that 30 percent of the top corporate elite were heirs of wealthy families, compared to our figure of 10 percent for 1980. (Indeed, even since 1980, Henry Ford II stepped down as chairman of Ford Motors, and David Rockefeller retired as chairman of Chase Manhattan.) How can we explain the rise to power of the corporate manager?

Today the requirements of technology and planning have greatly increased the need in industry for specialized talent and skill in organization. Capital is something that a corporation can now supply to itself. Thus, there has been a shift in power in the American economy from capital to organized intelligence. This is reflected in the decline of individual- and family-controlled large corporations and in an increase in the percentage of large corporations controlled by management.

Individual capitalists are no longer essential to the accumulation of capital for investment. Approximately three fifths of industrial capital now comes from retained earnings of corporations rather than from the investments of individual capitalists. Another one fifth of industrial capital is borrowed, chiefly from banks. Even though the remaining one fifth of the capital funds of industry comes from "outside" investments, the bulk of these funds are from large insurance companies, mutual funds, and pension trusts, rather than from individual investors. Indeed, the individual investor who buys stock in corporations provides only about 5 percent of total industrial capital. Liberal economist John Kenneth Galbraith summarizes the changes in America's economic elite:

> Seventy years ago the corporation was the instrument of its owners and a projection of their personalities. The names of these principals—Carnegie, Rockefeller, Harriman, Mellon, Guggenheim, Ford—were well known across the land. They are still known, but for the art galleries and philanthropic foundations they established and their descendants who are in politics. The men who now head the great corporations are unknown. Not for a generation did people outside Detroit in the automobile industry know the name of the current head of General Motors. In the manner of all men, he must produce identification when paying by check. So with Ford, Standard Oil, and General Dynamics. The men who now run the large corporations own no appreciable share of the enterprise. They are selected not by the stockholders but, in the common case, by a board of directors which narcissistically they selected themselves.[11]

How do you climb the corporate ladder? It is not easy, and most who begin the climb fall by the wayside at some point in their careers before reaching the top.

> Just to be in the running, a career riser must discipline himself carefully. He must become a seasoned decision-maker. He must cultivate an aura of success and sustain his upward momentum on the executive ladder. He must be loyal to a fault, tolerably bright, fairly creative, politically agile, always tough, sometimes flexible, unfailingly sociable and, in the minds of his company's directors, seem superior to a dozen men who are almost as good. He must also be lucky.[12]

Today, more than ever before, getting to the top requires the skills of a "technocrat"—knowledge of bureaucratic organization, technical skills and information, extensive formal education (including postgraduate degrees), and proven ability to work within legal constraints and governmental regulations. Very few sons and no daughters are taking over the presidencies of large corporations owned by their families. Fewer than 10 of the nation's 500 largest corporations are headed by

[11]John Kenneth Galbraith, *The New Industrial State* (Boston: Houghton Mifflin, 1967), p. 323.

[12]Howard Morgans, former president of Procter & Gamble, as quoted in "Proud to Be an Organization Man," *Forbes*, May 15, 1972, p. 241.

men whose families had previously run the corporation.[13] Top corporate management is drawn from the ranks of upper-middle-class, well-educated, white, and male, management, financial, and legal experts.

Perhaps the most significant change over the years has been the rising number of top corporate and governmental executives who have acquired graduate degrees. Today over half of the corporate presidents of the 500 largest corporations have advanced degrees, including M.B.A.s (masters of business administration), law degrees, and Ph.D.s. Less than 3 percent are not college educated. (See Chapter 7.)

An increasing number of top corporate leaders are coming out of finance and law, as opposed to production, operations, advertising, sales, engineering, or research. Lawyers and accountants now head two out of every five large corporations. This is further evidence that finance, taxation, and governmental regulation are the chief problems confronting large corporations. The problems of production, sales, engineering, and transportation have faded in relationship to the pressing problems of money and power.

But the "managers" who head the nation's largest corporations are not merely paid administrators. On the contrary, the vast majority of corporate presidents, and other top management personnel, own substantial shareholdings of their company's stock. According to *Fortune* magazine, 30 percent of the presidents of the 500 largest companies personally own $1 million or more in their own company's stock. Fully 45 percent own over one-half million dollars worth; 75 percent own at least $100,000 worth; and only 10 percent own none at all. The managers have a personal stake in their company's growth and profitability—a stake that extends beyond their jobs to their personal investments as well.

Getting to the top by climbing the ladder of the giant corporation is not only difficult, it is also risky. The percentage chances of any one individual making it to the top are infinitesimal.

> Yet hundreds of thousands of executives willingly devote entire careers to working their way up through these giant corporations. On the lower rungs of the ladder, when they are in their 20s, all of them dream of reaching the top. As they advance into their 30s, and receive more responsibility and more money, the dream flowers brightly. Some time in their 40s and 50s, however, most realize they aren't going to make it. They are sorely disappointed, but it's too late to change. Comfortable and secure, they stay. Then each year there are perhaps a dozen or so—the lucky men who go all the way.[14]

[13]Charles G. Burch, "A Group Profile of the Fortune 500 Chief Executives," *Fortune*, May 1976, p. 174. See also *Business Week*, October 23, 1987, p. 37.

[14]"Proud to Be an Organization Man," p. 244.

COUNTER-REVOLUTION: CORPORATE TAKEOVERS

Until recently, management control of corporate America was seldom challenged. But the astonishing rise in "hostile takeovers" in the last decade has profoundly altered the structure of power in corporate boardrooms. A hostile takeover involves the purchase of enough stock in a publicly held corporation to force the ouster and replacement of existing corporate management. Indeed, the threat of a hostile takeover may be the dominant force in the behavior of top managers today.

Corporate mergers and acquisitions mushroomed during the past decade; from less than $100 billion in 1984, the total value of merger deals grew to nearly $500 billion in 1988. Table 2–7 lists some of the largest recent mergers, including the giant RJR Nabisco buyout for $25 billion, the largest buyout to date.

Only a decade ago the top corporate managers of large publicly owned companies were considered impregnable; nothing short of bankruptcy could dislodge them. Corporate managers ran the American economy, perpetuating themselves in office; they ruled without much interference from stockholders, employees, or consumers. But the rise of "corporate raiders" like T. Boone Pickens, who specializes in oil companies, and Carl Ichan, who ranges over all kinds of businesses, now threatens the secure and cozy life of the boardroom.

A hostile takeover begins with a corporate raider buying the stock of a corporation on the open market, usually with money borrowed for this purpose. The raider may wish to keep his early purchases secret for a while to avoid rapid rises in the price of the stock; but federal Securities and Exchange Commission rules require disclosure when a person acquires 5 percent of a corporation's stock. The raider may then offer a takeover bid to existing management. Management may reject the bid

TABLE 2–7   Big Deals: Large Corporate Mergers and Takeovers, 1980–88

BUYER/BOUGHT	INDUSTRIES	DATE
RJR Nabisco/Kohlberg Kraris and Roberts	tobacco and food/investment	1988
Kraft/Philip Morris	food/tobacco	1988
RCA Corp./General Electric	communications/electronics	1986
Standard Oil of California/Gulf Oil	oil/oil	1984
Texaco/Getty Oil	oil/oil	1984
Du Pont/Conoco	obeneal/oil	1981
USX/Manhattan Oil	steel/oil	1981
Mobil/Superior	oil/oil	1984
Royal Dutch Shell/Shell Oil	oil/oil	1983
Capital Cities Communications/ABC	newspapers/TV	1985
Elf Aquitaine/Texas Gulf	oil/oil	1981

outright or try to buy back the stock purchased by the raider at a higher price, that is, to offer the raider "greenmail." If the raider and management cannot reach agreement, the hostile takeover proceeds. The raider arranges to borrow additional money—perhaps several billion dollars—to make a purchase offer to the target corporation's stockholders, usually at a price higher than the current stock exchange price. Management may search for a "White Knight"—someone willing to offer even more money to purchase the corporation from its stockholders but who promises to keep the existing management. If the raider wins control of the corporation, he replaces management.

Following a successful takeover, the corporation is heavily laden with new debt. The raider may have borrowed billions to buy out shareholders. The investment firms which provide the loans to finance the corporation's purchase then issue "junk bonds" with high interest rates to attract investors to these risky ventures. The corporation must pay off these bonds with its own revenues. Additionally there may be many millions of dollars in bond-sale commissions and attorneys' fees to pay out. The raider may be forced to sell off parts of the corporation or some of its valuable assets in order to help pay off part of the debt. Thus, the target corporation itself must eventually bear the burden of the takeover battle.

Of course, the raider originally targets the corporation because its stock price is low compared to the value of its assets and/or its potential for future profits. The raider believes that the low price of the stock is a product of poor management performance. The raider hopes that with new management the corporation can improve its performance, pay off its debt, and produce greater profits. And the raider must convince the investment firms who provide the takeover money of the accuracy of his predictions.

Why does a corporation emerge as a target of a hostile takeover? Why have takeovers become so pervasive in the last decade? One explanation is inflation: The cost of replacing existing assets far exceeds the value placed on these assets. It is therefore cheaper to buy existing plants, buildings, machinery, inventories, and the like, than to produce new ones. It is cheaper to buy known oil reserves held by oil companies than to search for new oil. Another explanation focuses on mismanagement by isolated, arrogant, lazy American management. Managers not only have allowed American industry to fall behind foreign competition but they also have failed to put the assets of their corporations to their most productive use. Return on invested capital and world market shares have dwindled. The corporate raiders offer a way to "throw the rascals out" of the boardroom and reinvigorate American enterprise.

Government antitrust and tax policies combine to encourage mergers and takeovers. Tax policies contribute by allowing corporations to deduct from their taxable income the interest on loans used to acquire other companies. Both the U.S. Department of Justice and the Federal Trade Commission are responsible for enforcing the nation's antitrust laws. These laws forbid "monopoly" and "combinations in restraint of trade" (Sherman Antitrust Act, 1887), "unfair method of competition" and "efforts to reduce competition" (Federal Trade Commission Act, 1914), and the acquisition by one corporation of another "where the effect of such acquisition is to substantially lessen competition" (Clayton Act, 1914). But the interpretations placed on these laws in recent years have given increasing attention to *world* market conditions. It is argued that increasing concentrations of corporate assets in the United States through mergers do *not* "substantially lessen competition" because these firms are competing in a world market against giant Japanese and European multinational corporations. Indeed, in such a world market, it is even argued that the U.S. government should *encourage* mergers of U.S. firms in order to strengthen them against foreign competition.

Still another explanation is greed. The banks and the Wall Street investment firms which finance hostile takeovers charge high fees and commissions on the transactions, and they levy excessive interest rates on the junk bonds. The "mergers and acquisitions" (M and A) division of these firms is where the action is for ambitious young men and women. Traditionally conservative commercial banks have been squeezed by deregulation: They no longer enjoy zero-interest checking accounts, once protected by regulatory agencies. Typical checking accounts now pay 5 or 6 percent interest to depositors and the costs of processing checks may add another 2 or 3 percent. Thus, to make a profit—to maximize the "interest spread" between what the bank pays for money and what it charges borrowers—banks must seek out high-risk loans on which high interest rates can be charged. Initially, banks turned to Third World foreign loans—Mexico, Brazil, Zaire, Argentina. But when these loans turned sour, the banks turned to junk bonds. "The American commercial bank is pinched by the shrinkage of its traditional sources of income and almost desperate to find borrowers willing to pay very high interest rates. And the raider who makes a hostile takeover bid is, of course, perfectly willing to promise very high interest rates; after all, he will not pay them—the company he is aiming to take over will, after it has succumbed."[15]

Are corporate takeovers good or bad for America? There is no easy answer to this important question. The raiders claim that their activities force improvements in efficiency and productivity. Even the potential threat of a takeover forces corporate managers to streamline

[15]Peter Ducker, "Corporate Takeovers—What Is to Be Done?" *The Public Interest,* 82 (Winter 1986), 9.

their operations, eliminate waste, increase revenues, raise profits, and distribute profits to their shareholders rather than spend them on the comforts of management. The raiders argue that American management has grown soft, lazy, and self-satisfied; that, as a result, the American corporation has lost its competitive edge in the world marketplace.

Opponents of the corporate-takeover movement argue that fear of the raider forces management to focus on near-term profits at the expense of long-range research and development. Management must keep the current price of its stock high in order to deter a takeover attempt. Even worse, management often resorts to "poison pills" to deliberately weaken its own corporation to make it unattractive to raiders; it may increase its debt, buy other poorly performing corporations, devalue stockholders' voting powers, provide itself with "golden parachutes" (rich severance benefits) in the event of ouster. The corporate raiders enrich the shareholders and speculators, but they do so at the expense of the industry itself.

The debt which is incurred in corporate takeovers is a concern to employees, consumers, and taxpayers. While the original stockholders are paid handsomely by the raider, the corporation must labor intensively to pay off the debt incurred. The corporation may be broken apart and its separate pieces sold, which may disrupt and demoralize employees. Consumers may be forced to pay higher prices. If the corporation cannot meet the high interest payments, bankruptcy threatens. The corporation's heavy interest payments are tax-deductible, thus depriving the U.S. Treasury of corporate tax revenues. And the diversion of American capital from productive investments to takeovers threatens to weaken future national productivity.

THE CORPORATE RAIDERS

Carl Ichan generates more fear in America's corporate boardrooms than any communist revolutionary. The dreaded corporate raider has attacked such fortresses as TransWorld Airlines, Gulf + Western, American Can, Uniroyal, Goodrich, and Phillips Petroleum. Ichan graduated from Princeton University and then dropped out of medical school before starting his Wall Street career in investment banking. He founded Ichan and Company with a half-million dollars borrowed from his uncle. He began his corporate raiding in 1978 with a bid to take over the old, undervalued Tappan Company, makers of kitchen stoves. Over the years, he became skilled in identifying corporations whose assets were greater than the market value of their stock, and then lining up the massive financial backing required to purchase the stock. Even when he fails to win control of a target corporation, Ichan usually reaps a large "greenmail" profit on the stock he has purchased.

In Ichan's opinion, the nation's top corporate managers have become a "new aristocracy." He sees himself as a champion of the rights of long-suffering stockholders. He deplores management's negligent and self-serving stewardship of America's industrial assets. Ichan truly believes that he is forcing American management to become more competitive, to eliminate waste and bureaucracy, to work harder and become more productive. He ridicules what he calls the "corpocracy":

> Just like college, where the president of the fraternity is a real likable guy, the president or the CEO of the company is usually a likable guy . . .
>
> But they're not the cleverest, because clever guys, intelligent guys, are often abrasive and they're not that well-liked . . . what has happened in management is that the guys who got to the top are the guys that the board liked.

Top management, he claims, feathers its own nest at the expense of the stockholders, employees, and consumers.

> They're out on their jet planes with their wives going on safari and the company is going to the dogs, and then they'll give parties for themselves to celebrate how great they are.
>
> We can't have people on the dole. But when you have ten layers of bureaucracy in a corporation, isn't that the same as the dole? You can't have people walking around, all giving paperwork to other people . . . They're not producing for our society.

Ichan does not believe that the current style of corporate governance through a board of directors provides the necessary accountability for management.

> I was on the board of one company and really it's a frightening thing. . . . Here's what goes on, Literally, half the board is dozing off. The other half is reading *The Wall Street Journal*. And they put up slides and nobody can understand the slides and when it get dark they all doze off.
>
> [The CEO] was in control of that board. I mean nobody would say anything.

Ichan believes that only the *owners* of corporations can provide truly responsible leadership, because their own money is at stake. He believes America is losing its competitive edge in the world because management has grown lazy and self-satisfied.

> In the days when our country was the top industrial power—and we are really losing that edge today—my argument is that there was accountability. Because of ownership. The Andrew Carnegies and Mellons and other

people who built us up made sure that there was accountability in the corporations they owned, because it was their money at stake.

So Ichan defends the role of the corporate raider in forcing America's corporate managers to perform better:

> The problem we have in our managerial society today is that there is no accountability because corporate democracy is a travesty. Except when a guy like Carl Ichan comes along or a few others and really holds them accountable, management really operates without any constraints.[16]

LEE IACOCCA: CELEBRITY CEO

No one has climbed the corporate ladder to as much success and celebrity as Lido Anthony Iacocca.[17] His father Nicola emigrated from Italy and began a rent-a-car business in Allentown, Pennsylvania, in the 1920s. He sent his son to nearby Lehigh University to study mechanical engineering. Lido graduated in 1945, changed his name to Lee, and joined an executive training program at Ford Motors. Ford allowed him to accept a fellowship at Princeton where he completed a masters degree in engineering before returning to Ford headquarters in Detroit.

At this time in Ford's corporate history, young Henry Ford II was trying to build a high-quality engineering department to change the reputation of the company for dull and unimaginative car designs. Ford recruited the nation's best young talent, the "Whiz Kids," including Robert McNamara (later secretary of defense) and Arjay Miller (later dean of Sanford's Business School). Iacocca was originally included in this gifted group, but he soon made a risky career decision to leave engineering for marketing. He left Ford headquarters for a job selling Ford trucks in Chester, Pennsylvania, not far from his home town. Detroit might never have heard from Iacocca again, except for the fact that he turned out to be the best car salesman in the nation's history.

Iacocca spent ten years in face-to-face sales work. He knew enough engineering to talk "nuts and bolts" to truck buyers. His first big success came in 1956 with a sales campaign slogan "56 in 56"—a monthly payment of $56 would buy a 1956 Ford. Iacocca's district sales office soared to tops in the nation; Ford vice-president Robert McNamara heard about it, ordered the campaign to be used nationwide, and called Iacocca back to Detroit.

Iacocca's skills in marketing have become legendary. On arriving in Detroit he pressed the company to develop a car that would appeal to the baby boom generation in high school and college in the early 1960s.

---

[16] Ichan as quoted in *Newsweek*, October 20, 1986, pp. 51–52.

[17] See Lee Iacocca, *Iacocca* (New York: Bantam Books, 1984).

McNamara wanted to stick with basic low-priced transportation, the Falcon, with an auto safety campaign. Iacocca argued with his mentor, "Safety doesn't sell," and urged the building of a new speedy convertible for the youth market.

Henry Ford II had been badly burned in the Edsel fiasco a few years earlier and was unwilling to devote capital to another new car concept. So Iacocca used parts and pieces of cars already in stock in designing what turned out to be the most successful Ford car since the original Model T—the Mustang. The Mustang was not really a new car from an engineering perspective; but Iacocca marketed it as a flashy, low-priced sporty car for America's youth. Later he topped his own success by introducing the Mark series of luxury cars, which became even more profitable than the Mustang.

Lee Iacocca's ambition, competitiveness, and skill in corporate politics, created enemies as well as admirers. His detractors describe him as a glorified car salesman who mercilessly drives his subordinates and frequently takes credit for their accomplishments. Eventually Iacocca's ambition inspired suspicion in the boss himself, Henry Ford II. Iacocca became Ford president in 1970 after Henry Ford II had abruptly fired Bunkie Knudson, whom Ford had earlier recruited from General Motors. But by 1975 the boss began to question Iacocca's leadership. Sales of the Mustang were fading, and the new Pinto was a disaster. Henry Ford denied Iacocca's $2 billion request to develop front-wheel-drive cars and ordered an investigation of his president's expense account. Finally, after a stormy exchange in 1978, Ford fired Iacocca. When Iacocca asked what he had done wrong, Ford snapped, "Nothing, I just don't like you."

Lee Iacocca later expressed his feelings about Henry Ford II in words that had to be bleeped out of a television documentary. But he also described his personal philosophy: "Don't get mad, get even." Three months after his dismissal from Ford, Lee Iacocca was named president of the Chrysler Corporation.

Chrysler has always been number three among the American automakers, following General Motors and Ford. When Iacocca took over, Chrysler was down to only 8 percent of the market. It had no small or fuel-efficient cars to compete in the new fuel-conscious market. Worst of all, Chrysler cars had a reputation for poor quality. Dealers were deserting the company in droves; Chrysler faced imminent bankruptcy.

The Chrysler turnaround, engineered by Lee Iacocca, is one of the most dramatic events in American corporate history. Iacocca moved decisively on many fronts to save the company—rolling back union wages, cutting inventories, slashing the work force by almost half, forcing suppliers to lower prices. By 1984 his drastic cutting placed the company in a position where it could make a profit on sales of 1.2 million cars versus the 2.3 million it needed in 1980. He placed union president Lane Kirkland on the Chrysler board of directors. He introduced new cars: first the front-wheel-drive K cars, later the first new convertibles to be produced by Detroit in over a decade, and still later a popular minivan. He revamped the company's quality-control procedures and introduced unprecedented guarantees to reclaim the confidence of Chrysler buyers. He purchased American Motors Corporation, producers of the Jeep line of vehicles, and doubled Chrysler's share of the truck market.

Iacocca became a national celebrity when he went on television to sell his cars and the "new" Chrysler Corporation. The advertising agency executives were at first skeptical, but they later realized that having a corporate president speak directly to the American people was the best way to restore confidence in the product. "People believe in him. He wasn't slick or made up. It was as if he had just come from the battlefield, which he had." Iacocca came across to the American public as just the man he was—brash, confident, tough-talking.

The most controversial aspect of Iacocca's efforts to save Chrysler was his federal "bail out" scheme. Iacocca asked the federal government for $1.2 billion in loan guarantees in 1979, after the nation's major banks had decided that the Chrysler Corporation was beyond help. Going hat-in-hand to Washington was a humiliating experience for the self-made champion of private enterprise. But Iacocca is a pragmatist: "U.S. aid for Central America. Hell, when I think of 'Central America' I think of Michigan, Ohio, Indiana." Very few people gave Chrysler much of a chance to survive even *with* federal assistance. In 1983, Iacocca paid back the federal loans—seven years ahead of schedule. Iacocca is firmly established as the champion of smokestack America. He popularized the "Buy America" idea at the same time that he was importing more Japanese cars than any of his domestic rivals. Through the same marketing wizardry, he persuaded buyers to forgive Chrysler for tampering with odometers merely by apologizing in a massive ad campaign.

THE INHERITORS: STARTING AT THE TOP

Unquestionably, the Rockefellers, Fords, du Ponts, Mellons, and other families still exercise great power over America's corporate resources. However, research on family holdings in large corporations is not easy. Table 2–8 lists major family holdings of large corporations as revealed in a variety of sources. It is an even more difficult task to learn whether a family really "controls" the operations of a corporation, or whether control has been passed on to the managers. It is possible for families who no longer hold active management positions in a corporation to

TABLE 2–8 Family Influence in Corporations

CORPORATION	FAMILY
E.I. du Pont de Nemours	du Pont
Ford Motor Co.	Ford
Aluminum Co. of America	Mellon
Carborundum Co.	Mellon
Gulf Oil Co.	Mellon, Scaife
Sun Oil Co.	Pew
Pittsburgh Plate Glass	Pitcairn
Exxon	Rockefeller
Mobil	Rockefeller
Standard Oil of California	Rockefeller
Sears, Roebuck & Co.	Rosenwald
Polaroid Corp.	Land
IBM	Watson, Fairchild
Dow Chemical Co.	Dow
Corning Glass Works	Houghton
International Paper Co.	Phipps
W.R. Grace & Co.	Grace, Phipps
Weyerhauser	Weyerhaeuser
Winn-Dixie, Inc.	Davis
Campbell Soup Company	Dorrance
H.J. Heinz Co.	Heinz
Wm. Wrigley Jr. Co.	Wrigley
Firestone Tire & Rubber	Firestone
Columbia Broadcasting Co. (CBS)	Paley
Olin Chemical	Olin
Ralston Purina Co.	Danforth
Hilton Hotels	Hilton
Howard Johnson Co.	Johnson
Great Atlantic & Pacific Tea Co. (A&P)	Hartford
Woolco	Woolworth
McDonnell Douglas Aircraft	McDonnell
International Harvester	McCormick
Coca-Cola	Woodruff
Eli Lilly & Co.	Lilly
Duke Power Co.	Duke
Rockwell Mfg. Co.	Rockwell
Gerber Products Co.	Gerber
Deere & Company	Deere
Borden Co.	Borden

Sources: Ferdinand Lunberg, *The Rich and the Super-Rich* (New York: Lyle Stuart, 1968); *Fortune*, June 15, 1967; update to *Fortune*, "Directory of the Largest 500 Corporations," June 1981; and Edward S. Herman, *Corporate Control, Corporate Power* (Cambridge, Mass.: Cambridge University Press, 1981), Table 2–7.

exercise "latent" power—that is, to use their control blocks of stock as a restraint on management. Sometimes families interfere only when something goes seriously wrong.

Some members of the corporate elite "start at the top." *Fortune* suggests that 150 of the largest 500 industrial corporations are controlled by one or more members of a single family.[18] True, most of these individual- or family-controlled corporations are ranked *below* the top 100. But if indeed 30 percent of American industrial corporations are controlled by individuals or family groups, then the claimed disappearance of the traditional American capitalist may have been exaggerated.

However, even family-controlled corporations recruit professional managers from the ranks. Indeed, nearly all of the directors of Ford, Alcoa, Gulf, Exxon, Chase Manhattan, du Pont, and other such corporations are professional managers recruited from outside the family.

It does not seem to matter much whether the inheritors or the managers really control America's largest corporations; the end policies appear to be the same. Management is motivated by considerations of growth, stability, and profit, and so are prudent family stockholders. Moreover, managers themselves usually acquire sizable blocks of stock in their own companies as they move up through the ranks. It is doubtful that the decisions of managers differ a great deal from those of inheritors. *Fortune* magazine agrees:

> It is expected that the demise of the owner-manager would markedly affect the conduct and performance of business. Some have predicted that the new managerial brass, as essentially non-owners, would lack the self-interested maximization of profits that inspired proprietors, would be inclined to curb dividends, and would be tempted to provide themselves with disproportionately large salaries and bonuses. . . .
>
> Despite these theories, it is extremely doubtful that ownership or the lack of it motivated the conduct of executives in such a direct way. Very few executives agree that the managers of a widely held company run their business any differently from the proprietors of a closely held company. Competition is a great leveler, and both managers and proprietors respond to its pressures with equal spirit and objectivity.[19]

After carefully comparing the performance of managerial-run corporations with owner-dominated corporations, Wharton Business School professor Edward S. Herman reaches the same conclusion:

[18] Robert Sheehan, "Family-Run Corporations: There Are More of Them Than You Think" *Fortune,* June 15, 1967, p. 179.

[19] Ibid., p. 183.

In sum, the triumph of management control in many large corporations has not left them in the hands of neutral technocrats. The control groups of these organizations seem as devoted to profitable growth as are the leaders of entrepreneurial and owner-dominated companies, past and present.[20]

HENRY FORD II: THE INHERITOR AS BOSS

Until 1980, Henry Ford II, grandson of the Ford Motor Company founder, served as chairman of the board. "The first thing you have to understand about the company is that Henry Ford is the boss. . . . He *is* the boss, he always was the boss since the first day I came in and he always will be the boss." These are the words of Arjay Miller, who spent twenty-three years climbing the rungs of Ford management to become president of the company, only to find that Henry Ford II actually ran things. Miller eventually resigned to become dean of the Graduate School of Business at Stanford University.[21]

Henry Ford II grew up in a very narrow society; he was a member of a rich, insulated family that was dominated by his grandfather, known to be an exceedingly suspicious, prejudiced, and willful man. Young Ford attended Hotchkiss School and later Yale University. However, he failed to graduate in 1940 after admitting that he had cheated on a term paper. He enlisted in the U.S. Navy and served until his father died in 1943; President Roosevelt directed the secretary of the navy to release Ford to return to the family business.

Ford started in the automobile industry at the age of twenty-five as vice-president of Ford Motors, serving under his aged grandfather. A year later he took over the presidency. His initial decisions were to replace the one-person autocratic rule of the company with a modern management structure, recruiting bright, young management types (the famous Ford "Whiz Kids," including Robert S. McNamara, who later resigned as Ford president to become secretary of defense; Lee Iacocca; Arjay Miller; and Charles B. Thornton, later to become chairman of Litton Industries). He also initiated a modern labor relations program and ended the company's traditional hostility toward labor unions. As commonplace as these policies appear today, they were considered advanced, enlightened, and liberal for the Ford Motor Company at the time.

Over the years Ford proved himself a capable director of the company, despite some occasional and even colossal mistakes. (The Edsel

[20]Herman, *Corporate Control, Corporate Power*, pp. 112–13.

[21]Quoted in Victory Lasky, *Never Complain, Never Explain* (New York: Richard Marek, 1981), p. 86.

fiasco cost the company over $300 million.) Ford worked long hours at the company headquarters in Detroit. He personally approved style changes in Ford cars and test-drove them himself. He was active on the board of the Ford Foundation, and conscientiously reviewed research and grant proposals with other board members. His younger brothers, Benson and William Clay, eventually became Ford vice-presidents and board members. (William Clay Ford married the daughter of tire manufacturer Harvey S. Firestone, Jr. and purchased the Detroit Lions professional football team.)

Henry Ford II helped launch the National Urban Coalition and organized the National Alliance of Businessmen to provide more jobs for minorities. He was a prime mover in Detroit's urban renewal and redevelopment program, Renaissance Center. It was Ford himself who convinced his old rival, General Motors, as well as Amoco, K-Mart, Parke-Davis, and Western International Hotels, to invest in the central city project. When cost overruns forced up the price of the project, Ford "arm-twisted" many Ford suppliers—U.S. Steel, Firestone, Budd Company—to come up with the additional funds.

Like many people born to wealth and power, Ford's personal style was far from that of the bland organizational person. He was frequently unpredictable, sometimes abrasive, often profane; he expressed his opinions directly. His public and private actions were often controversial. (He divorced his wife of many years and married a beautiful, young Italian actress in 1965; in 1980, he divorced her to marry an American model.)

The Ford Foundation was created before the death of the elder Henry Ford to protect the family fortune from inheritance taxes. Originally, it supported charities in the Detroit area; its assets were primarily Ford stock. As the company prospered, the value of the foundation assets increased. In 1951, Henry Ford II asked Robert Hutchins, chancellor of the University of Chicago, to take over the foundation and make it a national force in civic affairs. Hutchins immediately funded some projects that "the Chairman" did not like; Hutchins was cut loose to become head of the Fund for the Republic, a smaller, Ford-funded foundation. The Ford Foundation supported the moderate black civil rights organization, the Urban League, with Henry Ford II's approval. In 1966, McGeorge Bundy, Presidents Kennedy and Johnson's national security adviser, became the Ford Foundation head.

Bundy gradually sold off the Ford stock from the foundation assets. Bundy and Henry Ford clashed over the liberal programs of the foundation. Finally, in 1976, Ford resigned from his directorship of the Ford Foundation. In his resignation letter, he pointedly advised the foundation to direct more attention to strengthening the system. "The Foundation is a creature of capitalism. . . . I'm just suggesting to the trustees and the staff that the system that makes the Foundation possible very probably is worth preserving."[22]

By 1980, Henry Ford II faced many troubles. The Pinto car had to be recalled for a faulty gas tank—the largest recall in auto history. Brother Benson Ford died of a heart attack. The break with Lee Iacocca was troublesome. Henry went through another divorce and remarriage. His nephew, Benson Ford, Jr., sued him over his father's will and demanded a seat on the Ford board, which Henry denied him. And in 1980, the Ford Motor Company lost $1.5 billion—the largest annual loss in the history of any American corporation. (Of course, General Motors lost money that year, and Chrysler would have gone bankrupt without favorable U.S. government loan guarantees.) Henry Ford II resigned as chairman of the board of Ford Motors.

The Ford family continues to hold a large bloc of Ford Motor stock. Henry Ford II's son, Edsel B. Ford, and his nephew, William Clay Ford, Jr., are both promising Ford Company executives who might make it to the top. In 1980 Henry said that his son and nephew were still "a good ten years" away from top management. When Henry was reminded that he himself inherited the presidency at age twenty-six, he said only that "times have changed."

CHANGING OF THE GUARD

Top leadership in the corporate world changes slowly over time. A reasonably successful president or chairperson and chief executive officer can expect to run the corporation for eight to ten years. Management "climbers," those who have spent thirty years in the corporation, may become president or chairperson at age fifty-eight or sixty and may expect to serve to age sixty-five or sixty-seven. Of course, family "inheritors" may have much longer tenures at the top; Henry Ford II was the dominant figure at Ford Motors for over forty years.

Nonetheless, there is inevitably a "changing of the guard"—a succession to power—in the corporate world as elsewhere. At the beginning of the 1980s, it seemed as if a generation of powerful corporate leaders was stepping aside: Irving S. Shapiro of Du Pont, Thomas A. Murphy of General Motors, Reginald Jones of General Electric, J. Paul Austin of Coca-Cola, and Harold Geneen of ITT all announced their retirements. David Rockefeller retired as chairman of Chase Manhattan, and Henry Ford II retired as chairman of Ford Motors.

Despite a few highly publicized firings, top corporate directors are well insulated in their positions. Turnover rates are far lower than in

[22]*Newsweek,* January 24, 1977, p. 69.

TABLE 2-9   Stability and Change among the Corporate Giants: Largest Industrial Corporations by Size of Assets, 1940, 1952, 1970, 1986

1940		1952	
RANK		RANK	
1.	Standard Oil of N.J. (Exxon)	1.	Standard Oil of N.J. (Exxon)
2.	U.S. Steel	2.	General Motors
3.	General Motors	3.	U.S. Steel
4.	Socony Vacuum (Mobil)	4.	Socony Vacuum (Mobil)
5.	Du Pont	5.	Standard Oil (Ind.)
6.	Bethlehem Steel	6.	Ford
7.	Standard Oil (Ind.)	7.	Texas Corp. (Texaco)
8.	Ford	8.	Du Pont
9.	Texas Corp. (Texaco)	9.	Gulf Oil
10.	Standard Oil (Calif.)	10.	Bethlehem Steel
11.	Anaconda Cooper	11.	G.E.
12.	Gulf Oil	12.	Standard Oil (Calif.)
13.	G.E.	13.	Sears, Roebuck
14.	International Harvester	14.	Westinghouse
15.	Republic Steel	15.	International Harvester
16.	Kennecott Copper	16.	Union Carbide
17.	Shell Oil	17.	Cities Service
18.	Union Carbide	18.	Sinclair Oil
19.	Consolidated Oil	19.	Phillips Petroleum
20.	American Tobacco	20.	Chrysler

1970		1986	
RANK		RANK	
1.	Exxon	1.	General Motors
2.	General Motors	2.	Exxon
3.	Texaco	3.	IBM
4.	Ford	4.	Ford
5.	Gulf Oil	5.	Mobil
6.	IBM	6.	G.E.
7.	Mobil	7.	AT&T
8.	GTE	8.	Chevron
9.	ITT	9.	Texaco
10.	Standard Oil (Calif.)	10.	Du Pont
11.	U.S. Steel	11.	Shell
12.	G.E.	12.	Amoco
13.	Standard Oil (Ind.)	13.	BP America
14.	Chrysler	14.	Atlantic Rich
15.	Shell Oil	15.	Chrysler
16.	Atlantic Rich.	16.	USX
17.	Tenneco	17.	Philip Morris
18.	Western Electric	18.	Tenneco
19.	Du Pont	19.	RJR Nabisco
20.	Union Carbide	20.	Occidental

government. The average CEO still controls the directors, having selected most of them in the first place. Only a really disastrous corporate performance can inspire a revolution against management.

Corporate leadership is very stable not only because turnover among managers and directors is low but also because the nation's largest corporations are seldom displaced from their dominant positions in the marketplace. By and large, the nation's largest industrial corporations in the 1980s were the nation's largest industrial corporations in the 1940s (see Table 2–9). These large corporations, although not invulnerable, possess great power to protect and enlarge their positions over time. This power derives from various sources: obstacles to entry for new firms; their giant scale of operations and low marginal costs; worldwide access to raw materials and markets; ready access to money for expansion from their own profits and from large banks; and diversification which protects many of these giants from the vagaries of particular markets and allows them to shift resources to the most promising growth areas. Nonetheless, there are identifiable changes in the rankings of the largest industrial corporations: the growth of computer technology has permitted IBM to emerge as an industrial giant; world surpluses of copper have taken their toll on America's great copper companies, Anaconda and Kennicott; world competition has also contributed to the decline of the great steel companies—U.S. Steel (now USX), Bethlehem, and Republic. Yet overall, the industrial giants of fifty years ago are still the industrial giants of today.

THE LIMITS OF CORPORATE POWER

Elites do not like to acknowledge their own power. Kenneth Olsen, CEO of Digital Equipment, offered a typical elite response to the question of power: "I've got no power. All I can do is encourage people, motivate people to do things. I've got no power over them."[23] Why do elites say things like this? It is not merely modesty nor intent to deceive. "Power" in a democratic society has acquired a pejorative meaning—tyranny, arbitrariness, absolute rule. And this connotation conflicts with the requirements for successful corporate leadership today. Hence, corporate elites deny they have power; but they acknowledge that they have the principle responsibility for "how the company is run."

Yet top corporate elites feel more constrained today in the exercise of their authority than in the past. Many believe that the era of the all-powerful CEOs is over. No large corporation can be directed from the

[23]Quoted in *Forbes*, May 30, 1988, p. 120

top in the fashion of William Paley's CBS, Armand Hammer's Occidental Petroleum, or Harold Geneen's ITT.

The greatest constraint on corporate power is the global market. Thirty years ago the American market was isolated; each sector of industry was a self-contained oligopoly with three to eight major manufacturers competing in a limited fashion. Top corporate elites were relatively unconstrained in deciding about products and prices, technologies and innovations, capital flows and investments. But today, global competition severely limits American corporate decision-making. The United States remains the world's largest market (until 1992 when the

TABLE 2–10 Pressures on the Corporate Elite

OTHERS GAINING INFUENCE

Compared with five years ago, would you say that the following individuals or institutions have gained influence over decisions in companies such as yours, lost influence, or kept their influence?

	GAINED INFLUENCE	LOST INFLUENCE	KEPT INFLUENCE	NOT SURE
Institutions holding big stock blocs	47%	2%	42%	9%
Raiders and potential raiders	58	2	24	16
Investment bankers	46	13	36	5
Stock analysts	48	4	43	5
Government regulators	41	20	34	5
Environmentalists	37	14	40	9
Consumer groups	28	14	49	9
Labor unions	2	54	34	10

SHORT-TERM PRESSURE

Let me read you a list of people, institutions, and other factors that might be the source of pressure on companies to focus on the short term, rather than on long-term growth. Tell me which three or four you believe exert the most pressure on companies to focus on the short term.

Banks holding debt	12%
Bond-rating services	14
Boards of directors	15
Financial press	34
Institutional shareholders	58
Investment bankers, takeover advisers	45
Securities analysts	65

Source: Survey of 400 chief executives of corporations in the top 1,000, reported by *Business Week*, October 23, 1987, p. 28.

European Economic Community emerges as a unified market). But large shares of the U.S. market have been captured by foreign competition in nearly every industrial sector.

Top corporate elites believe their own power is more limited today than a few years ago. They believe other elites have gained in power relative to themselves. They acknowledge that labor unions have lost influence in American life, but they believe that institutional investors and bankers, Wall Street analysts, government regulators, and most of all, corporate raiders, are gaining power (see Table 2–10).

America's corporate elite has come under severe criticism for its failure to plan for the long term, to direct funds into research, and to develop strategies to confront the global competition. It is charged with myopic concerns with short-term profits, tomorrow's stock prices, and next quarter's earnings.

Elites agree that the criticism is justified, but they claim that their failure to focus on long-term growth strategies is a result of pressures from institutional investors, Wall Street analysts, and corporate raiders.

WHO OWNS AMERICA?

The managerial thesis—the notion that effective control of large corporations is now vested in the hands of the active managers rather than the passive stockholders—has become the conventional wisdom.[24] Nonetheless, a spirited minority of scholars have challenged the managerial thesis, which they contend has been overstated because of the absence of "up-to-date reliable evidence."[25] It is a very difficult task to learn exactly who "controls" a corporation. The concept of control may involve distinguishing between active and latent power where owners may intervene with management only when things go seriously astray. This latent power may be better understood as a constraint on management decision-making, similiar to the constraints of government regulation or union activism. The concept of control may also involve distinctions between policy initiation and "veto power." Owners may exercise control over only a limited sphere of company activity (quantity of borrowing, dividend payouts, sale of assets, and so on). The concept of control may also involve a distinction between "financial" control and "operating" control: Owners may exercise prevailing influence over external financial functions (raising and supplying capital funds, buying and selling

[24]Edward S. Herman, *Corporation: Control Corporate Power* (Boston: Houghton Mifflin, 1981), p. 14.

[25]Phillip H. Burch *The Managerial Revolution Reconsidered* (Lexington, Mass.: D.C. Heath, 1972), p. 9.

securities, merging and acquiring other corporations, and the like), while management exercises prevailing influence over the operating activities of the corporation (producing and selling automobiles, chemicals, or business machines).

The diffusion of ownership of the nation's largest corporations makes it possible to acquire power in the corporation by owning a very small percentage of the voting common stock. There is no specific percentage of ownership (under 50) which guarantees "control." Table 2–11 shows the five largest owners of each of the fifteen largest industrial corporations in 1981. Note that many of these largest owners own only 1 or 2 percent of the corporation's total common stock.

Who are these largest owners? Banks and their trust departments own nearly one quarter of the common stock in the Fortune 500 industrial corporations. While banks are owners of record, in many cases banks hold stock as trustees for other "ultimate" owners. It is not possible to trace all of the beneficiaries of banks' holdings. Banks often hold stock on behalf of employee stock-saving and profit-sharing plans (ESPs) as indicated on Table 2–11. Herman writes about ESPs: "I heavily discount bank power arising from the ESP trustee function. Because banks are dependent on management in all aspects of such plans, the ESP strengthens management control."[26]

Financial investment firms also hold about one quarter of the common stock of the nation's largest industrial corporations. Investment firms, like banks, very often hold these positions as trustees on behalf of other owners, and it is not possible to know who all of the ultimate owners may be. However, again we can identify ESPs as holders of about half of the positions under investment firms. Less important in ownership are the insurance companies, the pension funds, and industrial corporations themselves. Foreign ownership is confined to a small num-

TABLE 2–11 Strategic Ownership Positions in America's Largest Industrial Corporations, 1981

OWNERS	SHARES	BLOC PERCENTAGE
EXXON (outstanding shares: 453,205,000)		
Exxon Corporation		
Exxon Thrift Plan	9,481,047	2.09
Rockefeller Family	7,650,600	1.68
Chase Manhattan	6,792,848	1 ⌐
Manufacturers Hanover	4,451,394	
SAROFIM & Co.	4,385,00⌐	

[26]Herman, *Corporation: Control, Corporate Power*, p. 24.

TABLE 2–11 *(Continued)*

OWNERS	SHARES	BLOC PERCENTAGE
GENERAL MOTORS (outstanding shares: 286,869,000)		
National Detroit Corp.		
GM ESP	39,164,990	13.65
du Pont Family	20,080,830	7.00
TIAA-CREF	4,201,000	1.46
J.P. Morgan & Co.	3,684,000	1.28
Prudential Insurance	3,551,300	1.23
MOBIL (outstanding shares: 212,143,000)		
Bankers Trust NY		
Mobil ESP	13,337,399	6.28
J.P. Morgan & Co.	4,864,000	2.29
Rockefeller Family	4,193,438	1.97
Internorth Inc.	3,000,433	1.41
Bancoklahoma	2,637,250	1.24
STANDARD OIL INDIANA (outstanding shares: 292,335,000)		
First Chicago Corp.		
Standard Oil Indiana ESP	24,074,603	8.22
Blaustein Family	10,500,000	3.58
SAROFIM & Co.	4,707,027	1.60
Chase Manhattan	2,989,460	1.02
Mudd Family	2,844,165	.97
IBM (outstanding shares: 583,374,000)		
J.P. Morgan & Co.	13,747,000	2.35
Manufacturers Hanover	9,200,729	1.57
Bankers Trust NY	5,833,014	.99
Chase Manhattan	5,720,560	.98
TIAA-CREF	5,095,700	.97
GULF OIL (outstanding shares: 195,033,000)		
Mellon Family	21,453,630	11.00
Mellon National Corp.	4,221,703	2.16
Prudential	3,579,200	1.83
TIAA-CREF	2,883,400	1.47
First Tulsa	2,126,751	1.09
ATLANTIC RICHFIELD (outstanding shares: 236,244,000)		
Security Pacific		
Atlantic Richfield ESP	7,375,969	3.12
Citicorp	4,403,984	1.86
Manufacturers Hanover	4,063,515	1.72
Prudential	2,533,200	1.07
BankAmerica	2,499,335	1.03
FORD (outstanding shares: 177,262,000)		
Ford Family	71,624,938	40.40
Manufacturers National Corp.		
Ford ESP	30,994,661	17.48
Capital Group	3,301,700	1.86
Batterymarch Financial	1,972,250	1.11

TABLE 2–11 *(Continued)*

OWNERS	SHARES	BLOC PERCENTAGE
FIRESTONE (outstanding shares: 57,660,000)		
Firestone Family	12,685,200	22.00
Ameritrust Co.	8,301,851	14.39
Manufacturers Hanover		
Firestone ESP	3,740,037	6.48
Capital Group	1,928,500	3.34
Citicorp	1,051,409	1.65
DUPONT (outstanding shares: 144,718,000)		
du Pont Family	50,651,300	35.00
Delaware Trust	3,350,342	2.31
Capital Group	2,559,100	1.76
Prudential	2,144,900	1.48
Manufacturers Hanover	2,005,478	1.38
ITT (outstanding shares: 114,468,000)		
du Pont Family	4,112,900	3.58
Bankers Trust NY		
ITT ESP	4,025,435	3.51
Batterymarch Financial	2,702,004	2.35
TIAA-CREF	2,385,700	2.08
California Public Employees Retirement System	2,019,712	1.76
GENERAL ELECTRIC (outstanding shares: 226,335,000)		
General Electric Co.		
General Electric ESP	9,319,402	4.11
Eccles Family	3,377,951	1.49
TIAA-CREF	2,857,200	1.26
J.P. Morgan & Co.	2,310,000	1.02
Capital Group	2,302,000	1.01
U.S. STEEL (outstanding shares: 86,367,000)		
U.S. Steel Corp.		
U.S. Steel ESP	14,437,079	16.71
Capital Group	1,601,900	1.85
FMR Corp.	1,430,000	1.65
Batterymarch Financial	1,240,300	1.43
Manufacturers Hanover	1,226,415	1.42
SHELL OIL (outstanding shares: 308,839,000)		
Royal Dutch Shell	214,503,246	69.45
First City Bancorp Texas		
Shell Oil ESP	25,518,974	8.26
Shell Oil Co.	23,500,000	7.60
DOW CHEMICAL (outstanding shares: 181,007,000)		
Dow Family	15,957,548	8.81
Ameritrust Co.		
Dow ESP	6,091,267	3.36
National Detroit	3,742,538	2.06
Richardson Family	2,874,555	1.58
J.P. Morgan & Co.	2,435,000	1.34

ber of corporations; British Petroleum owns 55 percent of Standard Oil of Ohio, and Royal Dutch Shell owns 69.45 percent of Shell Oil.

Family and individual ownership is still very impressive. Families and individuals hold as many large blocs of stock in the Fortune 500 as banks or investment firms. Many of these family holdings are well known to students of American capitalism. The du Pont family holdings are more extensive and more valuable than any other. The du Ponts own large blocs in 24 of the Fortune 500 industrial corporations, positions worth a total of more than $5 billion. Their holdings include 35 percent of the Du Pont Corporation and 7 percent of General Motors. The Fords own 40.4 percent of Ford Motors, and the Gettys own 50.18 percent of Getty Oil.

THE SUPERRICH: DISTINGUISHING WEALTH FROM POWER

It is a mistake to equate *personal* wealth with economic power. Persons with relatively little personal wealth can exercise great power if they occupy positions that give them control of huge institutional resources. A president of a large company who came through the ranks of management may receive an income of only $600,000 or $800,000 a year, and possess a net worth of only $2 million or $3 million. Yet these amounts are small when you consider that this person may control a corporation with annual revenues of $2 *billion* and assets worth $10 *billion* or $20 *billion*. (The contrast is even greater in government where $60,000-a-year bureaucrats manage government expenditures of $50 *billion* a year!) The important point is that personal wealth in America is insignificant in comparison to corporate and governmental wealth.

One must occupy top *positions* in large corporate *institutions* to exercise significant economic power. The mere possession of personal wealth, even $100 million, does not guarantee economic power. Indeed, among America's 800 to 1,000 "centimillionaires"—individuals with personal wealth in excess of $100 million—there are many people such as widows, retired persons, and other inheritors who have never played any role in the family business. There are also many "independent operators" who have acquired great wealth in, say, independent oil operations or land speculation, but who do not occupy high positions in the corporate world. Of course, there are many centimillionaires whose personal wealth has come to them through their personal ownership of corporate shares. Familiar names—Ford, Rockefeller, du Pont, Mellon— are liberally sprinkled among the nation's top personal wealth-holders. However, their personal wealth is a *byproduct* of their role, or their ancestor's role, in the corporate structure.

Socialist critics of America usually do not comprehend the insignificance of personal wealth in relation to corporate and governmental resources. They direct their rhetoric against inequality in personal income in the nation, when in fact the greatest inequities occur in the comparisons between corporate and government resources and the resources of individuals.

Let us illustrate our point: If the personal wealth of every one of America's centimillionares was *completely confiscated* by government, the resulting revenue (about $100 billion) would amount to less than 10 *percent* of the federal budget for a *single year!*

The relationship between personal wealth and institutional power is described well by economist Adolf A. Berle:

> As of now, in the United States and in Western Europe, the rich man has little power merely because he is rich. . . . [He] amounts to little unless he connects himself with effective institutions. He must master past institutions or must create new ones. . . . However large his bank account, he can do nothing with it but consume. He can build or buy palaces, amuse himself at Mediterranean or Caribbean resorts, become a figure in Monte Carlo, Miami, or Las Vegas. He can amuse himself by collecting books or purchasing bonds. He can give libraries or laboratories to universities and have his name put on them. He can receive the pleasant but powerless recognition of decorations, honorary degrees, and even titles of nobility. None of these things entitle him to make decisions affecting other men or to give orders (outside his household) with any likelihood they will be fulfilled. Even when he seeks to give his son a career in business, he must ask the assistance of acquaintances and friends who will give the boy a fair chance—and can give him little more. Beyond that, he can leave his son nothing but the ability to live without work and to waste as long as his wealth holds out. All of this does not add up to power.
>
> So, if he wishes a power position, he must find it outside his bank account. He can, it is true, use the bank account to buy into, or possibly create, an institution. He can buy control of a small corporation. (Few rich men are left who are capable of buying individual control of really large ones.) He can undertake the management of that corporation. Then he can derive power from the institution—if, and only if, he is capable of handling it. Whatever power he has comes from the corporation or other institutions, and from such intellectual or organizing skill as he may have—not from his wealth, which is largely irrelevant. He at once discovers that he is subordinate to the institution. It operates under, and in conditions accepted or laid down or directed by, the paramount political power. Then he is tested, not by the dollar value of his wealth, but by his performance as director or manager of the institution.[27]

Even if personal wealth is not the equivalent of economic power, the nation's top wealth-holders are worthy of study. (See Table 2–12.) They include at least two categories—old and established families whose

[27]From Adolf A. Berle, *Power*, copyright © 1967, 1968, 1969. Reprinted by permission of Harcourt Brace Jovanovich, Inc.

TABLE 2-12 America's Superrich

1918 "WEALTHIEST AMERICANS"	1968 "CENTIMILLIONAIRES"	1987 "BILLIONAIRES"	FOUNDER
J.D. Rockefeller (oil)	J.P. Getty (oil)	S.M. Walton	self
H.C. Frick (coke, steel)	H. Hughes (aerospace)	J.W. Kluge	unrelated
A. Carnegie (steel)	H.L. Hunt (oil)	H. Ross Perot	self
G.W. Baker (banking)	E.H. Land (Polaroid)	David Packard	self
W. Rockefeller (oil, RRs)	D.K. Ludwig (shipping)	S.I. Newhouse, Jr.	father
E.S. Harkness (oil)	Alisa M. Bruce (Mellon)	D.E. Newhouse	father
J.O. Armour (meat packing)	P. Mellon (Mellon)	Lester Crown	father
H. Ford (cars)	R.K. Mellon (Mellon)	K.R. Murdoch	father
W.K. Vanderbilt (RRs)	N.B. Hunt (oil)	W.E. Buffet	unrelated
Ed. H.R. Green (banking)	J.D. McArthur (insurance)	L.H. Wexner	self
Mrs. E.H. Harriman (RRs)	W.L. McKnight (3M)	J.A. Pritzker	grandfather
V. Astor (real estate)	C.S. Mott (GM)	R.A. Pritzker	grandfather
J. Stillman (banking)	R.E. Smith (oil)	E.M. Bronfman	father
T.F. Ryan (transit, tobacco)	H.F. Ahmanson (banking)	Barbara C. Anthony	father
D. Guggenheim (mining)	C. Allen, Jr. (banking)	Ann C. Chambers	father
C.M. Schwab (steel)	Mrs. W.V. Clark, Sr. (Avon)	Ted Arison	self
J.P. Morgan (banking)	J.T. Dorrance, Jr. (soup)	A.A. Taubman	self
Mrs. R. Sage (banking)	Mrs. A.I. du Pont (Du Pont)	H.L. Hillman	father
C.H. McCormick (farm machinery)	C.W. Englehard, Jr. (mining)	M.H. Davis	father
J. Widener (transit)	S.M. Fairchild (cameras)	W.R. Hewlett	self
A.C. James (mining, RRs)	L. Hess (oil)	Harry Helmsley	self
Nicholas F. Brady (transit)	W.R. Hewlett (aerospace)	P.F. Anschutz	father
J.H. Schiff (banking)	D. Packard (aerospace)	Anheuser Bush, Jr.	remote
J.B. Duke (tobacco)	A. Houghton (Corning Glass)	J.T. Dorrance, Jr.	father's uncle

G. Eastman (cameras)
P.S. du Pont (gunpowder)
L.F. Swift (meat packing)
J. Rosenwald (mail orders)
Mrs. L. Lewis (oil)
H. Phipps (steel)

J.P. Kennedy (investments)
Eli Lilly (drugs)
F.E. Mars (candy)
S.E. Newhouse (newspapers)
Marjorie M. Post (foods)
Mrs. J. Mauze (Rockefeller)
D. Rockefeller
J.D. Rockefeller
L. Rockefeller
N. Rockefeller
W. Rockefeller
Cordelia S. May (Mellon)
R.M. Scaife (Mellon)
D. Wallace (Reader's Digest)
Mrs. C. Payson (Whitney)
J.H. Whitney

Name	Relationship
M.J. Petrie	self
E.M. Kauffman	self
Ray Lee Hunt	father
E.J. DeBartolo	self
W.H. Gates, III	self
D.L. Bren	father
S.J. LeFrak	father's uncle
R.M. Bass	father
E.L. Gaylord	father
F.E. Mars, Sr.	grandfather
F.E. Mars, Jr.	grandfather
J.F. Mars	grandfather
J.M. Vogel	self
H.C. Simmons	self
Sol Goldman	father
Margaret H. Hill	father's uncle
Sid R. Bass	father's uncle
Lee M. Bass	father
L.A. Tisch	father
P.R. Tisch	grandfather
David Rockefeller	father
L.N. Stern	self
C.H. Lindner, II	grandfather
Roger Milliken	husband
Joan B. Kroc	

Lists ranked in order of estimated wealth.

Sources: 1918—*Forbes Magazine*, March 2, 1918, reprinted in *Forbes*, Fall 1983; 1968—*Fortune*, May 1968; 1987—*Forbes*, Fall, 1987.

wealth is inherited from large corporate enterprise, and newly rich individuals whose wealth is derived from "independent" oil operations, real estate speculation, fast foods and discount merchanding, or aerospace and computer industries. In 1918, the first year for which a reasonable estimate of the nation's wealthiest Americans is available, virtually all of the names on the list are newly rich, having acquired great wealth within a single generation. These are the great entrepreneurs of America's Industrial Revolution—Rockefeller, Carnegie, Frick, Harkness, Ford, Vanderbilt, Morgan, and so on. Only a few of the wealthiest Americans in the early twentieth century were inheritors: for example, the Astors, whose original fortune was made in the North American fur trade; and the du Ponts, who manufactured gun powder in Delaware even before the Revolutionary War. However, by the second half of the century, the great families of the Industrial Revolution had become the nation's established wealth-holders. Their wealth was tied to the large corporations and banks which their ancestors had founded.

Millionaires in America are no longer considered rich. More than 2 million people have net worths exceeding $1 million. To be truly rich today, one must be worth more than $200 million. In 1988, *Forbes* magazine identified "The *Forbes* Four Hundred"—400 Americans with individual net worth of at least $200 million. Most of the nation's wealthy are reluctant to reveal their net worth; thus, any listing is only an estimate. There may be 200 individuals or families in the world worth over $1 *billion* dollars. *Forbes* magazine claims to have identified 192 billionaire individuals or families; only 68 of them are American.[28] Fortune identifies 129 billionaires of whom 49 are Americans.[29]

It is widely believed that great personal wealth in America today is inherited and that opportunities to acquire great personal fortunes dried up after the Industrial Revolution. C. Wright Mills wrote that "Wealth not only tends to perpetuate itself, but . . . tends also to monopolize new opportunities for getting great wealth. . . . In none of the latest three generations has a majority of the very rich been composed of men who have risen."[30] But Mills and other Marxist critics of American society are wrong. All of the available evidence points to considerable social mobility among the wealthiest Americans.

Today about half of America's top wealth-holders are self-made single-generation tycoons. On the lists of billionaires and centimillionaires, the names of self-made men and women rival the number of heirs to family fortunes, and first- and second-generation immigrants abound. Moreover, in every successive list of top wealth-holders over the

[28]Forbes, July 25, 1988, pp. 89–91

[29]*Fortune*, September 12, 1988, pp. 46–105

[30]C. Wright Mills, *The Power Elite* (New York: Oxford University Press, 1956), p. 105.

decades there are as many dropouts and newcomers as holdovers. It is true that America's great nineteenth-century industrial fortunes have held together remarkably well, despite inheritance taxes and family dispersions.[31] But in each generation, America produces a new crop of superrich entrepreneurs.

Representative of the newly rich in 1968 were the five wealthiest Americans—J. Paul Getty and H.L. Hunt, whose fabulous fortunes were amassed in independent oil operations; Howard Hughes, whose fortune was made in the aerospace industry; Edward H. Land, an inventor whose self-developing "Land" camera was the foundation of the Polaroid Corporation; and Daniel K. Ludwig, who wisely purchased war-surplus oil tankers in anticipation of U.S. dependence on foreign oil. By 1983, additional new names of the superrich emerged from the burgeoning computer industry—An Wang, who emigrated to the United States, completed a Ph.D. in physics at Harvard, and founded Wang Labs; H. Ross Perot, who founded Electronic Data Systems; the Bechtels, whose giant construction firm is the world's largest privately owned enterprise (see Chapter 8); and Ray Kroc, who founded McDonalds.

Even many of today's *billionaires* are self-made. *Fortune* lists Forrest Mars, the original creator of the Milky Way, and other candies, and his children as the richest American family; *Forbes* lists Sam Walton, who opened his first Wal-Mart Store in rural Arkansas in 1962. It is true that the fortunes listed by *Forbes* and *Fortune* include many familiar names: Annenberg, Bechtel, Cabot, Chandler, Dorrance, McCormick, Mellon, Pew, Phipps, Pitcairn, Pulitzer, Rockefeller, Uihlein, Upjohn, and Weyerhaeuser. But there are also larger numbers of self-made fortunes, from New York real estate mogul Donald Trump to the youthful computer wizard and Harvard dropout William Gates III, co-founder of Microsoft.

America offers *opportunity*, not income equality. Inequality is and has always been a significant component of the American social structure. The top fifth of income recipients in America accounts for over 40 percent of all income in the nation, while the bottom fifth accounts for only about 5 percent (see Table 2–13). Since the pre–World War II years, the income share of the top 5 percent of families has declined dramatically from 30 to 17 percent. However, the bottom fifth of the population still receives a very small share of the national income.

Inequality increased in America in the 1980s. While the increase was slight by historical standards, and the United States remains one of the most equalitarian nations in the world; nonetheless, this increase reverses the historical tendencies toward greater equality. Various theories have been put forward to explain this reversal: the decline of the

---

[31]See Michael Patrick Allen, *The Founding Fortunes* (New York: Dutton, 1987).

TABLE 2–13   The Distribution of Family Income in America

(BY QUINTILES AND TOP 5 PERCENT)

QUINTILES	1929	1936	1944	1950	1956	1962	1972	1976	1980	1986
Lowest	3.5	4.1	4.9	4.8	4.8	4.6	5.5	5.4	5.2	4.6
Second	9.0	9.2	10.9	10.9	11.3	10.9	12.0	12.0	11.6	10.8
Third	13.8	14.1	16.2	16.1	16.3	16.3	17.4	17.6	17.5	16.8
Fourth	19.3	20.9	22.2	22.1	22.3	22.7	23.5	24.1	24.1	24.0
Highest	54.4	51.7	45.8	46.1	45.3	45.5	41.6	41.0	41.5	43.7
Total	100.0	100.0	100.0	100.0	100.0	100.0	100.0	100.0	100.0	100.0
Top 5 percent	30.0	24.0	20.7	21.4	20.2	19.6	14.4	14.2	15.6	17.0

Source: U.S. Bureau of the Census, *Current Population Reports,* Series P-60; data for early years from Edward C. Budd, *Inequality and Poverty* (New York: W.W. Norton, 1967).

manufacturing sector of the economy with its relatively high-paying jobs; a rise in the number of two-wage-earning families, which makes single-headed households relatively less affluent; and demographic trends which include larger proportions of the aged as well as larger proportions of female-headed families. The popular notion that miserly government welfare and social insurance payment caused the increase in inequality is untrue; aggregate government transfer payments did not decline in the 1980s. Nor is there any evidence that income taxation has any significant effect on the distribution of income. Before-tax and after-tax income distribution are nearly identical.

SUMMARY

In later chapters, we will examine interlocking, recruitment, conflict, and consensus, as well as corporate involvement in national policy-making, in greater detail. Now, however, let us summarize our initial observations of corporate management as one of the key elites in the institutional structure of American society.

Economic power in America is highly concentrated. A small number of corporations control more than one half the nation's industrial assets; one half of all assets in communications and utilities; two thirds of all banking assets; and more than three quarters of all insurance assets. This concentration of economic power is increasing gradually over time, as the nation's largest corporations gain ever larger shares of total corporate assets.

Power over corporate assets rests in the hands of about 4,300 presidents and directors. These managers not the stockholders or the employees, decide major policy questions, choose the people who will carry out these decisions, and even select their own replacements. However, most of these presidents and directors have climbed the corporate ladder to their posts. They owe their rise to power to their skill in organizational life, and to their successful coping with the new demands for expertise in management, finance, technology, and planning. Individual capitalists are no longer essential in the formation of capital assets. Most industrial capital is raised either within the corporation itself or from institutional borrowing.

The greatest threat to the dominance of the corporate managers comes from the new corporate raiders. These modern tycoons, threatening hostile takeovers of even the largest U.S. corporations, have become an important force in the American economy. While they claim to reinvigorate American enterprise and competition, their critics claim they demoralize managers and workers and burden American corporations with excessive debts. Top corporate elites claim that they have less power today than only a few years ago, and they attribute their loss of power to the growing influence of corporate raiders, bankers, and Wall Street investment houses.

Managerial dominance of the corporate world is not complete. While corporate ownership is largely institutional—banks, investment firms, employee stock ownership trusts—family holdings are still important. The Rockefellers, du Ponts, Mellons, and other great entrepreneurial families still exercise power over corporate resources. But a majority of the directors of family-dominated firms have been brought in from outside the family, and only about 150 of the 500 largest corporations are family-dominated.

Corporate leadership is very stable over time. Turnover among top managers is low and the nation's largest corporations have the power and resources to protect their dominant positions.

Personal wealth is insignificant in relation to corporate (or governmental) wealth. It is necessary for individuals to achieve top corporate positions in order to exercise significant economic power.

Top corporate leaders generally display moderately liberal, socially responsible attitudes and opinions on public issues. They are not necessarily hostile to government, but generally share with government an interest in stable growth, the avoidance of disruption, and planned scientific and technological development. The notion of "corporate responsibility" involves a willingness to sacrifice some profits to exercise a larger role in social policy-making. Profits, however, remain essential to the accumulation of capital and the continued existence of the corporation.

CHAPTER THREE
THE GOVERNING CIRCLES

If there ever was a time when the powers of government were limited—when government did no more than secure law and order, protect individual liberty and property, enforce contracts, and defend against foreign invasion—that time has long passed. Today it is commonplace to observe that governmental institutions intervene in every aspect of our lives—from the "cradle to the grave." Government in America has the primary responsibility for providing insurance against old age, death, dependency, disability, and unemployment; for providing medical care for the aged and poor; for providing education at the elementary, secondary, collegiate, and postgraduate levels; for providing public highways and regulating water, rail, and air transportation; for providing police and fire protection; for providing sanitation services and sewage disposal; for financing research in medicine, science, and technology; for delivering the mail; for exploring outer space; for maintaining parks and recreation; for providing housing and adequate food for the poor; for providing job training and manpower programs; for cleaning the air and water; for rebuilding central cities; for maintaining full employment and a stable money supply; for regulating business practices and labor relations; for eliminating racial and sexual discrimination. Indeed, the list of government responsibilities seems endless, yet each year we manage to find additional tasks for government to do.

THE CONCENTRATION OF GOVERNMENTAL POWER

Governments do many things that cannot be measured in terms of dollars and cents. Nonetheless, government expenditures are the best available measure of the dimensions of government activity. Such expenditures in the United States amount to about 35 percent of the gross national product. This is an increase from about 8 percent of the GNP at the beginning of the century. (Years ago, the German economist Adolph Wagner set forth the "law of increasing state activity"; in effect, this law states that government activity increases faster than economic output in all developing societies.) The largest governmental cost is "income maintenance"—social security, welfare, and related social services. Defense spending is the second largest governmental cost, followed by education.

Of course, the observation that government expenditures now account for over one third of the nation's GNP actually understates the great power of government over every aspect of our lives. Government regulatory activity cannot be measured in government expenditures alone. Indeed, large segments of the economy come under direct federal regulation, notably transportation and utilities; yet these are officially classified as private industries and are not counted in the governmental proportion of the GNP.

Concentration of governmental resources is also evidenced in the growing proportion of *federal* expenditures in relation to *state* and *local* government expenditures. There are 83,217 separate governmental units operating in the United States today (U.S. government—1; state governments—50; counties—3,042; municipalities—19,205; townships—16,691; school districts—14,741; special districts—29,487). But only one of these, the U.S. government, accounts for *two thirds* of all governmental expenditures. This means that approximately 22 percent of the GNP is accounted for by federal expenditures alone.

We have defined our governmental elite as the top executive, congressional, military, and judicial officers of the *federal* government; the President and Vice-President; secretaries, undersecretaries, and assistant secretaries of executive departments; senior White House presidential advisers; congressional committee chairpersons and ranking minority members; congressional majority and minority party leaders in the House and Senate; Supreme Court Justices; and members of the Fed-

eral Reserve Board and the Council of Economic Advisers. In the pages
that follow we will try to describe some members of the governmental
elite, as well as to discuss the power they exercise, and how they came to
power.

THE POLITICIANS: STYLE AND IMAGE

The politician is a professional office-seeker. The politician knows how
to run for office—but not necessarily how to run the government. After
victory at the polls, the prudent politician turns to "serious men" to run
the government. Pulitzer Prize–winning writer David Halberstam reports a revealing conversation between newly elected President John F.
Kennedy and Robert A. Lovett in December 1960, a month before
Kennedy was to take office:

> On the threshold of great power and great office, the young man seemed
> to have everything. He was handsome, rich, charming, candid. The can-
> dor was part of the charm: he could beguile a visitor by admitting that
> everything the visitor proposed was right, rational, proper—but he
> couldn't do it, not this week, this month, this term. Now he was trying to
> put together a government, and the candor showed again. He was self-
> deprecating with the older man. He had spent the last five years, he said
> ruefully, running for office, and he did not know any real public officials,
> people to run a government, *serious men*. The only ones he knew, he
> admitted, were politicians. . . . Politicians *did* need men to serve, to run
> the government. The implication was obvious. Politicians could run Penn-
> sylvania and Ohio, and if they could not run Chicago they could at least
> deliver it. But politicians run the world? What did they know about the
> Germans, the French, the Chinese?[1]

Robert Lovett was "the very embodiment of the Establishment." His
father had been chairman of the board of Union Pacific Railroad and a
partner of the great railroad tycoon, E.H. Harriman. Lovett attended
Hill School and Yale, married the daughter of James Brown, the senior
partner of the great banking firm of Brown Brothers, and formed a
new and even larger Wall Street investment partnership, Brown Brothers, Harriman & Co. Lovett urged Kennedy to listen to the advice of
Lovett's partner and former governor of New York and ambassador to
the Soviet Union, Averell Harriman; to see "Jack McCloy at Chase"
(then chairman of the board of Chase Manhattan), and "Doug Dillon
too" (to become Kennedy's secretary of the treasury); to look up a
"young fellow over at Rockefeller, Dean Rusk" (to become Kennedy's

[1]David Halberstam, *The Best and the Brightest* (New York: Random House, 1969), pp.
3–4. [Italics added.]

secretary of state); and to get "this young man at Ford, Robert McNamara" (to become Kennedy's secretary of defense). Kennedy gratefully accepted the advice: he turned to these serious men to run the government.

The great majority of politicians—elective officeholders—have had little or no experience in heading major corporate enterprises. Most have devoted their lives to running for public office. They are specialists in vote-getting, public relations, image-making, bargaining and compromise, and coalition-building.

Most politicians in America are lawyers. But they are not usually top professional lawyers. (We will examine three "superlawyers" in Chapter 5.) Instead, the typical politician-lawyer uses his or her law career as a means of support—one that is compatible with political officeholding.

A significant number of top politicians have inherited great wealth. The Roosevelts, Rockefellers, Kennedys, Bushes, and others have used their wealth and family connections to support their political careers. However, it is important to note that *a majority of the nation's top politicians have climbed the ladder from relative obscurity to political success.* Many have acquired some wealth in the process, but most political leaders started their climb from very middle-class circumstances. Only two of the last nine presidents (John F. Kennedy and George Bush) were born to great wealth. Thus, as in the corporate world, we find more "climbers" than "inheritors" at the top in the world of politics.

RONALD REAGAN: THE QUICK-STUDY COWBOY

Ronald Wilson Reagan was always a "quick study"—he learned his acting lines easily and well. He made fifty-four movies over a period of twenty-seven years. He never won an Oscar; he was never even nominated for one. His best role was the legendary Notre Dame halfback, George Gipp ("win one for the Gipper") in the movie *Knute Rockne, All-American*, with Pat O'Brien in the title role. But Ronald Reagan was a steady, hardworking professional. He showed up on time, knew his lines, and took direction easily. He was comfortable—even modest—in front of the camera. The Hollywood crowd thought he was a square—no drugs, booze, or high living. He was a liberal and a Democrat, and in 1947 he was elected president of the Screen Actors Guild, a post he held through six terms.

Reagan's boyhood in small towns of the midwest—Tampico, Dixon, and Eureka, Illinois—was far removed from the glitter of Hollywood or the power of Washington. Reagan "climbed" the ladder of success: He was the child of a failed, alcoholic shoe salesman; he washed dishes at tiny, threadbare Eureka College; he won a partial athletic scholarship (football and swimming); he graduated in 1932 in the middle of the Great Depression; and he struggled for five years as sports announcer (beginning at five dollars per game) for radio station WHO in Des Moines, Iowa. Later, when WHO sent "Dutch" Reagan to California to cover spring training for the Chicago Cubs, Reagan contacted an agent who arranged a screen test for him. The test was shown to Jack Warner, resident tycoon at Warner Brothers, and "a star was born"— or more accurately, another grade-B movie actor was signed to a studio contract.

Reagan was never Humphrey Bogart or James Cagney or Errol Flynn. He served in the Army Air Corps in World War II making training films, and his acting career faded after the war. His marriage to actress Jane Wyman (who won the best-actress Oscar for her work in *Johnny Belinda*) also faded. The good acting roles went to other actors, and new stars—Brando, Newman, Holden—replaced the old. By 1957, Reagan was playing opposite a chimpanzee in *Bedtime for Bonzo*. He met and married an aspiring young actress, Nancy Davis, who was to stick by him in the lean years, all the way to the presidency.

Turning fifty, Reagan was rescued from obscurity by Ralph J. Cordiner, president of General Electric. G.E. was putting together a weekly network television show, *G.E. Theatre*, and Reagan was offered the job as host. Reagan believed that a television show would be the end of his Hollywood career, but he had little choice. Fortunately, *G.E. Theatre* turned out to be an Emmy Award—winning venture; it held a prime Sunday evening spot for seven years before being replaced by one of Reagan's own favorites, *Bonanza*.

More importantly, Reagan began making public appearances and pro-business speeches across the country on behalf of General Electric. Hollywood receded into the background as Reagan collected a vast array of three-by-five index cards filled with examples of federal bureaucracy run amok, social welfare programs wasting money and ruining lives, and the ever-increasing threat of socialism to America's free enterprise system. Reagan's early liberalism gave way to staunch conservatism.

Several new-money southern California millionaires decided that Reagan had a more promising future than merely speaking at Chamber of Commerce meetings. When *G.E. Theatre* was finally canceled, and Reagan was hosting *Death Valley Days* at a lower salary, his wealthy admirers came to his rescue. In 1964, Reagan was in debt; he had failed to invest his money when he was in Hollywood, and he owed back income taxes to the U.S. government. A group headed by Justin Dart (Dart Industries, Rexall Drugs, Kraft Foods); Holmes Tuttle (a Los Angeles Ford dealer); William French Smith (a wealthy Los Angeles attorney and later Attorney General of the United States); and A.C. (Cy) Rubel (chairman of Union Oil Co.) formed the Ronald Reagan Trust Fund to take over his personal finances and free him to concentrate on a political career. His first political venture was the production of a film to assist Republican presidential candidate Barry Goldwater in 1964. Reagan made the perfect pitch; the money rolled in, but Goldwater was overwhelmingly rejected at the polls. Nonetheless, Reagan won the hearts of conservatives throughout the country, who recognized a new and highly gifted media politician.

Two years later, Ronald Reagan took on the incumbent governor of California, Edmund G. "Pat" Brown (the father of Governor Jerry Brown), who had defeated Richard Nixon for the post in 1962. It was Reagan's first try for public office. Like so many other politicians, Brown underestimated Reagan's appeal. Reagan buried him with nearly a million-vote margin.

Reagan won the admiration of many as California's governor; he was willing to compromise; he was never angry or bitter; if he could not reduce the size of government, he was satisfied to slow its growth. He was described as a pleasant, charming, amicable "closet moderate" whose hard-line conservative speeches did not reflect his pragmatic approach to administration. He delegated responsibility and relied on his staff. He did not read books; he wanted one-page summaries of major issues. He worked in a relaxed manner, frequently ending his workday in the early afternoon. He built his Rancho del Cielo on weekends. Reagan was reelected in 1970 by another million-vote margin.

In the meantime, the Ronald Reagan Trust Fund turned a $65,000 investment in Malibu Canyon into $1.9 million by selling the land to Twentieth Century Fox Studios. The Fund also purchased Rancho California for $347,000 and sold it for $856,000. Reagan bought his Pacific Palisades residence for less than $50,000 and placed it on sale in 1981 for $1.9 million. By 1980, Reagan was worth over $2 million and had an annual income of over $500,000.

The camera is a tool of both of Ronald Reagan's trades—actor and politician. Newspaper journalists could never understand Reagan's success. Reporters wrote up his commonplace phrases and time-worn slogans—the simple messages on the old and yellowed three-by-five cards. The printed words were lifeless and uninspiring. Journalists missed Reagan's true appeal as a comfortable, pleasant, reassuring man of traditional American values.

In 1976, Gerald Ford was the Republican President, and it appeared unlikely that the Republican party would deny him renomination. However, Reagan decided to make a run for Ford's job (some say because Ford had bypassed Reagan for a "liberal," Nelson Rockefeller, as Vice-President). Reagan almost defeated Ford in the 1976 Republican convention. Ford lost to Carter, and conservatives throughout the country turned to Reagan for leadership in 1980.

The political landscape is littered with candidates who underestimated Reagan—the supposedly lightweight, "too-old" actor. President Carter hoped Reagan would win the Republican nomination in 1980, because Carter's aides thought Reagan would be the easiest person to beat! In the general election, however, Reagan skillfully turned his age from a liability to an asset. In 1980, the "good old days" never looked better. Reagan spoke of traditional values; he knew that America could be "great again." Carter mistakenly tried to portray Reagan as an unstable warmonger. But Reagan's polished style and charm—his appearance as a kindly, older, soft-spoken, western rancher—deflected Carter's attack. In the presidential debate, Reagan was the master of the stage: He was relaxed, smiling, even joking. He never said anything of great importance. He merely asked, "Are you better off now than you were five years ago?" Simple, yet highly effective.

In the final few days before the election, the media decided to publicize the first anniversary of the Iranian hostage-taking. This decision sealed Carter's fate. By reminding Americans of international humiliations, military weaknesses, and administrative blunders during the Carter years, the media set the stage for a Reagan landslide.

Just as Reagan's opponents underestimated his abilities as a campaigner, they also underestimated his skills as President. Yet with skillful personal appeals to Democrats and Republicans in Congress, and very successful national television appeals, Reagan rolled over his congressional opponents. He reduced proposed government spending and later pushed through the largest tax cut in the nation's history. In slowing the growth of social welfare programs, rebuilding national defenses, and cutting federal income taxes, Reagan changed the course of government more than any President since Franklin D. Roosevelt.[2]

The nation's oldest President could have retired to the ranch after his first term, secure in the knowledge that he had achieved most of his major goals. First Lady Nancy Reagan worried about the stresses on her husband and remembered the nearly successful assassination attempt. But Reagan himself seemed to thrive on the challenges of the job. He worked fewer hours than any other modern President, vacationed more, and kept himself in better physical condition. His personal popularity remained high despite any problems confronting his administration, causing his frustrated opponents to call him "the Teflon President."

During his campaign for reelection, the "Great Communicator" stumbled only once on the road to his landslide reelection. In the first of two televised debates with Walter Mondale, Reagan looked like a heavyweight champ who had gone soft against a hungrier challenger. Reagan appeared confused and out of touch as he stumbled over statis-

[2]See John L. Palmer and Isabel V. Sawhill, eds., *The Reagan Record* (Washington: Urban Institute, 1984).

tics and frequently lost his train of thought. Indeed, his performance was so bad that it raised an issue which Mondale was afraid to raise directly—the President's age. But in the second debate, almost as if he had set a trap for Mondale, the President regained his old mastery of the medium. When questioned whether he might be too old for the job, he answered, "I want you to know that I will not make age an issue in this campaign. I am not going to exploit for political purposes my opponent's youth and inexperience." Even Mondale had to laugh, along with millions of viewers. Mondale may have won a debate on the issues, but Reagan reassured his fans that he was still champion of the one-liner.

Liberals interpreted the Reagan landslide as a personal victory for a popular President. They did not wish to acknowledge that the American people might agree with Reagan on the issues—less government spending, lower taxes, a stronger national defense. And indeed, Reagan's failure to bring many Republicans into Congress on his coat-tails created many political obstacles in his second term.

Reagan's romantic nature—personally worrying over the fate of individual hostages—and his hands-*off* leadership style, eventually led to his only serious mistake—the Iran-Contra scandal. Despite the advice of the experienced heavyweights in his Cabinet, Secretary of State George Schultz and Secretary of Defense Casper Weinberger, Reagan set in motion the trading of arms to Iran for the release of hostages. He personally encouraged support for the "Contras," the democratic resistance in Communist Nicaragua, but he did not personally approve of the diversion of arms "profits" by Lt. Col. Oliver North.

Reagan's popularity tumbled during the various Iran-Contra investigations. But over time, the general public appeared to forgive the popular President, and by November 1988, Reagan had recovered in the opinion polls. Over eight years he had come to view his Vice-President, George Bush, as both a personal friend and the legitimate heir to the Reagan legacy. Reagan campaigned hard for Bush and took great satisfaction in Bush's election. Upon leaving office Ronald Reagan enjoyed the highest approval rating of any modern President. Asked to explain his own popularity, he replied: "Well, I genuinely like people, and I think perhaps, people can tell. But more importantly, I've always thought of myself as a citizen politician, speaking up for the ideas and values and common sense of everyday Americans. That's what I've always tried to do and maybe that's what they like."

TED KENNEDY: INHERITING A POLITICAL DYNASTY

John F. Kennedy once said of his brothers, "Just as I went into politics because Joe [the oldest Kennedy brother, killed in World War II] died, if anything happened to me tomorrow Bobby would run for my seat in the Senate. And if Bobby died, our young brother Ted would take over for him."

Edward M. "Ted" Kennedy's major qualifications for public office are his style, appearance, accent, and name. The deaths of his brothers John and Robert by assassins' bullets make the youngest Kennedy brother the sentimental favorite of millions of Americans, the last guardian of the Camelot legend.

The Kennedy dynasty began with the flamboyant career of Joseph P. Kennedy, a son of a prosperous Irish saloon-keeper and ward boss in Boston. Joseph Kennedy attended Boston Latin School and Harvard, receiving his B.A. in 1912. He started his career in banking, moved into stock market operations, dabbled in shipbuilding, formed movie-making companies (RKO and later Paramount), and married the daughter of the mayor of Boston. "Old Joe" made the major part of his fortune in stock market manipulations. With his associate, William Randolph Hearst, Kennedy provided key financial backing for the 1932 presidential campaign of Franklin D. Roosevelt. FDR later made Kennedy head of the Securities and Exchange Commission. But making a market speculator head of a commission that was designed to protect investors caused such public outcry that Kennedy was forced to resign after one year. FDR then appointed Kennedy head of the Maritime Commission, but rumors of extravagant subsidies to shipbuilding friends forced his resignation after only two months on the job. In 1937, FDR appointed him ambassador to England. His diplomatic career lasted three years and ended over differences with FDR regarding U.S. assistance to the Allies. Old Joe is said to have advised FDR of the likelihood of German victory and the advantages of placating Hitler.

Joseph P. Kennedy, Sr., was a family man, a prominent Catholic, and the father of nine children. (Joseph P., Jr., was killed as a World War II Navy pilot; President John F. Kennedy was assassinated; Senator Robert F. Kennedy was assassinated; Kathleen died in a plane crash; Rosemary is living in an institution for the mentally retarded; Eunice is married to Sargent Shriver, former director of the Peace Corps and the War on Poverty and replacement for Senator Thomas Eagleton as the Democratic vice-presidential nominee in 1972; Patricia, formerly married to actor Peter Lawford; Jean, wife of Stephen Smith; and the youngest, Edward M. "Ted" Kennedy.)

Although born to great wealth and accustomed to an upper-class style of living (he received his first communion from Pope Pius XII), Ted Kennedy acquired the sense of competition fostered in the large Kennedy household. In 1951, suspended from Harvard for cheating on a Spanish examination, he joined the Army and served two years in Germany. He was readmitted to Harvard, where he played on the Harvard football team and graduated in 1956.

Despite his family background, Harvard Law School rejected Ted Kennedy's application for admission. He enrolled instead in the University of Virginia Law School and completed his law degree in 1959. Following graduation and work on his brother's 1960 presidential campaign, he was appointed assistant district attorney for Suffolk County, Massachusetts.

When he was just thirty years old, the minimum age for a U.S. senator, he announced his candidacy for the Massachusetts Senate seat formerly held by his brother, who was then President. In the Democratic primary he faced Edward J. McCormack, nephew of the then Speaker of the House, John W. McCormack. During a televised debate, McCormack said to Kennedy, "You never worked for a living. You never held elective office. You lack the qualifications and maturity of judgment. . . . If your name were not Kennedy, your candidacy would be a joke." But Kennedy won overwhelmingly and went on to defeat the Republican candidate, George Cabot Lodge. (George Cabot Lodge was the son of U.S. Ambassador to South Vietnam and former U.S. Senator Henry Cabot Lodge, Jr. In 1916, Kennedy's grandfather, Boston Mayor John F. Fitzgerald, had been defeated in a race for the same Senate seat by Lodge's great-grandfather, Senator Henry Cabot Lodge.)

Kennedy performed better in the Senate than many had expected. He cultivated Senate friends, appeared at fund-raising dinners, and informed himself about several important policy fields. He worked hard learning about national health problems, problems of the elderly, and the activities of the National Science Foundation. In 1969 he was elected Senate Democratic whip by his colleagues.

His personal life, however, was marred by accident, tragedy, and scandal. He nearly died in a 1964 plane crash in which he suffered a broken back. An athletic and handsome six foot two inches, Kennedy was frequently the object of romantic gossip at Washington cocktail parties. On July 19, 1969, a young woman, Mary Jo Kopechne, died when the car Kennedy was driving plunged off a narrow bridge on Chappaquiddick Island after a late-night party. Missing for ten hours after the accident, Kennedy later made a dramatic national television appearance, saying that the tragedy had been an accident, that he had tried unsuccessfully to save Miss Kopechne, and that he had been too confused to report the tragedy until the next day. The official inquest has been kept secret, and many feel that there are still unresolved discrepancies in Kennedy's story.[3] Kennedy pled guilty to the minor charge of leaving the scene of an accident. Senate Democrats removed Kennedy from his position as majority whip. But the national news media never pressed the Chappaquiddick incident and continued favorable reporting of the still charismatic senator.

[3]See Robert Sherrill, "Chappaquiddick + 5," *New York Times Magazine,* July 14, 1974.

Kennedy deliberately avoided the Democratic presidential nomination in both 1972 and 1976. His advisers argued that the public's memory of Chappaquiddick was still too fresh for Kennedy to enter a campaign battle in which the issue of his personal life would certainly be raised. However, in late 1979, with Carter standing at an all-time low for Presidents in the opinion polls, Kennedy announced his presidential candidacy. Most observers thought that Kennedy was unbeatable, despite Carter's pledge "I'll whip his ass." But Carter was temporarily saved by the Iranian seizure of American embassy employees in Iran as hostages. Shortly thereafter, Soviet troops invaded neighboring Afghanistan. Support for the President was equated with support for America. Carter's approval ratings in the polls leaped upward, even though he failed to obtain either the early release of the hostages or Soviet withdrawal from Afghanistan. Nonetheless, these events provided a "rally round the flag" effect. Carter was temporarily transformed from a lackluster politician to commander-in-chief of all of the people. He defeated Kennedy in the Democratic primaries from the White House Rose Garden without even campaigning. The media focus was on the President, and the news from Iran simply obliterated the Kennedy campaign. But Ted Kennedy reestablished his leadership of liberal Democrats and polished his own charismatic image with a dramatic and inspiring speech at the 1980 Democratic National Convention. It was clearly Ted Kennedy's finest public performance.

Kennedy avoided the 1984 and 1988 presidential races, citing family affairs as his reason. And indeed, his family situation might have caused him political problems had he chosen to run. He was separated from his wife, Joan, and many stories were published in women's magazines portraying her as a victim of Ted's life style. At the same time, he felt responsible for the many sons and daughters of his deceased brother Robert as well as his own children. Several of these "third generation" Kennedys suffered serious personal problems;[4] David Anthony Kennedy dropped out of Harvard and died a drug-related death in a Miami motel in 1984.

Clearly, Ted Kennedy is an inheritor rather than a climber in the world of politics. His success rests upon his image and style more than upon his substantive contributions to public policy. He was elected to the Senate solely because he was a Kennedy, an inheritor of a famous political image. The image survived tragedy and scandal, although his fellow senators seem less impressed with his mystique than the general public.

Perhaps Ted Kennedy now senses that he missed his opportunity to become President, that he no longer possesses the motivation to con-

---

[4]See Peter Collier and David Horowitz, *The Kennedys: An American Dream* (New York: Summit, 1984).

front the many personal obstacles to a successful campaign. Perhaps he feels comfortable as the recognized leader of the liberal wing of the Democratic party. Perhaps he is prepared now to help pave the way for the next generation of the family political dynasty.

Joseph P. Kennedy II, son of the late Senator Robert F. Kennedy, leads the third generation of Kennedys. (There were twenty-six children born to John F. Kennedy, Robert F. Kennedy, Patricia Kennedy Lawford, Eunice Kennedy Shriver, and Edward M. Kennedy.) In 1986 young Joe inherited the Boston congressional seat of his Uncle Jack, when the venerable House Speaker Thomas P. "Tip" O'Neill conveniently retired. Joe had struggled through various private prep schools and dropped out of M.I.T. and the University of California at Berkeley, before finally getting a degree from the University of Massachusetts. He floundered for several years after graduation; he was the driver in a Jeep accident that crippled a passenger. Later he headed a nonprofit company to deliver heating oil to poor Bostonians. But when he announced his candidacy for Congress, the Kennedy name made him the instant front-runner, the focus of media attention, and the recipient of heavy campaign contributions. It will be interesting to observe whether political inheritance can span three generations of American life.

GEORGE BUSH: PATRICIAN PRESIDENT

Try as he may, George Bush cannot shed his upper-class "preppy" image. His personal mannerisms, his diction and dress, his Episcopalian morality, all belie his efforts to portray himself as a cowboy and "kick-ass" Texan.

George Bush is an inheritor in politics. His father, U.S. Senator Prescott Bush, was the managing partner in the great Wall Street investment firm of Brown Brothers, Harriman & Co. (see Table 2–5), as well as chairman of the board of Yale Corporation, which governs Yale University, and Republican U.S. senator from Connecticut from 1962 to 1972. George Herbert Walker Bush was born in 1924 and spent his boyhood in upper-class Greenwich, Connecticut. He attended the Greenwich Country Day School before entering Phillips Academy in Andover, Massachusetts, where he was captain of the soccer team and president of his senior class.

At age seventeen, in the dark days of World War II, George Bush set aside his admission to Yale in order to join the Navy. His worried father asked President Roosevelt to ignore the age requirements and allow George to be commissioned as an ensign in flight school. As the youngest pilot in the U.S. Navy, Bush was assigned to the light aircraft carrier U.S.S. *San Jacinto* in 1943. He flew fifty-eight combat missions.

He was awarded the Distinguished Flying Cross and three Air Medals for action in the Pacific. His torpedo bomber was shot down, his two crewmen were killed, and he was rescued at sea by a submarine. He returned home on leave to marry Barbara Pierce, daughter of the publisher of *Redbook* and *McCall's* magazines. He spent the rest of the war training Navy pilots.

George Bush entered Yale in September of 1945. He captained the baseball team and graduated in three years, Phi Beta Kappa in economics. His father wanted him to join Brown Brothers, Harriman in New York, but at twenty-five George wanted to strike out on his own. "On his own" turned out to be a job as vice-president of Dresser Industries, a Texas oil-drilling equipment firm of which his father was director. George Bush quickly became very successful in the Texas oil business. He formed several oil companies with financing from his uncle, Herbert Walker: Bush-Overby, Zapata Petroleum, and Zapata Offshore Oil. He served as a director of the First International Bank of Houston and London as well as of Eli Lilly, Texas Gulf, and Purolator. By the early 1960s Bush was a multimillionaire Texas oilman still in his thirties. Having conquered the world of business, he turned to politics.

Bush did not have the same easy success in politics that he enjoyed in business. Bush served a term as chairman of the Republican party in Harris County (Houston), and then in 1964 he plunged into a campaign to unseat Ralph Yarborough, U.S. senator from Texas and ally of President Lyndon Johnson. Bush fell victim to the Johnson landslide in that year but captured a larger share of the Senate vote (43.5 percent) than any previous Republican candidate in Texas. In 1966, Bush returned to the political fray to win election to Congress from a wealthy suburban Houston district. After serving two terms in the House, he set out again in 1970 to defeat Ralph Yarborough and win a Senate seat. But Yarborough was upset in the Democratic primary by another wealthy oilman, conservative Democrat Lloyd Bentsen. The Bush-Bentsen race was hard fought and expensive for both sides; Bush was edged out in a very close election. The unsuccessful Senate race cost Bush his safe seat in the House.

President Richard Nixon named Bush to the post of United Nations ambassador in 1970, where he served for two years. Following Nixon's reelection, the President named Bush as chairman of the Republican National Committee, a job which became very difficult as the Watergate scandal mushroomed. But most of the Watergate evils occurred under the Committee to Reelect the President (CREEP)—an organization which was separate from the Republican National Committee—and George Bush was successful in keeping the regular Republican organization free of scandal and his own name untarnished. A grateful President Gerald Ford asked Bush to pick his own post in the new administration, and Bush chose the newly created ambassadorship to the People's Republic of China. In 1975 President Ford asked him to return from China to head the U.S. Central Intelligence Agency.

George Bush took charge of the CIA at one of the low points of its history. The agency was under serious attack from the left in American politics and had allowed itself to be used in domestic politics by the Nixon White House. Bush drew up new guidelines for CIA activity, tried to restore morale, and worked to improve CIA relations with Congress.

George Bush inherited the support of the Eastern Establishment wing of the Republican party. These internationalist Wall Street Republicans had formed the foundation of Eisenhower's administration and had been led for many years thereafter by Nelson Rockefeller. Following Gerald Ford's defeat at the hands of Jimmy Carter, Bush began his own bid for the presidency. He hoped to combine his new Eastern Brahmin support with his Texas oil friends, thus bringing together the new wealth of the Sunbelt and the old wealth of the East. He recruited his friend Houston attorney James A. Baker, Ford's campaign manager, as his own and conducted a vigorous nationwide campaign. But Ronald Reagan had spent years building his political base among the southern and western Sunbelt Republicans. Following a Nashua debate in which Bush looked stiff and inflexible and Reagan relaxed and amiable, Bush narrowly lost the 1980 New Hampshire presidential primary. Although Bush went on to win primaries in Massachusetts, Connecticut, and Pennsylvania, he was "stunned" again by Reagan's victory in Bush's home state of Texas. Despite his many years in Texas, George Bush was unable to escape his Eastern preppy background to win the hearts of Texans.

At the Republican National Convention, following an awkward effort to get former President Ford as his vice-presidential running mate, Ronald Reagan wisely turned to George Bush. Bush balanced the Reagan ticket with his youth, foreign policy experience, and appeal to Republican moderates. Although Bush had attacked Reagan vigorously in the primary battles (labeling Reagan's tax cut plans as "voodoo economics"), Bush became a dedicated Reagan team player.

As Vice-President, George Bush attended many funerals (including those of Soviet Presidents Leonid Brezhnev and Yuri Andropov). But he was as close to the Oval Office as any Vice-President had ever been. He was head cheerleader in the Reagan reelection campaign. His praise of President Reagan was so effusive that many commentators speculated that Bush was trying to win over the conservative Republicans for his own expected presidential bid in 1988. Despite some off-color slips during the campaign, Bush was an effective spokesman for the ticket and is conceded to have outpointed Democratic vice-presidential candidate

Geraldine Ferraro in their nationally televised debate. Bush's personal life has been untouched by scandal; his marriage has lasted forty years, and he and his wife had six children, one of whom died of leukemia.

George Bush was a supremely loyal Vice-President. He steadfastly refused to differ with his President—even when he was being skewered by the media for the Iranian arms-for-hostages dealings. Indeed, George Bush was portrayed as a terminal second-banana with no principles or passions of his own, forever to be overshadowed by Ronald Reagan. *Newsweek* magazine even devoted its cover to branding Bush as a "wimp."[5]

George Bush never enjoyed the grubby work of campaigning for votes among the masses. With the exception of his Houston congressional seat, all of his high offices had come to him by appointment. Bush's patrician origins and easy ride to the top infuriated his primary opponent in 1988—the hard-working self-made farm boy from Kansas, Robert Dole. But Bush knew what he had to do to win the highest prize. He proceeded to gather around him the best media campaign team ever assembled in a presidential race.

At the beginning of the 1988 presidential campaign, the outlook was gloomy. It is true that the nation was experiencing peace and prosperity and, historically, "good times" had favored the candidate of the party in power. But, in the media age, candidate "image" dominates the voters' decision. Bush was behind in the polls by 17 percentage points in the early summer of the election year. His media image was a stiff, upper-class WASP with "an overstuffed resume." He mangled his sentences; he used preppy, goofy phrases like "deep doo doo"; his voice rose to squeaky heights when he became excited; and he was prone to jerky hand motions and awkward body language. His verbal gaffes made his own staffers wince, as for example when he referred to his Hispanic grandchildren as the "little brown ones."

The remaking of Bush's image began at the Republican National Convention. His World War II–Navy fighter pilot photos and film of his dramatic rescue from the water by a submarine helped overcome the wimp image. His support for President Reagan, even during the Iran-Contra scandal, was recast as a test of his loyalty to a popular President under fire. In his acceptance speech, an astonishingly new and telegenic George Bush emerged—warm, relaxed, authoritative, even presidential. He spoke more slowly in a deeper voice, and with modest and witty phrases. He was a more "likable" George Bush; he distinguished his own vision of America from that of Ronald Reagan; and he called for a "kinder, gentler nation." His children and grandchildren crowded to the podium in an orgy of familism.

[5]*Newsweek*, October 19, 1987.

Andover teaches its boys to fight hard to win. George Bush was prepared to do what was necessary to defeat the Democratic challenger, Massachusetts Governor Michael Dukakis. The media campaign strategy called for a series of hard-hitting "attack" videos linking Dukakis to unpopular liberal policy positions. The Bush team succeeded in creating an image of Dukakis as an unpatriotic liberal who furloughed murderers, befouled harbors, spurned the American flag, and belonged to an organization (the ACLU) that defended child pornography. Even before the first televised debate, Dukakis' lead in the polls had evaporated.

Bush's handlers were more worried over the potential outcome of the presidential debates than the Dukakis team was. Their fear was that in the relatively unstructured, ninety-minute give-and-take of a live appearance, Bush would revert to his old excitable, gaffe-prone, preppy self. Dukakis had experience moderating a Boston PBS debate show, and it was unlikely that the cool and articulate challenger would make any big mistakes. The Bush team carefully limited the debates to two between the presidential candidates and one between the vice-presidential contenders.

George Bush won the presidential election in the second televised debate with the most polished performance of his career. On television, *image* triumphs over *issues*. And Bush emerged from the second debate as likable, occasionally goofy, warm, personal, and spontaneous. Dukakis emerged as competent yet cool, intense yet personally detached, almost arrogant. The media commentators were forced to report a clear Bush victory. Bush leaped ahead in the polls. His margin over Dukakis expanded from 4 to 5 points to 8 to 10 points. The media pronounced the election over.

In the end, George Bush's loyalty to his President paid off. Ronald Reagan recovered his popularity in his final year. Eight years of peace and prosperity were rewarded at the polls. Bush was perceived as the legitimate heir to the Reagan legacy, both in the primary elections where he swept away his Republican challengers, and in the general election where Michael Dukakis failed to convince Americans that their well-being was a temporary illusion.

The Bush presidency reflects all of the moderation, temperance, worldly sophistication, and patrician conservatism that were so appreciated at Andover. Bush eschews the ideological fervor of the early Reagan years. His call for a kinder, gentler America reflects upper-class paternalism more than middle-class competitive ambition. Bush seeks compromise over confrontation, not only because he faces a Democratic Congress but also because of his innate moderation. Most importantly, George Bush sees the presidency on the world stage. He will deal with domestic issues because he cannot avoid them. But his real interest is foreign affairs and national security. He could fulfill the highest expectations of his patrician upbringing by negotiating a significant reduction in the world's strategic nuclear weapons.

THE ASPIRING POLITICOS

For people of great ambition in American politics, there is only one goal—president of the United States. Aspiring political leaders will cultivate a style and an image that encourage others to think of them as "presidential timber," and they will prepare themselves to seize the opportunity when it arises. Both Edward M. Kennedy and George Bush are inheritors in the world of politics; they were blessed with personal wealth, Ivy League educations, and family connections to help establish their careers. Most others are climbers in the political world—those of relatively modest backgrounds who have devoted themselves to the quest for the presidency.

Mario Cuomo. No American politician can inspire so much passion among his followers, or so much fear among his enemies, as Mario Matthew Cuomo. He casts a giant shadow over the presidential ambitions of all of his fellow Democrats. He won reelection as governor of New York in 1986 by the widest margin (65 percent) in the state's history. His speeches can stir audiences as no other orator in recent times. Many political strategists agree that he could have won the Democratic presidential nomination in 1988 and given George Bush a much tougher race than Michael Dukakis. Yet Cuomo remained darkly brooding on the sidelines. "This is not the year," he said. "It doesn't feel right."

No one in national politics today has climbed so far from such humble beginnings as Mario Cuomo. His father immigrated from Salerno, Sicily, in the 1920s and sold goods from a pushcart in the borough of Queens in New York City. Later, he opened an Italian grocery store where young Mario and his brothers and sisters worked long hours each day. Cuomo attended Catholic schools in Queens and won a scholarship to the local St. John's University. He briefly tried semiprofessional baseball, playing one summer with the Brunswick Georgia Pirates. But he stayed at St. John's for both his bachelors and law degrees. Cuomo believes that his working-class Italian background and nonprestigious educational credentials kept him out of the big New York law firms. Instead he joined a Brooklyn firm and began working his way up through the political machinery of the New York Democratic party. His old St. John's Law School friend, Governor Hugh Carey of New York, offered him the post of secretary of state in 1975. From that post Cuomo entered the New York City mayor's race in 1977 against six rivals seeking to run the near-bankrupt metropolis. In a bitter run-off election, Cuomo lost to Ed Koch, who would later restore the city to solvency and becomes its longest serving mayor. In 1978 Cuomo won election as Governor Carey's lieutenant governor, but their political partnership soon dissolved in petty squabbling. In 1982 Carey announced that he would not seek a third term and endorsed Mayor Koch for the governorship.

Cuomo was an underdog against the popular mayor in the governor's race. But Koch's devotion to his beloved city of New York got him in trouble up-state. (Koch publically described life outside of New York City as "sterile" and a "joke.") Again Cuomo and Koch waged a bitter personal campaign against each other for the votes of Democrats. Cuomo squeaked out a close victory over Koch, only to face a strong Republican opponent, drugstore magnate Lewis E. Lehrman. Lehrman castigated Cuomo for sending his own children to Catholic schools yet supporting publically funded abortions and opposing tuition tax credits for parochial schools. Cuomo barely survived the attacks in the heavily Democratic state and won only a narrow victory over Lehrman.

As governor, Cuomo combined liberal rhetoric with conservative administration to win both the hearts and minds of New Yorkers. He kept his liberal support with national speeches portraying himself as a champion of ethnics, minorities, and the poor. Yet he won moderate and conservative support with tax cuts, deficit reductions, spending restraint, and tougher criminal penalties. He reinvigorated traditional liberal themes by appealing to the symbols of family, community, and opportunity in America.

Yet Cuomo is frequently combatitive, and occasionally arrogant in dealing with his critics, including the press. He is extremely sensitive, even hot tempered, in dealing with perceived ethnic slurs. He does not accept criticism gracefully. People react emotionally to Cuomo's inspirational messages about family, helping others, and living out the American dream. He rarely troubles his audiences with specifics. In short, he would make a formidable presidential candidate.

Michael Dukakis.   Michael Dukakis' campaign biography is subtitled "The Man Who Would Be President." Once bitten by the presidential bug, the fever often returns in four-year cycles. This is particularly true for people who convince themselves that their quest for the Oval Office is inspired by righteous, high-minded principles.

Dukakis has lived all of his life in Brookline, Massachusetts, an upper-class yankee refugee suburb of Boston. Dukakis' claim that he is the son of Greek immigrants is technically true; his father was a prosperous Boston physician, a Bates College and Harvard Medical School graduate, who assimilated into old-line Boston Brahmin society. When the Dukakis family moved to Brookline, it was the richest suburb in America. Young Michael went to Brookline High School, where he earned a reputation as an "earnest nerd"[6]—serious, studious, an Eagle Scout, a band member, a straight A student, student council president,

[6]*Newsweek*, July 25, 1988, p. 25.

and president of the honor society. His yearbook labels him "Most Brilliant" as well as "Big Chief Brain in the Face."[7]

While many of his classmates migrated across town to Harvard, Dukakis chose Swarthmore College, a small prestigious liberal arts college in Pennsylvania. He graduated Phi Beta Kappa, as had his mother, but instead of medicine he chose political science as his major. He spent a summer in Peru and learned Spanish. While still in college, he worked in the "reform" campaign of Philadelphia mayor and later U.S. Senator Joe Clark. When his student draft deferment ended, he joined the Army for a two-year enlistment. He was sent to Korea in 1955, two years after the fighting had ended. It appears that the Army did not recognize Michael Dukakis' brilliance, assigning him menial tasks as a lowly specialist-third class. Dukakis reportedly hated army life and retained his animosity toward the military throughout his career. When he returned, he enrolled in Harvard Law School, commuting from his home in Brookline. While still in law school, he won a seat in the Brookline Town Meeting.

Michael Dukakis has been an intense, driven, over-achiever throughout his life. He internalized the upward strivings of his immigrant parents, both of whom had brilliant scholastic records and successful professional careers. (Dukakis' older brother died in 1973 after years of psychiatric care and multiple suicide attempts.) He also displayed the arrogance and self-righteousness typical of people who believe they are "the best and the brightest." Liberal reform politics appeal to such people. He joined the American Civil Liberties Union and following graduation from Harvard, he organized a slate of "reform" Democrats to take over control of the Brookline Democratic Committee and oust the older Irish machine politicians. In 1962 he won an open seat for the Massachusetts state legislature. When his father died, Dukakis came into a multimillion-dollar trust fund. He nourishes an image of frugality, and in truth he has devoted his life to the quest for power and high office, not financial reward.

Dukakis led the reform "goo goo" (good government) faction in the legislature. He ran for attorney general in 1966 and lieutenant governor in 1970 and lost both elections. But he was not discouraged. In 1974 he ran for the governorship, capitalizing on the state's heavy taxes, high unemployment, and deficit spending; he defeated the incumbent Republican governor.

"Duke I," as his first term as governor was labeled, is acknowledged by everyone to have been a total failure. By all accounts Dukakis was "imperial," arrogant, self-righteous, closeminded, and unresponsive to the pleas and advice of his aides and co-workers. He was "lonely, misunderstood, and roundly disliked."[8] When he ran for reelection in 1978, he

[7]Richard Gaines and Michael Segal, *Dukakis: The Man Who Would Be President* (New York; Avon Books, 1988), p. 26.

[8]Gaines and Segal, *Dukakis*, p. 188.

was defeated in his own party's primary election by a lackluster old Irish politician, Ed King. Even Dukakis' liberal friends deserted him.

Dukakis is said to have brooded over what he called his "public death" and vowed to remodel himself into a winner. He accepted a post at Harvard's John F. Kennedy School of Government. He was not a popular teacher; students complained that he would not listen to any voice other than his own. When he began his reelection campaign in 1982, he publically apologized for his previous priggish style and promised to be a new "sensitive" governor. In the meantime Ed King had cut both spending and taxing in Massachusetts, and with the help of a voter referendum "Proposition $2^{1}/_{2}$," the state's reputation as "Taxachussetts" was moderated. The economic recovery that would be called the "Massachusetts miracle" was already underway. But political liberals were incensed by King's budget-cutting, and Dukakis ran a hard-hitting campaign, attacking King's billing of the state for lobster dinners. Dukakis won the Democratic primary and then rolled over token Republican opposition in the general elections. By all accounts "Duke II" was indeed mellower. And during his second term the state enjoyed an economic renaissance, for which Dukakis claimed credit. He was easily reelected to his third term in 1986.

At the start of the 1988 presidential campaign, the Dukakis team chose "competence" as its theme. Dukakis intoned the theme in a very effective acceptance speech—"This election is about competence, not ideology." By casting the theme in this fashion, Dukakis hoped to deflect attention from his liberal positions on taxing, spending, the death penalty, and other unpopular social and domestic policies he had espoused. He wanted to sell himself as a pragmatist, not a liberal, as a manager, not an ideologue. But Bush's media managers would not let Dukakis run away from his record. They launched a series of "attack videos," paid television ads designed to link Dukakis with unpopular liberal policy positions. Bush's skilled handlers had previously identified "hot button" issues by electronically recording the reactions of small "focus groups" of citizens to various themes. The most effective videos focused on the flag salute issue (Dukakis had vetoed a bill mandating the flag salute in public schools); the furlough of murders and rapists (a Massachusetts prison furlough program gave a convicted murder, Willy Horton, the opportunity to rape and murder a woman while on furlough); and Dukakis' opposition to defense spending. Dukakis himself had tried to pose as a supporter of defense efforts by having himself videotaped riding around in a tank; he looked so silly that the Bush team used the tape to illustrate his inexperience in defense policy. Dukakis' image as an environmentalist was destroyed by graphic pictures of garbage floating in Boston harbor.

The Bush-Dukakis televised debates in 1988 were crucial to the presidential election. Public opinion was volatile; large shifts in poll results had followed the televised Democratic and Republican conventions; and more than one-third of the voters remained undecided or only weakly committed to a candidate. Going into the debates, George Bush held only a very narrow edge over his opponent.

In the first debate both Bush and Dukakis performed extraordinarily well. Bush succeeded in reinforcing a major campaign theme: Dukakis was a big-spending, tax-raising liberal, "out there, out of the mainstream." Bush touched all of the hot-button social issues: crime, abortion, and the death penalty. Dukakis hammered back on Bush's role in the Iran-Contra scandal, the qualifications of his running mate, Senator Dan Quayle, and his prior association with the Panamanian drug-trafficking strongman Noriega. Bush was relaxed, occasionally joking, and gaffe-free. Dukakis was intense, occasionally eloquent, but passionless. The most common post-debate media verdict on the first debate was that Dukakis had outpointed Bush by a narrow margin.

But in the second presidential debate, Dukakis insured his defeat with a cold, impersonal performance. His media advisers tried to "de-ice" their candidate prior to the debate. They began hitting back hard in attack videos of their own, implying that Bush was lying about their man's record, that Bush furloughed murderers, too, and that Bush was cozy with drug-trafficking dictators. They coached Dukakis to show warmth and "likability," yet at the same time to hit back hard on drugs, "Noriega," and Quayle, and if possible, to portray Bush as an opponent of social security. But the very first question exposed Dukakis' cool, seemingly uncaring demeanor. CNN anchorman Bernard Shaw opened with a question that touched on every viewer's raw emotions: "Governor, if Kitty Dukakis were raped and murdered would you favor an irrevocable death penalty for the killer?" The question demanded an emotional reply but the detached candidate responded with an impersonal recitation of his stock positions on crime, drugs, and law enforcement.

The Dukakis team fought back in the last weeks of the campaign with a new populist theme: "We're on your side." Bush was subjected to harsh attacks as a "liar," and, at the same time, was blamed for the nastiness of the campaign. The television network anchors joined in the attacks by claiming the campaign was the most negative on record. Dukakis embraced the liberal label but defined it in terms of "Roosevelt, Truman, and Kennedy." These last-minute appeals to traditional Democratic voters succeeded in tightening the race in a few big states. when the popular vote was counted on election day, the results were very close to the final polls. Bush won the popular vote 54 percent to 46 percent and swept the electoral college.

Jack Kemp.   Jack Kemp's "game plan" for politics was to "get first downs, and the touchdowns will come up and hit you in the face." A former quarterback for the Buffalo Bills and the AFL's Most Valuable Player in 1965 made a great many political "first downs" since first winning election to Congress in 1970. But in 1988 he went for the "long bomb"—a presidential primary campaign to take the Republican nomination away from George Bush—but failed to put points on the board.

He gave up his sure congressional seat during the campaign. But George Bush, seeking to unite Republicans in his administration, named Kemp to his Cabinet as secretary of housing and urban development. The boyishly handsome, athletic Jack Kemp remains a favorite among Republican conservatives.

Kemp grew up in Los Angeles, where his father owned a small trucking firm. Kemp admits to being "totally tunnel-visioned" about his early goal in life—"to play football." Kemp chose smaller Occidental College, rather than USC or UCLA, to ensure that he would get a lot of playing time. He was only an average student, majoring in physical education. But as an outstanding quarterback, he was drafted by the Detroit Lions. He spent thirteen years with various professional teams, but his best years were with the Buffalo Bills in 1963, 1964, and 1965, when he led the team to three consecutive Eastern division titles and two AFL championships. Kemp compiled a number of AFL records and served as co-founder and president of the AFL Players Association. But by 1970, he had accumulated two broken ankles, two broken shoulders, a broken knee, and eleven concussions. When he quit, the Buffalo Bills permanently retired his jersey number.

Kemp moved directly from the playing field to the political arena. Buffalo Republicans urged him to run for a suburban congressional seat held by the Democrats. Kemp's high name recognition and his success as the home-team quarterback helped him win a narrow victory over the incumbent. In later elections, his margin of victory soared to over 75 percent of the vote.

In his first years in Washington, Kemp was regarded as an "ex-jock" and a "lightweight." Kemp took advantage of these years by informing himself about a wide range of social, economic, military, and foreign policy issues. Kemp was especially impressed with the ideas of Arthur B. Laffer, an economist at the University of Southern California. Laffer argued that high federal tax rates have reached a point of diminishing returns. Taxes are so high that they are undermining incentives to produce and save; lowering tax rates might actually increase federal revenues if more people were encouraged to work and save.

Kemp became the leading congressional spokesman for the new "supply-side" economics. "If you tax something, you get less of it. If you subsidize something, you get more of it. In America we tax work, growth, investment, employment, savings, and productivity. We subsidize nonworking, consumption, welfare, and debt." In 1978, Kemp, together with Republican Senator William V. Roth of Delaware, proposed an across-the-board slash in income taxes by 30 percent in three years. This "Kemp-Roth" tax bill was at first ridiculed in Establishment circles. (The Brookings Institution called it "the most irresponsible financial policy ever suggested in U.S. history.") But in 1980 it was incorporated into the Republican platform. When Ronald Reagan captured the White House, his first priority was economic recovery, and Jack Kemp's tax plan became a key part of the President's program. The 1981 Reagan tax cuts included a 25-percent reduction in personal income taxes over three years, only a slight modification of Kemp's original plan. Jack Kemp became a recognized leader in the Congress.

Jack Kemp's presidential hopes rested on his ability to unify the conservative wing of the Republican party on behalf of his candidacy; to portray George Bush as an upper-class, Eastern-Establishment, Republican moderate; and to capture the hearts of the Reagan voters in both the primary and general elections. Kemp's populist brand of conservatism certainly appealed to the ideological right more than Bush or Dole centrism But the Rev. Pat Robertson entered the race to claim the religious right and Pierre S. Du Pont, governor of Delaware, claimed the intellectual conservatives. And the Reagan loyalists decided that George Bush was indeed the true heir to the Reagan legacy. Jack Kemp's bid for the presidency collapsed shortly after the first New Hampshire primary.

Kemp gave up his sure Congressional seat to make his presidential bid, and his loss left him out of public office for the first time since his quarterbacking days. He was oblidged to seek a Cabinet post from his primary opponent. In the spirit of party unity, Bush agreed; but the post given Kemp—Secretary of Housing and Urban Development—is not a highly visible or influential one. It remains to be seen whether Jack Kemp can remain in the presidential hunt.

Dan Quayle.   Like George Bush, Dan Quayle is an "inheritor" in politics—the beneficiary of a family fortune and name which propelled him into the U.S. Senate and the vice-presidency. But unlike George Bush, Quayle never excelled in school or college nor performed heroic deeds in war nor compiled much of a record of public service.

J. Danforth Quayle III inherited the wealth and power of the Pullman newspaper publishing family—owners of the *Indianapolis Star and News*, the *Arizona Republic*, the *Phoenix Gazette*, and the *Huntington Herald Press*. The Quayle family lived a relatively simple life on a horse farm in Indiana, and young Dan attended a public high school. He enrolled at DePauw University, a small liberal arts college heavily endowed by his father. By all reports, he was a poor student, a hard-partying fraternity man, and an excellent golf-team member. Upon graduation he received his draft notice; the Vietnam War was at its height. Like many of his contemporaries, Quayle sought an honorable alternative. His family eased his way into the Indiana National Guard where he served in a headquarter public relations unit. His poor college grades initially caused the University of Indiana Law School to reject his admission application. But he personally convinced the admissions dean at the Indianapolis branch to admit him to night classes. His father got him a clerk's job in the Indiana attorney general's office; he later joined the governor's staff. He met and married Marilyn Tucker, a law school classmate, and in 1974 they set up practice in Huntington as Quayle and Quayle.

Quayle and Quayle apparently attracted very little legal business. Quayle's father named him associate publisher of the city's newspaper, but he did very little newspaper work. He perfected his golf game, which was reported to be near-professional in quality. In 1976, the Republican county committee chairman asked Quayle to run for Congress against a heavily favored incumbent Democrat. "I'll have to call my dad," Quayle responded.[9] Apparently dad approved.

Quayle won his congressional seat in an upset victory. He seemed to find his calling as a young, handsome office seeker. He was an energetic campaigner and won reelection by a wide margin in 1978. In 1980 Quayle was ready to take on U.S. Senator Birch Bayh, a liberal Democrat. Bayh was targeted for defeat by conservative political action committees in Washington and anti-abortion groups. Bayh's ultra-liberal voting made him more popular in Washington elite circles than back home in Indiana. With the help of the Reagan presidential landslide in 1980, Quayle unseated Bayh and went to Washington as a U.S. senator.

George Bush reportedly never sat down face to face with Dan Quayle to assess the young senator's understanding of the issues and his competence to be Vice-President. Instead, Bush is said to have looked only at his superficial political qualifications: He had won election to the House twice and election and reelection to the U.S. Senate; his youth was expected to appeal to the large baby-boom generation of voters; his good looks were expected to appeal to women voters; his midwestern conservatism was expected to balance Bush's Eastern image. Bush was personally wary of his old competitors, Dole and Kemp; he wanted a Vice-President who would be as loyal to him as he had been to Reagan. But less than twenty-four hours after Quayle's selection as running mate, Bush and his campaign team knew they had made a mistake. They reluctantly decided that dropping him from the ticket would be more costly politically than suffering through the campaign with him.

The initial media attack on Quayle—that he had sought to avoid duty in Vietnam by joining the Indiana National Guard—was easily deflected. The vast majority of Quayle's age group had also sought honorable alternatives to Vietnam. Quayle was coached to turn the issue to his advantage: "I am proud of my service in the Indiana National Guard." But Quayle's experience and competence paled in comparison to Dukakis' wily choice of a running mate—the distinguished U.S. senator from Texas who had defeated George Bush for his seat, Lloyd Bentsen.

Whatever credibility Quayle had as a vice-presidential candidate was destroyed by the crafty Bentsen in their televised debate. Quayle stumbled badly when repeatedly asked what he would do if he became President. But the knockout punch was delivered by Bentsen himself when Quayle (accurately) compared his experience in Congress with that of John F. Kennedy in 1960. "Senator, I served with Jack Kennedy. Jack Kennedy was a friend of mine. Senator, you're no Jack Kennedy."

[9]*New York Times*, August 26, 1988, p. 8.

This brief sound bite captured Quayle's problem: He was regarded as a featherweight by the media and a drag on the Bush ticket. He was promptly put in deep freeze by Bush's campaign managers. As Vice-President he is likely to give new meaning to the term oblivion.

Bill Bradley. When William Warren Bradley graduated from the public high school in Crystal City, Missouri, he could have gone to any college in the nation. His father was president of the local bank. Bradley was a six-foot five-inch high school All-American center, averaging over thirty points per game, and academically, he stood at the top of his class. Wisely, he chose Princeton over the basketball powerhouse schools; he went on to become an All-American, a gold-medal winner in the 1964 Tokyo Olympics, and a Rhodes Scholar. He obtained an M.A. at Oxford before returning to the United States. He played ten years in the NBA with the New York Knicks, including two NBA championships. He wrote a book about these years, *Life on the Run*, widely acclaimed as a classic in sports literature.

Upon his retirement from basketball in 1978, Bradley capitalized on his celebrity to move directly into politics. He successfully challenged the Democratic party machine in New Jersey to win a U.S. Senate nomination with 61 percent of the vote in the primary election. He went on to win 56 percent of the vote in the general election against a conservative Republican. His Senate colleagues were initially suspicious of his sports celebrity, but he soon impressed Capitol Hill with his hard work and knowledge of the issues. Indeed, as one commentator put it: "The only Democratic think tank in this town is Bill Bradley's head." In the Senate he has led efforts in tax reform, supported defense modernization, and firmly established himself as a leader of moderate Democrats. He was reelected in 1986 in a 64 percent landslide.

Many commentators consider Bradley the Democrats' best hope to win the presidency. Liberals in the party refuse to believe that ideology has played a crucial role in defeating the party's presidential candidates. Despite losing five of the last six presidential elections, liberals continue to maintain control of the nominating process. Each defeat is given ad hoc explanations, for example, Reagan came across better on TV than Mondale, Bush ran a "dirty" campaign. But serious political analysts understand that the Democratic party must return to its roots: It must nominate a candidate in the mold of Harry Truman and John F. Kennedy—a strong supporter of national defense as well as civil rights, an advocate of tax reform and economic growth as well as opportunity for the less advantaged. There are few who doubt that if Bradley could wrest the Democratic presidential nomination from the party's ideologues and special interests, he could win the general election.

EXECUTIVE DECISION-MAKERS: THE SERIOUS PEOPLE

Politicians deal in style and image. However, the responsibility for the initiation of national programs and policies falls primarily upon the top

White House staff and the heads of executive departments. Generally, Congress merely responds to policy proposals initiated by the executive branch. The President and his key advisers and administrators have a strong incentive to fulfill their responsibility for decision-making: In the eyes of the American public, they are responsible for everything that happens in the nation regardless of whether or not they have the authority or capacity to do anything about it. There is a general expectation that every administration, even one committed to a "caretaker" role, will put forth some sort of policy program.

The President and Vice-President, White House presidential advisers and ambassadors-at-large, Cabinet secretaries, undersecretaries, and assistant secretaries constitute our executive elite. Let us take a brief look at the careers of some of the people who have served in key Cabinet positions in recent presidential administrations.

SECRETARIES OF DEFENSE

Charles E. Wilson. (1953–57). President and Chairman of the board of directors of General Motors.

Neil H. McElroy. (1957–59). President and Chairman of the board of directors of Procter & Gamble; member of the board of directors of General Electric, Chrysler Corp., and Equitable Life Assurance Co.; member of the board of trustees of Harvard University, the National Safety Council, and the National Industrial Conference.

Thomas S. Gates. (1959–60). Secretary of the Navy, 1957–59; chairman of the board and chief executive officer, Morgan Guaranty Trust Co.; member of the board of directors of General Electric, Bethlehem Steel, Scott Paper Co., Campbell Soup Co., Insurance Co. of North America, Cities Service, SmithKline and French (pharmaceuticals), and the University of Pennsylvania

Robert S. McNamara. (1961–67). President and Chairman of the board of directors of the Ford Motor Co.; member of the board of directors of Scott Paper Co.; president of the World Bank, 1967–81.

Clark Clifford. (1967–69). Senior partner of Clifford & Miller (Washington law firm); member of board of directors of the National Bank of Washington and the Sheridan Hotel Corp.; special counsel to the President, 1949–50; member of the board of trustees of Washington University in St. Louis.

Melvin Laird. (1969–73). Wisconsin Republican congressman, and former chairman of Republican conference in the House of Representatives.

James R. Schlesinger. (1973–77). Director, Central Intelligence Agency; former chairman of Atomic Energy Commission; formerly assistant director of the Office of Management and Budget; economics professor; and research associate of the RAND Corp.

Harold Brown. (1977–81). President of the California Institute of Technology. A member of the board of directors of International Business Machines (IBM) and the Times-Mirror Corp. Former secretary of the air force under President Lyndon Johnson, and U.S. representative to the SALT I talks under President Richard Nixon.

Caspar W. Weinberger. (1981–89). Vice-president and director of the Bechtel Corporation, the world's largest privately owned corporation. A member of the board of directors of Pepsico and Quaker Oats Co. Former secretary of health, education, and welfare under President Richard Nixon; former director of the Office of Management and Budget; former chairman of the Federal Trade Commission. A former San Francisco attorney and California State legislator.

Richard B. Cheney. Congressman and chairman of the House Republican Conference; assistant to the President, Gerald Ford; chairman of the Cost of Living Council; director of Office of Economic Opportunity under President Richard Nixon. Attorney.

SECRETARIES OF STATE

John Foster Dulles. (1953–60). Senior partner of Sullivan & Cromwell, and member of the board of directors of the Bank of New York, Fifth Avenue Bank, American Bank Note Co., International Nickel Co. of Canada, Babcock and Wilson Corp., Shenandoah Corp., United Cigar Stores, American Cotton Oil Co., United Railroad of St. Louis, and European Textile Corp. He was a trustee of the New York Public Library, Union Theological Seminary, the Rockefeller Foundation, and the Carnegie Endowment for International Peace; also a delegate to the World Council of Churches.

Dean Rusk. (1961–68). President of the Rockefeller Foundation.

William P. Rogers. (1969–73). U.S. attorney general during Eisenhower Administration; senior partner in Royall, Koegal, Rogers and Wells (one of the twenty largest Wall Street law firms).

Henry Kissinger. (1973–77). Special assistant to the president for national security affairs; former Harvard professor of international affairs, and project director for Rockefeller Brothers Fund and for the Council on Foreign Relations.

Cyrus Vance. (1977–80). Senior partner in the New York law firm of Simpson, Thacher & Bartlett. A member of the board of directors of IBM and Pan American World Airways; a trustee of Yale University, the Rockefeller Foundation, and the Council on Foreign Relations; former secretary of the army under President Lyndon Johnson.

Alexander M. Haig, Jr. (1981–82). President of United Technologies Corporation, and former four-star general, U.S. Army. He was former Supreme Allied Commander, NATO forces in Europe; former assistant to the President under Richard Nixon; former deputy assistant to the President for national security under Henry Kissinger; former deputy commandant, U.S. Military Academy at West Point; former deputy secretary of defense.

George P. Shultz. (1982–89). President of the Bechtel Corporation. Former secretary of the treasury, former secretary of labor, and former director of Office of Management and Budget under President Richard Nixon. Earned Ph.D. in economics from M.I.T. Former dean of the school of business, University of Chicago. Former director of General Motors, Borg-Warner, and Dillon, Read & Co.

SECRETARIES OF TREASURY

George M. Humphrey. (1953–57). Former chairman of the board of directors of the M.A. Hanna Co.; member of board of directors of National Steel Corp., Consolidated Coal Co. of Canada, and Dominion Sugar Co.; trustee of M.I.T.

Robert B. Anderson. (1957–61). Secretary of the navy, 1953–54; deputy secretary of defense, 1945–55; member of board of directors of Goodyear Tire and Rubber Co. and Pan American World Airways; member of the executive board of the Boy Scouts of America.

Douglas Dillon. (1961–63). Chairman of the board of Dillon, Read & Co. (one of Wall Street's largest investment firms); member of New York Stock Exchange; director of U.S. and Foreign Securities Corp. and U.S. International Securities Corp.; member of board of governors of New York Hospital and the Metropolitan Museum of Art.

David Kennedy. (1969–71). President and chairman of the board of Continental Illinois Bank and Trust Co.; director of International Harvester Co., Commonwealth Edison, Pullman Co., Abbott Laboratories, Swift and Co., U.S. Gypsum, and Communications Satellite Corp.; trustee of the University of Chicago, the Brookings Institution, the Committee for Economic Development, and George Washington University.

John B. Connally. (1971–72). Secretary of the navy, governor of Texas, administrative assistant to Lyndon B. Johnson; attorney for Murcheson Brothers Investment (Dallas); former director of New York Central Railroad.

George P. Shultz. (1972–74). Secretary of labor and director of the Office of Management and Budget; former dean of the University of Chicago Graduate School of Business; former director of Borg-Warner Corp., General American Transportation Co., and Stein, Roe & Farnham (investments).

William E. Simon. (1974–77). Director of Federal Energy Office, and former deputy secretary of the treasury; formerly a senior partner of Salomon Brothers (one of Wall Street's largest investment firms specializing in municipal bond trading).

Warner Michael Blumenthal. (1977–79). President of the Bendix Corporation; former vice-president of Crown Cork Co.; trustee of Princeton University and the Council on Foreign Relations.

G. William Miller. (1979–81). Chairman and chief executive officer of Textron Corporation. Former partner in Cravath, Swaine & Moore (one of the nation's twenty-five largest and most prestigious law firms); a former director of Allied Chemical and Federated Department Stores; former chairman of the Federal Reserve Board.

Donald T. Regan. (1981–85). Chairman of the board and chief executive officer of Merrill Lynch & Co. Inc. (the nation's largest investment firm); former vice-chairman of the New York Stock Exchange; a trustee of the University of Pennsylvania and the Committee for Economic Development, and a member of the policy committee of the Business Roundtable.

James A. Baker III. (1985–89). Wealthy Houston attorney whose father owned Texas Commerce Bank. Former undersecretary of commerce in the Ford administration and campaign chairman for George Bush's unsuccessful presidential race in 1980. President Reagan's White House chief of staff in his first term.

Nicholas Brady. (1989 to date). Former chairman of Dillon Read & Co., a director of Purolator, NCR, Georgia International, ASA, and Media General.

It makes relatively little difference whether a President is a Democrat or a Republican. The same type of "serious men" must be called upon to run the government (see Table 3–1 on page 94).

THE WASHINGTON INSIDERS

George Bush is the first truly patrician president since Franklin D. Roosevelt. (By patrician we mean born into a family of many generations of wealth, power, and prestige.) Despite his years of loyal support to Ronald Reagan and his often awkward efforts to portray himself as a Texas conservative, George Bush is an *Establishment* Republican. The key posts in his administration are filled by the people who share patrician, privileged, noblesse oblige sentiments of the Bushes of Connecticut.

The Bush inner circle is composed of prep-school, Ivy League accommodationists, familiar with power, wealth, and privilege. The President attended Andover and Yale; close friend and Secretary of Treasury Nicholas Brady attended St. Mark's School, Yale, and Harvard Business School; Secretary of State James A. Baker was born to old Texas money but was educated at The Hill School and Princeton before getting his law degree at the University of Texas; OMB Director Richard Darman attended The Rivas School, Harvard College, and Harvard Business School; attorney General Richard Thornberg attended Mercersburg Academy and Yale before going to the University of Pittsburgh Law School.

The corporate and governmental experience and educational credentials of these "serious" decision-makers greatly exceed those of most members of Congress or other elected officials. When presidents turn from the task of *running for office* to the task of *running a government*, they are obliged to recruit higher quality leadership than typically found among political officeholders.

The Bush administration appears divided into an inner and an outer circle. In addition to Baker, Brady, Thornberg, and Darman, the inner circle includes National Security Adviser Brent Scowcroft, educated at West Point and Columbia University; John Sununu with a B.S., M.S., and Ph.D. from M.I.T.; and Richard Cheney, the only insider without Establishment credentials. The outer circle appear far less privileged in background. It includes Cabinet officials chosen for their political experience and appeal to various constituencies. The outer circle includes two Hispanics, former Congressman Manuel Lujan and former Texas A&M President Lauro F. Cavazus; one black, HHS Secretary Louis W. Sullivan (see Chapter 7); and two women, Labor Secretary Elizabeth Dole and Trade Representative Carla Hills.

The Bush Cabinet possesses more experience in government than any recent administration; Washington "insiders" dominate. Eight members held Cabinet-level posts *before* Bush took office; five served in the Congress; two were governors (see Table 3–1).

The educational credentials of the twenty Cabinet-level officials

TABLE 3–1 The Washington Insiders

NAME (YEAR OF BIRTH)	GOVERNMENT POSTS	PRIVATE POSTS	EDUCATION
J. Danforth Quayle III Vice-President (1947)	U.S. Senate (1981–88); U.S. Congress (1977–80); administrative assistant to governor of Indiana (1971–73)	Associate publisher, *Huntington* (Ind.) *Herald Press*	DePauw; University of Indiana Law School
James A. Baker III Secretary of State (1930)	Secretary of treasury (1985–89); White House chief of staff (1981–85); undersecretary of commerce (1975–76)	Houston oilman and attorney	Princeton; University of Texas Law School
Nicholas Brady Secretary of Treasury (1930)	Secretary of treasury (1989 to date), appointed by Reagan, continued by Bush	Chairman, Dillon, Read & Co. (Wall Street investment firm); a director of Purolator, NCR, Georgia International, Wolverne, WorldWide, ASA, Media General	Yale; Harvard, M.B.A.
Richard B. Cheney Secretary of Defense (1941)	U.S. Congress (1979–89); chairman of House Republican Conference; assistant to the president (1975–77); deputy assistant to the president (1974–75); Cost of Living Council (1971–73); Office of Economic Opportunity (1969–70)	Attorney; Bradley Woods & Co.	University of Wyoming, B.A. and M.A.; post graduate, University of Wisconsin

Richard Thornberg Attorney General (1932)	Attorney general (1988 to date), appointed by Reagan, continued by Bush; governor, Pennsylvania (1979–87); assistant U.S. attorney general (1975–77); U.S. attorney for Western Pennsylvania (1969–75)	Yale; University of Pittsburgh Law School
Robert Adam Mosbacher Secretary of Commerce (1927)	President and chairman, Mosbacher Energy Co.; a director of Texas Commerce Bankshares, New York Life	Washington and Lee
Jack French Kemp Secretary of Housing and Urban Development (1935)	Professional football player; co-founder AFL Players Association	Occidental College
Elizabeth Hanford Dole Secretary of Labor (1936)	Secretary of transportation (1983–88); assistant to the President (1981–83); commissioner, Federal Trade Commission (1973–79); deputy director, Office of Consumer Affairs (1971–73); director, President's Commission for Consumer Interests (1968–71)	Duke; Harvard, M.A., J.D.

(Continued)

TABLE 3-1 The Washington Insiders (Continued)

NAME (YEAR OF BIRTH)	GOVERNMENT POSTS	PRIVATE POSTS	EDUCATION
Samuel K. Skinner Secretary of Transportation (1938)	Chairman, Northwestern Illinois Regional Transportation Authority (1984–89); U.S. attorney (1968–84)	Attorney and senior partner, Sidley and Austin	University of Illinois; DePaul University Law School
Manuel Lujan, Jr. Secretary of Interior (1928)	U.S. Congress (1969–89)	Family insurance business	College of Santa Fe
Louis W. Sullivan Secretary of Health and Human Services (1933)		Dean, Morehouse School of Medicine (1978–89); professor of hematology, Boston University Medical School (1968–78); instructor and researcher, Harvard Medical School, New Jersey College of Medicine	Morehouse College; Boston University Medical School
Lauro F. Cavazus Secretary of Education (1927)	Secretary of education (1988 to date), appointed by Reagan, continued by Bush	President, Texas Tech University; professor of anatomy; director of Diamond Shamrock, R&M Inc.	Texas Tech; Iowa State, Ph.D.
Clayton Keith Yeutter Secretary of Agriculture (1930)	U.S. trade representative (1985–89); deputy special trade representative (1975–77); U.S. Department of Agriculture (1970–75).	Chairman, Chicago Mercantile Exchange; professor, University of Nebraska; rancher, farmer	University of Nebraska, B.S., J.D., Ph.D.

96

Name / Position	Career	Education
James D. Watkins Secretary of Energy (1927)	Chief of naval operations (1982–86); CINCPAC (1981–82); Navy admiral	U.S. Naval Academy; Naval Postgraduate M.S.
Edwin J. Derwinski Secretary of Veterans Affairs (1926)	Undersecretary of state (1985–89); U.S. Congress (1959–85); Illinois state legislator (1957–59)	Loyola
Brent Scowcroft National Security Advisers (1925)	Chairman, President's Commission on Strategic Alternatives (Scowcroft Commission) (1983); national security adviser (1975–77); deputy national security adviser (1973–75); military assistant to President (1972–73); lt. general, U.S. Air Force	U.S. Military Academy; Columbia, M.A.; Georgetown University, Ph.D.
Partner, Kissinger and Associates, international consultants; director, National Bank of Washington		
John Sununu Chief of Staff (1939)	Governor, New Hampshire (1983–88); New Hampshire legislator (1973–74)	M.I.T., B.S., M.S., Ph.D.
Associate dean, professor, College of Engineering, Tufts University; president, Ergring Co. and Thermal Research		

(Continued)

TABLE 3-1 The Washington Insiders (Continued)

NAME (YEAR OF BIRTH)	GOVERNMENT POSTS	PRIVATE POSTS	EDUCATION
Richard G. Darman Director Office of Management and Budget (1943)	Deputy secretary of treasury (1985–87); assistant to President (1981–85); assistant secretary, Department of Commerce (1976–77); special assistant to attorney general (1973); assistant to secretary of defense (1973); deputy assistant secretary HEW (1972–72)	Managing director, Shearson, Lehman Bros. (Wall Street investment firm); director, American Capital and Research Corp.	Harvard; Harvard Business School, M.B.A.
Carla A. Hills Special Trade Representative (1934)	Secretary of HUD (1975–77); assistant attorney general (1974–75); assistant U.S. attorney, Los Angeles (1958–61)	Attorney and partner, Latham, Watkins & Hills, a director of IBM, Corning Glass, American Airlines, Federal National Mortgage Association, Henely Group, Chevron	Stanford; Yale Law School
William J. Bennett Director, National Drug Control Policy (1943)	Secretary of education (1985 to date), appointed by Reagan, continued by Bush; chairman, National Endowment for the Humanities (1981–85)	Director, Humanities Center of North Carolina; assistant to president of Boston University	Williams; Harvard Law School; University of Texas, Ph.D.

(fourteen secretaries, together with the Vice-President, attorney general, White House chief of staff, OMB director, national security adviser, and U.S. trade representative) are also very impressive. Sixteen Cabinet officials (80 percent) have advanced degrees: five hold Ph.D.s, one a medical degree, and seven hold law degrees. Ivy League degrees predominate: Eleven top officials (55 percent) hold at least one degree from a private prestigious university or West Point or Annapolis. Harvard degrees are most numerous (four), closely followed by Yale (three, or four if the President is counted).

Corporate and Wall Street connections are numerous. Secretary of Treasury Nicholas Brady was chairman of Dillon, Read & Company; Agriculture Secretary Clayton Yeutter was chairman of the Chicago Mercantile Exchange; OMB Director Richard Darman was a top official at Shearson, Lehman. In all, nine (45 percent) have held directorships in large corporations or banks.

THE PROFESSIONAL BUREAUCRATS

The federal bureaucracy has grown to nearly 3 million civilian employees. The professional federal executives who supervise this giant bureaucracy occupy a uniquely influential position in American society. They advise the President on decisions he must make; they present and defend legislative recommendations before the Congress; and they supervise the day-to-day decisions of the hundreds of departments, agencies, commissions, and boards that influence the lives of every American. These federal executives comprise a powerful bureaucratic elite—particularly the secretaries, assistant secretaries, and undersecretaries of the fourteen federal departments (State, Treasury, Defense, Justice, Health and Human Services, Education, Interior, Agriculture, Commerce, Labor, Housing and Urban Development, Energy, Veteran's Affairs, and Transportation); administrators of important independent agencies in the executive office of the President (including the Office of Management and Budget, the National Security Council, and the Council of Economic Advisers); and members of key regulatory commissions and boards (Federal Reserve Board, Civil Aeronautics Board, Federal Communications Commission, Federal Power Commission, Federal Trade Commission, Interstate Commerce Commission, National Labor Relations Board, and Securities and Exchange Commission). Most of these top federal executive positions are filled by presidential appointment with Senate confirmation.

What kind of people head the federal bureaucracy? In an interesting early study[10] of over 1,000 persons who occupied the positions listed

[10]David T. Stanley, Dean E. Mann, and Jameson W. Doig, *Men Who Govern* (Washington: Brookings Institution, 1967).

above during the presidential administrations of Roosevelt, Truman, Eisenhower, Kennedy, and Johnson, the Brookings Institution reported that 36 percent of these top federal executives came up through the ranks of the government itself, 26 percent were recruited from law, 24 percent from business, 7 percent from education, and 7 percent from a variety of other fields. A plurality of top federal executives are *career bureaucrats.* Moreover, most of these people served in only one government agency and slowly acquired seniority and promotion in the agency in which they eventually became chief executives. A total of 63 percent of the top federal executives were federal bureaucrats at the time of their appointment to a top post; only 37 percent had no prior experience as federal bureaucrats.

Thus, the federal bureaucracy itself is producing its own leadership, with some limited recruitment from business and law. (Later in this volume, see Table 7–4, we will compare our own data for 1970 and 1980 on governmental and military elites with the earlier Brookings Institution's data, but we can say now that our figures are roughly comparable.) The federal bureaucracy, then, is an independent channel of recruitment to positions of governmental power in America.

Top federal bureaucrats are recruited primarily from the middle- and upper-middle classes of the population, as are leaders in other sectors of society. The Brookings Institution reported that the percentage of college-educated top executive bureaucrats rose from 88 percent in the Roosevelt administration to 99 percent in the Johnson Administration. Moreover, 68 percent had advanced degrees—44 percent in law, 17 percent with earned masters degrees, and 11 percent with earned doctorates. However, the class composition of the top bureaucrats was better reflected in information on *which* schools and colleges were attended. The Brookings Institution reported that the Ivy League schools plus Stanford, Chicago, Michigan, and Berkeley educated over 40 percent of the top federal executives, with Yale, Harvard, and Princeton leading the list.[11] Moreover, this tendency was increasing over time; there are larger proportions of Ivy Leaguers in top posts today than in years past. Perhaps more importantly, the Brookings study reported that 39 percent of the top federal executives attended *private* schools (compared to only 6 percent of the U.S. population); and 17 percent went to one of only eighteen "name" prep schools.[12]

There is little difference between Republican and Democratic administrations in the kind of people who are appointed to top executive

[11]Stanley, Mann, and Doig, *Men Who Govern,* p. 21.
[12]Avon Old Farms, Choate, Deerfield, Groton, Hill, Hotchkiss, Kent, Lawrenceville, Loomis, Middlesex, Milton, Phillips Andover, Phillips Exeter, St. George's, St. Mary's, St. Paul's, Taft, Thatcher.

posts. It is true, of course, that Republican Presidents tend to appoint Republicans to top posts, and Democratic Presidents tend to appoint Democrats; only about 8 percent of the top appointments cross party lines. However, there are few discernible differences in the class backgrounds, educational levels, occupational experiences, or previous public service of Democratic or Republican appointees.

One troublesome problem at the top of the federal bureaucracy is the shortness of tenure of federal executives. *The median tenure in office of top federal executives is only two years.*[13] Such a short tenure at the top has obvious disadvantages; it is generally estimated that a top federal executive needs a year or more to become fully productive, to learn the issues, programs, procedures, technical problems, and personalities involved in his or her work. If he or she resigns after the second year, the federal bureaucracy is not getting continuous, knowledgeable direction from its top officials. The data on short tenure suggest that we have created too many conflicting pressures on top federal executives—from the White House, Congress, interest groups, other government agencies, and particularly the mass media. Top federal executive positions are becoming less attractive over time.

THE MILITARY ESTABLISHMENT

In his farewell address to the nation in 1961, President Dwight D. Eisenhower warned of "an immense military establishment and a large arms industry." He observed:

> In the councils of government, we must guard against the acquisition of unwarranted influence, whether sought or unsought, by the military-industrial complex.

While radicals view the military-industrial complex as a conspiracy to promote war and imperialism, it is not really anything like that. Liberal economist John K. Galbraith portrays the military-industrial complex as a far more subtle interplay of forces in American society:

> It is an organization or a complex of organizations and not a conspiracy. . . . In the conspiratorial view, the military power is a coalition of generals and conniving industrialists. The goal is mutual enrichment: they arrange elaborately to feather each other's nests.
>
>   There is some enrichment and some graft. Insiders do well. . . . Nonetheless, the notion of a conspiracy to enrich the corrupt is gravely damaging to an understanding of military power. . . .

[13]Stanley, Mann, and Doig, *Men Who Goverrn,* p. 57.

The reality is far less dramatic and far more difficult of solution. The reality is a complex of organizations pursuing their sometimes diverse but generally common goals. The participants in these organizations are mostly honest men. . . . They live on their military pay or their salaries as engineers, scientists, or managers, or their pay and profits as executives, and would not dream of offering or accepting a bribe. . . .

The problem is not conspiracy or corruption, but unchecked rule. And being unchecked, this rule reflects not the national need but the bureaucratic need. . . .[14]

What are the real facts about the military-industrial complex? Today, even with a defense buildup underway, total defense spending runs about $300 billion per year—only 27 percent of the federal government's budget and only *6 percent of the gross national product.* The 100 largest industrial corporations in the United States depend on military contracts for *less than 10 percent of their sales.* In other words, American industry does *not* depend upon war or the threat of war for any large proportion of its income or sales.

Nonetheless, there are a few powerful companies that depend heavily on defense contracts—Lockheed Aircraft, General Dynamics, Rockwell, McDonnell Douglas, Boeing, Litton, Thiokol, Hughes Tool, and Grumman Aircraft.[15] These firms, however, are not really the nation's largest corporations. (Of the top 100 industries in Table 2–1, Boeing is listed as 26, Rockwell as 36, McDonnell-Douglas as 38, Lockheed as 56, General Dynamics as 68, and Litton as 71. The others do not appear in the top 100 at all.) Other companies among the corporate giants also accept defense contracts (AT&T, Chrysler, GM, IBM, and so on), but their military sales are only a small proportion of total sales. Yet there is enough military business to make it a real concern of certain companies, the people who work for them, the communities in which they are located, and the members of Congress and other public officials who represent these communities.

For many years, however, the military-industrial complex was notably *unsuccessful* in influencing the federal budget. Federal spending for defense *declined* from 49.8 percent of the budget in 1960, to 40.8 percent in 1970, and down to 25 percent of the budget in 1978. Federal spending for social security and welfare surpassed defense spending long ago. Only after 1978, when Soviet superiority in both conventional and nuclear weapons was very clear and threatening, did U.S. defense spending begin to increase very slowly. First Jimmy Carter, and later

[14]John K. Galbraith, *How to Control the Military* (New York: Signet Books, 1969), pp. 23–31.

[15]These corporations are listed as the largest military contractors by Ralph E. Lapp in *The Weapons Culture* (New York: W.W. Norton, 1968).

Ronald Reagan, proposed increased defense budgets for the early 1980s. Defense spending edged upward to 29 percent of the budget in 1986, but has since declined to less than 27 percent. The long-term decline of U.S. defense spending suggests that the American military-industrial complex is *not* a very powerful conspiracy.

It seems clear in retrospect that C. Wright Mills placed too much importance on the military in his work, *The Power Elite*.[16] Mills was writing in the early 1950s when military prestige was high following victory in World War II. After the war, a few high-level military men were recruited to top corporate positions to add prestige to corporate boards. But this practice ended in the 1950s.[17] Indeed, the contrast between the political prestige of the military in the 1950s and in the post-Vietnam years is striking: The Supreme Allied Commander in Europe in World War II, Dwight D. Eisenhower, was elected President of the United States; the U.S. Commander in Vietnam, William Westmoreland, was defeated in his bid to become governor of South Carolina!

Moreover, in contrast with corporate and governmental elites, military officers do *not* come from the "upper-classes" of society. Janowitz reports that a general infusion of persons from lower- and lower-middle-class backgrounds has occurred in all branches of the Armed Services (particularly the Air Force). He also reports that military leaders are more likely to have rural and Southern backgrounds than corporate or governmental elites.

Brent Scowcroft. One of the few military men to acquire a top institutional position in recent years is former Air Force Lt. General Brent Scowcroft, the national security adviser to President George Bush. (another is General Alexander M. Haig, Jr., who served as White House chief of staff under President Nixon and briefly as secretary of state under President Reagan.[18]) Yet Scowcroft's success can be attributed more to his political acumen than to his military skills.

Scowcroft was born and educated in Ogden, Utah, in a conservative Mormon family. He won an appointment to the U.S. Military Academy at West Point; he was commissioned in the newly separate U.S. Air Force in 1947 and earned his pilot's wings. But he was seriously injured in a plane crash, which ended his flying career. He was given a series of lackluster desk jobs, after which he decided to refuel his ambitions by studying international relations at Columbia University. He received his M.A. degree and was appointed assistant professor on the faculty at West Point. He continued his Russian language studies and was assigned

[16]C. Wright Mills, *The Power Elite* (New York: Oxford, 1956).

[17]Morris Janowitz, *The Professional Soldier* (New York: Free Press, 1960), p. 378.

[18]See Thomas R. Dye, *Who's Running America? The Conservative Years* (Englewood Cliffs, N.J.: Prentice Hall, 1986), pp. 95–96.

to the U.S. embassy in Belgrade, Yugoslavia. He returned to the faculty of the newly opened U.S. Air Force Academy in Colorado Springs. Scowcroft earned a Ph.D. in international relations at Georgetown University while serving as a staff officer at U.S. Air Force headquarters in Washington, D.C. He taught at the National War College and served in a variety of Pentagon jobs.

Scowcroft's big break came in 1971 when National Security Adviser Henry Kissinger, under President Nixon, selected the young colonel as a military aid to accompany the President's delegation to the People's Republic of China. Nixon's historic trip to China was followed by the Nixon-Brezhnev summit and the signing of the SALT I Agreement. Scowcroft's fluency in Russian gave him an important role on the negotiating team. He was promptly promoted to brigadier general and tapped by Kissinger to serve as his deputy.

Scowcroft became Kissinger's friend and trusted aid at the National Security Council during the Nixon years. When Kissinger was eventually named Secretary of State, he turned over the NSC to Scowcroft. Scowcroft resigned his commission as Air Force Lt. General to serve as national security adviser to President Gerald Ford, 1975–77. When President Jimmy Carter came to the White House, Scowcroft returned to civilian life as a private consultant in international relations with his old boss in Kissinger and Associates, Inc.

Many conservatives regarded Scowcroft's role in the SALT negotiations and his closeness to Henry Kissinger as an indication of his softness toward the Soviets. He was not offered a formal post in the Reagan administration. However, when Reagan floundered over the MX missile, Scowcroft was called in to forge a sensible policy for the modernization of land-based ballistic missile forces. He headed the nonpartisan Commission on strategic forces, which recommended the development of a small, mobile missile dubbed the "Midgetman." Scowcroft himself won praise from both Democrats and Republicans for his cool professional judgement and ability to bring together various political viewpoints. He next served on the three-member Tower Commission investigation of the Iran-Contra affair; the commission issued a scathing report criticizing the President directly as well as his NSC staff. Thus, Scowcroft was well positioned in Washington politics to return to his old post as national security adviser when George Bush came to the White House.

THE CONGRESSIONAL ESTABLISHMENT

While policy initiatives are usually developed outside Congress, Congress is no mere "rubber stamp." Key members of Congress do play an independent role in national decision-making; thus, key congressional leaders must be included in any operational definition of a national elite.

Many important government decisions, particularly in foreign and military affairs, are made without any direct participation by Congress.

The President, with the support of top people in the administration, can commit the nation to foreign policies and military actions that Congress can neither foresee, prevent, nor reverse. Détente with the Soviet Union, new relationships with Communist China, the U.S. role in the Middle East, the Grenada invasion, and similarly important policy directions are decided with little congressional participation. Often congressional leaders are told of major foreign policy decisions or military actions only a few minutes before they are announced on national television.

Congress is more influential in domestic affairs and budgetary decisions than in foreign or military policy. Executive agencies must go to Congress for needed legislation and appropriations. Congressional committees can exercise power in domestic affairs by giving or withholding the appropriations and the legislation wanted by these executive agencies.

Finally, congressional committees are important communication links between governmental and nongovernmental elites; they serve as bridges between the executive bureaucracies and the major nongovernmental elites in American society. Congressional committees bring department and agency heads together with leading industrial representatives—bankers, cotton producers, labor leaders, citrus growers, government contractors.

Political scientists have commented extensively on the structure of power *within* the Congress (see Table 3–2). They generally describe a hierarchical structure in both houses of the Congress—a "congressional establishment" which largely determines what the Congress will do. This establishment is composed of the speaker of the House and president pro tempore of the Senate; House and Senate majority and minority leaders and whips; and committee chairpersons and ranking minority members of House and Senate standing committees. Party leadership roles in the House and Senate are major sources of power in Washington. The speaker of the House and the majority and minority leaders of the House and Senate direct the business of Congress. Although they share this task with the standing committee chairpersons, these leaders are generally "first among equals" in their relationships with committee chairpersons. But the committee system also creates powerful congressional figures, the chairpersons of the most powerful standing committees—particularly the Senate Foreign Relations, Appropriations, and Finance committees, and the House Rules, Appropriations, and Ways and Means committees.

"Policy clusters"—alliances of leaders from executive agencies, congressional committees, and private business and industry—tend to emerge in Washington. Committee chairpersons, owing to their control over legislation in Congress, are key members of these policy clusters.

TABLE 3–2   The Congressional Establishment, 1989–91

SENATE LEADERSHIP

President Pro Tempore	Robert C. Byrd, W.Va.
Majority Leader	George J. Mitchell, Maine
Majority Whip	Alan Cranston, Cal.
Minority Leader	Robert Dole, Kan.
Minority Whip	Alan K. Simpson, Wyo.

HOUSE LEADERSHIP

Speaker	Thomas S. Foley, Wa.
Majority Leader	Richard A. Gephardt, Mo.
Majority Whip	William H. Gray, Pa.
Minority Leader	Robert H. Michael, Ill.
Minority Whip	Newt Gingrich, Ga.

SENATE COMMITTEE LEADERS

Agriculture, Nutrition and Forestry: Patrick J. Leahy, Vt.; *Richard G. Lugar, Ind.*

Appropriations: Robert C. Byrd, W.Va.; *Mark O. Hatfield, Ore.*

Armed Services: Sam Nunn, Ga.; *John W. Warner, Va.*

Banking, Housing and Urban Affairs: Donald W. Riegle Jr., Mich.; *Jake Garn, Utah*

Budget: Jim Sasser, Tenn.; *Pete V. Domenici, N.M.*

Commerce, Science and Transportation: Ernest F. Hollings, S.C.; *John C. Danforth, Mo.*

Energy and Natural Resources: J. Bennett Johnston, La.; *James A. McClure, Idaho*

Environment and Public Works: Quentin N. Burdick, N.D.; *John H. Chafee, R.I.*

Finance: Lloyd Bentsen, Texas; *Bob Packwood, Ore.*

Foreign Relations: Claiborne Pell, R.I.; *Jesse Helms, N.C.*

Governmental Affairs: John Glenn, Ohio; *William V. Roth Jr., Del.*

Judiciary: Joseph R. Biden Jr., Del.; *Strom Thurmond, S.C.*

Labor and Human Resources: Edward M. Kennedy, Mass.; *Orrin G. Hatch, Utah.*

Rules and Administration: Wendell H. Ford, Ky.; *Ted Stevens, Alaska*

Select Ethics: Howell Heflin, Ala.; *Warren B. Rudman, N.H.*

Select Indian Affairs: Daniel K. Inouye, Hawaii; *John McCain, Ariz.*

Select Intelligence: David L. Boren, Okla.; *William S. Cohen, Maine*

Small Business: Dale Bumpers, Ark.; *Rudy Boschwitz, Minn.*

Special Aging: David Pryor, Ark.; *John Heinz, Pa.*

Veterans' Affairs: Alan Cranston, Calif.; *Frank H. Murkowski, Alaska*

HOUSE COMMITTEE LEADERS

Agriculture: E. "Kika" de la Garza, Texas; *Edward R. Madigan, Ill.*

Appropriations: Jamie L. Whitten, Miss.; *Silvio O. Conte, Mass.*

Armed Services: Les Aspin, Wis.; *William L. Dickinson, Ala.*

Banking, Finance, and Urban Affairs: Henry B. Gonzalez, Texas; *Chalmers P. Wylie, Ohio*

Budget: Leon E. Panetta, Calif.; *Bill Frenzel, Minn.*

District of Columbia: Donald V. Dellums, Calif.; *Stan Parris, Va.*

Education and Labor: Augustus F. Hawkins, Calif.; *Bill Goodling, Pa.*

Energy and Commerce: John D. Dingell, Mich.; *Norman F. Lent, N.Y.*

Foreign Affairs: Dante B. Fascell, Fla.; *William S. Broomfield, Mich.*

TABLE 3–2 The Congressional Establishment, 1989–91 (Continued)

HOUSE COMMITTEE LEADERS

Government Operations: John Conyers Jr., Mich.; *Frank Horton, N.Y.*

House Administration: Frank Annunzio, Ill; *Newt Gingrich, Ga.*

Interior and Insular Affairs: Morris K. Udall, Ariz.; *Don Young, Alaska*

Judiciary: Jack Brooks, Texas; *Hamilton Fish Jr., N.Y.*

Merchant Marine and Fisheries: Walter B. Jones, N.C.; *Robert W. Davis, Mich.*

Post Office and Civil Service: William D. Ford, Mich.; *Benjamin A. Gilman, N.Y.*

Public Works and Transportation: Glenn M. Anderson, Calif.; *John Paul Hammerschmidt, Ark.*

Rules: Claude Pepper, Fla.; *James H. Quillen, Tenn.*

Science, Space and Technology: Robert A. Roe, N.J.; *Robert S. Walker, Pa.*

Select Aging: Edward R. Roybal, Calif.; *Matthew J. Rinaldo, N.J.*

Select Children, Youth and Families: George Miller, Calif.; *Thomas J. Bliley Jr., Va.*

Select Hunger: Mickey Leland, Texas; *Bill Emerson, Mo.*

Select Intelligence: Anthony C. Beilenson, Calif.; *Henry J. Hyde, Ill*

Select Narcotics Abuse and Control: Charles B. Rangel, N.Y.; *Benjamin A. Gilman, N.Y.*

Small Business: John J. LaFalce, N.Y.; *Joseph M. McDade, Pa.*

Standards of Official Conduct: Julian C. Dixon, Calif.; *John T. Myers, Ind.*

Veterans' Affairs: G.V. "Sunny" Montgomery, Miss.; *Bob Stump, Ariz.*

Ways and Means: Dan Rostenkowski, Ill; *Bill Archer, Texas*

Majority Democrats, minority Republicans in italics.

One policy cluster might include the chairpersons of the House and Senate Agriculture committees, the secretary of agriculture, and the leaders of the American Farm Bureau Federation. Another vital policy cluster would include the chairpersons of the House and Senate Armed Services committees; the secretary and undersecretaries of defense; key military leaders, including the joint Chiefs of Staff; and the leadership of defense industries such as Lockheed and General Dynamics. These alliances of congressional, executive, and private elites determine most public policy within their area of concern.

Viewed within the broader context of a *national elite*, congressional leaders appear "folksy," parochial, and localistic. Because of the local constituency of a member of Congress, he or she is predisposed to concern him or herself with local interests. Members of Congress are part of local elite structures "back home"; they retain their local businesses and law practices, club memberships, and religious affiliations. Members of Congress represent many small segments of the nation rather than the nation as a whole. Even top congressional leaders from safe districts, with many years of seniority, cannot completely shed their local interests. Their claim to *national* leadership must be safely hedged by attention to their local constituents. Consider, for example, the parochial backgrounds of the following top congressional leaders.

Thomas S. Foley. After two successive House speaders (Thomas P. "Tip" O'Neill and Jim Wright) whose hard ball politics engendered conflict and partisanship, the elevation of the tall, soft-spoken Tom Foley to the speakership promises a new era of conciliation in the House of Representatives. Unlike his predecessors, Foley is well-liked and highly-respected by both Democrats and Republicans. While he is expected to advance the Democratic Party program in the House, he is also expected to uphold the integrity of the House of Representatives.

Foley's father was a Washington State Superior Court judge and a close political associate of the state's senior U.S. Senator, Henry M. "Scoop" Jackson. Young Tom Foley completed his B.A. and law degrees at the University of Washington, served briefly as an assistant state attorney, and then went to Washington to serve on Senator Jackson's staff. In 1964, after only three years in the capitol, the Democratic state committee asked Foley to run against a long-term incumbent Republican, Walter F. Horan, in a conservative district which included the city of Spokane.

Foley was only expected gain campaign experience and fill out the Democratic slate, but to everyone's surprise he squeaked out a narrow victory over the heavily-favored incumbent. Foley's victory was generally attributed to the coattail effects of President Lyndon B. Johnson's landslide election. But in subsequent congressional elections, Foley held on to his seat by close margins. In 1978 he won with only 48 percent of the vote in a three-way contest. In recent years, however, he has won by large margins.

Foley's experience as a Democrat representing a conservative district may help explain his success in the Congress as a conciliator. He gradually built a reputation within the institution as a man who understood and respected his opponents' point of view. When the reform-minded, post-Watergate Democrats flooded Congress in 1974, they elected Foley to Chairman of the Agricultural Committee; at the time he was the youngest person ever to chair a major committee. By most accounts, Foley was a strong yet cautious chairman. He was elected Democratic whip in 1981 and moved up to House Majority Leader in 1985 when Speaker "Tip" O'Neill retired and former Majority Leader Jim Wright became speaker.

For a brief period, Jim Wright was one of the strongest speakers in the history of the U.S. House of Representatives. He challenged Republican presidents and Democratic senators for control of national policy. He undertook direct foreign policy negotiations with Latin American governments and he was directly responsible for the collapse of the Contra forces in Nicuragua and the strengthening of the Communist regime of Daniel Ortega. Indeed, Wright's abrasive style infuriated most Republicans and alienated many Democrats. When the House Ethics Committee brought charges against him regarding his personal financial affairs, Wright had very little personal support to fall back on. Tom Foley publicly supported his embattled speaker and did nothing to assist in his downfall. Yet the presence of the respected, telegenic Foley as next in line for the Speakership, doubtlessly contributed to the movement to oust Wright.

It is Foley's task to restore public confidence in the House of Representatives and to develop a record of Democratic legislative accomplishments that will help his party retain its large majority.

George Mitchell.   The rise of George Mitchell (D. Maine) to majority leader of the U.S. Senate was very rapid by historic standards. First elected to the Senate in 1980, Mitchell quickly established himself as a soft-spoken, serious leader of liberal Democrats. The collapse of the crusty old Democratic Senate leadership of Robert Byrd in 1988, left a power vacuum that Mitchell skillfully exploited. His career defies the conventional wisdom that Senate leadership requires a long institutional apprenticeship.

Mitchell graduated from Maine's Bowdoin College with a degree in history, served two years in the U.S. Army in Europe, and went to Georgetown University for his law degree. He served a brief stint as a Justice Department attorney before attaching his star to Maine Senator Edward S. Muskie. He was Muskie's top congressional aide and campaign manager for both his vice-presidential bid in 1968 and his disastrous presidential effort in 1972. Returning to Portland, Maine, as a lawyer, Mitchell spent most of his time building a personal political following as Democratic state party chairman and national committeeman. He easily won the Democratic nomination for governor in 1974, but despite Democratic post-Watergate sweeps elsewhere, he was upset by the only Independent candidate to win a governorship in modern times, James Longley. President Carter appointed Mitchell U.S. attorney for Maine in 1977 and made him a federal judge in 1979. When Muskie resigned from the U.S. Senate to become Carter's secretary of state, Mitchell was appointed to Muskie's seat. With the advantage of incumbency, he won election to the seat with 61 percent of the vote in 1982. Early on, he organized Senate liberals to oppose Majority Leader Robert Byrd, a staunch defender of West Virginia coal industry, on the issue of acid rain. He led liberals in their opposition to lower income-tax rates in the Tax Reform Act of 1986. By 1988 liberals dissatisfied with Robert Byrd had been joined by many others who believed Byrd's rustic television image was hurting the Democratic party's cause nationally. Senator Daniel Inoyue was in line for the leadership post, but Inoyue was embarrassed by the fine performance of Lt. Col. Oliver North in the nationally televised Iran-Contra hearings. The only Democrat to effectively counter the Marine hero was George Mitchell. Mitchell went on to win the secret ballot vote of his Democratic Senate colleagues for the post of majority leader.

Robert J. Dole.   (R. Kansas) Senate minority leader. Dole left the family farm in Kansas to join the Army during World War II and suffered serious wounds in Italy. He was nearly blown apart by mortar and machine-gun fire and was left for dead on the battlefield for twenty-four hours. Later he was paralyzed from the neck down; he spent three years in hospitals recovering from wounds, and even today he cannot use his right arm. He married his physical therapist and completed a law degree at tiny Washburn Municipal University in To-peka in 1952. But even before he finished law school, Dole won a seat in the Kansas legislature at the age of twenty-six. He has not been out of public office since. He was district attorney for Russell County, Kan-sas, for four terms, and then a Kansas congressman for four terms. In 1988 he was elected to the U.S. Senate, then reelected in 1974, 1980 and 1986. In 1976 he was Gerald Ford's running mate on the unsuccess-ful Republican ticket. It was in that vice-presidential campaign that Dole appeared to be a "hatchet man" compared to the boy scout image of his opponent, Walter Mondale. Dole is perhaps one of the wittiest elected officials in Washington, but on television his quips seem bitter and caustic. Dole is generally a moderate on policy issues; he supports big spending programs for his farm constituents as well as for veterans and handicapped persons. He divorced his first wife in 1972 and married Elizabeth Hanford Dole, a member of the Federal Trade Commission, in 1975. She later became secretary of transportation in the Reagan ad-ministration. As chairman of the Senate Finance Committee, Dole helped to shepherd Reagan's tax cuts through Congress. When Republi-can leader Howard Baker retired from the Senate, Dole emerged the winner in a heated fight for the leadership post. Dole's presidential ambitions looked bright very early in 1988. Bush had been labeled a "wimp" by the media and even though he led in the opinion polls his support was considered "soft." Dole's hopes to unseat the forthcoming Vice-President depended on an early win in the Iowa caucuses, followed by an upset victory in the New Hampshire primary. Dole won Iowa on the strength of his long-standing support for farmers, but he was am-bushed by slick Bush TV ads in New Hampshire attacking his willing-ness to raise taxes to reduce the deficit. Dole was personally embittered; he frequently contrasted his own hard scramble in life to Bush's upper-class ease. It remains to be seen how well Dole supports the Bush administration in Congress.

Robert H. Michel. (R. Illinois). House minority leader. The son of a French immigrant factory worker, Michel attended tiny Bradley Uni-versity. He began his career in politics fresh out of college as an admin-istrative assistant to Congressman Harold H. Velde. When Velde retired in 1956, Michel, with several years experience as a congressional aide, decided to run for the office himself. He won in a close race and has represented the city of Peoria in Congress since 1957. One of his constit-uents was the Senate Republican leader Everett Dirksen, who helped him on Capitol Hill. Dirksen's son-in-law, Howard H. Baker, who also became a Senate Republican leader, became a close friend. The wives of Baker and Michel attended college together. Early in his career, Michel was appointed to a seat on the powerful House Appropriations Commit-tee. Over the years, Michel has been described as "a party man and a conservative." He almost always voted with the Republican majority and with the conservative coalition. He was described as "a plodder rather than a thinker." The *Congressional Quarterly* described him as in the "Mr. Nice Guy" tradition—unpretentious, self-effacing, Rotary Club glad hander with a gee-whiz vocabulary and a rambling speaking style."[19] In 1980, the long-time Republican House leader John Rhodes (R. Arizona) voluntarily stepped down. Michel, the conservative party workhorse, found himself in a struggle for Republican leadership with Guy Vander Jagt (R. Michigan), a moderate with an impressive speaking style. Michel won, even though Vander Jagt was better known throughout the nation. Michel immediately set to work to win over his conservative friends in the Democratic party. He was very effective during President Reagan's first term in combining Republican and conservative Democratic votes to win support for tax and spending cuts, frequently embarrassing Democratic Speaker Thomas P. "Tip" O'Neill But in Reagan's second term, the loss of Republican House seats combined with the Iran-Contra scandal's adverse impact on Reagan's popularity, undermined Michel's power. Moreover, the new Democratic Speaker Jim Wright was much more aggressive and partisan in squelching the Republican minority in the House.

Lloyd Bentsen. Lloyd Bentsen's power in the U.S. Senate (D. Texas) has been greatly enhanced by his fine performance as the Democratic vice-presidential candidate in 1988. Opinion polls showed him personally more popular than anyone else on either national ticket. As chairman of the Senate Finance Committee, he will have a major role in determining how the United States copes with its deficit problem. Bentsen is the son of a wealthy, self-made Rio Grande Valley rancher, cattleman, and banker, "Big Lloyd." Lloyd Jr. graduated from the University of Texas Law School, enlisted in the Army Air Corps, and flew combat missions in Europe in World War II, winning the Distinguished Flying Cross and returning home as a colonel. He promptly won a county judicial election, and then in 1948 at age twenty-two he became the youngest member of Congress. He served three terms in the House but then became bored with life as a young congressman. He returned to Texas, and with $7 million from his father he formed Consolidation Life Insurance Company, and later Lincoln Consolidated, a holding company which acquired businesses banks, oil fields, and ranches. He acquired a number of prestigious corporate directorships, including the Lockheed Corporation. Having conquered the world of business, he returned to politics in 1970, defeating the incumbent liberal U.S. Senator Ralph Yarborough in the Democratic primary, and then defeating fellow oil man Republican Congressman George Bush in the general election. In the Senate the elegantly dressed baritone-voiced Bentsen has been the leading defender of the oil interests, using his power as chair-

---

[19]Congressional Quarterly, *Weekly Report*, December 3, 1988, p. 3436.

man of the Senate Finance Committee to insure that the oil companies retain their special tax treatments. He was notably unsuccessful in his fight against the Tax Reform Act of 1986, but he managed to retain most of the oil industry's favorite tax loopholes. Bentsen is the largest recipient of PAC campaign contributions in the Congress. In 1988 Texas voters helped send Bush to the White House and at the same time reelected Bentsen.

THE JUDGES

Nine people—none of whom is elected and all of whom serve for life— possess ultimate authority over all the other institutions of government. The Supreme Court of the United States has the authority to void the acts of popularly elected Presidents and Congresses. There is no appeal from their decision about what is the "supreme law of the land," except perhaps to undertake the difficult task of amending the Constitution itself. Only the good judgment of the Justices themselves—their sense of "judicial self-restraint"—limits their power over government elites. It was the Supreme Court, rather than the President or Congress, that took the lead in important issues such as eliminating segregation from public life, ensuring voter equality in representation, limiting the powers of police, and declaring abortion to be a fundamental right of women.

Social scientists have commented on the class bias of Supreme Court Justices. John R. Schmidhauser reports that over 90 percent of the Supreme Court Justices serving on the Court between 1789 and 1962 were from socially prominent, politically influential, upper-class families.[20] Over two thirds of the Supreme Court Justices ever serving on the Court attended well-known or Ivy League law schools (most notably, Harvard, Yale, Columbia, Pennsylvania, NYU, Michigan, Virginia). No blacks had served on the Supreme Court until the appointment of Associate Justice Thurgood Marshall in 1967. No women had served until the appointment of Sandra Day O'Connor in 1981. Henry Abraham depicts the typical Supreme Court justice: "White; generally Protestant . . . ; fifty to fifty-five years of age at the time of his appointment; Anglo-Saxon ethnic stock . . . ; high social status; reared in an urban environment; member of a civic-minded, politically active, economically comfortable family; legal training; some type of public office; generally well educated."[21] Of course, social background does not necessarily determine judicial philosophy. But as Schmidhauser observes,

[20] John R. Schmidhauser, *The Supreme Court* (New York: Holt, Rinehart and Winston, 1960), p. 59.

[21] Henry Abraham, *The Judicial Process* (New York: Oxford University Press, 1962), p. 58.

"If . . . the Supreme Court is the keeper of the American conscience, it is essentially the conscience of the American upper-middle class sharpened by the imperative of individual social responsibility and political activism, and conditioned by the conservative impact of legal training and professional legal attitudes and associations."[22]

Not all Justices, however, conform to this upper-class portrait. Indeed, several current Justices of the Supreme Court are middle class rather than upper class in social origin. Their appointments to the Supreme Court have been more closely related to their political activities than either their social backgrounds or their accomplishments in the law.

William H. Rehnquist. Chief Justice, U.S. Supreme Court. Raised in an upper-middle class suburb of Milwaukee, Rehnquist attended Stanford University as an undergraduate, earned a Masters degree in political science at Harvard, and then returned to Stanford for his law degree in 1952. He did his clerkship with U.S. Supreme Court Justice Robert H. Jackson and then settled in Phoenix, Arizona, to practice law. He became active in Arizona Republican politics, together with Richard Kleindienst, who later became President Richard Nixon's attorney general. Kleindienst brought Rehnquist to Washington as assistant attorney general. He was serving in that post when Nixon appointed him Associate Justice in 1971. Aty age forty-seven he was the youngest as well as the most conservative of the Court's justices. In 1986 President Ronald Reagan elected him to the post of Chief Justice upon the retirement of Warner F. Burger.

Byron R. White. U.S. Supreme Court Justice. Son of the mayor of Wellington, Colorado. Attended public schools and the University of Colorado. At Colorado, he was Phi Beta Kappa, a Rhodes Scholar, and an All-American halfback. Attended Yale Law School while playing halfback for the Pittsburgh Steelers and Detroit Lions; was the NFL leading ground gainer in 1938. In World War II he served in the Navy in the Pacific, where he met John F. Kennedy. After the war, White completed his law degree at Yale, served legal clerkship under U.S. Supreme Court Chief Justice Fred M. Vinson, and opened a law practice in Denver, Colorado. His law practice was undistinguished, but in 1960 the Kennedys called on him to organize Colorado for JFK's presidential campaign. White was credited with delivering Colorado's convention votes to Kennedy. He was JFK's only appointment to the Supreme Court.

Thurgood Marshall. U.S. Supreme Court Justice. Son of a Pullman car steward. Educated at Lincoln University and Howard University Law School. Shortly after graduation in 1933, Marshall became counsel for the Baltimore chapter of the NAACP. From 1940 to 1961, he served as director and chief counsel of NAACP's semiautonomous

[22] Schmidhauser, *The Supreme Court,* p. 59.

Legal Defense and Educational Fund. During that period, he argued thirty-two cases before the Supreme Court, winning twenty-nine. His notable victory (indeed, perhaps the most notable judicial victory for blacks ever) came in *Brown* v. *Board of Education of Topeka* in 1954. President Kennedy chose Marshall as a judge for the U.S. Circuit Court of Appeals in 1961; President Johnson appointed him U.S. solicitor general in 1965. As the latter, Marshall argued nineteen more cases before the U.S. Supreme Court. When President Johnson announced Marshall's appointment to the Supreme Court in 1967, he accurately noted that "probably only one or two other living men have argued as many cases before the court—and perhaps less than half a dozen in all the history of the nation."

SUMMARY

Governmental power may be even more concentrated than corporate power in America. One indicator of its growing concentration is the increasing proportion of the gross national product produced by government. All governmental expenditures now account for more than one third of the GNP, and *federal* expenditures account for nearly two thirds of all government expenditures.

Running for office is not the same as running a government. Presidents must depend on serious men to run government. Skill in campaigning does not necessarily prepare individuals for the responsibility of governing. Key government executives must be recruited from industry, finance, the law, universities, and the bureaucracy itself. These serious men do not appear to differ much in background or experience from Republican to Democratic administrations.

While a significant number of top politicians have inherited wealth and power, most have climbed the ladder from relative obscurity to political success. Among current leaders, Kennedy and Bush inherited great wealth and power, but Reagan, Cuomo, and Kemp climbed to prominence from very modest backgrounds. Most politicians are lawyers but not top corporate or professional lawyers.

The "military-industrial complex"—the Defense Department, the corporations with large military contracts, and the members of Congress with defense-oriented constituencies—is an important influence in Washington, but defense spending is only 6 percent of the nation's GNP and only a few corporations are dependent upon defense contracts. Defense spending declined to less than 25 percent of the federal budget in the 1970s and is only 27 percent today. Military leadership does not enjoy the same prestige as in the years after World War II. Military leaders are more likely to come from middle- and lower-class backgrounds than other leaders.

Congress seldom initiates programs, but rather it responds to the initiatives of the President, the executive departments, influential interest groups, and the mass media. Power *within* Congress is concentrated in the House and Senate leadership and in the chairperson and ranking minority members of the standing committees. Compared to other national elites, congressional leaders appear localistic. Their claim to national leadership must be safely hedged by attention to their local constituencies. Members of Congress are frequently recruited from very modest, middle-class backgrounds.

The Supreme Court is the most elitist branch of government. Its nine members are not elected, and they serve life terms. They have the authority to void the acts of popularly elected Presidents and Congresses. It was the Supreme Court, rather than the President or Congress, that took the lead in eliminating segregation from public life, ensuring voter equality in representation, limiting the powers of police, and declaring abortion to be a fundamental right of women. Although most justices have been upper class in social origin, their appointment has generally been related to their political activities rather than to their experience in the law.

CHAPTER 4
THE NEWSMAKERS

Television is the major source of information for the vast majority of Americans, and the people who control this flow of information are among the most powerful in the nation. Indeed, today the leadership of the mass media has successfully established itself as equal in power to the nation's corporate and governmental leadership.

The rise of the mass media to a position of preeminence among institutions of power is a relatively recent phenomenon. It is a direct product of the development of a national television communication network extending to nearly every home in America. (In 1952, only 19.9 percent of all American homes had television sets, compared to 99.8 percent by 1972).[1] Newspapers had always reported wars, riots, scandals, and disasters, just as they do today. But the masses of Americans did not read them—and fewer still read their editorials. But television reaches the masses: It is really the first form of *mass* communication devised. It also presents a *visual* image, not merely a printed word.

The mass media, particularly television, sets the agenda for public discussion. It determines what we think about and talk about. Political journalist Theodore White asserts:

[1]*Statistical Abstract of the United States*, 1973, p. 693.

116

The power of the press in America is a primordial one. It sets the agenda of public discussion; and this sweeping political power is unrestrained by any law. It determines what people will talk about and think about—an authority that in other nations is reserved for tyrants, priests, parties, and mandarins.[2]

As children, Americans spend more time in front of television sets than in school. As adults, Americans spend half of their leisure time watching television. In the average home, the television set is on seven hours a day. More than two thirds of Americans report that they get all or most of their "news" from television. More importantly, television is the "most trusted" medium of communication.[3]

Network television news not only reaches a larger audience than newspapers, but perhaps more importantly, it reaches children, functional illiterates, the poor, and the uneducated. The television viewer *must* see the news or else turn off the set; the newspaper reader can turn quickly to the sports and comics without confronting the political news. But the greatest asset of television is its *visual* quality—the emotional impact that is conveyed in pictures. Scenes of burning and looting in cities, dead American GIs being loaded on helicopters, and terrorists holding frightened hostages, all convey *emotions* as well as *information.* Television tells Americans what to *feel* as well as what to *think about.*

AGENDA-SETTING: CREATING THE NEWS

The power to decide what will be decided—agenda-setting—is crucial to politics. Indeed, deciding what will be the nation's "problems" is even more important than deciding what will be the solutions. Many civics textbooks imply that agenda-setting just "happens," that in a pluralist democracy any issue can be discussed and placed on the agenda of government decision-makers by anyone. It is true, of course, that we can say whatever we want to say about our society. But will anyone *listen?* Not if we do not have access to the mass media.

In reality, political issues do not just "happen." Creating an issue, dramatizing it, calling attention to it, and pressuring government to do something about it are important political tactics. These are the tactics of agenda-setting. These tactics are employed by influential individuals, organized interest groups, political candidates, government leaders, and, most of all, by the mass media.

[2]Theodore White, *The Making of the President, 1972* (New York: Bantam, 1973), p. 327.

[3]"America's Watching: Public Attitudes toward Television" (New York: Television Information Office, 1987), p. 18.

The mass media set the agenda for conversation among people and debate among leaders. The media create some issues and obscure others. They spotlight some personalities and condemn others to anonymity. They define some conditions in society as "problems" or even "crises," and allow other conditions to go unnoticed. "TV is the Great Legitimator. TV confers reality. Nothing happens in America, practically everyone seems to agree, until it happens on television."[4]

Most Americans believe that the media have an important impact on politics and public opinion, and certainly politicians and their professional advisers behave as if they believe it. But many political scientists deny that the media are very influential. This is because early voter studies showed that few people *change* their voting intentions based on newspaper endorsements of candidates. But even though the media may not change attitudes once they are formed, the media determine what topics people will form attitudes on. "In short, the mass media may not be successful in telling us what to think, but they are stunningly successful in telling us what to think *about*."[5]

PREPLANNED NEWS. Topics for television "news" must be selected well in advance of scheduled broadcasting. It is impossible to put together a half-hour television show in twelve hours. The network "assignment desk" must decide days or weeks in advance of broadcasting what will be newsworthy, so that crews, cameras, and correspondents can be sent to the scene of the event. Videotapes must be shot and later transported, processed, and edited. "Understanding how things operate enables good assignment-desk editors to suggest stories for coverage even before they happen."[6] Many stories languish in the "bank" of already-prepared news stories awaiting broadcasting time.

Television news can be categorized as either "spontaneous" or "preplanned." Spontaneous news includes fires, floods, accidents, shootings, and so on, which actually occurred the day of the news broadcast and were not planned by the media to occur on that day. In contrast, preplanned events may have occurred days or weeks before the broadcast, or may have been planned by the media and others for coverage on that day. The most common preplanned events are congressional hearings and investigations, meetings of government leaders, and press conferences. These are usually coordinated by government press agents and

[4]William A. Henry, "News as Entertainment," in *What's News,* ed. Elie Abel (San Francisco: Institute for Contemporary Studies, 1981) p. 134.

[5]Bernard C. Cohen, *The Press and Foreign Policy* (Princeton, N.J.: Princeton University Press, 1963), p. 13. See also Maxwell E. McCoombs and Donald L. Shaw, "The Agenda Setting Function of the Press." in *Media Power in Politics,* ed. Doris Graber (Washington: Congressional Quarterly Inc., 1984), p. 66.

[6]Av Westin, "Inside the Evening News," *New York,* October 18, 1982, p. 52.

network producers. Ideally, they try to predict "slow" news days to schedule these media events. They are not always successful; if a hurricane, an assassination, or a violent eruption occurs (and if film of it is available), then a spontaneous event may push the preplanned event off the evening news.

Almost 70 percent of all television news stories are preplanned. One careful study of stories presented on ABC, NBC, and CBS weekday evening newscasts in 1978 reported the following breakdown of stories:[7]

	PERCENT OF TIME
Preplanned events	31.8
Commentary on preplanned events	38.1
Spontaneous events	19.8
Commentary on spontaneous events	10.3
	100.0

The requirement to preplan television news helps create the "media event"—an activity arranged primarily for media coverage. It is not only the press secretaries, public relations professionals, "spokespersons," and politicians who benefit from media events. It is also the network executives and producers who are searching for dramatic, sensational, or bizarre activities to videotape, and who appreciate notification well in advance of these activities so they can assign camera crews and broadcast time.

THE LINE-UP. Early on the day of broadcasting the executive producer distributes the "line-up"—what "news" is scheduled, where it will originate, what priorities it will have, what graphics must be produced, what scripts need to be written, what commercials are scheduled for broadcast, and finally in what order and for how long each story is to run. Without these early decisions, the "news" would be chaos. Of course, "Change the line-up!" is a common directive during the day as "spontaneous news" arrives.

THE MYTH OF THE MIRROR. Top executives in the news media do not doubt their own power. They generally credit themselves with the success of the civil rights movement: The dramatic televised images of the nonviolent civil rights demonstrators of the early 1960s being attacked by police with night-sticks, cattle prods, and vicious dogs helped to awaken the nation and its political leadership to the injustices of

---

[7]Robert Rutherford Smith, "Mythic Elements in Television News," *Journal of Communication,* 29 (Winter 1979), 78–82.

segegation. These leaders also credit TV with "decisively changing America's opinion of the Vietnam War," and forcing Lyndon Johnson out of the presidency.

Television news, together with the Washington press corps, also lays claim, of course, to the expulsion of Richard Nixon from the presidency. The *Washington Post* conducted the "investigative reporting" that produced a continuous flow of embarrassing and incriminating information about the President and his chief advisers. But it was the television networks that maintained the continuous nightly attack on the White House for nearly two years and kept Watergate in the public eye. Richard Nixon's approval rating in public opinion polls dropped from an all-time high of 68 percent in January 1973 following the Vietnam Peace Agreement to a low of 24 percent less than one year later.

Yet publicly the leadership of the mass media claim that they do no more than "mirror" reality. Although the "mirror" argument contradicts many of their more candid claims to having righted many of America's wrongs (segregation, Vietnam, Watergate), the leadership of the three television networks claim that television "is a mirror of society." Frank Stanton, president of CBS, told a House committee: "What the media does is hold a mirror up to society and try to report it as factually as possible."

Of course, the mirror analogy is nonsense. Newspeople decide what the news will be, how it will be presented, and how it will be interpreted. As David Brinkley explained, "News is what I say it is. It's something worth knowing by my standards."[8] Newspeople have the power to create some national issues and ignore others, elevate obscure people to national prominence, reward politicians they favor, and punish those they disfavor. In a book significantly entitled *News from Nowhere,* Edward J. Epstein explains:

> The mirror analogy further tends to neglect the components of "will," or decisions made in advance to cover or not to cover certain types of events. A mirror makes no decisions, it simply reflects what occurs in front of it; television coverage can, however, be controlled by predecisions or "policy." . . .
> Policy can determine not only whether or not a subject is seen on television but also how it is depicted. . . .
> Intervention by the producer or assistant producers in decisions on how to play the news is the rule rather than the exception.[9]

[8]*TV Guide,* April 11, 1964.
[9]Epstein, *News from Nowhere,* pp.16–17.

CONCENTRATION OF POWER IN MEDIA CORPORATIONS

American television is dominated by three private corporations—Capital Cities–ABC Inc. (ABC); CBS, Incorporated (CBS); and the National Broadcasting Company (NBC), which is a division of General Electric Corporation. Most of the 968 local commercial television stations are forced to affiliate with one or another of these networks because of the high cost of producing news and entertainment programs. Local stations restrict themselves to local news coverage and then broadcast the network "feeds" of the "Evening News," rebroadcasting it in shorter form as part of their late news program. In addition, each network owns five stations itself, the maximum number under the rules of the Federal Communications Commission (FCC). These network-owned stations are found in the largest "market" cities and they cover 38 percent of all "TV households" in the nation.

Television has eroded newspaper circulation over the years. There are fewer daily newspapers today than thirty years ago, and circulation has declined from 36 to 26 percent of the population. The nation's 1,657 daily newspapers get most of their national news from the Associated Press (AP) wire service, although the larger newspapers and newspaper chains also disseminate their own national news. Radio stations also rely heavily on AP. Of course, local newspapers can "rewrite" national news stories to fit their own editorial slant, and they usually write their own headlines on the national news. But the news itself is generated from an extremely small cadre of people at the top of the media industry.

Concentration of newspaper ownership is increasing, as more and more local papers are being taken over by the major newspaper chains. Fifteen newspaper empires account for more than one-half of the total newspaper circulation in the United States. (See Table 4–1.)

The traditional dominance of the television networks may be eroding. Cable and satellite technology confront the corporate giants of the media with a new challenge. Or, as the flamboyant, antiestablishment entrepreneur of cable news, Ted Turner, boasts, "The networks are in stark terror of us."[10] Indeed, in 1988 one-half of all television homes in the United States were cable subscribers, and that number is steadily increasing. ABC, NBC, and CBS combined still draw about 70 percent of total TV viewing, but this figure is down from the 95 percent enjoyed only a few years ago. The challenges of CNN (Turner's Cable News Network); pay television channels such as HBO; specialized chan-

[10]*Time*, August 9, 1981, p. 50.

TABLE 4–1   The News Empires

	DAILY CIRCULATION (000)	NUMBER OF DAILIES
Gannet Co. Inc.	5,508	90
Knight-Ridder Newspapers	3,627	27
Newhouse Newspapers	2,933	26
Tribune Co.	2,638	8
Dow Jones & Co. Inc.	2,470	23
Times Mirror Co.	2,448	8
News America Pub. Corp.	1,947	4
New York Times Co.	1,693	26
Scripps-Howard Newspapers	1,616	21
Thomson Newspapers	1,452	90
Cox Enterprises	1,210	19
Hearst Newspapers	1,125	15
Capital Cities Communications Inc.	933	8
Freedom Newspapers	892	29
Central Newspapers Inc.	809	7
Washington Post Co.	791	2

Total U.S. daily circulation 62,502,000. Figures for 1986.

Source: James L. Rowe, Jr., "Chains Seen Buying More Papers," *Washington Post*, 1 (June 1986), F2.

nels presenting only children's programming, or sports (ESPN), or music (MTV); "superstations" such as Turner's TNT in Atlanta broadcast via satellite; and new low-power local stations—all combined to threaten the media giants.

Media corporations are prime takeover targets in the arena of corporate mergers and acquisitions. The media are very profitable. Return on invested capital in media corporations averages above 25 percent annually, more than twice the average return for industry generally. Moreover, the media ownership grants celebrity; investors are lured to the media by the promise of fame as well as fortune.

Capital Cities Communications acquired ABC in 1985 for $3.5 billion. The takeover was "friendly," that is, supported by ABC management, which was worried about a possible hostile takeover by Ted Turner. In 1986, General Electric merged with RCA Corporation, owners of NBC, in a $6 billion deal.

CBS remained the only independent network and it fought valiantly against various takeover efforts. It sought to use its political clout with the Securities and Exchange Commission to protect itself from prospective buyers. (It may seem ironic that CBS claims freedom of the press to protect itself from government regulation but seeks the protection of government to fight off corporate buyers.) A Fairness-in-Media group, with the assistance of conservative Republican Senator Jesse Helms, urged conservatives throughout the nation to buy CBS stock in order to become "Dan Rather's boss." But the real threat was a massive buyout offer by Ted Turner. In order to escape "Terrible Ted," CBS management invited billionaire hotel owner Lawrence A. Tisch to buy a controlling interest and become chairman of the board. The deal had the blessing of the aging CBS founder, William S. Paley. CBS remains independent, but Tisch has turned out to be more "bottom-line" oriented than the previously pampered network producers and reporters would prefer. The network superstars grumbled when their limousines, staff, and other perks were reduced.

THE MEDIA MOGULS

Who are the people who govern the flow of information to the nation? The top network executives—presidents, chairpersons, and corporate directors—do not make the day-to-day decisions about the news, but they choose the producers, anchors, and reporters who do. Let us examine a few brief sketches of those in the top leadership positions in the major media institutions.

William S. Paley. Former chairman of the board of CBS Inc. and a director and major shareholder. Attended Western Military Academy, University of Pennsylvania. Began work in father's cigar company, but in 1928 at age twenty-seven he purchased CBS for $400,000. Recruited Edward R. Murrow to develop a news policy for CBS, and supported Murrow's successful efforts to make television news an independent political force in America. Paley actively opposed creation of the Federal Communications Commission and over the years helped to prevent its intrusion into network broadcasting. He established the first regular schedule of television broadcasting in the United States in 1941. A trustee of the Museum of Modern Art, Columbia University, Resources for the Future, Inc., and the Bedford-Stuyvesant Restoration Corp. Past chairman of the United Jewish Appeal.

Arthur Ochs Sulzberger. Publisher and president of the *New York Times*. Son of the *Times* board chairman and grandson of the newspaper's founder. Attended Loomis School and Columbia University. A corporal in World War II, but was assigned as headquarters aide to General Douglas MacArthur. He began as a reporter with the *Times* in 1953 and became president in 1963. A director of the New York Times Co., the Chattanooga Publishing Co., the Spruce Falls Power and Paper Co. of

Toronto, and the Gaspesia Pulp and Paper Company of Canada. A trustee of the Boy Scouts of America, the American Association of Indian Affairs, Columbia University, and the Metropolitan Museum of Art.

Lawrence A. Tisch. Self-made billionaire, chairman of the board of CBS Inc., and "white knight" who purchased controlling interest in CBS to save the network from Ted Turner. Protégé son of a New York garment manufacturer, Tisch graduated from NYU at age eighteen and obtained an M.B.A. from Wharton School at the University of Pennsylvania at nineteen. Served in the OSS (precursor to the CIA) in World War II; sampled Harvard Law School in 1946, but then left to purchase a series of resort hotels in New York and New Jersey. Expanded hotel empire to Manhattan and Florida and purchased Loews Theatre Company to obtain prime downtown locations to build more hotels. Later purchased Lorrilland, fifth largest cigarette company in the United States; CNA Financial Corporation; Bulova Watch Company; as well as oil tankers and real estate around the world. Upon taking control of CBS, Tisch shocked staffers by firing top management and cutting back the lavish perks previously enjoyed by newsroom personalities. But he does not direct news or program content. He is a director of the Bulova Watch Company, Automatic Data Processing Inc., Macy & Co., and Petrie Stores. He is a trustee of the United Jewish Appeal, the Whitney Museum, the Metropolitan Museum of Art, the New York Public Library, the Carnegie Corporation, and New York University.

Thomas S. Murphy. Chairman of the board of Capital Cities–ABC. A Cornell University and Harvard M.B.A. graduate, who rose within Capital Cities Communications to become CEO in 1966. He presided over the acquisition of ABC—a major undertaking inasmuch as Capital Cities was only a medium-sized newspaper and magazine publisher when it swallowed the much larger network. Murphy is also a director of Texaco, Johnson & Johnson, IBM, and General Housewares.

Ted Turner. Owner and chairman of Turner Broadcasting Inc., including Cable News Network (CNN), Superstation TNT, and MGM United Artists. He also owns the Atlanta Braves baseball team, the Atlanta Hawks basketball team, and the Atlanta Omni. The independent, flamboyant "Terrible Ted" has been the bête noire of the media industry for over a decade. Reportedly a mischievous child with a difficult upbringing, Turner was sent to the Georgia Military Academy before entering Brown University. He was expelled for various infractions and served a brief tour with the U.S. Coast Guard before entering the family's billboard advertising company. When the business floundered and his father committed suicide, young Ted took over and began building his empire. He used the restored profits from the billboard company to buy television stations and invest in the new satellite technology. With FCC deregulation of satellite broadcasting in 1975, Turner was well positioned to challenge the major networks. Turner's Atlanta station was the first "superstation" beaming its program via satellite throughout the nation. He purchased the Atlanta Braves and the Atlanta Hawks to help feed his programing as well as his mountainous ego. His most important contribution to the media is CNN's twenty-four-hour news broadcasting, which he began despite predictions of financial failure. Turner created panic at CBS with an unsuccessful hostile-takeover effort. In 1986 he purchased MGM/UA Entertainment in order to obtain its extensive film library (including *Gone with the Wind*) to use on WTBS. To finance the deal, he sold Turner stock to Cable broadcasters, bringing them on to his board of director's and diluting his own authority. Despite his successes in capitalism, Turner is decidely pro-Soviet in his views; when the United States boycotted the Moscow Olympics in 1984, Turner produced his own Olympics, "The Goodwill Games," in Moscow with the aid of the Soviet leadership.

Thorton Bradshaw. Former chairman of the board of Radio Corporation of America who was added to the GE board when it acquired RCA and the NBC television network. Attended Phillips Exeter Academy, Harvard, and has a Harvard M.B.A. After a few years of teaching at the Harvard Business School, Bradshaw joined the Atlantic Richfield Oil Company and rose to president in 1964. Later he was named an outside director of RCA, and its subsidiary NBC. In 1981, after several years in which NBC ranked lowest in network-viewing ratings, Bradshaw took over the reins of the parent company, RCA, and replaced NBC president Fred Silverman with Grant Tinker. Bradshaw is also director of Atlantic Richfield, Champion International, the First Boston Corp., the Los Angles Philharmonic, and the American Petroleum Institute.

KATHERINE GRAHAM: THE MOST POWERFUL WOMAN IN AMERICA

Katherine Graham, the owner and publisher of the *Washington Post* and *Newsweek* magazine, was probably the most powerful woman in America even *before* Watergate. But certainly her leadership of the *Post,* which did more than any other publication to force the resignation of the President of the United States, established Graham as one of the most powerful figures in Washington. The *Washington Post* is the capital's most influential newspaper, and it vies with the *New York Times* as the world's most influential newspaper. These are the papers read by all segments of the nation's elite, and both papers feed stories to the television networks and wire services.

Graham inherited her position from her father and husband, but since 1963, when she became president of the Washington Post Company, she has demonstrated her own capacity to manage great institutional power. She is the daughter of a wealthy New York banker, Eugene Meyer. Like many elites, her education was in the fashionable private preparatory schools; she also attended Vassar College and the University of Chicago. In 1933 her father bought the *Washington Post* for less than $1 million. Katherine Meyer worked summers on her father's paper, and then took a job as a reporter with the *San Francisco News*. After one year as a reporter, she joined the editorial staff of the *Washington Post*. "Father was very strong. There was a great deal of emphasis on not behaving rich and a lot of emphasis on having to *do* something. It never occurred to me that I didn't have to work."[11]

In 1940, she married Philip L. Graham, a Harvard Law School graduate with a clerkship under Supreme Court Justice Felix Frankfurter. After service in World War II, Philip Graham was made publisher of the *Washington Post* by his father-in-law. Meyer later sold the paper to the Grahams for one dollar. The Washington Post Company proceeded to purchase other competitive papers in the nation's capital; it also bought *Newsweek* magazine from the Vincent Astor Foundation, as well as five television stations and several pulp and paper companies.

In 1963, Philip Graham committed suicide, and Katherine Graham took control of the *Washington Post–Newsweek* enterprises. By the early 1970s the *Washington Post* was challenging the *New York Times* as the nation's most powerful newspaper.

Indeed, the Washington Post Company's domination of the Washington scene gives it great power over federal officials and agencies. As conservative columnist Kevin Phillips observes:

> We might note the quasi-governmental role played by the Washington Post Company. The Post Company has a five-level presence in Washington—a newspaper (the *Washington Post*), a radio station (WTOP), a television station (WTOP-TV), a news magazine *(Newsweek)*, and a major news service (L.A. Times—Washington Post). Not only does the Washington Post Company play an unmatched role as a federal government information system—from the White House to Congress to the bureaucracy and back—it serves as a cue card for the network news, and it plays a huge role in determining how the American government communicates to the American people.[12]

Graham is a director of Bowaters Mersey Paper Company, the John F. Kennedy School of Government of Harvard University, and a member of the Committee for Economic Development. She is a trustee of George Washington University, the American Assembly, the University of Chicago, and the Urban Institute.

[11]*Current Biography* (1971), p. 170.
[12]Kevin Phillips, "Busting the Media Trusts," *Harpers* (July 1977), p. 30.

THE NETWORK CELEBRITIES

Each night nearly 40 million Americans watch one of three men—Dan Rather, Tom Brokaw, or Peter Jennings. No other individuals—Presidents, movie stars, popes—have such extensive contact with so many people. These network celebrities are recognized and heard by more people than anyone else on the planet. "The networks demand that an anchor be the network's premier journalist and principal show-man, top editor and star, symbol of news excellence and the network's single most important living logo."[13]

The anchors are both celebrities and newsmen. They aspire to both journalistic power and ratings supremacy. Occasionally, they and their shows are torn between journalistic and commercial values. They must attract viewship, that is, keep their "ratings" high, and at the same time influence the course of national events.

The anchors are chosen for their mass appeal, but they must also bring journalistic expertise to their jobs. Dan Rather and Tom Brokaw are managing editors of their shows and Peter Jennings is senior editor of his show. Their views on what is news shape their nightly reports. Rather and Brokaw have veto power over their broadcasts.

The anchors must select from thousands of hours of videotapes and hundreds of separate stories, which stories and visuals will be squeezed into the twenty-two minutes of nightly network news. (Eight minutes are reserved for commercials.) Each minute represents approximately 160 spoken words. The total number of words on the entire newscast is fewer than a single newspaper page. These restrictions of the medium itself give great power to the anchors and their executive producers in selecting what Americans will see and hear about their world each night.

All three network anchors are middle-aged, Anglo-Saxon, male Protestants. All share liberal, reformist social values and political beliefs. Rather and Brokaw command multimillion-dollar star salaries and Jennings only slightly less.

The Canadian-born Jennings projects an image of thoughtful, urbane sophistication. He is widely traveled (his father was a journalist), but his formal education ended in the tenth grade. ABC's *World News Tonight with Peter Jennings* devotes slightly more time to international news than its rival news shows.

Dan Rather deliberately projects an image of emotional intensity. He is tense yet commanding in his broadcasts. His intensity creates both strong attachments and heated animosities among his audiences. Some

---

[13]Alex S. Jones, "The Anchors," *New York Times Magazine*, July 27, 1986, p. 14.

surveys have shown that he is the most "trusted" among the news anchors (see Table 4–2). Yet he is also the most despised by conservatives because of his undisguised, passionate liberal views. He is the most recognizable newsman in the world, easily beating out Brokaw and Jennings on identification by the general public.[14] Rather worked his way up through the ranks of CBS news following graduation from Sam Houston State College in Huntsville, Texas. He was a reporter and news director for the CBS affiliate station in Houston, then chief of the CBS London Bureau and later Vietnam correspondent. He came to national prominence in 1966 as CBS White House correspondent. In 1981 Rather took over the anchor position at CBS from the legendary Walter Cronkite. But he has not been able to maintain the ratings lead for *The CBS Evening News with Dan Rather* which Cronkite had previously given the network. Although Rather's ratings are still as good as those of his competitors, the drop from the Cronkite years at CBS has created anxieties for Rather and the CBS news staff.

Tom Brokaw gives a calm and unemotional delivery of the news, with occasional wry humor. He is comfortable, smooth, and authoritative, yet never overbearing or hostile toward guests. He has been gaining in stature relative to his competitors; his exclusive interview with

TABLE 4–2   Believability of the Anchors

ANCHORS	PERCENT RATING "HIGHLY BELIEVABLE"
Walter Cronkite	57%
Dan Rather	44%
Peter Jennings	40%
Tom Brokaw	37%
REPORTERS	
Ted Koppel	41%
Mike Wallace	35%
Sam Donaldson	30%
Barbara Walters	30%
Diane Sawyer	28%
OTHERS	
Ronald Reagan	28%
Phil Donahue	23%

Source: Derived from figures in *The People and the Press* (Times Mirror, 1986), p. 2.

[14]See Michael Robinson, "Dan Rather Wins the Battle of the Network News Stars," *Public Opinion* (December–January 1986), pp. 41–42.

Soviet General Secretary Gorbachev in 1987 was a prestige grabber even though it flopped in the ratings. Brokaw graduated from the University of South Dakota and started his career at an Omaha television station. He anchored local news in Atlanta and Los Angeles before moving up to the post of NBC White House correspondent in 1973. He hosted the NBC *Today Show* from 1978 to 1982. His show-biz and talk-show host experience have served him well as anchor of the *NBC Nightly News* since 1982. He is less ideological than Rather or Jennings. He can appear relaxed and friendly, singing Christmas carols with Nancy Reagan, chatting with the President during a Super Bowl broadcast, or emceeing a presidential debate.

BAD NEWS AND GOOD PROFITS

The primary function of the mass media is to attract and hold large audiences so that they may be sold to advertisers. On any average night, about 70 million people will be watching television at 7:30 P.M.; that number will increase steadily to nearly 100 million at 9:00 P.M. and then gradually drop to 50 or 60 million by 11:00 P.M. Advertisers must pay $100,000 or more for a thirty-second prime-time spot on any one of the three networks. Networks present six minutes of their own paid commercials per hour during regular programs, seven minutes during movies and sports events, and allocate an additional three-and-one-half minutes for local affiliated stations to advertise and promote upcoming shows. This means that a network's revenue for one hour of prime time is $1 to $1.5 million. Advertisers pay the networks on the basis of ratings, compiled by independent services, the most popular of which is the A.C. Nielson Company. By placing electronic boxes in a national sample of television homes, Nielson calculates the proportion of all "TV homes" that watch a program (the "rating") as well as the proportion of TV homes with their sets turned on that watch a specific program (the "share"). The economic pressure on the networks is to attract and hold as large an audience as possible.

Bad news makes good video, because bad news attracts big audiences. The principal source of bias in television news is not the liberal politics of the newsmakers themselves, but rather the need to capture audience attention with drama, action, and confirmation. Topics are *not* selected for their social or political significance, but rather for their ability to attract the attention of large audiences. This means an emphasis on violence, conflict, scandal, fear, and the personal lives of celebrated people.

Bad news drives out the good. It is true that the nation's media elite is the most liberal of the nation's elite groups (see Table 4–3). But

TABLE 4–3 **Attitudes of the Media Elite**

	PERCENT AGREEING WITH VIEWPOINT		
SOCIAL ISSUE AND VIEWPOINT	BUSINESS LEADERS	NEWSMAKERS	ENTERTAINMENT PRODUCERS
Economic Liberalism			
Government should redistribute income.	23	68	69
Government should guarantee jobs.	29	48	45
Big corporations should be publicly owned.	6	13	19
Private enterprise is fair.	89	70	69
People with more ability should earn more.	90	86	94
Reformism			
Structure of society causes alienation.	30	49	62
Institutions need overhaul.	28	32	48
Social Liberalism			
Strong affirmative action for blacks.	71	80	83
Women have the right to abortions.	80	90	97
Homosexuals should not teach in schools.	51	15	15
Homosexuality is wrong.	60	25	20
Adultery is wrong.	76	47	49

Sources: Lichter and Rothman, "Media and Business Elites," *Public Opinion* (October–November 1981), pp. 42–46; Lichter, Lichter, and Rothman, "Hollywood and America: The Odd Couple," *Public Opinion* (December–January 1983), pp. 54–58.

the most pervasive bias is toward the negative in American life—in government, business, the military, politics, education, and everything else. Media analyst Michael Robinson writes: "The problem is not nearly so much new class values as old-time sensationalism and competitiveness. Ratings and circulation are the issue here, not radical chic." He reports that in a lengthy study of network "Evening News" broadcasts, a study which classified news stories about presidential candidates as positive or negative, *bad news stories outnumbered good news stories by three to one.*[15] All political candidates (with the exception of Jesse Jackson in 1988) receive more bad coverage than good. A study of network commentary and

[15]Michael Robinson, "Just How Liberal Is the News," *Public Opinion* (February–March 1983), pp. 55–60.

feature reporting on the Reagan presidency showed that the ratio of *un*favorable reporting to favorable was thirteen to one.[16]

The network's concentration on scandal, abuse, and corruption in government has not always produced the desired liberal, reformist notions in the minds of the masses of viewers. Contrary to the expectations of network executives, their focus on governmental scandals—Watergate, illicit CIA activities, FBI abuses, congressional sex scandals, Pentagon waste, and power struggles between Congress and the executive branch—has produced feelings of general political distrust and cynicism toward government and "the system." These feelings have been labeled "television malaise"—a combination of social distrust, political cynicism, feelings of powerlessness, and disaffection from parties and politics which seems to stem from television's emphasis on the negative aspects of American life[17].

Network executives do not *intend* to create "television malaise" among the masses. But scandal, sex, abuse of power, and corruption attract large audiences and increase "ratings." "Bad" news is placed up front in the telecast, usually with some dramatic visual aids. Negative television journalism " . . . is concerned with what is *wrong* with our governmental system, our leaders, our prisons, schools, roads, automobiles, race relations, traffic systems, pollution laws, every aspect of our society. In Europe, there is much less emphasis on exposing what is wrong, much more satisfaction with the status quo.[18] The effect of negative television coverage of the American political system is to turn off the masses from participation in government. The long-run effects of this elite behavior may be self-defeating in terms of elite interest in maintaining a stable political system.

LIBERAL BIAS IN THE NEWS

When TV newscasters insist that they are impartial, objective, and unbiased, they may sincerely believe that they are, because in the world in which they live—the New York and Washington world of newspeople, writers, intellectuals, artists—the established liberal point of view has been so uniformly voiced. TV news executives can be genuinely shocked

[16]Michael Robinson, Maura Clancey, and Lisa Grand, "With Friends Like These . . . ," *Public Opinion* (June–July 1983),pp. 2–3.

[17]Michael Robinson, "Public Affairs Television and the Growth of Political Malaise," *American Political Science Review,* 70 (June 1976), 409–32; and "Television and American Politics," *The Public Interest* (Summer 1977), pp. 3–39.

[18]Merritt Panitt, "America Out of Focus," *TV Guide,* January 15, 1972, p. 6.

and affronted when they are charged with slanting the news toward the prevailing established liberal values.

Network entertainment programming, newscasts, and news specials are designed to communicate established liberal values to the masses. These are the values of the media elite; they include a concern for liberal reform and social welfare, an interest in problems confronting the poor and blacks, a desire to educate the ignorant and cure the sick, and a willingness to employ governmental power to accomplish these ends.

There is very little diversity in television news. All three networks—ABC, CBS, and NBC—present nearly identical "packages" each evening. They are "rivals in conformity."[19] Liberal and conservative views can be found in newspapers and magazines—for example, the *New York Times* versus the *Wall Street Journal, Newsweek* versus *U.S.News and World Report, Harpers* versus the *National Review.* But a standard liberal position is presented on all three television networks in both news and entertainment programming.

The owners and directors of the major media corporations usually share the moderate conservatism of the big business community; but the executives, producers, reporters, and other media professionals are clearly liberal and "left-leaning" in their political views. Generally, newsmakers in the larger, or prestigious organizations—CBS, ABC, NBC, *New York Times, Washington Post–Newsweek*—are more "liberal" in their social, cultural, and political values than those in smaller, regional organizations, including individual television stations.

The media elite—the top journalists and broadcasters in the most influential media outlets—is composed mainly of white males in their thirties or forties. Only one in twenty is nonwhite and one in five female. They are highly educated: almost all have college degrees, and over half have attended graduate school as well. These newsmakers are mostly either Democrats or liberal independents; very few are Republicans. Most classify themselves ideologically as "left-leaning" rather than "middle of the road," and certainly not "right-leaning." Most of the media elite enjoyed socially privileged upbringings. Fewer than one in five came from working-class families.

The responses of the newsmakers to various economic, social, and foreign policy questions confirms their upper-class liberalism. Few of them are outright socialists; they overwhelmingly reject the idea that major corporations should be taken over by the government. Most reject rigid egalitarianism and support the idea that people with more ability should be paid more money. Most believe that free enterprise is fair to

[19]Doris Graber, *Mass Media and American Politics* (Washington: Congressional Quarterly Inc., 1980), p.68.

workers and that deregulation of business is generally good for the country. However, the media elite is strongly committed to the welfare state. They believe the government should reduce income differences between the rich and the poor, and nearly half believe that the government should guarantee jobs. They favor affirmative action and believe environmental problems are serious. They are liberals on social issues such as abortion and homosexuality.

Of course, the argument by many newsmakers is that they do not allow their personal values to affect the news. But newsmakers, like all of us, must rely on our personal values in making decisions, including decisions about what is "newsworthy." Newsmakers must choose from an almost infinite number of stories in the real world which stories will be presented as "news." Even as broadcast time approaches, hundreds of hours of film and videotape are available for selection as "news." Most of these stories must be rejected; there is simply not enough time to report all of the news. It would be impossible for the newsmakers own values *not* to influence the selection of news.

Political scientist Doris A. Graber writes: "The political orientations of the personnel frequently are reflected in the overall tone of the media. Economic and social liberalism prevails, as does a preference for an internationalist foreign policy, caution about military intervention, and some suspicion of the ethics of established large institutions, particularly the government." However, she adds that during general election campaigns the media try to treat major party candidates evenly "in anticipation of scrutiny and criticism in this area."[20]

PRIME-TIME: SOCIALIZING THE MASSES

Prime-time entertainment programming suggests to Americans how they ought to live and what values they ought to hold. Socialization—the learning, accepting, and approving of customs, values, and life styles—is an important function of the mass media. Network television entertainment is the most widely shared experience in the country. America's favorite TV shows average over 25 million viewers (see Table 4–4). This is two-and-one-half times the average audience for network news. The network executives who decide what will be shown as entertainment have a tremendous impact on the values, aspirations, and life styles of Americans.

Throughout the 1970s no one had a more direct effect on the themes of television entertainment than Fred Silverman. Silverman was vice-president for programming at CBS-TV from 1970 to 1975, presi-

[20]Ibid., p. 41.

TABLE 4–4 America's Favorite Television Programs in 1988

PROGRAM	AVERAGE NUMBER OF HOUSEHOLDS VIEWING (MILLIONS)
1. "The Cosby Shows"	34.0
2. "Family Ties"	31.8
3. "Cheers"	26.7
4. "Night Court"	25.6
5. "Golden Girls"	24.2
6. "Murder, She Wrote"	23.5
7. "60 Minutes"	23.4
8. "Who's the Boss?"	21.3
9. "Dallas"	21.2
10. "Moonlighting"	21.2

Source: A. C. Nielsen, as reported in *The World Almanac 1988* (New York: Newspaper Enterprises Association, 1988), p. 362.

dent of entertainment for ABC-TV from 1975 to 1978, and president of NBC-TV from 1978 to 1981. It was Silverman who championed liberal programming with *M.A.S.H.* (antiwar), *All in the Family* (antira-cist), and later *Roots* (black experience). He favored the producer Norman Lear, whose work—*All in the Family, Maude, The Jeffersons, One Day at a Time,* and *Mary Hartman, Mary Hartman*—emphasized different and often controversial life styles. When Silverman moved to ABC, he boldly predicted that he would raise a lackluster network to number one in viewing audience; he did just that. It was Silverman, more than anyone else, who introduced sex-oriented shows to prime-time television with *Charlie's Angels* and *Three's Company.* He also went after young audiences—*Happy Days* and *Laverne and Shirley*—with the notion that children in the family really control the TV dial. Silverman was never accused of overestimating the intelligence of TV audiences.

When he moved to NBC, Silverman faced the problem of beating his own program line-ups on CBS and ABC. By 1978, NBC had dropped to third in the audience ratings. Its biggest success was *The Tonight Show,* and the star of that show, Johnny Carson, was demanding a reduction in his workload and threatening to move to another network. Silverman held on to Carson. He made numerous changes in program line-ups to try to restore NBC audience ratings, but he failed. He spent millions on poor shows, and in 1981 NBC was still in the network cellar. It lost a chance to televise the Moscow Olympics when the United States boycotted the games. Its only long-run, top-ten show, *Little House on the Prairie,* predated Silverman's tenure and emphasized traditional family values. When a new chairman, Thornton Bradshaw, took over the reins of NBC's parent company, RCA, Silverman was encouraged to resign. His replacement was Grant Tinker.

Tinker had founded MTM Enterprises with his former wife, Mary Tyler Moore. He had produced shows generally considered superior to those of Silverman: *The Mary Tyler Moore Show*, *Phyllis*, *Rhoda*, and *Lou Grant*. These shows emphasized feminism, liberalism, and crusading journalism.

When Tinker took over the chairmanship of NBC in 1981, the network's prime-time ratings were the lowest in its history. Five years later Tinker had propelled the network to the top of the ratings again and sent corporate profits soaring. He mastered late night TV by keeping Johnny Carson with a shorter show and adding the popular David Letterman show. The NBC *Today Show* already captured most of the early morning viewers. He brought the award-winning *Hill Street Blues* to NBC, and its upscale viewship grew. He fed a younger audience's thirst for violence with the hip *Miami Vice*. And he hooked the entire country on *The Cosby Show*, which quickly became the nation's number one prime-time television show. He added *Cheers*, *Family Ties*, *The Golden Girls* and *Night Court*.

Despite his success at NBC, Tinker left his post in 1986 to start another independent television production company. He walked away, he says, to avoid the pressure and the repetition of network management.[21] No one exercised greater influence over prime-time television broadcasting for more than two decades than Grant Tinker.

Silverman, Tinker, and other top network executives and producers are generally "coast oriented" in their values and life styles; that is, they reflect popular culture in New York and California. Typical themes include tolerance toward sexual relations, including interracial affairs and homosexuality, and toward divorce, and feminism. Network executives and producers are genuinely perplexed when it is charged that their programming does not reflect the values of a majority of Americans.[22]

The prime-time programmers—the television producers, production company executives, and network vice-presidents responsible for program selection—are the most liberal segment of the nation's elite.[23] Almost all are from the big cities of the East and West coasts. Almost all

[21]Diane K. Smith, "Starting Over: TV's Grant Tinker," *New York Times Magazine*, October 23, 1987.

[22]See Michael Robinson, "Prime-Time Chic," *Public Opinion*, 2 (March–May 1979), 42–47.

[23]See Linda S. Lichter, S. Robert Lichter, and Stanley Rothman, "Hollywood and America: The Odd Couple," *Public Opinion* (December–January 1983), pp. 54–58.

are white males. A majority are Jewish. They are well-educated, extraordinarily well-paid, and independent or Democratic in their politics. They are *not* radicals or socialists: Almost all believe that "people with ability should earn more," and most support free enterprise and oppose government ownership of the economy. However, these television programmers are very critical of government and business; they believe strongly that society is unfair to women, blacks, and minorities; and they are socially very liberal, in terms of their views on abortion, homosexuality, and adultery.

More importantly, perhaps, the programmers believe that they have a responsibility to change America's views to fit their own. They believe that television should "promote social reform." (Fully two thirds of the programmers interviewed agreed with this definition of their role in society). "This is perhaps the single most striking finding in our study. According to television's creators, they are not in it just for the money. They also seek to move their audience toward their own vision of the good society."[24]

Much of our learning is subconscious. We learn how New York cab drivers live from *Taxi*, how Texas oil families live from *Dallas*, how waitresses live from *Alice*, and so on. If these televised images are inaccurate, we end up with wrong impressions of American life. If television shows emphasize sex and violence, we come to believe that there is more sex and violence in America than is actually the case.

For millions of Americans, television is a way of keeping in touch with their environment. Both entertainment and advertising provide model ways of life. People are shown products, services, and life styles that they are expected to desire and imitate. By creating these desires and expectations, the media help to define how Americans should live.

SUMMARY

The people who control the flow of information in America are among the most powerful in the nation. Television network broadcasting is the first form of truly *mass* communication; it carries a visual image with emotional content as well as information. Television news reaches virtually everyone, and for most Americans it is the major source of information about the world.

The power of mass media is primarily in agenda-setting—deciding what will be decided. The media determine what the masses talk about and what the elite must decide about. Political issues do not just "hap-

[24]Ibid., p. 58.

pen." The media decide what are issues, problems, even crises, which must be acted upon.

Control of the television media is highly concentrated. Three private corporations (CBS, NBC, and ABC) determine what the people will see and hear about the world; they feed 968 local TV stations that account for 80 percent of the news and entertainment broadcasts. Most of the nation's 1,657 daily newspapers receive their news from the AP wire service. The fifteen largest newspaper empires account for more than one half of the total newspaper circulation in the country.

Those at the top of the mass media include both inheritors and individuals who worked their way up the management ladder. Among the media elite are the heads of CBS, NBC, and ABC; the *New York Times; Washington Post–Newsweek;* Time, Inc.; and the fifteen largest newspaper empires.

The mass media must attract large audiences to sell to advertisers. The principal source of bias in the news originates from the need to capture large audiences with drama, action, and confrontation. The result is an emphasis on "hard" news—unfavorable stories about prominent people and business and government. However, media attention to scandal, abuse, violence, and corruption has not always produced liberal reformist values. Many scholars believe it has produced "television malaise"—distrust, cynicism, and disaffection from public affairs caused by negative reporting on American life. This reporting may also be contributing to the public's decline in confidence in the media.

The media elite is the most liberal segment of the nation's elite. While this elite supports the free enterprise system and reward based on merit, it favors government intervention to reduce income differences and aid women, blacks, and minorities. News executives claim only to "mirror" reality, yet at the same time they take credit for civil rights laws, ending the Vietnam War, and expelling Richard Nixon from the White House. Prime-time programming executives are even more liberal in their views, and they acknowledge that their role is to "reform" society.

CHAPTER 5
THE CIVIC ESTABLISHMENT

In a complex, industrial society, there are many specialized institutions and organizations that exercise power. In addition to economic organizations (corporations, banks, insurance companies, and investment houses), governmental and military bureaucracies, television networks and news organizations, there are other less visible institutions which also provide bases of power in American society. An operational definition of a national elite must include individuals who occupy positions of power in influential law firms, major philanthropic foundations, recognized national cultural and civic organizations, and prestigious private universities. We shall refer to these institutions collectively as the "civic establishment."

The identification of a civic establishment involves many subjective judgments. We shall try to defend these judgments, but we recognize that equally valid defenses of alternative judgments might be made in many cases.

THE "SUPERLAWYERS"

As modern societies grow in scale and complexity, the need for rules and regulations increases geometrically, and so does the power of people whose profession is to understand those rules and regulations. As early as 1832, deTocqueville felt that the legal profession in this country would become the "new aristocracy" of the Republic. C. Wright Mills asserts that lawyers are indeed a key segment of the nation's aristocracy of power:

> The inner core of the power elite also includes men of the higher legal and financial type from the great law factories and investment firms who are professional go-betweens of economic, political, and military affairs, and who thus act to unify the power elite.[1]

The predominance of lawyers among political elites has already been noted. Within the corporate elite—presidents and directors of the nation's largest industries, banks, utilities, and insurance companies—over 15 percent are lawyers. But neither the politician-lawyer nor the businessperson-lawyer really stands at the top of the legal profession. The "superlawyers" are the senior partners of the nation's most highly esteemed New York and Washington law firms. These are the firms that represent clients such as General Motors, AT&T, Du Pont, CBS, and American Airlines,[2] not only in the courts but, perhaps more importantly, before Congress and the federal regulatory agencies. Of course, the nation's largest corporate and financial institutions have their own legal departments; but attorneys in these departments, known as "house counsels," usually handle routine matters. When the stakes are high, the great corporations turn to the superlawyers.

Sociologist Erwin O. Smigel argued persuasively that the largest New York and Washington law firms were emerging as the dominant force in the legal profession:

> As our society has grown increasingly complex, the legal tools for social control have indeed increased beyond the possible total comprehension of a single individual. And the lawyers, like the scientists, have increasingly, although on a much smaller scale, met the problem of specialization within large law firms.[3]

Identification of the "top" New York and Washington law firms is necessarily a subjective task. Professional ethics prevent firms from listing their clients, so we cannot be certain what firms actually represent the nation's largest corporations. The listing in Table 5–1 was compiled from a variety of sources and represents our best estimate of

[1]C. Wright Mills, *The Power Elite* (New York: Oxford, 1956), p. 289.

[2]Quoted as clients of Covington & Burling by Joseph C. Goulden, *The Superlawyers* (New York: Dell, 1971),p.27.

[3]Erwin O. Smigel, *The Wall Street Lawyer* (New York: Free Press, 1964), p. 9.

TABLE 5–1   The Top Law Firms

WALL STREET	WASHINGTON
Shearman & Sterling	Arnold & Porter
Cravath, Swaine & Moore	Covington & Burling
White & Case	Arrent, Fox, Kintner, Plotkin & Kahn
Dewey, Ballantine, Bushby, Palmer & Wood	Wilmer, Cutler & Pickering
Simpson, Thacher & Bartlett	Clifford, Warnke, Glass, McIlwain & Finney
Davis, Polk, & Wardwell	Fried, Frank, Harris, Shriver & Kampelman
Milbank, Tweed, Hadley & McCloy	Rodgers & Wells
Cahill, Gordon & Reindel	
Sullivan & Cromwell	
Chadbourne, Parke, Whiteside & Wolff	
Breed, Abbott & Morgan	
Winthrop, Simpson, Putnam & Roberts	
Cadwalader, Wickersham, & Taft	
Wilkie, Farr & Gallagher	
Donovan, Leisure, Newton & Irvine	
Lord, Day & Lord	
Dwight, Royall, Harris, Koegel & Caskey	
Mudge, Rose, Guthrie & Alexander	
Kelley, Drye & Warren	
Cleary, Gottlieb, Steen & Hamilton	

These firms were selected on the basis of reputed power and prestige. If gross revenues were considered, the following firms would be at the top of the list: Skadden, Arps, Slate, Meagler & Flom (New York); Finley, Kumble, Wagner, Heine, Underberg, Manley, Meyerson & Casey (New York); Baker and McKenzie (Chicago); Gibson, Dunn & Crutcher (Los Angeles); O'Melveny & Myers (Los Angeles).

the nation's legal elite. The senior partners of these firms are our superlawyers.

These selected firms represent the nation's largest banks and corporations. A partial listing of their clients include:[4]

> Cravath, Swaine & Moore
>   IBM, CBS, Chemical Bank
> Davis, Polk & Wardwell
>   ITT, LTV, Morgan Guaranty
> Donovan, Leisure, Newton & Irvine
>   Mobil, Westinghouse
> Milbank, Tweed, Hadley & McCloy
>   Chase Manhattan, Rockefellers
> Shearman & Sterling
>   United Technologies, Citibank

[4]James B. Stewart, *The Partners: Inside America's Most Powerful Law Firms* (New York: Simon & Schuster, 1983).

Simpson, Thacher & Bartlett
  Paramount Communications, Manufacturers Hanover
Sullivan & Cromwell
  Exxon, General Foods, GE

The names of the firms themselves, of course, do not always identify the senior partners. Firms often retain the names of deceased
founders, and most large firms have so many senior partners (twenty or
thirty is not uncommon) that it would be impossible to put all their
names in the title of the firm. Then, too, some firms change names
upon the resignation of partners, so it is sometimes difficult to maintain
the identity of a firm over time.[5]

The great law firms are, of course, the "spokespersons" for big
business.[6] But it would be naive to believe that they oppose government
regulation, consumer laws, antitrust laws, labor laws, or corporate tax
legislation. On the contrary, the top law firms gain in power and influence as the interaction between business and government heightens.
New laws mean new business for lawyers. Even the founder of one of
Washington's most conservative and dignified firms, Judge J. Harry
Covington of Covington & Burling, confided before his death: "I dis-
agreed with the New Deal strongly. But it was a great benefit to lawyers because so many businessmen all over the country began squeal-
ing about what was happening and had to have lawyers. So when you
ask me about bureaucracy, I say, 'Oh, I'm for it. How would I eat
otherwise?' "[7]

The senior partners of the nation's top law firms generally feel an
obligation to public service. According to superlawyer Arthur Dean, the
experience of serving in such a firm provides "an exceptional opportu-

---

[5]For example, Mudge, Stern, Baldwin & Todd placed the name of Richard M.
Nixon at the head of the firm during his Wall Street years, and later added John Mitchell's name to the firm. The result was "Nixon, Mudge, Rose, Guthrie, Alexander &
Mitchell." When Nixon became President and Mitchell became attorney general, the firm
went back to Mudge, Rose, Guthrie & Alexander. Despite the legal difficulties of its
former partners, the firm remains one of the most powerful on Wall Street. Likewise,
when one of Arnold, Fortas & Porter's clients, Lyndon Johnson, became President of the
United States, and named his personal attorney Abraham Fortas to the Supreme Court
(and then later tried unsuccessfully to make him Chief Justice), the Fortas name was
removed from the firm. The firm is now Arnold & Porter, but it is still one of the most
powerful in Washington.

[6]Prestigious law firms do not provide lists of clients, claiming that to do so would
violate lawyer-client "confidentiality." Nonetheless, a partial listing of the clients of the
Washington firm of Arnold & Porter confirms the big business orientation of the major
firms: Allis Chalmers, BankAmerica, Braniff, Coca-Cola, Federated Department Stores,
Gulf + Western, Koppers, LTV, Martin Marietta, Xerox. See Jonathan Cotten, "Washington Pressures," *National Journal* (January 8, 1972), p. 46.

[7]Quoted in Goulden, *The Superlawyers*, p. 36.

nity to acquire a liberal education in modern government and society. Such partnerships are likely in the future, as they have in the past, to prepare and offer for public service men exceptionally qualified to serve." The arrogance of such an assertion has too much basis in fact to be dismissed as mere self-congratulation.

Superlawyers among the serious men who have been called upon for governmental leadership include:

> John Foster Dulles, secretary of state (Sullivan & Cromwell)
> Dean Acheson, secretary of state (Covington & Burling)
> Clark Clifford, secretary of defense (Clifford, Warnke, Glass, McIlwain & Finney)
> William P. Rogers, secretary of state (Rodgers & Wells)
> Cyrus Vance, secretary of state (Simpson, Thacher & Bartlett)

In an even earlier era, the New York Wall Street law firms supplied presidential candidates:

> John W. Davis, Democratic party nominee for President of the United States, 1924 (Davis, Polk, Wardwell, Sunderland & Kiendl)[8]
> Wendell Willkie, Republican party nominee for President of the United States, 1940 (Willkie, Farr, Gallagher, Walton & Fitzgibbon)
> Thomas E. Dewey, Republican party nominee for President of the United States, 1944 and 1948 (Dewey, Ballantine, Bushby, Palmer & Wood)

Equally important are the top lawyers who are called upon to represent the United States itself in periods of crisis where matters are too serious to be left to State Department bureaucrats.

Paul Warnke.   Arms control and disarmament adviser under President Carter. U.S. negotiator in the Strategic Arms Limitation Talks (SALT). Partner in Clifford, Warnke, Glass, McIlwain & Finney. Former assistant secretary of defense, 1967–69. A member of the Trilateral Commission and a director of the Council on Foreign Relations.

John J. McCloy.   Special adviser to the President on disarmament, 1961–63. Chairman of the Coordinating Committee on the Cuban Crisis, 1962. Member of the President's commission on the assassination of President Kennedy. U.S. high commissioner for Germany, 1949–52. President of the World Bank, 1947–49. Partner in Milbank, Tweed,

---

[8]Davis unsuccessfully argued the case for racial segregation on behalf of the Board of Education of Topeka, Kansas, in the famous case of *Brown* v. *Board of Education* (1954); opposing counsel for Brown, of course, was Thurgood Marshall, later to become Supreme Court Justice.

Hadley & McCloy. Member of the board of directors of Allied Chemical Corp., AT&T, Chase Manhattan Bank, Metropolitan Life Insurance Co., Westinghouse Electric, and E.R. Squibb and Sons. Member of the board of trustees of the Ford Foundation, the Council on Foreign Relations, and Amherst College.

Arthur H. Dean. Chairman of the U.S. delegation on Nuclear Test Ban Treaty. Chief U.S. negotiator of the Korean Armistice Agreement. Partner, Sullivan & Cromwell. Member of the board of directors of American Metal Climax, American Bank Note Co., National Union Electric Corp., El Paso Natural Gas Co., Crown Zellerbach Corp., the Lazard Fund, Inc., and the Bank of New York. Member of the board of trustees of New York Hospital, Cornell Medical Center, Cornell Medical College, Cornell University, the Carnegie Foundation, and the Council on Foreign Relations.

Still other superlawyers are called upon from time to time to head major domestic programs.

R. Sargent Shriver, Jr. Former director of the Peace Corps, the Office of Economic Opportunity (President Johnson's "war on poverty"), and Democratic vice-presidential nominee in 1972. Canterbury School, Yale, Yale Law School. Senior partner in the Washington Law firm of Fried, Frank, Harris, Shriver, and Kampelman. Married Eunice Kennedy, sister of John F., Robert F., and Edward M. Kennedy. He began work for Joseph P. Kennedy after World War II and eventually married his boss's daughter. He managed the Kennedys' Merchandise Mart in Chicago until President John F. Kennedy asked him to organize the Peace Corps. The Peace Corps was a popular success, so President Lyndon Johnson asked him to organize the "war on poverty" in 1964. But the poverty program was less successful, and Shriver was shipped off as ambassador to France in 1968. He was McGovern's second choice for Vice-President in 1972, after Senator Thomas Eagleton revealed a history of mental illness. Shriver was defeated by Jimmy Carter in the Democratic presidential primaries in 1976. He settled into his Washington law practice and remains an influential superlawyer today. He is a member of the Council on Foreign Relations.

Elliot L. Richardson. Former secretary of health, education and welfare and former attorney general under President Nixon. Senior partner in Milbank, Tweed, Hadley, & McCloy. Harvard, Harvard Law School, and clerkship with Supreme Court Justice Felix Frankfurter. He began as a partner in the old Boston firm of Ropes & Gray and served briefly as assistant to U.S. Senator Everett Saltonstall. He was elected lieutenant governor of Massachusetts. He took over the Justice Department in May 1973 during the Watergate crisis, but in October 1973 Nixon fired him in the "Saturday Night Massacre" because he supported

Watergate Special Prosecutor and old Harvard law professor Archibald Cox. He returned to government under President Ford, serving as ambassador to Great Britain and secretary of commerce. He is a member of the board of overseers of Harvard College and the John F. Kennedy School of Government, and a director of the Council on Foreign Relations.

The typical path to the top of the legal profession starts with a Harvard or Yale Law School degree, clerkship with a Supreme Court Justice, and then several years as an attorney with the Justice Department or a federal regulatory commission. Young government lawyers who are *successful* at defeating a top firm in a case are *more* likely to be offered lucrative junior partnerships than those who lose to big firms. Poorly paid but talented younger government lawyers are systematically recruited by the top firms.

CLARK CLIFFORD: WASHINGTON SUPERLAWYER

Consider the style of the nation's top Washington lawyer, Clark Clifford:

> There is one point I wish to make clear. This firm has no influence of any kind in Washington. If you want to employ someone who has influence, you will have to go somewhere else. . . . What we do have is a record of working with the various departments and agencies of the government, and we have their respect and confidence, and that we consider to be a valuable asset.[9]

Clifford's "valuable assets" have brought him clients such as Standard Oil of California, American Broadcasting Company, Hughes Tool Co. (Howard Hughes), Time, Inc., General Electric, Penn Central Railroad, Du Pont Corporation, Phillips Petroleum, W.R. Grace Shipping, El Paso Natural Gas, TWA, and so forth. A former personal client was John F. Kennedy. The Clifford firm is Clifford, Warnke, Glass, McIlwain & Finney.

Clifford is the son of an auditor for the Missouri-Pacific Railroad. He attended Washington University St. Louis Law School, graduating in 1928. He promptly established a successful law practice in St. Louis, and included in his contacts Missouri Senators Harry S Truman and Stuart Symington. Clifford enlisted in the Navy in World War II, but when Truman became President, he was called to the White House as counsel to the President. Clifford's title never changed, but he soon became a dominant figure on Truman's staff. He supervised foreign and domestic policy in the White House, as well as Truman's successful 1948 presi-

[9]Quoted in Goulden, *The Superlawyers*, p. 78.

dential campaign. In 1950, he left the White House, after five years of service, to open his own Washington firm. The decision to leave was fortunate, since the White House staff was shortly thereafter shaken by scandal.

Bureaucrats had become accustomed to answering Clifford's phone calls when they came from the White House, so they answered them when he called from his firm. His first big clients were Phillips Petroleum, Pennsylvania Railroad, Standard Oil of California, and Howard Hughes. Even during the Republican years under President Dwight Eisenhower, Clifford prospered: His close friend Senator Stuart Symington was chairman of the Senate Armed Forces Committee. McDonnell Douglas Aircraft became a Clifford client. After Du Pont had lost its complex ten-year antitrust case and was ordered to sell its ownership of General Motors, it called upon Clifford in desperation. (Covington & Burling had unsuccessfully represented Du Pont.) If Du Pont were forced to sell its stock in GM immediately, the price of GM stock would plummet, and income from the sale would be heavily taxed. Clifford obtained passage of a special congressional act allowing distribution of the GM stock to Du Pont stockholders as a capital gain—and a tax savings to Du Pont of $.5 billion (which of course was a tax loss to the U.S. Treasury of an equal amount).

When President Kennedy prepared to take over the reins of government from his predecessor, Dwight Eisenhower, he sent his personal attorney, Clark Clifford, to arrange the transition. He also sent Clifford to investigate the Bay of Pigs disaster and reorganize the CIA and Defense intelligence operations. Later he sent Clifford to the headquarters of U.S. Steel to force a rollback of steel prices by threatening tax audits, contract cancellations, and FBI investigations. But Clifford did not accept any formal government appointment under Kennedy.

When the Vietnam War controversy had shattered the Johnson administration and Robert McNamara was forced to resign as secretary of defense, Johnson persuaded his friend Clark Clifford to assume leadership of the Defense Department. Clifford reluctantly accepted the position of secretary of defense, reversed the policy of escalation in Vietnam, and began America's slow and painful withdrawal. Thus, the policy of military disengagement from Southeast Asia had already been started under Clifford when the Nixon administration came to Washington in 1969.

Clifford returned to his Washington law firm; he subsequently accepted the directorships of Phillips Petroleum and the Knight-Ridder newspapers. His partner, Paul Warnke, was arms control and disarmament adviser to President Carter, with special responsibilities for the SALT negotiations with the Soviet Union. When President Carter's personal friend and banker, Bert Lance, whom Carter had named as director of the Office of Management and Budget, was charged with banking irregularities, Lance turned to Clifford to get him out of trouble. Lance was forced to resign his office, but he avoided conviction under banking laws. Clifford himself remains at the top of the hierarchy of Washington superlawyers.

LAWRENCE WALSH: SUPERPROSECUTOR

The Washington Establishment was extremely unhappy to learn that a lowly Marine lieutenant colonel on the National Security Council staff had bypassed a congressional prohibition in order to keep alive the "Contra" resistance to the Communist regime in Nicaragua. And when Oliver North embarrassed his congressional critics and their high-priced attorneys in nationally televised hearings in the summer of 1987, it became even more important to bring down the outspoken Marine. A three-judge federal appeals court panel, functioning under the independent prosecutor law, called for the appointment of an outside attorney to investigate and prosecute allegations of unlawful conduct of high government officials. Lawrence E. Walsh was selected for the critical task of prosecuting Lt. Col. Oliver L. North; former National Security Adviser, Admiral John M. Poindexter; and arms dealers Richard V. Secord and Albert Hakim.

Walsh had retired as a senior partner in the prestigious New York law firm of Davis, Polk, & Wardwell. His long legal career began when he graduated from Columbia University Law School in 1936 and went to work for New York District Attorney Thomas E. Dewey. When Dewey became governor, Walsh was his chief counsel. Walsh would most likely have become attorney general of the United States if Dewey had defeated Truman in 1948. When Walsh's friend William Rogers became attorney general under President Dwight Eisenhower (Rogers later would become secretary of state under President Richard Nixon), Walsh became his chief deputy. When Eisenhower left office in 1961, Walsh became a Wall Street superlawyer at Davis, Polk, & Wardwell with clients that included AT&T, ITT, and General Motors. In 1969 President Nixon asked him to join the U.S. delegation at the Vietnam Peace Conference in Paris. He also served as president of the American Bar Association.

As a Republican superlawyer, Walsh was ideally suited to secure the conviction of Colonel North. To insure that outcome, Walsh had a multimillion-dollar budget and recruited an army of legal and investigative talent larger than most Washington law firms, including twenty-eight lawyers, eighteen FBI agents, and eight IRS investigators.[10] Walsh

[10]*New York Times Magazine*, October 25, 1987, p. 67.

understood the political nature of this prosecution. He had successfully prevented President Reagan, who once referred to Oliver North as a "national hero," from granting him a pardon before leaving office. But the White House denied the use of secret documents at the trial and forced Walsh to limit his prosecution to the more mundane charges of lying to Congress. The jury acquitted North on most of Walsh's charges but convicted the ex-Marine on charges of shredding government documents and illegally accepting a gratuity—a security fence around his home. Walsh spent over forty million investigating and prosecuting North. Appeals and prosecutions of others involved in the affair are expected to continue for years.

THE FOUNDATIONS

The power of the nation's largest foundations derives from their support of significant *new* research projects in social problems, arts, and humanities. Actually, the foundations spend far less for research and development than does the federal bureaucracy. But the principal research components of the federal bureaucracy—the National Science Foundation, U.S. Public Health Service, the National Institute of Education—are generally conservative in their support of social research. These government agencies frequently avoid sensitive, controversial issues and avoid projects that would lead to major social innovations. Thus, it has been the role of the nation's largest foundations to support and direct innovations in the scientific, intellectual, and cultural life of the nation.

The major foundations consider themselves to be in the forefront of national policy-making. "The foundations' best role," said Dr. Douglas D. Bond of the W.T. Grant Foundation, "is to identify, support, and bring to fruition certain ideas that government may later implement. . . . Government is beset by crises of a social and political nature that divert it and its money from the nurturing of new ideas and new discoveries. It is the foundation's task to remain steady in its aim and to sacrifice immediate goals for the more distant."[11]

The foundations channel corporate and personal wealth into the policymaking process, providing both financial support and direction for university research and the activities of various policy-planning groups. Foundations are tax-exempt: Contributions to foundations may be deducted from federal corporate and individual income taxes, *and* the foundations themselves are not subject to federal income taxation.

Foundations can be created by corporations or by individuals.

[11]"Medicine's Philanthropic Support," *Medical World News,* December 8, 1972, p. 65.

These corporations or individuals can name themselves and their friends as directors or trustees of the foundations they create. Large blocs of corporate stock or large amounts of personal wealth can be donated as tax-exempt contributions to the foundations. The foundations can receive interest, dividends, profit shares, and capital gains from these assets without paying any taxes on them. The directors or trustees, of course, are not allowed to use foundation income or assets for their personal expenses, as they would their own taxable income. Otherwise, however, they have great latitude in directing the use of foundation monies—to underwrite research, investigate social problems, create or assist universities, establish "think tanks," endow museums, theaters, operas, symphonies, and so on.

According to *The Foundation Directory*, there were 4,063 foundations large enough to deserve recognition and listing; these are the foundations with at least $1 million in assets or $100,000 in yearly distributions. (There are tens of thousands of other smaller foundations and trusts, some established as tax dodges by affluent citizens and therefore not having any appreciable effect on public policy except to reduce tax collections.) These foundations controlled $47.5 billion in assets.

But as in other sectors of society, these foundation assets are concentrated in a small number of large foundations. *The Foundation Directory* reports: "One of the outstanding facts concerning assets is the degree of their concentration in a small number of large organizations."[12] The fifty largest foundations control over 40 percent of all foundation assets in the nation (see Table 5–2).

Historically, the largest and most powerful foundations have been those established by the nation's leading families—Ford, Rockefeller, Carnegie, Mellon, Pew, Duke, Lilly, Danforth. Over the years, some foundations—for example, the Ford Foundation and the Carnegie Corporation—have become independent of their original family ties; independence occurs when the foundation's own investments prosper and new infusions of family money are not required. However, some Rockefellers, Mellons, Lillys, Danforths, and other wealthy individuals still sit on the boards of directors of their family foundations. A number of foundations limit their contributions to specific fields; the Johnson Foundation, for example, sponsors research in medicine, and the Lilly Endowment supports advances in education and religion. This specialization, however, tends to reduce a foundation's power to shape national goals and policy directions. In contrast, the Ford and Rockefeller foundations deliberately attempt to focus on key national policy areas. These foundations play a more influential role in national policy-making, be-

---

[12]*The Foundation Directory,* 3rd ed. (New York: Russell Sage Foundation, 1967), p. 16.

TABLE 5–2   The Fifty Leading Foundations (Ranked by Assets)

RANK	FOUNDATION	ASSETS (MILLIONS)
1	Ford Foundation	$4,758
2	Getty Trust	3,690
3	Kellog Foundation	3,108
4	MacArthur Foundation	2,271
5	Lilly Endowment	1,913
6	Johnson Foundation	1,803
7	Rockefeller Foundation	1,605
8	Pew Memorial Trust	1,550
9	Mellon Foundation	1,477
10	Kresge Foundation	1,047
11	Duke Endowment	797
12	Mott Foundation	733
13	Carnegie Corporation	715
14	McKnight Foundation	711
15	Keck Foundation	647
16	Gannett Foundation	576
17	Hewlett Foundation	565
18	Mellon Foundation	564
19	New York Community Trust	527
20	Sloan Foundation	482
21	Knight Foundation	460
22	Starr Foundation	460
23	Marin Community Foundation	430
24	Irvine Foundation	423
25	Penn Foundation	421
26	Meadows Foundation	419
27	Cleveland Foundation	415
28	Kaiser Foundation	387
29	Houston Endowment	371
30	Ahmanson Foundation	364
31	Brown Foundation	361
32	Clark Foundation	348
33	Bush Foundation	344
34	Weingart Foundation	339
35	Bradley Foundation	336
36	Pew Freedom Trust	331
37	Heinz Endowment	315
38	Surdna Foundation	291
39	Norton Simon Foundation	288
40	Noble Foundation	270
41	Joyce Foundation	269
42	Mabee Foundation	264
43	Meyer Charitable Trust	252
44	Gund Foundation	241
45	Warren Foundation	239
46	Welch Foundation	238
47	Chicago Community Trust	237
48	Longwood Foundation	235
49	Hearst Foundation	228
50	Skillman Foundation	228

Source: *The Foundation Directory*, 12 ed. (New York: Russell Sage Foundation, 1987), p. xv.

cause they concentrate their attention on broad social issues such as poverty, health care, welfare reform, and foreign affairs.

THE ROCKEFELLER FOUNDATION. A glance at some of the people who serve on the Rockefeller Foundation board of trustees confirms its ties in other top institutions.

Robert V. Roosa. Partner, Brown Brothers, Harriman & Co. (investment firm); and a director of American Express, Owens-Corning Fiberglas, Texaco, and the Brookings Institution.

Richard H. Jenrette. Chairman of the board of Equitable Life.

Arthur Levitt. Chairman of the American Stock Exchange.

Eleanor Holmes Norton. Former chairman of the U.S. Equal Employment Opportunities Commission; a director of the Council on Foreign Relations and the Ford Foundation.

W. Michael Blumenthal. Former secretary of treasury. Former president of Bendix Corporation. Chairman of the Burroughs Corporation; and a director of Equitable Life, Pillsbury, and Chemical New York Corp.

Harold Brown. Former secretary of defense. Former president of Cal Tech. A director of AMAX, CBS, and IBM.

Eleanor B. Sheldon. A sociologist who is a director of the Rand Corporation, Equitable Life Assurance Society, Citicorp, and Mobil Oil.

THE FORD FOUNDATION. The president of the Ford Foundation is Franklin A. Thomas, a black New York attorney (Columbia Law School), who made his mark as president of the Bedford Stuyvesant Restoration Corporation (urban renewal). He is a director of Citicorp, CBS, Aluminum Company of America, Allied Stores, and Cummins Engine; he is also a trustee of Columbia University. Recent trustees of the Ford Foundation have included:

Alexander Heard. Chairman of the board of the Ford Foundation. President of Vanderbilt University, and a director of Time, Inc.

Henry B. Schacht. Chairman of the board of Cummins Engine, and a director of AT&T, CBS, and Chase Manhattan. He is also a trustee of the Brookings Institution and Yale University.

Irving S. Shapiro. Former chairman of the board of Du Pont Corporation; and a director of Citicorp, IBM, and Continental American Insurance.

Donald S. Perkins. Chairman of the board of Jewel Co.; a director
of Time, Inc., AT&T, Inland Steel, Corning Glass, Cummins Engine,
and G.D. Serle; and a trustee of the Brookings Institution.

Hedley Donovan. Former editor-in-chief of Time, Inc.

Robert S. McNamara. Former president of Ford Motor Co., secretary of defense, and president of the World Bank.

A. Bartlett Giamatti. Former president of Yale University, and
presently commissioner of baseball.

THE CULTURAL ORGANIZATIONS

The identification of the nation's leading cultural and civic institutions
requires qualitative judgments about the prestige and influence of a
variety of organizations. Five cultural organizations were selected:

Metropolitan Museum of Art
Museum of Modern Art
Lincoln Center for the Performing Arts
Smithsonian Institution
John F. Kennedy Center for the Performing Arts

It is difficult to measure the power of particular institutions in the
world of art, music, and theater. Certainly there are a number of viable
alternatives that might be added to or substituted for our choices.

THE METROPOLITAN MUSEUM OF ART. This organization in New
York City is the largest art museum in the United States, with a collection of nearly one-half million *objects d'art*. Decisions of the Metropolitan
Museum regarding exhibitions, collections, showings, and art objects
have tremendous impact on what is or is not to be considered valued art
in America. These decisions are the formal responsibility of the governing board. This board includes names such as:

C. Douglas Dillon. Trustee emeritus. Former secretary of the treasury, undersecretary of state, and a director of Chase Manhattan.

Mrs. Vincent Astor. Trustee emeritus. Wealthy philanthropist and
trustee of the New York Public Library, the New York Zoological Society,
the Pierpont Morgan Library, and Rockefeller University.

Arthur Ochs Sulzberger. Chairman of the board of trustees of the

Metropolitan Museum of Art. Chairman of the board of the New York Times Co.

Lawrence A. Tisch.   Chairman of the board of CBS.

John F. Akers.   Chairman of the board of IBM, a director of the New York Times Company, and former chairman of the Business Roundtable.

Henry A. Kissinger.   Former secretary of state.

Mrs. Henry J. Heinz II.   Spouse of the chairman of the H.J. Heinz Company.

Richard S. Perkins.   Former chairman of the board of Citicorp; and a director of Allied Chemical, New York Life Insurance, Southern Pacific, ITT, and Hospital Corporation of America.

THE MUSEUM OF MODERN ART.   This museum in New York City is the leading institution in the nation devoted to collecting and exhibiting contemporary art. It houses not only paintings and sculpture but also films, prints, and photography. Its loan exhibitions circulate art works throughout the world. The determination of what is to be considered "art" in the world of modern art is extremely subjective. The directors of the Museum of Modern Art, then, have great authority in determining what is or is not to be viewed as art. Its directors include illustrious names such as:

William S. Paley.   Chairman. Former chairman of the board of CBS.

Mrs. John D. Rockefeller III.   Widow of the oldest of four sons of John D. Rockefeller, Jr.

David Rockefeller.   Former chairman of the board of Chase Manhattan.

Frank T. Cary.   Former chairman of the board of IBM.

Thomas S. Carroll.   President of Lever Brothers.

Peter G. Peterson.   Former chairman of the board of Lehman Brothers, Kuhn Loeb (investments); and a director of RCA, General Foods, Minnesota Mining & Manufacturing, Black and Decker, and Cities Service.

THE LINCOLN CENTER FOR THE PERFORMING ARTS.   The Lincoln Center in New York City is a major influence in the nation's serious theater, ballet, and music. The Lincoln Center houses the Metropolitan Opera, the New York Philharmonic, and the Julliard School of Music. It also supports the Lincoln Repertory Company (theater), the New York State Theater (ballet), and the Library-Museum for Performing Arts.

The Metropolitan Opera, which opened in 1883, is the nation's most influential institution in the field of serious operatic music. Decisions about what operas to produce influence greatly what is, or is not, to be considered serious opera in America, and indeed, in the world. Such decisions are the formal responsibility of a board that includes luminaries such as the following:

William Rockefeller. Chairman of the Metropolitan Opera. A cousin of the Rockefeller brothers. Senior partner in Shearman & Sterling, a top Wall Street law firm.

Stephen Samas. Former vice-president of Exxon. President of the New York Philharmonic, and a trustee of Harvard College and the Council on Foreign Relations.

Richard R. Shinn. Chairman of the board of Metropolitan Life.

Norborne Berkeley, Jr. President of Chemical Bank of New York.

Anthony A. Bliss. Senior partner in Milbank, Tweed, Hadley & McCloy.

John T. Conner. Former chairman of the board of Allied Chemical; and a director of General Motors, Chase Manhattan, ABC, and Warner Lambert.

THE SMITHSONIAN INSTITUTION. The Smithsonian Institution in Washington supports a wide variety of scientific publications, collections, and exhibitions. It also exercises nominal control over the National Gallery of Art, the John F. Kennedy Center for the Performing Arts, and the Museum of Natural History, although these component organizations have their own boards of directors. The Smithsonian itself is directed by a board consisting of the Vice-President of the United States, the Chief Justice of the Supreme Court, three U.S. senators, three U.S. representatives, and nine "private citizens."

Its "private citizens" turn out to be people such as:

J. Paul Austin. Former chairman of the board of the Coca-Cola Company.

Carlisle H. Humelsine. Chairman of the board of Colonial Williamsburg Foundation.

Anne Armstrong. Former U.S. ambassador to Great Britain, and a director of General Motors, Halliburton, General Foods, Boise Cascade, and First City Bancorp. of Texas.

Murray Gell-Man. Nobel Prize winner, Cal Tech professor of physics.

William G. Bowen. President of Princeton University, and a director of NCR Corp., Merck & Co., and Reader's Digest, Inc.

Samuel C. Johnson. Chairman of the board of Johnson Wax Co., and a director of Deere & Co. and Mobil Oil.

THE JOHN F. KENNEDY CENTER FOR THE PERFORMING ARTS. The Kennedy Center in Washington, which was begun in 1964, also has considerable influence on the arts in America. It describes itself as a "national showcase for the performing arts" (music, opera, drama, dance). It is officially part of the Smithsonian Institution, but it is administered separately by a forty-five member board, most of whom are appointed by the President. The board is largely "political" in origin and includes:

Roger L. Stevens. Chairman of the board of the John F. Kennedy Center for the Performing Arts. Producer of *West Side Story, Cat on a Hot Tin Roof, Bus Stop, Tea and Sympathy, A Man for All Seasons.* Former chairman of the National Endowment for the Arts. A director of the Metropolitan Opera.

Mrs. Bob Hope. Spouse of the prominent entertainer and heavy financial contributor to political campaigns.

Joan Mondale. Spouse of the former Vice-President.

Cary Grant. Actor.

Mrs. J.W. Marriott. Spouse of the president of Marriott Motor Hotels, a heavy financial contributor to political candidates.

Charles H. Percy. U.S. senator from Illinois.

Mrs. Howard H. Baker, Jr. Spouse of the former Republican leader of the U.S. Senate.

Abe Fortas. Former U.S. Supreme Court Justice.

J. William Fulbright. Former U.S. senator.

Patricia Roberts Harris. Former secretary of health, education and welfare; and senior partner in a top Washington law firm.

Melvin R. Laird. Former secretary of defense.

Mrs. Jean Kennedy Smith. Sister of John F., Robert F., and Edward M. Kennedy.

THE CIVIC ASSOCIATIONS

Our judgments about power and influence in the civic arena are necessarily qualitative, as they were for cultural organizations. We shall focus particular attention on the political power of the nation's leading policy-planning organizations—the Council on Foreign Relations, the Business Roundtable, and the Brookings Institution—both in this chapter and later in Chapter 9. These organizations are central coordinating mechanisms in national policy-making. They bring together people in top positions from the corporate world, the universities, the law firms, and the government, to develop explicit policies and programs for submission to Congress, the President, and the nation.

THE COUNCIL ON FOREIGN RELATIONS. The most influential policy-planning group in foreign affairs is the Council on Foreign Relations. The origins of the CFR go back to the Versailles Treaty in 1919 ending World War I. Some Americans, including Woodrow Wilson's key adviser, Edward M. House, believed that top leadership in the United States was not sufficiently informed about world affairs. The Council on Foreign Relations was founded in 1921 and supported by grants from the Rockefeller and Carnegie foundations and later the Ford Foundation. Its early directors were internationally minded Wall Street corporation lawyers such as Elihu Root (who was secretary of state), John W. Davis (1924 Democratic presidential nominee), and Paul Cravath (founder of the famous law firm of Cravath, Swaine & Moore); as well as Herbert Hoover (later to become President), Yale University President Charles Seymour, Harvard professor Archibald Cary Coolidge, and Columbia professor James T. Shotwell.

The CFR is designed to build consensus among elites on foreign policy questions. It initiates new policy directions by first commissioning scholars to undertake investigations of foreign policy questions. Its studies are usually made with the financial support of foundations. Upon their completion, the CFR holds briefings and discussions among its members and between its members and top government officials.

The history of the CFR accomplishments is dazzling: It developed the Kellogg Peace Pact in the 1920s, stiffened U.S. opposition to Japanese Pacific expansion in the 1930s, designed major portions of the United Nations' charter, and devised the "containment" policy to halt Soviet expansion in Europe after World War II. It also laid the groundwork for the NATO agreement and devised the Marshall Plan for European recovery. While originally supporting U.S. involvement in Vietnam, the CFR worked out the plan that became the U.S. negotiating position at the Paris Peace Talks, which led to U.S. withdrawal in 1973. The CFR planned the Carter administration's "human rights" campaign, as well as restrictions on international arms sales. Even before the election of Ronald Reagan, the CFR was calling for reassessment of U.S.–Soviet relations in view of the large Soviet arms build-up.

CFR publishes the journal *Foreign Affairs,* considered throughout the world to be the unofficial mouthpiece of U.S. foreign policy. Few important initiatives in U.S. policy have not been first outlined in articles in this publication. It was in *Foreign Affairs* in 1947 that George F. Kennan, chief of the policy-planning staff of the State Department, writing under the pseudonym of "X," first announced U.S. intentions of "containing" Communist expansion in the world. When top elites began to suspect that the United States was over-reliant on nuclear weapons in the 1950s and unable to fight theater-type wars, the CFR commissioned a young Harvard professor to look into the matter. The result was Henry Kissinger's *Nuclear Weapons and Foreign Policy,* urging greater flexibility of response to aggression. Current CFR concerns, as reflected in the pages of *Foreign Affairs,* the *Annual Report,* and other public sources, are discussed in Chapter 9.

The CFR by-laws limit membership to 1,900 individuals who are proposed by existing members and who meet "high admissions standards." However, there is a long waiting list of individuals seeking membership in this prestigious organization. The CFR's list of former members includes every person of influence in foreign affairs from Elihu Root, Henry Stimson, John Foster Dulles, Dean Acheson, Robert Lovett, George F. Kennan, Averill Harriman, and Dean Rusk, to Henry Kissinger, Cyrus Vance, Alexander Haig, George Schultz and George Bush. The CFR describes itself as "a unique forum for bringing together leaders from the academic, public, and private worlds."

For almost two decades the CFR chairman was David Rockefeller, then chairman of the board of Chase Manhattan Bank (see Chapter 6). The international investment activity of Chase and the foreign policy influence and expertise of CFR dovetailed neatly in the person of the chairman. Rockefeller became "honorary chairman" in 1985 and turned over the reins of power to Peter G. Peterson. The CFR board of directors has always been a compendium of power and prestige:

Peter G. Peterson. Chairman of the board of directors of CFR, chairman of the board of Bell and Howell Co., and former secretary of commerce. A director of Minnesota Mining & Mfg., General Foods, and Federated Department Stores. Trustee of the Museum of Modern Art and the University of Chicago.

Cyrus R. Vance. Director emeritus of CFR. Former secretary of state. Former chairman of the Rockefeller Foundation; senior partner in the prestigious Wall Street law firm of Simpson, Thacher & Bartlett.

Juanita Kreps. Former secretary of commerce. A director of the New York Stock Exchange, RJR Nabisco, Eastman Kodak, Citicorp, Armco, Allegis Corp, AT&T, J.C. Penny, and Chrysler Corp.

Brent Scowcroft. National security adviser to President George Bush. Former national security adviser to President Gerald Ford. Partner in Kissinger & Associates. Former Air Force lieutenant general.

Harold Brown. Former secretary of defense. Former president of California Institute of Technology.

William D. Rogers. Former secretary of state. Senior partner in Rogers & Wells.

Clifton R. Wharton, Jr. Former chancellor of the State University of New York; and a director of Ford Motors, Burroughs Corp., and Equitable Life.

Paul A. Volcker. Former chairman of the Federal Reserve Board.

B.R. Inman. Chairman of the board of Westmark. Former deputy director of the CIA and former director of the National Security Agency. Admiral, U.S. Navy.

THE BUSINESS ROUNDTABLE. The Business Roundtable provides direct representation of the chief executive officers of the nation's 200 largest corporations in the policy process. Unlike other policy-planning groups, which emphasize policy formation and consensus-building, the Roundtable engages in direct lobbying on behalf of specific bills it wants passed by the Congress and supported by the President. The Roundtable was formed in 1972 to successfully lobby Congress on labor laws in the construction industry. Later, the Roundtable was successful in defeating the establishment of a consumer protection agency in both the Ford and Carter administrations. The Roundtable has been instrumental in making "deregulation" a key item in the Washington policy agenda in recent years. It has also supported social spending cuts, general tax cuts, and faster depreciation schedules for business tax purposes.

The Roundtable has formed task forces on a wide variety of policy issues—antitrust, energy, environment, inflation, government regulation, health, social security, taxation, welfare, and so on. These task forces submit their policy recommendations to a powerful policy committee. The strength of the organization is derived from the willingness of its member chiefs to appear *in person* in Washington. In 1989 its leadership consisted of:

> **Roger B. Smith.**   Chairman of the Business Roundtable, and chairman of the board of General Motors.
>
> **John F. Akers.**   Chairman of the board of IBM.
>
> **Edmund T. Pratt.**   Chairman of the board of Pfizer.
>
> **Theodore F. Brophy.**   Chairman of the board of GTE.

together with fifty-one other CEOs on its policy committee.

THE BROOKINGS INSTITUTION. Over the years, the foremost policy-planning group in domestic affairs has been the Brookings Institution. Since the 1960s, it has overshadowed the CED (Council on Economic Development), the American Enterprise Institution, the American Assembly, the Twentieth Century Fund, the Urban Institute, and all other policy-planning groups. Brookings has been extremely influential in planning the war on poverty, welfare reform, national health care, defense programs, and taxation programs. The Brookings Institution is generally regarded as moderate-to-liberal in its policy orientation. The American Enterprise Institute (AEI) was reorganized in the 1970s to try to offset Brookings' influence by providing moderate-to-conservative advice on public policy. While the AEI has enjoyed a resurgence in Washington in the Reagan administration, its long-term influence is no match for the well-established Brookings Institution.

The Brookings Institution's directors today are as impressive a group of top elites as assembled anywhere:

> **Louis W. Cabot.**   Chairman of the board of trustees of the Brookings Institution. Chairman of the board of the Cabot Corporation. A director of Owens-Corning Fiberglas, and New England Telephone, and chairman of the Federal Reserve Bank of Boston. A trustee of the Carnegie Corporation, M.I.T., and Northeastern University; and a member of the Council on Foreign Relations.
>
> **Robert V. Roosa.**   Honorary trustee and former chairman of the Brookings Institution. Senior partner, Brown Brothers, Harriman & Co. (New York investment firm). He is director of American Express, Ana-

conda Copper, Owens-Corning Fiberglas, and Texaco. He is a former undersecretary of the treasury and a director of the Council on Foreign Relations. Roosa has an earned Ph.D. in economics from the University of Michigan and was a Rhodes scholar. A trustee of the Rockefeller Foundation.

James D. Robinson. Chairman of the board of American Express.

Alden W. Clausen. Chairman and chief executive officer of BankAmerica; former president of the World Bank.

William T. Coleman. Former secretary of transportation; and a director of IBM, Chase Manhattan, Pepsico, American Can, and Pan American World Airways.

B.R. Inman. Chairman of the board of Westmark. Former deputy director of the CIA and former director of the National Security Agency.

Henry B. Schacht. Chairman of the board of Cummins Engine, and a director of AT&T, CBS, and Chase Manhattan.

Vernon E. Jordon, Jr. Executive director of the National Urban League, and a director of Bankers Trust New York Corp., Celenese Corp., J.C. Penney, and Xerox.

Robert F. Erburu. Chairman of the board of the Times Mirror Company of Los Angeles, and a director of the Council of Foreign Relations and the Business Roundatable.

If the names are growing repetitious by now, it is for good reason. Those who occupy top posts in the leading corporate, governmental, and mass media institutions are frequently the same individuals who direct the leading foundations, cultural organizations, and civic associations. The purpose of "naming names," even when they become repetitive, is to suggest frequent interlocking of top elites in different institutional sectors. In Chapter 6, we will examine interlocking in greater detail.

THE UNIVERSITIES

The growth of public higher education since World War II—the creation of vast state university, state college, and community college systems in every state in the nation—has diminished the influence of the prestigious private universities. There are now nearly 3,000 separate institutions of higher education in America, enrolling over 12 million students—more than one half of all high school graduates. Only about one quarter of these students are enrolled in *private* colleges and universities. Moreover, some leading public universities—for example, the University of California at Berkeley and the University of Michigan— are consistently ranked with the well-known private universities in terms of the quality of higher education offered. Thus, the leading private universities in the nation no longer exercise the dominant influence over higher education that they did before World War II.

Nonetheless, among private colleges and universities it is possible to identify those few top institutions which control most of the resources available to private higher education. The twenty-five universities listed in Table 5–3 control two thirds of all private endowment funds in higher education; this was the formal basis for their selection. (Only three *public* universities rank with the top twenty-five private universities in endowments. These are the University of Texas, the University of California, and the University of Virginia.) Moreover, they are consist-

TABLE 5–3 Private Universities with Largest Endowments

RANK		ASSETS (MILLIONS)
1	Harvard University	$4,018
2	Princeton University	2,829
3	Yale University	2,098
4	Stanford University	1,677
5	Columbia University	1,387
6	Washington University	1,200
7	Massachusetts Institute of Technology	1,170
8	University of Chicago	913
9	Rice University	857
10	Northwestern University	802
11	Emory University	798
12	Cornell University	725
13	University of Pennsylvania	648
14	University of Rochester	556
15	Rockefeller University	542
16	Dartmouth College	537
17	Johns Hopkins University	534
18	Vanderbilt University	509
19	New York University	504
20	University of Notre Dame	456
21	California Institute of Technology	409
22	University of Southern California	401
23	Duke University	364
24	Brown University	347
25	Case Western Reserve University	341

Source: *Chronicle of Higher Education,* June 1, 1988, p. A35.

ently ranked among the "best" educational institutions in the nation. Finally, as we will see, a disproportionate number of the nation's top leaders attended one or another of these institutions.

We have already acknowledged the growing importance in higher education of the nation's leading *state* universities. Is there any reason to believe that their rise to prominence since World War II has distributed power in education more widely and opened positions of authority to persons whose elite credentials are not necessarily as impressive as the ones we have seen again and again in our lists of top leaders? Our answer is a very qualified "yes": State boards of regents for state universities are on the whole composed of individuals who would probably *not* be among the top institutional elites according to our definition in Chapter 1. Many of these regents hold directorships in smaller corporations, smaller banks, and smaller utility companies; they frequently have held state rather than national political office; their legal, civic, cultural, and foundation affiliations are with institutions of state rather than with prestigious and powerful national institutions.[13]

University presidents, particularly the presidents of the nation's top institutions, are frequently called upon to serve as trustees or directors of other institutions and to serve in high government posts. Most university presidents today have come up through the ranks of academic administration, suggesting that universities themselves may offer channels for upward mobility into the nation's elite. (Harvard's president, Derek Curtis Bok, rose through the ranks of Harvard's law school faculty; Yale's former president, A. Bartlett Giamatti, rose from Yale's English faculty; and Chicago's president, Hanna H. Gray, rose from professor of history at Chicago through administrative posts at Northwestern and Yale.) We must keep in mind, however, that presidents are hired and fired by the trustees, not the students or faculty.

THE AMERICAN ESTABLISHMENT

Is there a unifying Establishment in this nation, separate from business and government, which seeks to use its power, prestige, and wealth to further its own vision of America? The notion of an Establishment—with its old school ties, inherited wealth, upper-class life style, position, and privilege—flourishes even in a democratic society. Harvard historian Mark Silk and his brother, *New York Times* columnist Leonard Silk, write:

[13]David N. Smith, *Who Rules the Universities?* (New York: Monthly Review Press, 1974), pp. 30–33.

Although the origins of the Establishment are ecclesiastical and aristocratic, in America it is firmly joined to both democratic and capitalist institutions. But its ambitions go beyond: it seeks to protect and advance social, moral, and aesthetic values that transcend the interests of any single person, economic group, or political constituency or organization; it affects to be a harmonizer, an arbiter, a wise instructor of the nation—and particularly of its political and business leaders.[14]

This Establishment traces its roots, and even its name, to the established church in early Massachusetts. The nation's earliest democrats sought to ensure that there would be "no establishment of religion" by writing these words into the First Amendment of the Constitution. But in the early years the First Amendment applied only to the national government and not to the states; Massachusetts supported the established Congregationalist church well into the nineteenth century. Harvard College was the center of established religion, even after the more rigid Calvinists abandoned it in favor of more orthodox instruction at newer Yale College. This early schism in the established church was partly due to the greater openness, humanism, and tolerance of dissent at Harvard, traits which are supposed to characterize the Establishment even today.[15]

The Establishment today is said to "inhabit" the nation's most influential institutions. The Establishment is not an institution itself but rather a "collective entity" or "third force" (the other two being business and government) which links together various institutions in separate segments of society. The Establishment is concerned with maintaining a public ethos—a civic morality emphasizing toleration, individual liberty, and goodness. The institutions which it "inhabits" are said to be:

Harvard University
New York Times
Ford Foundation
Brookings Institution
Council on Foreign Relations
Committee for Economic Development

Not every person associated with these institutions is a member of the

[14]Leonard Silk and Mark Silk, *The American Establishment* (New York: Basic Books, 1980), p. 325.

[15]According to the Silks, Harvard represented a middle religious ground between the Calvinists at Yale and the Enlightenment Deists of the Virginia planters, notably Thomas Jefferson. Only six of the fourteen faculty members at Harvard in 1831 were Unitarians; the faculty even included three Roman Catholics and a Quaker. See Silk and Silk, Ibid., p. 13.

Establishment. And there are other institutions which also possess Establishment connections:

> Yale University
> Princeton University
> Columbia University
> University of Chicago
> Stanford University
> Carnegie Endowment for International Peace
> RAND Corporation
> Twentieth Century Fund
> Russell Sage Foundation
> Century Club
> Metropolitan Museum of Art
> Museum of Modern Art
> Metropolitan Opera [16]

But these institutions do not define the Establishment. Instead, the Establishment is defined as "a national force, outside government, dedicated to truth, liberty, and however defined, the broad public interest."[17]

SUMMARY

Using the term "civic establishment," we refer collectively to the nation's top law firms, its major foundations, its national cultural institutions, influential civic organizations, and prestigious private universities. At the top of the legal profession, the senior partners of the nation's best-known New York and Washington law firms exercise great power as legal representatives of the nation's largest corporations. These super-lawyers are frequently called upon for governmental leadership, particularly when high-level, delicate negotiations are required. Most superlawyers have been educated at Ivy League law schools and serve apprenticeships in governmental agencies before entering law firms.

The power of the nation's large foundations rests in their ability to channel corporate and personal wealth into the policy-making process. They do this by providing financial support and direction over university research and the activities of policy-oriented, civic associations. There is great concentration of foundation assets. There is also a great deal of overlapping among the directorates of the leading foundations

[16]Silk and Silk, Ibid., p. 18.
[17]Silk and Silk, Ibid., p. 20.

and corporate and financial institutions, the mass media, universities, policy-planning groups, and government.

A small number of cultural organizations exercise great power over the nation's art, music, theater, and ballet. A brief glance at the directors of these institutions confirms that they are the same group of people identified earlier as influential in business, finance, government, and the mass media.

The civic associations, particularly the leading policy-planning groups—the Council on Foreign Relations, the Business Roundtable, and the Brookings Institution—play key roles in national policy-making. They bring together leaders at the top of various institutional sectors of society to formulate recommendations on major policy innovations. More will be said about the important role of policy-planning groups in Chapter 9. But we have noted here that the directors of these groups are top leaders in industry, finance, government, the mass media, law, and the universities.

There may not be as much concentration of power in higher education as in other sectors of American life. The development of state universities since World War II has diminished the influence of the private, Ivy League–type universities. However, among *private* universities, only twenty-five institutions control over two thirds of all private endowment funds.

Commentators have speculated about an American "Establishment," separate from business and government, which inhabits influential civic organizations, universities, and foundations.

CHAPTER 6
INTERLOCKING
AND SPECIALIZATION
AT THE TOP

CONVERGENCE OR SPECIALIZATION AT THE TOP?

Is there a convergence of power at the top of an institutional structure in America, with a single group of individuals, recruited primarily from industry and finance, who occupy top positions in corporations, education, government, foundations, civic and cultural affairs, and the military? Or are there separate institutional structures, with elites in each sector of society having little or no overlap in authority and many separate channels of recruitment? In short, is the structure of power in America a pyramid or a polyarchy?

Social scientists have differed over this important question, and at least two varieties of leadership models can be identified in the literature on power.[1] A *hierarchical model* implies that a relatively small group of

---

[1]This literature is voluminous, and any characterization of positions results in some oversimplification. For good summary statements of positions, see the works of Mills, Hunter, Berle, Kolko, and Dahl, cited elsewhere in chapter notes. See also Arnold M. Rose, *The Power Structure* (New York: Oxford University Press, 1967); Suzanne Keller, *Beyond the Ruling Class* (New York: Random House, 1963); G. William Domhoff, *Who Rules America?* (Englewood Cliffs, N.J.: Prentice-Hall, 1967); Nelson Polsby, *Community Power and Political Theory* (New Haven: Yale University Press, 1963); and David Ricci, *Community Power and Democratic Theory* (New York: Random House, 1971).

individuals exercises authority in a wide variety of institutions—forming what has been called a "power elite." In contrast, a *polyarchical model* implies that different groups of individuals exercise power in various sectors of society and acquire power in separate ways.

The hierarchical model derives from the familiar "elitist" literature on power. Sociologist C. Wright Mills argues that "the leading men in each of the three domains of power—the warlords, the corporation chieftains, and the political directorate—tend to come together to form the power elite of America."[2] According to Mills, leadership in America constitutes "an intricate set of overlapping cliques." And Floyd Hunter, in his study *Top Leadership, U.S.A.,* concludes: "Out of several hundred persons named from all sources, between one hundred and two hundred were consistently chosen as top leaders and considered by all informants to be of national policy-making stature."[3] The notion of interlocking directorates has widespread currency in the power elite literature. Gabriel Kolko writes that "interlocking directorates, whereby a director of one corporation also sits on the board of one or more other corporations, are a key device for concentrating corporate power. . . ."[4] The hierarchical model also implies that top leaders in all sectors of society—including government, education, civic and cultural affairs, and politics—are recruited primarily from business and finance.

In contrast, pluralist writers have implied a polyarchical leadership structure, with different sets of leaders in different sectors of society and little or no overlap, except perhaps by elected officials responsible to the general public. According to this view, leadership is exercised in large measure by "specialists" who limit their participation to a narrow range of societal decisions. These specialists are believed to be recruited through separate channels—they are not drawn exclusively from business and finance. Generally, pluralists have praised the dispersion of authority in American society. Robert A. Dahl writes: "The theory and practice of American pluralism tends to assume, as I see it, that the existence of multiple centers of power, none of which is wholly sovereign, will help (may indeed be necessary) to tame power, to secure the consent of all, and to settle conflicts peacefully."[5]

SOURCES OF ELITE COHESION

It is the responsibility of elitist scholars to demonstrate the cohesiveness of the nation's leadership, and to counter the pluralist argument that elites

[2]C. Wright Mills, *The Power Elite* (New York: Oxford University Press, 1956), p. 9.

[3]Floyd Hunter, *Top Leadership, U.S.A.* (Chapel Hill: University of North Carolina Press, 1959), p. 176.

[4]Gabriel Kolko, *Wealth and Power in America* (New York: Praeger, 1962), p. 57.

[5]Robert A. Dahl, *Pluralist Democracy in the United States* (Chicago: Rand McNally, 1967), p. 24.

are plural, specialized, relatively independent, frequently competitive, and occasionally conflictual. Elite theorists postulate several different mechanisms which provide the necessary cohesion among the leaders of different institutions in American society:

INTERLOCKING DIRECTORATES. Institutions are linked by a network of interlocking memberships, whereby the directors of various industrial corporations, banks, foundations, newspapers and television networks, civic and cultural corporations, sit on the governing boards of more than one institution. Banks and other financial institutions are often considered central to this network. Banks may function to mediate in intercorporate conflict since they usually have investments in many different segments of the economy.[6]

AN INNER GROUP. An "inner group" thesis suggests that even though most corporate leaders have a direct interest in only a single corporation, a relatively small group of business leaders have broader interests which transcend the boundaries of industrial corporations to encompass the long-term interests of business as a whole.[7]

INSTITUTIONAL EXPERIENCES. In addition to *concurrent* interlocking where individuals hold more than one top institutional post at the same time, members of the elite may enjoy *sequential* interlocking, where individuals hold a number of leadership positions over their lifetime. This is especially important in securing cohesion between governmental and corporate elites: Government officials are usually expected to resign their corporate directorships when they assume a government post, but many top government leaders bring their corporate experience to government and even return to corporate life after their government work.

CLASS BACKGROUNDS, EDUCATION, CLUBS, KINSHIP. Still another source of cohesion may be the shared social class backgrounds which transmit relatively uniform upper- and upper-middle-class values and aspirations to future elite members. These class values are reinformed with uniform educational experiences for a large proportion of elite members, including attendance at prestigious private prep schools and Ivy League universities. These social class and educational ties are frequently reinforced through marriage and family relations. Finally, elite cohesion is

[6]See, for example, Beth Mintz and Michael Swartz, "Interlocking Directorates and Interest Group Formations," *American Sociological Review,* 46 (1981), 851–69; Ronald F. Burt, "A Structural Theory of Interlocking Corporate Directorates," *Social Networks,* 1 (1979), 415–35; Ronald S. Burt, et al., "Testing a Structural Theory of Corporate Cooptation: Intraorganizational Directorate Ties," *American Sociological Review,* 45 (1980), 821–41; Thomas Koenig, "Interlocking Corporate Directorates as a Social Network," *American Journal of Economics and Sociology,* 40 (1981) 37–50.

[7]See, for example, Maurice Zeitlin, "Corporate Ownership and Control," *American Journal of Sociology,* 79 (1974), 1073–119; Michael Useem, "The Inner Group of the American Capitalist Class," *Social Problems,* 25 (1978), 225–40.

abetted through a network of private prestigious social clubs, which purposefully encourage interaction and solidarity within the elite.[8]

SHARED ATTITUDES AND BELIEFS. The result of shared social class backgrounds, similar educational experiences, and numerous social, family, and business ties, is broad agreement on societal values. Elites agree on the goals and purposes of public policies; disagreement is limited to specific means for achieving these goals and purposes. Elite consensus includes support for the free enterprise system, limited government, and rewards based on individual merit; a devotion to personal liberty, due process of law, and equality of opportunity; opposition to discrimination; a desire to mitigate the worst effects of poverty and ill-health; an impulse to do good and instill middle-class values in all citizens; a desire to exercise influence in international affairs and spread Western cultural values throughout the world. The range of disagreement among elites is relatively narrow compared to this broad consensus on fundamental values.[9]

PRIVATE POLICY-PLANNING ORGANIZATIONS. Planning, coordination, and consensus-building in national policy is achieved through a complex process which ensures that major policy directions are determined *before* the "proximate policy-makers"—Congress, the White House, administrative agencies, and so on—become directly involved. Central to this process are a small number of private, policy-planning organizations. These organizations bring together leaders from corporate and financial institutions, universities, foundations, the mass media, the top law firms, and government, in order to set the agenda of national decision making, direct research into policy questions, and most importantly, try to reach a consensus on the major policy directions for the nation.[10]

These potential sources of elite cohesion are discussed in the remainder of this volume. In Chapter 6 we shall examine interlocking directorates, the "inner group," and the institutional experiences of our national elite. In Chapter 7 we shall examine the social class origins of the top elites, their educational experiences, and their social activities. In Chapter 8, we assess the extent of consensus and factionalism among the nation's elite. In Chapter 9 we describe the policy-planning process and the role of the private policy-planning organizations.

---

[8]See, for example, G. William Domhoff, *The Bohemian Grove and Other Retreats* (New York: Harper and Row, 1974); Gwen Moore and Richard D. Alba, "Class and Prestige Origins in the American Elite," in *Social Structure and Network Analysis*, eds. Peter V. Marsden and Nan Lin (Beverly Hills, Calif.: Sage, 1982).

[9]See Richard Hofstadter, *The American Political Tradition* (New York: Knopf, 1948).

[10]See, for example, Thomas R. Dye, "Oligarchic Tendencies in National Policy-Making," *Journal of Politics*, 40 (May 1978), 309–31; G. William Domhoff, *The Powers That Be* (New York: Vintage, 1979); Michael Useem, "The Social Organization of the American Business Elite and Participation of Corporate Directors in the Governance of American Institutions," *American Sociological Review*, 44 (August 1979), 553–72.

"INTERLOCKERS" AND "SPECIALISTS"

Earlier we identified 7,314 top institutional positions in 12 different sectors of society which we defined as the nation's elite (see Chapter 1). Individuals in these positions control more than one half of the nation's industrial and financial assets, nearly half of all the assets of private foundations, and two thirds of the assets of private universities; they control the television networks, the news service, and leading newspapers; they control the most prestigious civic and cultural organizations; and they direct the activities of the executive, legislative, and judicial branches of the national government.

These 7,314 top positions were occupied by 5,778 individuals. In other words, there were fewer top individuals than top positions—indicating multiple holding of top positions by some individuals. Table 6–1 presents specific data on this phenomenon, which we shall call *interlocking.*

Approximately 15 percent of those we identified as the nation's elite held more than one top position at a time. These are our "interlockers." Most of them held only two top positions, but some held five, six, seven, or more! Eighty-five percent of the people at the top are "specialists"—individuals who hold only one top position. Many of these specialists hold other corporate directorships, governmental posts, or civic, cultural, or university positions, but not *top* positions as we have defined them. Thus, our "specialists" may assume a wide variety of lesser positions: directorships in corporations below the top 100; positions on governmental boards and commissions; trusteeships of less well-known colleges and foundations; and directorships of less influential civic and cultural organizations. We will also observe that over a lifetime, many of our specialists tend to hold a number of top positions, serially, rather than concurrently.

About 32 percent of all top *positions* are interlocked with other top positions. The reason that 32 percent of the top positions are interlocked, but only 15 percent of the top individuals hold more than one position, is that some individuals are "multiple interlockers"—they hold three or more positions.

The multiple interlockers turned out to be individuals of considerable stature, as the listing in Table 6–2 indicates. This list was compiled from extensive data collected and analyzed in 1980–81. These individuals comprised our top group of multiple interlockers—individuals occupying *six or more* top positions concurrently. By any criteria whatsoever, these individuals must be judged important figures in America. The fact that our investigation of positional overlap revealed such impressive names lends some face validity to the assertion that interlocking is a source of authority and power in society. However, despite the impressive concentration of interlocking authority in this top group, it should be remembered

TABLE 6–1 Interlocking and Specialization in Top Institutional Positions

	NUMBER OF TOP INSTITUTIONAL POSITIONS	PERCENT OF TOTAL POSITIONS	NUMBER OF INDIVIDUALS IN TOP POSITIONS	PERCENT OF TOTAL INDIVIDUALS
Total	7,314	100.0	5,778	100.0
Specialized	4,981	68.1	4,911	85.0
Interlocked	2,333	31.9	867	15.0
Number of Interlocks:				
Two	1,046	14.3	520	9.0
Three	614	8.4	202	3.5
Four	278	3.8	69	1.2
Five	197	2.7	40	0.7
Six	110	1.5	17	0.3
Seven or more	88	1.2	11	0.2

TABLE 6–2 Multiple Interlockers in Top Institutional Positions, 1980

A. Robert Abboud.   President, Occidental Petroleum. Former chairman of the board of First National Bank of Chicago; a director of Hart Schaffner & Marx, Inland Steel, Standard Oil of Indiana. A director of the Committee for Economic Development, a trustee of the University of Chicago, and member of the Council on Foreign Relations.

J. Paul Austin.   Chairman of the board of Coca-Cola Co. A director of Federated Department Stores, Morgan Guaranty Trust, General Electric, Trust Company of Georgia, Dow Jones & Co.

Thorton Bradshaw.   Chairman of the board of RCA. Former president of Atlantic Richfield. A director of Security Pacific Corp., NBC, Los Angeles Philharmonic, Aspen Institute, American Petroleum Institute, and a trustee of Howard University.

Andrew F. Brimmer.   President of Brimmer & Co. A director of BankAmerica, American Security Bank, International Harvester, United Airlines, Du Pont Corp., the Trilateral Commission, the Committee for Economic Development, the Ford Foundation, the Urban League, and the Council on Foreign Relations.

Ralph Manning Brown, Jr.   Chairman of the board of New York Life Insurance Co. A director of Union Carbide, Morgan Guaranty Trust, A&P, and Avon Products. A trustee of the Sloan Foundation, and Princeton University; and a director of the Metropolitan Museum of Art.

Edward W. Carter.   Chairman of the board of Carter Hawley Hale Stores (including Nieman Marcus, Bergdorf, and so on). A director of AT&T, Del Monte, Lockheed Corp., Pacific Mutual Life Insurance, Southern California Edison, Western Bancorp. A trustee of the Brookings Institution, the Committee for Economic Development, Rockefeller University, Howard University.

Frank T. Cary.   Chairman of the board of IBM. A director of J.P. Morgan & Co. and the American Broadcasting Company. A director of the Brookings Institution, the Business Roundtable, and the Committee for Economic Development.

Catherine B. Cleary.   Former chairman of the board of First Wisconsin Corp. A director of Northwestern Mutual Life Insurance, General Motors, Kohle Corp., Kraft.

William T. Coleman.   Former secretary of transportation. Washington attorney. A director of IBM, Chase Manhattan, Pepsi Co., American Can, Pan American World Airways, Philadelphia Electric. A trustee of the Brookings Institution and Harvard University, and a member of the Trilateral Commission and the Council on Foreign Relations.

John D. Debutts.   Former chairman of the board of AT&T. A director of Citicorp, U.S. Steel, Kraft, General Motors, Hospital Corporation of America. A trustee of the Brookings Institution, the Business Roundtable, the Duke Endowment, and Duke University.

Clifton C. Garvin.   Chairman of the board of Exxon. A director of Citicorp, Pepsi Co., Sperry Rand. Chairman of the Business Roundtable. A trustee of the Committee for Economic Development, Memorial Sloan-Kettering Cancer Center, and Vanderbilt University.

J. Richardson Dilworth.   Chairman of the board of the Rockefeller Center. A director of R.H. Macy & Co., Chase Manhattan, Chrysler. A trustee of colonial Williamsburg and Yale University.

(Continued)

TABLE 6–2   Multiple Interlockers in Top Institutional Positions, 1980 (Continued)

Harry Jack Gray. Chairman of the board of United Technologies. A director of Exxon, Citicorp, Aetna Life & Casualty, Carrier Corp., Otis Elevator, Pratt & Whitney.

Fred L. Hartley. Chairman of the board of Union Oil Co. A director of Rockwell International, Union Bank, Daytona International Speedway. A trustee of Cal Tech Pepperdine University, the Council on Foreign Relations, and the Committee for Economic Development.

Gabriel Hauge. Former chairman of the board of Manufacturers Hanover Trust. A director of New York Life Insurance, Amax, N.Y. Telephone, Chrysler, Royal Dutch Petroleum. A trustee of the Committee for Economic Development and the Juilliard School of Music.

Robert S. Hatfield. Chairman of the board of Continental Can. A director of Citicorp, Johnson & Johnson, the New York Stock Exchange, Kennecott Copper, General Motors, Eastman Kodak. A director of the Business Roundtable, and a trustee of the Committee for Economic Development and Cornell University.

Carla A. Hills. Former secretary of housing and urban development. Washington attorney. A director of IBM, American Airlines, Signal Companies, Standard Oil of California. A trustee of the Brookings Institution and the University of Southern California.

George P. Jenkins. Chairman of the board of Metropolitan Life. A director of Citicorp, ABC, St. Regis Paper, Bethlehem Steel, W.R. Grace & Co., and a trustee of the University of Southern California.

Howard W. Johnson. Former president of M.I.T. A director of Federated Department Stores, John Hancock Mutual Life Insurance, Du Pont Corp., Morgan Guaranty Trust, Champion International. A trustee of the Committee for Economic Development and Radcliffe College.

J. Paul Lyet. Chairman of the board of Sperry Rand Corp. A director of Armstrong Cork, Continental Can, Manufacturers Hanover Trust, Hershey Trust, Eastman Kodak, and a trustee of the University of Pennsylvania.

Lee L. Morgan. Chairman of the board of Caterpillar Tractor. A director of 3M, Commercian National Bank, Mobil Oil.

Ellmore C. Patterson. Former chairman of the board of Morgan Guaranty Trust. A director of General Motors, Bethlehem Steel, Acheson Topeka and Santa Fe Railroad, J.P. Morgan & Co., Standard Brands, and Comsat. A trustee of the Alfred P. Sloan Foundation, Memorial Sloan-Kettering Cancer Center, the University of Chicago, and M.I.T.

Donald S. Perkins. Chairman of the board of Jewel Companies. A director of Time Inc., AT&T, Inland Steel, Corning Glass, Cummins Engine. A trustee of the Ford foundation, the Business Roundtable, and the Brookings Institution.

Richard S. Perkins. Former chairman of the board of Citicorp. A director of Allied Chemical, New York Life, Southern Pacific, ITT, the Hospital Corporation of America. A trustee of Chapin School, Miss Porter's School, and the Metropolitan Museum of Art.

Peter G. Peterson. Chairman of the board of Lehman Brothers, Kuhn Loeb Inc. Former secretary of commerce. A director of RCA, Black & Decker, Cities Service, 3M Co., General Foods, Federated Department Stores. A trustee of the Museum of Modern Art, the Council on Foreign Relations, and the University of Chicago.

TABLE 6–2   Multiple Interlockers in Top Institutional Positions, 1980 (Continued)

Edmund T. Pratt.   Chairman of the board of IBM. A director of Chase Manhattan, International Paper Co., General Motors. A trustee of the Committee for Economic Development and Duke University.

David Rockefeller.   Chairman of the board of Chase Manhattan Bank. Chairman of the Council on Foreign Relations. A trustee of the Rockefeller Foundation, the Museum of Modern Art, Rockefeller Center, Downtown Lower Manhattan Association, the University of Chicago, and Howard University.

Robert V. Roosa.   Senior partner, Brown Brothers, Harriman & Co. A director of American Express, Owens-Corning Fiberglas, Texaco. Chairman of the Brookings Institution. A trustee of the Rockefeller Foundation, Memorial Sloan-Kettering Cancer Center, and the National Bureau of Economic Research.

Irving Saul Shapiro.   Chairman of the board of E.I. du Pont de Nemours & Co. A director of Citicorp, Bank of Delaware, IBM, Continental American Insurance. A director of the Business Roundtable; and a trustee of the Conference Board, the University of Delaware, and the Ford Foundation.

Richard R. Shinn.   Chairman of the board of Metropolitan Life Insurance. A director of Allied Chemical, Sperry Rand, Norton Simon. A director of the Business Roundtable and the Committee for Economic Development. A trustee of the Metropolitan Opera and the University of Pennsylvania.

Rawleigh Warner.   Chairman of the board of Mobil Oil. A director of Caterpillar Tractor, AT&T, Chemical Bank of New York, American Express, Wheelabrator. A trustee of Princeton University.

that most of the remaining 85 percent of top position-holders were specialists.

THE INNER GROUP: AN ELITE WITHIN THE ELITE

Let us label these multiple interlockers as the *inner group* of the nation's institutional leadership.[11] These individuals are only a small percentage of the total number of leaders we identified, but they are in a unique position to communicate and coordinate the activities of a variety of institutions. The members of the inner group have significant "connections" with corporations, banks, media, cultural organizations, universities, foundations, and civic associations. The inner group is really a metaphor, and the boundary between it and other top leaders is not sharp. The individuals listed in Table 6–2 have *six* or more *top* institutional positions; they cer-

[11]Maurice Zeitlin, "Corporate Ownership and Control," *American Journal of Sociology,* 79 (September 1974), 1073–119; Michael Patrick Allen, "Continuity and Change within the Core Corporate Elite," *Sociological Quarterly,* 19 (Autumn 1978), 510–21.

tainly can be thought of as the central core of the inner group. But we might also picture concentric rings surrounding the inner group—those persons with five, four, three, or two interlocking positions.

The existence of a "core elite," or an "elite within the elite," has been suggested by several social scientists.[12] However, there is no clear-cut definition of these terms. Our notion of an *inner group* involves not only multiple directorships of large corporate and financial institutions but also the governance of large, influential foundations, universities, cultural organizations, and civic associations.

Members of the inner group are differentiated from other leaders in that their multiple position-holding encourages them to take a broader view of business problems. "They move from the industrial point of interest and outlook to the interest and outlook of the class of all big corporate property as a whole."[13] Indeed, members of the inner group cannot take narrow positions based upon the interests of a single firm, but instead they must consider the well-being of a wide range of American institutions.

Members of the inner group know each other socially. They come together not only in multiple corporate boardrooms but also at cultural and civic events, charitable endeavors, foundation meetings, and university trustee and alumni get-togethers. They are also members of the same exclusive social clubs—the Links, Century, Knickerbocker, Burning Tree, Metropolitan, Pacific Union.

Most importantly, the inner group plays a major role in linking the corporate world with government, foundations, universities, cultural organizations, and civic associations. Members of the inner group are highly valued and generally preferred as members, advisers, and trustees of government and nonprofit organizations. "The multiple corporate connections place inner group members in an exceptionally good position to help mobilize the resources of many firms on behalf of policies they favor—and institutions whose governance they assist—making inner group members preferable to other businessmen when appointments to positions of governance are decided."[14] Indeed, it turns out that multiple corporate directors have a participation rate in government and nonprofit organizations which is more than twice the participation rate of single directors (specialists).

Interlocking of directorates appears to have declined modestly since the early 1970s. In 1970, we estimated that about 20 percent of all top leaders were interlockers. In 1980, our estimate was only 15 percent.

[12]W. Lloyd Warner and James D. Abegglen, *Big Business Leaders in America* (New York: Harper, 1955); Allen, "Continuity and Change within the Core Corporate Elite."

[13]Mills, *The Power Elite*, p. 121.

[14]Useem, "The Social Organization of the American Business Elite," p. 557.

While the two samples are not exactly comparable (1980 is larger), we believe that this modest decline in interlocking is "real," and not merely a product of methodology.[15] Over time, increasing proportions of top leaders are specialists.

PREVIOUS INSTITUTIONAL EXPERIENCE OF INDIVIDUALS AT THE TOP

How many positions of authority in all types of institutions have top leaders *ever held* in a lifetime? We carefully reviewed the biographies of our top position-holders to see how many authoritative positions—president, director, trustee, and so on—were ever held by these people. Their record of leadership turned out to be truly impressive. The average corporate leader held 10.5 positions in a lifetime; the average foundation trustee, 10.2; the average civic group leader, 11.4; the average governmental leader, 8.0 (see Table 6–3). Of course, these positions are not all in *top-ranked* institutions. But it is clear that top leaders occupy a number of institutional positions in their lifetime.

This impressive record of position-holding is found among leaders in all sectors of society. (The only exception is military leaders, whose experience is generally limited to the military itself.) Table 6–3 shows the average number of authoritative positions ever held by top leaders in each sector of society. Leaders in government have held somewhat fewer top positions in their lifetime than leaders in the corporate world, but nonetheless their record of leadership experience is impressive. However, governmental leaders tended to gain their experience in *governmental* or *public interest* positions—over 70 percent of governmental leaders had held previous governmental posts and had held posts in the public interest sector. Only about one quarter of top governmental elites had previously held any top positions in the corporate world.

The tradition of public service is very much alive among top institutional leaders in every sector. Both corporate and governmental elites reported one or more public appointments during their lifetime. Nearly 40 percent of corporate elites held at least one government post at some time during their careers.

As we might expect, corporate directorships are common among top leaders in industry, communications, utilities, and banking. It is common for these individuals to have held four or more directorships in a lifetime.

---

[15]However, for evidence that interlocking among all corporations remained fairly constant from 1935 to 1970, see Michael Patrick Allen, "The Structure of Interorganizational Elite Corporation: Interlocking Corporate Directorates," *American Sociological Review,* 39 (June 1974), 393–406.

TABLE 6–3 Institutional Experience of Top Leaders

	CORPORATE						PUBLIC INTEREST				GOVERNMENT		
	INDUSTRY	BANKING	UTILITIES	INSUR-ANCE	INVEST-MENT	MEDIA	LAW	FOUNDA-TION	EDUCA-TION	CIVIC	GOVERN-MENT	MILITARY	ALL
Average number of positions ever held:													
Total	10.5	6.6	10.9	9.1	4.6	7.1	7.9	10.2	7.9	11.4	8.0	1.0	9.3
Corporate	5.9	4.1	6.0	5.1	3.1	2.1	2.0	5.2	3.2	6.0	1.0	.0	5.2
Public interest	3.8	2.0	3.9	3.1	1.2	3.8	4.2	4.0	3.8	4.2	3.8	0.8	3.1
Governmental	.8	.5	1.0	.9	.3	1.2	1.7	1.0	.9	1.2	3.2	0.2	1.0
Percent having ever held positions in:													
Corporate	99.8	88.8	99.6	86.5	72.4	48.1	46.8	96.2	76.2	98.6	25.2	.0	80.2
Public interest	76.9	59.0	72.5	69.1	59.6	76.5	80.2	88.0	70.8	82.2	72.2	38.6	78.4
Governmental	39.2	24.8	40.6	38.0	19.2	40.2	56.5	45.1	42.5	58.6	76.6	14.5	42.3

In contrast, top government officials have *not* held many corporate directorships. Their experience in institutional positions is derived mainly from public service and government.

AT&T: EVIDENCE OF CONVERGENCE

Our aggregate data indicate that a majority of the people at the top are specialists, that corporate and governmental elites are not closely locked, and that there appear to be multiple, differentiated structures of power in America. Earlier we suggested that many corporate, governmental, and public interest leaders were self-made managerial elites rather than inheritors who started at the top. All of these findings tend to undermine confidence in the hierarchical model, at least as it is represented in the traditional power elite literature.

Nonetheless, there are important concentrations of combined corporate, governmental, and social power in America. The best evidence of concentration is found in interlocking directorates of major corporations. Figure 6–1 is our own diagram of the interlocking of AT&T directors with industrial corporations, banks, and insurance companies in 1984.

It might be possible to greatly expand Figure 6–1 and observe all of the corporate interlocks of corporations that interlock with AT&T. We might observe "indirect" interlocking of AT&T with any corporation that has an interlocking board member with any of the corporations in Figure 6–1. An indirect interlock does not mean that a director serves on two boards (this is a direct interlock); it means instead that a director of one corporation and a director of another both belong to the board of a third corporation. For example, AT&T and IBM are competitors in satellite communications. The AT&T and IBM boards are *not* interlocked. However, an AT&T director and an IBM director may meet on the board of an oil company. Is this evidence of collusion? Probably not. It requires "a touch of paranoia" to believe that indirect interlocks can create a concentration of power that would threaten the corporate structure.

The pattern of interlocking directorates with AT&T is illustrative of relationships and interests in the boardrooms of major corporations. AT&T, like many other giant corporations, has direct contacts with a wide variety of industrial corporations—oil, autos, steel, retail stores, foods, clothing, publishing, and so on—as well as banks and insurance companies.

The forcible break-up of AT&T, previously the world's largest corporation, significantly reduced concentration of resources in corporate America. In order to end a seven-year antitrust suit brought by the U.S. Department of Justice, AT&T agreed to divest itself of twenty-two telephone-operating companies, comprising over two thirds of its total

AT&T AND ITS FRIENDS

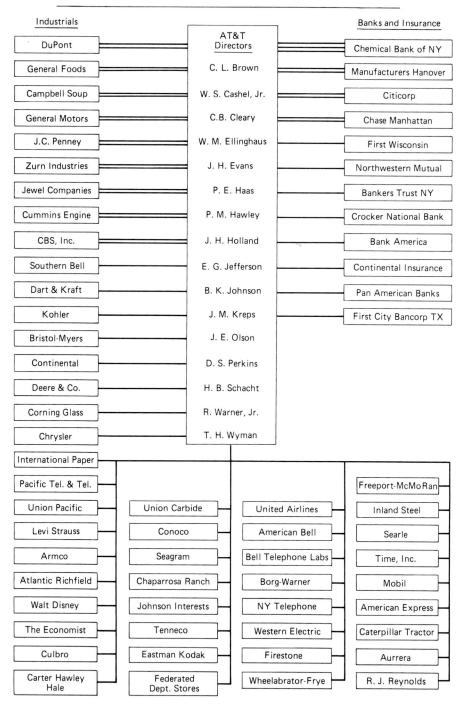

FIGURE 6–1 AT&T and Its Friends. Each line represents an interlocking directorship with AT&T in 1984. A double or triple line represents two or three interlocks with AT&T. Board members for 1984 are listed.

corporate assets. While it is true that AT&T itself remains the nation's largest utility company, and the seven new telephone holding companies created out of AT&T themselves are utility giants (see Table 2–2), nonetheless, this government-imposed action reduces the power of AT&T directors and creates new multiple centers of power in the new regional companies. In brief, the AT&T break-up contributes to polyarchy in corporate America.

THE ROCKEFELLERS: END OF A DYNASTY?

Historically the greatest concentration of power in America centered on the Rockefeller empire—a network of industrial, financial, political, civic, and cultural institutions, under the control of the Rockefeller family. Until recently this empire was actively directed by David Rockefeller. But David Rockefeller retired as chairman of the board of the core financial institution of the Rockefeller empire, Chase Manhattan Bank, in 1981. He gradually relinquished direct control over New York's Rockefeller Center and various Rockefeller investment holding companies, including Rockefeller Group Inc. and the Rockefeller Brothers Fund. Earlier he had set the Rockefeller Foundation on an independent course. Finally, in 1985 he gave up his chairmanship of the Council on Foreign Relations. No other member of the Rockefeller family, numbering nearly 100 today, has stepped forward to hold the empire together. Nonetheless, the Rockefeller empire, as it evolved over the last century, remains our best illustration of convergence of power in America.

The Rockefeller family fortune was founded by John D. Rockefeller, originator of the Standard Oil Company. With his partners, H.M. Flagler and S.V. Harkness, Rockefeller created the company that controlled 90 percent of the nation's oil production by the 1880s. A series of antitrust cases, culminating in the Supreme Court in *U.S.* v. *Standard Oil* (1911), resulted in the forced dissolution of the company into several separate corporations: Exxon, formerly Standard Oil of New Jersey (the nation's number-two-ranked industrial corporation); Mobil (ranked number 5); Chevron (ranked number 8); Atlantic Richfield (ranked number 14); and other large oil companies.[16] The Rockefeller family continues to hold large blocks of stock in each of these companies. But gradually the center of Rockefeller power shifted to banking and finance.

The core financial institution of the Rockefeller family was Chase Manhattan Bank, which David Rockefeller supervised for nearly thirty years. However, the family was also interested in Citicorp, which was headed for many years by James Stillman Rockefeller, a cousin of David's.

---

[16]See Table 2–1 for rankings.

The Rockefeller financial influence in corporate decision-making was felt in several ways: by giving or withholding loans to corporations, by placing representatives on corporate boards of directors, and by owning or controlling blocks of common stock of corporations. Chase Manhattan directors (there are 25 of them) were interlocked with more than 100 major industrial corporations, banks, utilities, and insurance companies. These included giants such as Exxon, AT&T, ITT, Metropolitan Life, Equitable Life, and United States Steel. In addition, Chase Manhattan owned or held in trust over 5 percent of the corporate stock of many other large companies, including Eastern Airlines, Pan American World Airways, Boeing, TWA, Mobil Oil, and CBS. The rules of the Securities and Exchange Commission presume that 5 percent of a corporation's stock can give the holder dominant influence in the corporation.

The Rockefeller interest in foreign affairs was particularly strong. The oil companies, which were the industrial core of Rockefeller holdings, required constant attention to foreign sources of supply. In addition, Chase Manhattan was deeply involved in overseas banking and investment activities. The Rockefellers supplied many of the top foreign affairs personnel for the nation, including Secretaries of State John Foster Dulles, Dean Rusk, and Henry Kissinger. Dulles, secretary of state under President Eisenhower, was a senior partner in the Wall Street law firm of Sullivan & Cromwell, whose principal client for many years was the Standard Oil Company (Exxon). Dulles was also chairman of the trustees of the Rockefeller Foundation. Dean Rusk, secretary of state under Presidents Kennedy and Johnson, served seven years as president of the Rockefeller Foundation. John J. McCloy, a Chase Manhattan director, served as U.S. high commissioner for Germany during the postwar occupation; in 1962, he was chairman of the Coordinating Committee on the Cuban Missile Crisis. Henry Kissinger was personal adviser on foreign policy to Nelson Rockefeller before becoming national security adviser and later secretary of state under President Richard Nixon. Cyrus Vance, secretary of state under President Carter, was a Wall Street lawyer and a director of the Rockefeller Foundation, as well as of Pan American World Airlines, Aetna Life Insurance, and IBM. Zbigniew Brzezinski, President Carter's national security adviser, was director of the Trilateral Commission—David Rockefeller's influential group of top leaders from industrialized nations of the world. David Rockefeller himself served as chairman of the influential Council on Foreign Relations, which has been responsible for many of the nation's most important foreign policy initiatives (see the section "The Policy-Planning Establishment" in Chapter 9).

For many decades, the single most powerful private citizen in America was David Rockefeller—"the only man for whom the presidency of the United States would be a step down." David Rockefeller is the youngest of five sons of John D. Rockefeller, Jr., himself the only son of the founder of the Rockefeller empire, John D. Rockefeller. Despite the seniority of his brothers,[17] it was recognized that David was the serious and scholarly one. It was to David that the family wisely entrusted its wealth.

David was raised with his brothers at the Rockefellers' 3,500-acre Pocantico Hills estate, east of Tarrytown, New York. He attended nearby Lincoln School. As a child, he traveled about to Rockefeller holdings—the Seal Harbor, Maine retreat, the Virgin Islands estate, the Venezuela ranch, the Grand Teton Mountains ranch—and collected beetles as a hobby. It soon became clear to David's father and grandfather that Nelson, Lawrence, and Winthrop were more interested in politics and pleasure than hard work, and that John D. III was content to pursue cultural interests. The elder Rockefellers wanted a businessman to care for the family fortune, and they were successful in motivating David in this direction.

David's undergraduate career at Harvard was undistinguished. But later he spent a year at the Harvard Graduate School of Business and a year at the London School of Economics. He married Margaret "Peggy" McGrath, whose father was a senior partner in the esteemed Wall Street law firm of Cadwalader, Wickersham & Taft. He enrolled at the Rockefeller-funded University of Chicago and *earned* a Ph.D. in economics in 1940. He returned to New York for a short stint in public service as an unpaid assistant to Mayor Fiorello La Guardia. In 1942 he enlisted in the Army as a private, went through Officers Training School, and served in North Africa and Europe as an intelligence officer. He was fluent in French, Spanish, and German.

After the war he began his banking career in his uncle Winthrop W. Aldrich's bank, the Chase Manhattan. His first post was assistant manager of the foreign department; three years later he became vice-president and director of the bank's business in Latin America. When his uncle became ambassador to England in 1952, David became successively executive vice-president, vice-chairman of the board, and finally, president and chairman of the board.

Of course, David Rockefeller was active in civic and cultural affairs. He was chairman of the Museum of Modern Art, president of the Board of Overseas Study of Harvard University, a trustee of the Carnegie Endowment for International Peace, a trustee of the University of Chicago, a trustee of the John F. Kennedy Library, and so forth.

Above all, David Rockefeller was an internationalist. His active intervention in American foreign policy produced remarkable results. He was personally involved in Nixon's arrangement of détente with the USSR, the

[17]John D. III (deceased), former chairman of the Rockefeller Foundation and the Lincoln Center for the Performing Arts; Nelson A. (deceased), former Vice-President of the United States and four-term governor of New York; Lawrence S., family dilettante in "venture capitalism" and "conservationist"; and Winthrop (deceased), former governor of Arkansas and cattle rancher.

Strategic Arms Limitations Talks (SALT), and the "normalization" of U.S. relations with the mainland People's Republic of China. He was chairman of the board of the Council on Foreign Relations, and he formed the Trilateral Commission in 1972. Through the CFR, Rockefeller was instrumental in most of the nation's important foreign policy initiatives of recent years: from the Paris Peace Agreement ending the Vietnam War, through "détente" with the Soviet Union and the international "human rights" campaign, to new concerns over U.S.–Soviet relations in the 1980s. David Rockefeller was personally involved in the decision to permit the Shah of Iran to come to the United States for medical treatment, the decision not to hand over the dying Shah to ransom the U.S. hostages, and the financial agreement that finally secured the release of the hostages.

Under David Rockefeller's direction, Chase Manhattan developed a reputation in the business world for "social responsibility," which included the active recruitment and promotion of blacks, women, and other minorities; the granting of a large number of loans to minority-owned business enterprises; and active involvement in a variety of social projects. Indeed, this may be one reason why Chase Manhattan fell as the nation's leading bank. Another reason for Chase's performance may be that David Rockefeller was so deeply involved in national and international affairs that he did not devote full attention to banking matters.

David Rockefeller exercised great power but always with *modesty,* of course, as one would expect of a man who has no reason to try to impress anyone. Indeed, he consistently understated his own power:

> I feel uncomfortable when you ask how I exert power. We accomplish things through cooperative action, which is quite different than exerting power in some mysterious and presumably evil way. I have no power in the sense that I can call anybody in the government and tell them what to do. Because of my position, I'm more apt to get through on the telephone than somebody else, but what happens to what I suggest depends on whether they feel this makes sense in terms of what they are already doing.[18]

Of course, what Rockefeller was really saying is that when David Rockefeller called, people answered their phone; when he asked them to serve on a committee, they were flattered to be asked; when he suggested that they do something, they did it.

Yet it may be that all great family dynasties eventually splinter and disperse. Despite the best efforts of the founders, the passage of time and the multiplication of family inheritors, together with an erosion of the entrepreneurial spirit in generations born to great wealth, gradually dissolve family concentrations of wealth and power.[19]

---

[18]"Beyond Wealth, What?" *Forbes,* May 15, 1972, pp. 250–52.

[19]For argument to the contrary, see Michael Patrick Allen, *The Founding Fortunes* (New York: Dutton, 1988).

POLYARCHY: INTERLOCKING CORPORATE GROUPS

The Rockefeller story is suggestive of concentration of industrial, financial, governmental, and social power. Yet there is also considerable evidence of polyarchy—multiple, differentiated groupings of corporate power. This evidence can be gleaned from close observation of the network of interlocking directorates in corporate America. Recent advances in the application of statistical methods allow us to observe some interesting groupings of corporate interlocks.[20] These groupings suggest the existence of a series of corporate groupings—industries, banks, utilities, and insurance companies—centered around distinct *geographic* areas.

Ten major interlocking groupings observed in the 1970s are in Table 6–4. These groupings, described by sociologist Michael Patrick Allen,[21] indicate the most heavily interlocked groupings, the location of each corporation, the total number of interlocks each corporation maintains with other corporations, and the number of interlocks it maintains with corporations within its own grouping.

There is an obvious tendency for corporations to maintain interlocks with other corporations in the same geographic area, even though many New York–based corporations occur across the board. Five interlocking groups involve corporations based primarily in Chicago, Pittsburgh, Los Angeles, Philadelphia, and Detroit. Four others are based primarily in New York. This finding, generally supportive of the polyarchical model of corporate power, suggests that geography rather than financial or family interests plays a major role in creating concentrations of corporate power.

However, another way of identifying the interlocking corporate groups in Table 6–4 would be by the major banks which provide the largest number of interlocking directors within each group. The banks which appear to lead corporate groupings include Citicorp, Chase Manhattan, Mellon, Morgan Guaranty, Chemical New York, Continental Illinois, Western Bancorp, and the National Bank of Detroit.

Thus, the systematic analysis of corporate interlocking suggests (1) multiple concentrations of financial and industrial power, (2) based in part upon geographic proximity, and (3) dominated by large commercial banks.

SUMMARY

The question of hierarchy versus polyarchy in America's elite structure is a familiar one in the literature on power. The elitist literature describes a

---

[20] A variation of factor analysis applied to sociometric data permits the extraction of a matrix of relationships based on interlocking among corporations. The matrix systematically identifies relatively independent and cohesive cliques. See Duncan MacRae, Jr., "Direct Factor Analysis of Sociometric Data," *Sociometry*, 23 (1960), 360–71; also Philip M. Lankforth, "Comparative Analysis of Clique Identification Methods," *Sociometry*, 37 (1974), 287–305.

[21] Michael Patrick Allen, "Economic Interest Groups and the Corporate Elite Structure," *Social Science Quarterly*, 58 (March 1978), 597–615.

TABLE 6-4   Ten Principal Interlock Groups

GN	CORPORATION	LOCATION	TI	GI
1	Chemical New York	New York	47	12
	New York Life	New York	32	8
	Consolidated Edison	New York	22	11
	Southern Pacific	San Francisco	24	4
	Equitable Life Assurance	New York	41	6
	Borden	New York	12	5
2	Continental Illinois	Chicago	29	15
	International Harvester	Chicago	22	11
	Commonwealth Edison	Chicago	12	10
	First Chicago Corp.	Chicago	25	11
	Sears Roebuck	Chicago	18	5
	Standard Oil (Indiana)	Chicago	11	6
	Inland Steel	Chicago	10	6
	Illinois Central, Inc.	Chicago	18	5
	Borg-Warner	Chicago	10	5
3	Mellon National Bank	Pittsburgh	30	14
	Gulf Oil	Pittsburgh	11	10
	Aluminum Co. of America	Pittsburgh	10	6
	Pittsburgh Plate Glass, Inc.	Pittsburgh	7	6
	Westinghouse Electric	Pittsburgh	19	4
4	Morgan Guaranty Bank	New York	38	11
	General Electric	New York	26	7
	General Motors	Detroit	27	5
	Continental Oil	New York	20	4
	Scott Paper	Philadelphia	12	4
	U.S. Steel	New York	27	3
	Procter & Gamble	Cincinnati	18	4
5	Citicorp	New York	51	11
	Monsanto	St. Louis	13	6
	National Cash Register	Cleveland	17	5
	Westinghouse Electric	Pittsburgh	19	3
	Kimberly-Clark	Milwaukee	7	5
	Pan American World Airways	New York	22	4
	AT&T	New York	33	2
6	Republic Steel	Cleveland	21	13
	Avco	Greenwich	13	10
	Metropolitan Life	New York	39	7
	Standard Oil (Ohio)	Cleveland	9	4
	Chemical New York	New York	47	7
	International Business Machines	Armonk	25	7
	Illinois Central, Inc.	Chicago	18	6
	Olin	Stamford	9	6
7	Chase Manhattan	New York	37	9
	General Foods	New York	20	5
	Metropolitan Life	New York	39	5
	International Paper	New York	15	5
	AT&T	New York	33	4
8	Western Bancorporation	Los Angeles	19	6
	Southern California Edison	Los Angeles	11	9

TABLE 6–4   Ten Principal Interlock Groups (Continued)

GN	CORPORATION	LOCATION	TI	GI
	Union Oil of California	Los Angeles	18	6
	BankAmerica	San Francisco	17	5
	North American Rockwell	Los Angeles	13	6
	Security Pacific National Bank	Los Angeles	13	5
	Getty Oil	Los Angeles	14	5
9	Pennsylvania Mutual	Philadelphia	21	12
	First Pennsylvania	Philadelphia	11	7
	Girard	Philadelphia	8	6
	Philadelphia Electric	Philadelphia	10	8
	Philadelphia National Bank	Philadelphia	7	5
	Atlantic Richfield	New York	15	4
10	National Bank of Detroit	Detroit	21	10
	Burroughs	Detroit	8	6
	Detroit Edison	Detroit	10	4
	National Steel	Detroit	10	4
	Bendix	Detroit	7	4
	S.S. Kresge	Detroit	7	4

Legend GN = Group Number
       TI = Total Interlocks
       GI = Group Interlocks

Source: Michael Patrick Allen, "Economic Interest Groups and the Corporate Elite Structure," *Social Science Quarterly,* 58 (March 1978), 608–9.

convergence of power at the top, with a single group of leaders recruited primarily from industry and finance, exercising power in many different sectors of society. The pluralist literature describes many separate structures of power in different sectors of society with little or no overlap in authority and many separate channels of recruitment.

Our findings do not all fit neatly into either the elitist or the pluralist leadership model. The fact that roughly 7,000 persons in 6,000 positions exercise formal authority over institutions that control over half of the nation's resources is itself an indication of a great concentration of power. But despite institutional concentration of authority, there is considerable specialization among these leaders. Eighty-five percent of them hold only one "top" position. Only 15 percent are interlockers—holders of two or more top positions. However, because of these interlockers, about 30 percent of all top positions were found interlocked with another top position. Moreover, the top multiple interlockers (those people with six or more top positions) turned out to be impressive figures in America, lending support to the notion of an inner group of national leaders.

There is very little concurrent interlocking among people at the top of the governmental and military sectors of society. To the extent that high government officials are interlocked at all, it is with civic and cultural and educational institutions. It is *within* the corporate sector that interlocking is most prevalent. If there is a "coming together" of corporate, governmental, and military elites as C. Wright Mills contends, it does not appear to be by means of interlocking directorates.

The notion of hierarchy is strengthened, however, if we examine the record of leadership experience of top institutional elites *over a lifetime*. Most top leaders have held more than one top position in their career. Governmental leaders, however, have generally gained their leadership experience in governmental positions or in the law; only one quarter of top governmental leaders have ever held high positions in the corporate world.

These aggregate figures suggest specialization rather than convergence at the top of the nation's institutional structure. However, we agree that there are special cases of concentrated corporate, governmental, and social power. AT&T, for example, is linked through its board of directors to a wide variety of manufacturing companies, as well as to banks and insurance companies. A few years ago, the Rockefeller family, through its dominance of Chase Manhattan Bank and its family holdings in many large corporations, utilities, and insurance companies; together with its activities in cultural organizations, universities, foundations, and civic associations; represented a very important concentration of power. Nonetheless, there is also evidence of polyarchy in identifiable groupings of corporations with extensive interlocking directorates. These groupings each appear to be geographically defined yet dominated by large banks.

CHAPTER 7
ELITE RECRUITMENT: GETTING TO THE TOP

A RULING CLASS OR AN OPEN LEADERSHIP SYSTEM?

Are there opportunities to rise to the top of the institutional structure of America for individuals from all classes, races, religions, and ethnic groups, through multiple career paths in different sectors of society? Or are opportunities for entry into top circles limited to white, Anglo-Saxon Protestant, upper- and upper-middle-class individuals whose careers are based primarily in industry and finance?

Social scientists have studied data on the social backgrounds of corporate and governmental leaders for many years. But there is still disagreement on the interpretation of the data. A "ruling class" school of thought stresses the fact that elites in America are drawn disproportionately from among wealthy, educated, prestigiously employed, socially prominent, "WASP" groups in society. These ruling-class social scientists are impressed with the fact that leadership in industry, finance, government, education, the law, the mass media, and other institutional sectors is recruited primarily from society's upper social classes. Many of the elite have been educated at a few esteemed private prep schools and gone to Ivy League colleges and universities. They have joined the same private clubs, and their families have intermarried. Moreover, a disproportionate share of the top leadership in all sectors of society has made its career mark in industry and finance. Ruling-class social scientists infer that these similarities contribute to cohesion and consensus among the institutional leaders in America.

By contrast, pluralists describe an open leadership system that enables a significant number of individuals from the middle and lower classes to rise to the top. High social background, or wealth, or WASPishness *itself* does not provide access to top leadership positions. Instead, top institutional posts go to individuals who possess outstanding skills of leadership, information, and knowledge, and the ability to organize and communicate. Admittedly, opportunities to acquire such qualities for top leadership are unequally distributed among classes. But lower-class origin, the pluralists believe, is not an insurmountable barrier to high position.

Classical elitist writers such as Mosca acknowledge that some "circulation of elites" is essential for the stability of a political system. The opportunity for the brightest among the lower classes to rise to the top siphons off potentially revolutionary leadership, and the elite system is actually strengthened when talented and ambitious individuals enter top positions. The fact that only a minority of top leaders are drawn from the lower classes is not really important. It is the availability of a modicum of opportunity that encourages talented people to believe they can rise to the top and strengthens support for the system throughout all social classes.

Defenders of the pluralist theory also argue that social background, educational experience, and social group membership are poor predictors of decision-making behavior. Members of the social elite often hold very different views about policy questions, differences that can be attributed to a variety of factors, all of which are more influential than social background. Among these are the nature of the top position occupied; the individual's perception of his or her own role; the institutional constraints placed upon the individual; systems of public accountability; interest-group pressures; public opinion; and so forth. Thus, pluralists argue that the class homogeneity among top leaders that is reported in many social background studies is meaningless, since the class background–decision-making behavior linkage is weak.

In contrast, the evidence of social class influence on behavior is truly impressive.[1] Social scientists have shown that social background affects whether or not you shoplift[2] or use LSD.[3] It has an important

[1] The following evidence was compiled from the numerous sources cited by psychologist Richard L. Zweigenhart, "Who Represents America?" *The Insurgent Socialist,* 5, no. 3 (1975), p. 119.

[2] George Won and George Yamamoto, "Social Structure and Deviant Behavior: A Study of Shoplifting," *Sociology and Social Research,* 53, no. 1 (1968), 44–45.

[3] Reginald G. Smart and Dianne Fejer, "Illicit LSD Users: Their Social Backgrounds,

influence on whom you date and marry,[4] how happy your marriage is likely to be,[5] how you vote,[6] how many children you have,[7] and how you go about raising them.[8] It largely determines your values,[9] how happy you are,[10] and how long you're likely to live.[11] It can even influence how large you think the circumference of a quarter is![12] In our opinion, it would be most unlikely that social class membership could affect all these varied attitudes and behaviors and *not* affect decision-making behavior.

The recruitment of some non-upper-class individuals to elite positions may be essential to society, because these individuals bring new and different perspectives to societal problems. Sociologist Suzanne Keller speaks of "two irreconcilable tendencies in social life—the need for order and the need for change":

> If the social leadership becomes so conservative as to be immune to new ideas and social developments, the pressure for unfulfilled needs mounts until that leadership declines, resigns, or is violently displaced. If it is so receptive to the new as to neglect established traditions, social continuity is endangered.[13]

Thus, we would expect to find some recruitment of non-upper-class individuals to elite positions even in an essentially hierarchical society.

Drug Use and Psychopathology," *Journal of Health and Social Behavior*, 10, no. 4 (1969), 297–308.

[4]A.B. Hollingshead, *Elmtown's Youth: The Impact of Social Classes on Adolescents* (New York: John Wiley, 1949).

[5]William J. Goode, "Marital Satisfaction and Instability: A Cross-Cultural Class Analysis of Divorce Rates," *International Social Science Journal*, 14, no. 3 (1962), 507–26.

[6]P.F. Lazarsfeld, B. Berelson, and H. Caudit, *The People's Choice* (New York: Columbia University Press, 1948). Also G. J. Selznick and Stephen Steinberg, "Social Class, Ideology, and Voting Preferences: An Analysis of the 1964 Presidential Election," in *Structural Social Inequality: A Reader in Comparative Social Stratification*, ed. Celia S. Heller (New York: Macmillan, 1969).

[7]Dennis H. Wrong, "Trends in Class Fertility in Western Nations," *The Canadian Journal of Economics and Political Science*, 24, no. 2 (May 1958), 216–29.

[8]R.R. Scars, E. MacCoby, and H. Levin, *Patterns of Child Rearing* (New York: Harper & Row, 1957).

[9]Herbert H. Hyman, "The Value Systems of Different Classes: A Social Psychological Contribution to the Analysis of Stratification," in *Readings on Social Stratification*, ed. Melvin M. Tumin (Englewood Cliffs, N.J.: Prentice-Hall, 1970), pp. 186–203.

[10]Alex Inkeles, "Class and Happiness," in Tumin, *Readings on Social Stratification*, pp., 180–86.

[11]I.M. Moriyama and L. Guralnick, "Occupational and Social Class Differences in Mortality," in Tumin, *Readings on Social Stratification* pp. 170–78.

[12]J.S. Bruner and L. Postman, "Symbolic Value as an Organizing Factor in Perception," *Journal of Social Psychology*, 27 (1948), 203–8.

[13]Suzanne Keller, *Beyond the Ruling Class: Strategic Elites in Modern Society* (New York: Random House, 1968), p. 172.

The question remains, *how much* opportunity exists in America for middle- and lower-class individuals to climb to the top?

GETTING AHEAD IN THE SYSTEM

The American ideal is not a classless society, but rather a society in which individuals are free to get ahead on the basis of merit, talent, hard work, and good luck. Upward mobility is valued very highly in American culture. The nation is portrayed in its own literature as a "land of opportunity" where individuals can better themselves if they work at it.

And, indeed, there is a great deal of upward social mobility in

TABLE 7–1   Social Mobility in America

YEAR AND FATHER'S OCCUPATION	SON'S CURRENT OCCUPATION						FATHER'S PERCENTAGE TOTALS
	UPPER WHITE COLLAR	LOWER WHITE COLLAR	UPPER MANUAL	LOWER MANUAL	FARM	TOTAL	
1962							
Upper white collar	53.8	17.6	12.5	14.8	1.3	100.0	16.5
Lower white collar	45.6	20.0	14.4	18.3	1.7	100.0	7.6
Upper manual	28.1	13.4	27.8	29.5	1.2	100.0	19.0
Lower manual	20.3	12.3	21.6	43.8	2.0	100.0	27.5
Farm	15.6	7.0	19.2	36.1	22.2	100.0	29.4
Son's percentage totals	27.8	12.4	20.0	32.1	7.7	100.0	100.0
1973							
Upper white collar	52.0	16.0	13.8	17.1	1.1	100.0	18.2
Lower white collar	42.3	19.7	15.3	21.9	0.8	100.0	9.0
Upper manual	29.4	13.0	27.4	29.0	1.1	100.0	20.5
Lower manual	22.5	12.0	23.7	40.8	1.0	100.0	29.7
Farm	17.5	7.8	22.7	37.2	14.8	100.0	22.6
Son's percentage totals	29.9	12.7	21.7	31.5	4.1	100.0	100.0

Mobility from father's (or other family head's) occupation to current occupation: U.S. men in the experienced civilian labor force aged 20 to 64 in 1962 and 1973. Figures in percentages.

The basic source of information is from David Featherman and Robert Hauser, *Opportunity and Change* (New York: Academic Press, 1978). Data are from March 1962 and March 1973 current population surveys and occupational changes in a generation survey. Occupation groups are upper white collar: professional and kindred workers and managers, officials and proprietors, except farm; lower white collar: sales, clerical and kindred workers; upper manual: craftspeople, forepersons and kindred workers; lower manual: operatives and kindred workers, service workers, and laborers, except farm; farm: farmers and farm managers, farm laborers, and forepersons.

America. The results of a typical study of social mobility are shown in Table 7–1. A majority of the sons of upper-white-collar fathers (53.8 percent in 1962 and 52 percent in 1973) are themselves in upper-white-collar occupations. This means that slightly less than half of these sons have descended to less prestigious occupations than their fathers. At the other end of the scale, only about 40 percent of the sons of lower manual workers (43.8 percent in 1962 and 40.8 percent in 1973) end up in the same manual occupations as their fathers. This means that nearly 60 percent of these sons have risen to more prestigious occupations than their fathers. There is more upward mobility than downward mobility in the American system, a pattern that can be attributed to economic growth.

SOCIAL CHARACTERISTICS OF INSTITUTIONAL LEADERS

What do we know about the people who occupy *top* institutional positions in American society? There are a number of excellent studies of the social backgrounds of political decision-makers,[14] federal government executives,[15] military officers,[16] and corporate executives.[17] These studies consistently show that top institutional leaders are *atypical* of the American public. They are recruited from the well-educated, prestigiously employed, older, affluent, urban, white, Anglo-Saxon, upper- and upper-middle-class male populations of the nation. We had expected our top institutional elites to conform to the pattern, and we were not at all disappointed (see Table 7–2).

AGE. The average age of all the corporate leaders identified in our study is sixty. Leaders in foundations, law, education, and civic and cultural organizations are slightly older—average age sixty-two. Top positions in the governmental sector are filled by slightly younger people—average age fifty-six. This means that America's elites in the 1980s were born in the 1920s and grew up during the Great Depression. World War II was an important event in their early careers; over half of our elites report military service.

SEX. The feminine sector of the population is seriously underrepresented at the top of America's institutional structure. Male dominance

---

[14]Donald R. Matthews, *The Social Background of Political Decision-Makers* (New York: Doubleday, 1954).

[15]David T. Stanley, Dean E. Mann, and Jameson W. Doig, *Men Who Govern* (Washington: Brookings Institution, 1967).

[16]Morris Janowitz, *The Professional Soldier* (New York: Free Press, 1960).

[17]Lloyd Warner and James C. Abegglen, *Big Business Leaders in America* (New York: Harper & Row, 1955).

TABLE 7–2 Social Characteristics of Top Leaders

	CORPORATE							PUBLIC INTEREST			GOVERNMENT		
	INDUSTRY	BANKING	UTILITIES	INSUR-ANCE	INVEST-MENT	MEDIA	LAW	FOUNDA-TION	EDUCA-TION	CIVIC	GOVERN-MENT	MILITARY	ALL
Average age	61	61	61	62	58	61	64	62	62	60	56	56	60
Female %	2.4	2.3	4.3	1.1	0.9	6.8	1.8	14.7	10.6	9.0	7.7	0	4.3
Education													
Non-College %	3.0	5.8	7.6	5.0	0.9	18.4	0	5.1	4.3	3.6	8.8	4.7	5.7
College %	42.7	43.0	40.6	42.7	51.3	39.2	100.0	24.9	32.8	37.0	10.7	30.2	37.4
Law %	22.6	22.2	25.1	22.6	8.8	20.9	100.0	26.9	28.1	24.8	41.0	9.3	25.8
Advanced %	29.8	29.0	26.7	29.8	39.0	21.6	5.3	43.1	34.7	34.7	33.5	55.8	31.1
Schools													
Public %	25.3	28.5	28.3	25.3	21.2	28.5	8.4	13.7	15.5	21.4	37.9	23.3	24.9
Private %	18.2	20.7	18.8	18.2	17.7	13.9	8.4	19.8	10.2	17.9	17.2	7.0	16.9
Prestigious* %	54.9	49.5	51.0	54.9	61.1	51.9	83.2	66.5	73.7	59.7	41.9	20.9†	56.1

*Harvard, Yale, Chicago, Stanford, Columbia, M.I.T., Cornell, Northwestern, Princeton, Johns Hopkins, Pennsylvania, and Dartmouth

†U.S. Military Academy (West Point) and U.S. Naval Academy (Annapolis) account for an additional 48.8 percent.

in top positions is nearly complete in the corporate world. But even in government, women hold less than 10 percent of the key posts. Only in cultural affairs, education, and foundations are women found in significant numbers among the top position-holders.

ETHNICITY.   WASPs are preeminent in America's institutional structure. Our own data do not include ethnic identification, but the work of sociologists Richard D. Alba and Gwen Moore confirm the disproportionate representation of WASPs in high positions in business and government. Their studies revealed that WASPs (who made up only 22.9 percent of all persons born before 1932) made up 57.3 percent of top business leaders and 53.4 percent of Congress. ("Other Protestants" increase these figures to 79.4 percent for business and 72.4 percent for Congress.) However, ethnics have made some inroads: 37 percent of union leaders are Irish Catholics, and 25.8 percent of mass media leaders are Jews. A WASP background, they conclude, is an "incremental advantage" in achieving elite status.[18]

EDUCATION.   Nearly all our top leaders are college-educated, and more than half hold advanced degrees. Some 25.8 percent hold law degrees, and 31.1 percent hold advanced academic or professional degrees. (These are earned degrees only; there are a host of honorary degrees that were not counted.) Governmental leaders are somewhat more likely to hold advanced degrees than corporate leaders. What is even more impressive is the fact that 54 percent of the corporate leaders and 42 percent of the governmental leaders are graduates of twelve heavily endowed, prestigious "name" private universities—Harvard, Yale, Chicago, Stanford, Columbia, M.I.T., Cornell, Northwestern, Princeton, Johns Hopkins, Pennsylvania, and Dartmouth. Elites in America are notably Ivy League.[19]

URBAN.   Most of our top leaders were urban dwellers. Governmental leaders (notably members of Congress) are somewhat more likely to be drawn from rural areas than are leaders in business, finance, and law, but less than one third of the key government posts in our study were found to be filled by individuals from rural areas.

PREPPY.   Elites are notably "preppy." At least 10 percent of the corporate leaders and 6 percent of the governmental leaders attended

---

[18]Richard D. Alba and Gwen Moore, "Ethnicity in the American Elite," *American Sociological Review*, 47 (June 1982).

[19]Our figures are confirmed in a separate study of over 55,000 top executives by Standard & Poor's Corporation, showing that half received degrees from these twelve universities. See *Chronicle of Higher Education*, September 29, 1980, p. 1.

one of only 33 prestigious private prep schools before entering college.[20] (Actually, the proportion of "preppies" among top leaders may be double these figures—up to 20 percent for corporate leaders and 10 percent for government leaders. The reason for suggesting these higher figures is that less than half of known preppies reported their prep school affiliation to *Who's Who in America*.[21] Thus, their prep school backgrounds would be overlooked in our biographical search.) It is astonishing to realize that these proportions of top leaders went to only thirty-three prep schools, since these schools educate an infinitesimal proportion of the nation's population. As *The Official Preppy Handbook* explains: "There are preparatory schools and then there are Prep Schools, those institutions that bless you with a certain luster along with your diploma."[22]

Among the Eastern Establishment, the phrase "old school ties" refers to prep schools, not to colleges or universities. It is considered more prestigious to have attended Groton, Hotchkiss, Phillips Exeter, Loomis, Phillips at Andover, or Choate, than to have attended Harvard, Yale, Princeton, or Columbia. Most of the prestigious prep schools are in the northeast, although Woodberry Forest is in Virginia, Cate is in California, and St. Mark's is in Texas.

These social background characteristics suggest a slight tendency for corporate elites to be more "upper class" in origin than government elites. Among governmental leaders there are slightly fewer Ivy Leaguers. Moreover, there is a slight tendency for governmental leaders to have had more advanced professional education.

CLASS: A TOUCHY SUBJECT

All known societies have some system of ranking individuals along a superiority-inferiority scale. Yet in America, the ideological assertion "All men are created equal" is so pervasive that people are reluctant to even acknowledge the existence of social classes. Most Americans describe themselves as "middle class"; nearly nine out of ten will choose "middle class" when they are asked in surveys to choose between this term and

[20]Andover, Buckley, Cate, Catlin, Choate, Cranbrook, Country Day, Deerfield, Episcopal, Exeter, Gilman, Groton, Hill, Hotchkiss, Kingswood, Kent, Lakeside, Lawrenceville, Lincoln, Loomis, Middlesex, Milton, St. Andrew's, St. Christopher's, St. George's, St. Mark's, St. Paul's, Shattuck, Taft, Thatcher, Webb, Westminster, Woodberry Forest. Listing courtesy of G. William Domhoff.

[21]Unpublished reports by Michael Useem and G. William Domhoff, November 1980.

[22]Lisa Birnbach, ed., *The Official Preppy Handbook* (New York: Workman, 1980), p. 50.

either upper class or lower class.[23] Sociologists use measures of occupation, income, and education to assess class position and to study social classes. But members of America's upper classes avoid using the term "class" altogether. In her *Women of the Upper Class,* sociologist Susan A. Ostrander reports that her interviewees preferred describing themselves as "being from an old family," "established," or "respected in the community."

> I hate [the term] upper class. Its so non-upper class to use it. I just call it "all of us," those of us who are well-born.

> I hate to use the word "class." We're responsible, fortunate people, old families, the people who have something.[24]

According to writer Paul Fussell, a tendency to get very anxious about discussions of social class—"It's the dirtiest thing I ever heard of"— reveals a middle-class outlook toward social classes.[25] Upper-class members will discuss class in subtle terms; lower-class members will discuss class in terms of humor and derision ("snobs," "fat cats," "fancy pants"). The middle class prefers to avoid the topic altogether. Fussell also contends that people reveal their own class by the way they define class: The lower classes believe class is defined by the amount of money a person has; the middle class grant that money has something to do with it, but think that education and occupation are more important; the upper class thinks that taste, values, style, and behavior define class, regardless of money or education or occupation.

The ambiguities about class in America make it difficult to assess the role of class in elite composition. We must avoid the circularity of saying "the power elite is the upper class" and then defining the upper class as "the power elite." We have already defined our elite as individuals who occupy the top positions in the institutional structure of society. Certainly these people are granted high status and accorded great deference by virtue of the institutional positions they occupy. But their institutional status cannot itself be synonymous with upper social class; upper social class must have some independent meaning if it is to have any meaning at all.

[23]Robert W. Hodge and Donald J. Treiman, "Class Identification in the United States," *American Journal of Sociology,* 73 (March 1968), 535–47.

[24]Susan A. Ostrander, "Upper-Class Women," in *Power Structure Research,* ed. G. William Domhoff (Beverly Hills, Calif.: Sage, 1980), pp. 78–79; see also Ostrander, *Women of the Upper Class* (Philadelphia: Temple University Press, 1984).

[25]Paul Fussell, *Class: A Guide Through the American Status System* (New York: Summit Books, 1983).

One of the few class analysts to recognize this distinction between class and power is sociologist G. William Domhoff:

> The upper class as a whole does not rule. Instead class rule is manifested through the activities of a wide variety of organizations and institutions. . . . Leaders within the upper class join with high-level employees in the organizations they control to make up what will be called the *power elite*. This power elite is the leadership group of the upper class as a whole, but it is not the same thing as the upper class. It is the members of the power elite who take part in the processes that maintain the class structure.[26]

To demonstrate upper-class "dominance" of the elite, Domhoff employs several upper-class "indicators": (1) listing in the *Social Register,* (2) attendance at a private prestigious preparatory school, or (3) membership in a private prestigious club. But Domhoff fails to acknowledge that listing in the *Social Register* and membership in a prestigious club usually come to an individual *after* he or she has attained high institutional position. In other words, one may attain these indicators of upper social class as a result of climbing the institutional ladder from a middle-class background. We certainly cannot contend that the upper class "dominates" the elite, if it turns out that elite membership is what determined upper-class status.

The only way to avoid circularity in studying the class composition of an elite group is to focus on social *origins.* Are top institutional positions largely limited to the sons and daughters of upper-class families?

Our own estimate is that approximately *30 percent* of our total institutional elite are upper class in social origin. This estimate derives from a sample of our elite for whom we endeavored to learn their parents' class circumstances. We attributed *upper-class social origin* on the basis of the following: (1) attendance at a private prestigious preparatory school; (2) parent is an officer or a director of a major corporation, bank, insurance company, or utility; (3) parent is a high government official or general in the military; (4) parent is an attorney in a top law firm, a newspaper owner or director, or a university president or trustee of a university, foundation, or major civic or cultural association.

Certainly individuals with upper-class family origins are disproportionately represented in institutional leadership positions. (Far less than 1 percent of the general population would meet our definition of upper-class origin.) But we cannot conclude that the upper class "dominates" on the basis of our estimate of 30 percent upper-class origins. On

[26]G. William Domhoff, *Who Rules America Now?* (Englewood Cliffs, N.J.: Prentice-Hall, 1983), p. 2.

the contrary, 70 per cent of our institutional elite appeared to be middle class in family origin; their parents were able to send them to college, but there is no indication that their parents ever achieved high institutional position.

BLACKS AT THE TOP

There are very few blacks in positions of power in America. We are able to identify only 20 blacks in 7,314 positions of authority in top-ranked institutions. It is possible, of course, that some may have escaped identification in our biographical search.

Blacks are noticeably absent from top positions in the corporate world. In 1979 only 3 of 1,700 senior executives of Fortune "1000" companies were black. A 1985 follow-up study found only 4 blacks, 6 Asians, and 3 Hispanics among 1362 senior executives.[27] Corporations say that the main reason that blacks are not found in top management positions is that they did not enter the corporate ranks until the late 1960s, and it takes anyone, white or black, over twenty years to rise to the top. However, many blacks feel that discrimination continues to play a major role in obstructing black progress up the corporate ladder. White corporate executives feel more comfortable in dealing with other whites, and they do not aggressively recruit blacks into management. The Equal Employment Opportunity Commission, and other federal agencies assigned to investigate job discrimination, focus their attention on entry-level cases rather than on very subtle discrimination in the ranks of top corporate management. Instead of assigning promising black executives to key operating posts, many corporations tend to move them to positions overseeing personnel or affirmative action programs. This removes blacks from the "fast track" in corporate promotions.

Edward W. Jones Jr., a black business consultant and former AT&T executive, argues that "colorism"—"a predisposition to act in a certain manner because of a person's skin color"—is the major obstacle to black advancement to top corporate positions. He distinguishes "colorism" from "racism", which he defines as overt bigotry and hatred. "All people possess stereotypes, which act like shorthand to avoid mental overload. . . . a decision about a promotion is a subjective thing. For blacks, colorism adds an extra layer of subjectivity."[28]

Illustrative of blacks who have gained positions at the top of the corporate structure are:

[27]See Edward W. Jones Jr., "Black Managers: The Dream Deferred," *Harvard Business Review* (May–June, 1986), 84–93.

[28]*Ibid.*, p. 88

William T. Coleman. Former secretary of transportation under President Gerald Ford. Senior partner, O'Melveny & Myers, Washington. Attended the University of Pennsylvania and Harvard Law School. Chairman of the board of the NAACP Legal Defense and Education Fund. A director of IBM, Chase Manhattan, Pepsico, American Can, Pan American World Airways; Philadelphia Electric. A director of the Brookings Institution, a member of the Council on Foreign Relations and the Trilateral Commission, and a trustee of Harvard University.

Andrew F. Brimmer. Independent financial consultant. A director of BankAmerica, International Harvester, United Airlines, and Du Pont. A graduate of the University of Washington with a Ph.D. (economics) from Harvard. He taught at the Wharton School of the University of Pennsylvania and moved on to be assistant secretary of commerce and later a member of the Federal Reserve Board. He now heads Brimmer and Company, an independent financial and managerial consulting firm. He is a member of the Council on Foreign Relations and the Trilateral Commission, and he is a trustee of Atlanta University, Tuskegee Institute, the Urban League, and the Ford Foundation.

Vernon E. Jordon, Jr. Executive director of the National Urban League. A graduate of DePauw University and Howard University Law School. He began his career in civil rights affairs as the Georgia field secretary of the NAACP in the early 1960s, and later became director of the Vote Education Project of the Southern Regional Council, leading black voter registration drives in the south. He served briefly as executive director of the United Negro College Fund before becoming head of the National Urban League in 1972. In recent years he has accepted directorships of Bankers Trust of New York, Celanese Corporation, J. C. Penney Co., and the Xerox Corporation. He is also a trustee of the Rockefeller Foundation and the Brookings Institution.

Franklin A. Thomas. President of the Ford Foundation. Former president of the Bedford Stuyvesant Restoration Corporation in New York. He received his B.A. and law degree from Columbia University, and served as deputy police commissioner under New York's Mayor John Lindsay. He is a director of Citicorp, Columbia Broadcasting System, New York Telephone, Cummins Engine, and New York Life Insurance. He is also a director of the Carnegie Corporation, Lincoln Center for the Performing Arts, and the Urban Institute.

Clifton R. Wharton, Jr. Former chancellor of the State University of New York. Educated at the private prestigious Boston Latin School and later Harvard and Johns Hopkins; he received his Ph.D. (economics) from the University of Chicago. Former president of Michigan State University. A director of Ford Motors, Burroughs Corp., Equitable Life. A director and later chairman of the board of the Rockefeller Foundation. A director of the Carnegie Corporation and the Council on Foreign Relations.

No blacks have ever been *president* of a major industrial corporation, bank, utility, insurance company, investment firm, or communication network. Black leadership has been confined to a small number of board members.

One black served in the Ford Cabinet (Secretary of Transportation William T. Coleman, see above). One black served in the Carter Cabinet:

> ***Patricia Roberts Harris***. Former secretary of health, education, and welfare. The daughter of a railroad dining-car waiter and a graduate of Howard University (B.A., 1945). Received a law degree from George Washington University in 1960. She began her career as a YWCA director in Chicago and later as executive director of Delta Sigma Theta, a national black sorority. She was a delegate to the Democratic National Convention in 1964, and seconded the nomination of Lyndon Johnson; President Johnson appointed her ambassador to Luxembourg (1965–67). She returned to a brief, troubled tenure as dean of Howard University Law School and resigned during student protests. She became a law partner of Sargent Shriver (Kennedy brother-in-law) and a prominent Washington attorney. She was appointed a director of IBM, Chase Manhattan, and Scott Paper Co. She is a member of the Council on Foreign Relations and the NAACP Legal Defense Fund.

President Reagan's Cabinet included one black:

> ***Samuel R. Pierce***. Secretary of housing and urban development. Pierce was a senior partner in the New York law firm of Fowler, Jaffin, Pierce & Kneel and a governor of the American Stock Exchange. Pierce received his law degree from Cornell in 1949 and began his long career as an assistant district attorney in New York. He was named an assistant U.S. attorney under President Eisenhower and later assistant to the undersecretary of labor. He was a Ford Foundation fellow at Yale for a year, and a New York City judge. Under Nixon, he was general counsel for the U.S. Department of the Treasury (1970–73). He has served as trustee for NAACP fund-raising and for the Rand Corporation, Cornell University, Mt. Holyoke College, and the Hampton Institute. He was a director of General Electric, Prudential Insurance, First National Boston Corp., International Paper, and U.S. Industries.

The Bush Cabinet includes:

> ***Dr. Louis W. Sullivan***. Secretary of health and human services. A graduate of Morehouse College and Boston University Medical School, Sullivan took his residency at Cornell Medical Center in New York, and then Massachusetts General Hospital. He served in a number of teaching and research positions at Harvard's Thorndike Labs, and Harvard and Boston University Medical Schools. In 1978 he was named the first dean and founding director of the Morehouse School of Medicine; Barbara Bush serves as a trustee of the school.

In government today the most powerful black leader is U.S. Representative William H. Gray III. Gray is now Majority Whip, the third-ranking House Democrat; he served four years as chairman of the House Budget Committee. Gray began his career as a minister, graduating from Franklin and Marshall College in Pennsylvania and earning theological degrees at Drew University and Princeton University. He began his preaching at the large Bright Hope Baptist Church in Philadelphia, which had been founded by his grandfather and led for many years by his father. (Gray's father had received his Ph.D. from the University of Pennsylvania and had also served as president of several black universities.) Gray took over the family church in 1972 when his father died. Gray's congressional district had long been represented by a black, Robert N.C. Nix. In 1976, Gray sought to unseat the elderly Nix; he lost by a slim margin but overwhelmed the older man two years later. Gray regularly wins the Democractic primary by 75 percent or more of the vote and is frequently unopposed in the general election. Gray is reported to be very effective in behind-the-scenes congressional maneuvering; he has a liberal voting record plus the support of key moderate Democracts.

JESSE JACKSON: CHASING RAINBOWS

JESSE: From charity to parity—our time has come. From aid to trade, from welfare to our share, from slaveship to championship—our time has come. From outhouse to White House—our time has come.

CHORUS: Run, Jesse, Run!

Jesse Jackson, so gifted in rhyme and alliteration, inspired millions of black voters in 1984 and 1988. Jackson was not the first black to run for President. (That distinction belongs to Representative Shirley Chisholm of New York, who ran for the Democratic nomination in 1972.) But Jackson demonstrated conclusively that a black man could be a serious contender for the presidency. His vision was a Rainbow Coalition of "the desperate, the damned, the disinherited, the disrespected, and the despised."

Jackson was born and raised in the segregated South. His mother, "Miss Helen," married Charles Jackson when Jesse was a small boy, and Jackson adopted him. Jesse attended the all-black school of Greenville, South Carolina, where he excelled in sports. He played quarterback on the state championship team and won a football scholarship to the University of Illinois. But Jackson's first experiences far from home on a predominantly white campus were unhappy ones. He learned that a black had no real chance of playing quarterback at the University of Illinois in the early 1960s. So he returned to the South, to black North Carolina A&T University in Greensboro. He played four years as quarterback at A&T and was student body president as well. More importantly, Jackson led the North Carolina A&T students in a successful campaign of marches and sit-ins to desegregate downtown Greensboro. Jackson became one of the nation's youngest recognized civil rights leaders.

Like many black leaders before him, Jackson chose the ministry as a vocation. But while completing his divinity studies at Chicago Theological Seminary, he was chosen by Martin Luther King, Jr. to lead the Southern Christian Leadership Conference's "Operation Breadbasket" in Chicago. This activity was part of King's effort in the late 1960s to bring the civil rights movement north to the urban ghettoes and to spotlight the economic problems confronting blacks. Jackson was in Memphis with King on the day he was assassinated in 1968.

Jackson transformed the SCLC Operation Breadbasket in Chicago into his own independent organization—Operation PUSH (People United to Save Humanity). Jackson preached the values of hard work, dedication, and self-confidence to ghetto youth: "I am somebody!" PUSH also threatened boycotts against large corporations whose employment policies were not in its judgment sufficiently "affirmative." Jackson negotiated "trade agreements" with Coca-Cola, Heublein, and Burger King to hire and promote more blacks.

But Jackson's role within the nation's black leadership was frequently controversial. Southern black leaders originally questioned Jackson's decision to make PUSH independent of the Southern Christian Leadership Conference. Many charged that PUSH was more self-promotion by the mercurial Jackson than economic promotion for Chicago blacks. Jackson frequently displayed a disrespect bordering on arrogance toward older, more established black leaders and organizations. When Harold Washington was campaigning to become Chicago's first black mayor, he found it necessary to banish the publicity-seeking Jackson from the campaign, although later Jackson would claim credit for Washington's election. When Jackson announced his candidacy for President in 1984, his critics said what he really wanted was to be president of black America.

Yet in two presidential elections Jackson captured the aspirations for power and self-determination of millions of blacks from the rural South to the Northern urban ghettoes. He pushed himself into national black leadership, stepping over the more experienced black politicans— Andrew Young of Atlanta, Tom Bradley of Los Angeles, Wilson Goode of Philadelphia. But these leaders were eventually swept along by the feelings of racial pride that Jackson's campaign unleashed.

Jackson's politics were *not* the coalition politics of established black leaders. He alienated Jews and white civil libertarians with his embrace of Yasser Arafat and the Palestinian terrorists; and his inadvertent reference to Jews as "hymies" during the campaign did not help him, even though he publicly apologized for the slip. The Black Muslim Louis Farrakhan and his paramilitary bodyguards provided "security" for Jackson throughout the campaign. His proposals to dismantle the U.S. military and his closeness to Fidel Castro placed him to the political left of most black leaders.

In 1984 Jackson won 18.2 percent of all of the votes cast in Democratic presidential primary elections held that year. In 1988 he expanded his political base: He won 29.3 percent of all the votes in Democratic primaries, and he finished second to the Democratic nominee, Michael Dukakis.

The Jackson campaigns turned out millions of new black voters. He had very little money to spend and no real organization. But with his gifted oratory and his flair for the dramatic, he commanded free televison news coverage nearly every day. He accomplished at least three objectives: increasing black voter registration, heightening black political awareness and skills, and making the Democractic party more responsive to black concerns. The passion and pride he stirred among black masses were real. Jesse Jackson became America's preeminant black political leader.

WOMEN AT THE TOP

The nation's institutional elite are predominately male. Less than 5 percent of top institutional leaders—presidents, directors, and trustees of the nation's largest industrial corporations, banks, utilities, insurance companies, television networks and newspaper chains, foundations, universities, civic and cultural organizations; full partners in the nation's leading law firms and investment houses; and top elected and appointed federal government officials—are women. Out of the 7,314 top institutional positions in 12 separate sectors of society, only 318 (or 4.3 percent) were occupied by women in 1980. As low as this proportion of female leadership may be, it represents more than double the proportion of women (1.9 percent) found in top institutional positions in 1970.

Most corporate boardrooms continue to resemble all-male clubs. In 1980, only 32 of the 100 largest *industrial corporations* had even one female member; the other 68 industrials remained exclusively male-directed. The nation's two largest industrial corporations, Exxon and General Motors, had women on their boards of directors: Martha Peterson was an Exxon director, and General Motors had two female directors, Anne L. Armstrong and Catherine B. Cleary. However, overall, in 1980 only 36 women occupied top industry positions out of 1,499 positions identified in the 100 largest industrial corporations (see Table 2–1). This means that women occupied only 2.4 percent of the top industrial leadership posts. No woman served as a president or chief executive officer of any of the 100 largest industrial corporations. Nonetheless, these figures are an improvement over the 3 women who served as directors of the 100 largest industrial corporations in 1970, an infinitesimal 0.2 percent of the industrial leadership of America.

Women have also improved their leadership position in *banking*. In 1980, twenty-one of the nation's fifty largest banks had at least one female director, including BankAmerica and Citicorp, the nation's two largest financial institutions. Yet women held only 2.3 percent of the total number of big bank directorships. One major bank, First Wisconsin Corporation, had a female president—Catherine B. Cleary. Again, these figures represent an improvement over the *two* women (0.2 percent) who served on the boards of directors of major banks in 1970.

The nation's largest *utilities* and *communication* corporations appear to have moved a little faster and further in recruiting women to top institutional positions than have industry, banking, or insurance. AT&T, the nation's largest corporation of any kind, appointed banker Catherine B. Cleary to its board of directors in the early 1970s. In 1980 a total of twenty-nine (or 4.3 percent) of the directors of this sector were women; there were *no* women identified as directors in this sector in 1970.

Only eight of the fifty largest *insurance* companies had a woman on their board of directors. Only nine women (or 1.1 percent) could be identified among the insurance company presidents and directors. However, the three largest companies—Prudential, Metropolitan, and Equitable—had women among their directors.

Large numbers of women are currently entering the *legal profession*. However, few women have yet managed to penetrate the inner circles of the nation's largest and most prestigious New York and Washington law firms. These firms generally have forty or fifty or more full partners, but in 1980 only 1.8 percent were women. Seventeen of the twenty-five top firms had at least one women partner. Washington's two top firms, Arnold & Porter, and Covington & Burling, led the way with three female partners each. It is important to note that there has been only a very modest increase in women as partners in top firms between 1970 and 1980. Indeed, the corporate sector has admitted more women to their boardrooms than the top law firms have admitted to full partnerships.

Women are still difficult to find on Wall Street. The nation's largest *investment* and *security* dealers do not include women as officers or directors, nor do they appear to be moving in that direction. In 1980, there were only five women (0.9 percent) among the full partners in the nation's top investment firms.

Women have been more successful in the *mass media* than in law, investments, industry, utilities, banking, or insurance. In 1980, women held 6.8 percent of the officer and director posts in the seventeen leading media corporations. For nearly twenty years, Katherine Graham, owner of the *Washington Post* and *Newsweek* magazine empire had served as chairman of the board of the Washington Post Company. Three women served on the board of directors of the New York Times Co.; all of them were "outside" directors. Each of the three television broadcasting networks has one woman on its board.

The nation's leading private *universities* have begun to appoint more women to their governing boards of trustees. In 1980, over 10 percent of the governing trustees of the nation's leading private universities were women, an increase over the 2 percent found in 1970. Six of Harvard's thirty-one trustees are women. All of the leading universities had at least one woman trustee.

Women are frequently encountered on the governing boards of trustees of leading *foundations*. Among the nation's fifty largest foundations, thirty had at least one woman trustee in 1980. The Ford and Rockefeller foundations each had three women trustees, and the Carnegie Corporation had six women trustees on its sixteen-member board. Some women, of course, have long served as foundation trustees because of their family associations: Mary Ethel Pew, Pew Memorial Trust; Doris Duke, Duke Endowment; Harriet Bush Melin, Bush Foundation; Mary Moody Northern, Moody Foundation; Josephine Hartford Bryce, Hartford Foundation; Mary Ann Mott Meynet, Mott Foundation; Ida Calloway, Calloway Foundation; Drue M. Heinz, Heinz Endowment.

Women are frequently encountered as trustees of *cultural organizations*. The influential *civic associations* may have one or two women trustees; for example, the Council on Foreign Relations and the Brookings Institution each had two women trustees in 1980. But the nation's leading cultural institutions appoint significant numbers of women to their governing boards. The John F. Kennedy Center for the Performing Arts had ten women on its twenty-five member board of trustees in 1980. Unlike most of the women in the corporate world who list themselves by their own name, many women in cultural organizations list themselves by their husband's name (for example, Mrs. Howard H. Baker, Jr.; Mrs. Edward Finch Cox; Mrs. Jean Kennedy Smith; Mrs. Bob Hope; Mrs. Vincent Astor; Mrs. Henry J. Heinz II). Overall, about 9 percent of the trustees of the leading cultural and civic associations are women.

Women have made greater inroads in *government* than in the corporate world. Women attained more *top* leadership positions in the Reagan administration than in any previous presidential administration. Three women served in Cabinet-level positions under President Reagan: *Margaret Heckler* (secretary of health and human services. Catholic College, Boston College law degree. Fourteen years a Republican congresswoman from Massachusetts); *Elizabeth Hanford Dole* (secretary of transportation. Duke University and Harvard Law School. Commissioner, Federal Trade Commission; later assistant to President Reagan); *Jeanne Kirkpatrick* (U.N. ambassador. Barnard College, Columbia University Ph.D. political science. Georgetown University professor).

The Bush Cabinet includes two women, both of whom are Washington "insiders" who have served in previous Cabinet posts. *Elizabeth Dole* resigned as Reagan's secretary of transportation in 1988 in order to assist her husband's presidential campaign. The political rivalry between George Bush and Robert Dole became very intense during the primary campaign, and both men exchanged bitter personal barbs. Following his election, George Bush endeavored to heal the breach with the Senate Republican leader; his success in persuading Elizabeth Dole to join his Cabinet was widely viewed as an important step in rebuilding Republican political unity. Bush also persuaded *Carla Anderson Hills* to accept a Cabinet-level post as U.S. trade representative. She had formerly served as secretary of housing and urban development in the Ford administration. She was a prominent Washington lawyer and a director of IBM, Corning Glass, American Airlines, Chevron, and the Signal Corporation. She was a member of the Council on Foreign Relations and the Trilateral Commission; she was once a trustee of the Brookings Institution, but later became an advisor to the American Enterprise Institute. She was also chairman of the board of trustees of the Urban Institute. She earned her bachelors at Stanford and her law degree at Yale.

Overall, only about 8 percent of the top positions in the federal government are filled by women, a figure that has remained the same over the last several presidential administrations.

The few women at the top deserve closer observation. This list of top women leaders includes:

Katherine Graham. Chairman of the board of the Washington Post Company. (See "Katherine Graham: The Most Powerful Woman in America" in Chapter 4).

Patricia Roberts Harris. Former secretary of health, education and welfare. (See "Blacks at the Top" in this chapter.)

Catherine B. Cleary. President and director of First Wisconsin Corporation. Earned a bachelors degree from the University of Chicago and a law degree from the University of Wisconsin. She served as assistant treasurer of the United States in the Eisenhower administration. She is a director of General Motors, AT&T, Kraft, and Northwestern Mutual Life Insurance.

Martha E. Peterson. Former president of Barnard College, and president of Beloit College. Has B.A., M.A., and Ph.D. degrees from the University of Kansas. A director of Exxon, Metropolitan Life Insurance, First Wisconsin Corporation, United Banks of lllinois, and R.H. Macy & Co. A trustee of the University of Notre Dame and Chatham College, and a member of the Committee on Economic Development.

Marina VonNeumann Whitman. Chief economist for General Motors Corporation and a director of Manufacturers Hanover Trust, Westinghouse Electric, and Procter & Gamble. Earned a bachelors degree from Radcliffe and a Ph.D. from Columbia. A director of the Council on Foreign Relations, and a member of the Trilateral Commission.

Anne L. Armstrong. A director of General Motors, Braniff International, First City Bankcorp. of Texas, General Foods, Halliburton Company, and Boise Cascade. Has a bachelor's degree from Vassar College. Former cochairperson of the Republican National Committee and former U.S. ambassador to Great Britain. A member of the Council on Foreign Relations. A trustee of the Smithsonian Institution and Southern Methodist University.

Jane Cahill Pfeiffer. Former chairman of the board of the Na tional Broadcasting Company. A director of International Paper Com pany, J.C. Penney Company, Chesebrough-Ponds Inc., and the Bach investments group. A member of the Council on Foreign Relations Earned a bachelors degree from the University of Maryland. Forme vice-president of IBM. A trustee of the University of Notre Dame Catholic University, and the Rockefeller Foundation.

Jewel Stradford Lafontant. Partner in Lafontant, Wilkins & Butler (Chicago law firm). Former solicitor general of the United States. Has a bachelors degree from Oberlin College and a law degree from the University of Chicago. A director of Trans World Airlines, Continental Bank, Bendix Corporation, and Equitable Life Assurance.

SOCIAL CHARACTERISTICS OF WOMEN LEADERS

Women leaders, like their male counterparts, are disproportionately upper class in social origin. More than half of the nation's women leaders attended *prestigious* private colleges. About one-quarter of them attended one of the "Seven Sisters": Vassar, Radcliffe, Smith, Wellesley, Barnard, Bryn Mawr, or Mt. Holyoke. Another one-quarter attended one of the traditional prestigious private universities: Harvard, Yale,

Chicago, Stanford, Columbia, Cornell, Northwestern, Princeton, Johns Hopkins, or Pennsylvania.

The educational level of top women leaders is very high; nearly half possess earned masters or doctorate degrees, and an additional quarter possess law degrees. (Honorary degrees were not counted.) Thus, a total of 71 percent of the women leaders earned advanced degrees; the comparable figure for male leaders is 55.8 percent. This strongly suggests that women need more education than men to compete effectively for top posts. (Only one woman in our entire group failed to indicate that she held a bachelors degree. Marian Sulzberger Heiskell, the daughter of the owner of the *New York Times*, and a director of the New York Times Co., Consolidated Edison, Ford Motors, and Merck & Co., does not list an earned degree in her biography.)

The average age of top women leaders was fifty-four in 1980. This is younger than the average age of men in comparable positions, which was sixty-one. We suspect that this difference is largely a product of the recent appointment of many of the women leaders to their positions. Newer members of an elite can be expected to be younger than established members.

An examination of the career backgrounds of women leaders reveals a number of separate recruitment paths. Table 7–3 includes the principal lifetime occupational activity of women at the top of each sector of society.

In the corporate world—industrials, banks, utilities, insurance companies, and investment firms—a surprising percentage of women are recruited to boards of directors from *universities*. Only 19 percent of female corporate directors were recruited from the corporate world itself; over 40 percent were recruited from universities. (This is *not* the pattern of recruitment of male corporate directors, most of whom [89 percent] are recruited from corporations, and few of whom [0.6 percent] come from universities.) This leads to the suspicion that many corporations deliberately reached out to universities in the 1970s to find talented women to join their boards. The corporations, in brief, raided the universities.

In contrast, women leaders in government tend to be recruited through government itself (58.8 percent). Only 17.6 percent of female governmental leaders are recruited from the corporate world. Likewise, top female lawyers are recruited through law firms, and top female leaders in the mass media are recruited from news organizations. The career backgrounds of civic, cultural, foundation, and educational leaders are balanced between various sectors of society. The largest single source of female leadership in these institutions is the academic world, supplying approximately one-third of the trustees of the largest and most influential institutions.

TABLE 7–3 Social Characteristics of Women in Top Institutional Positions

	TOTAL	CORPO-RATE	GOVERN-MENT	LAW, NEWS	CIVIC, CULTURAL, EDUCATION
Average age	54	55	49	55	54
Career					
Corporate %	15.9	19.0	17.6	-0-	4.3
Government %	19.6	8.5	58.8	9.1	17.4
Law %	13.1	11.9	5.9	18.2	21.7
News %	15.0	14.2	5.9	54.5	13.0
Education %	29.9	40.5	11.8	18.2	34.8
Other %	6.5	4.8	-0-	-0-	8.7
Education					
Advanced degree %	46.7	47.6	47.0	18.2	52.2
Law degree %	24.3	23.8	23.5	18.2	34.8
Bachelor's degree %	28.0	28.6	29.4	54.5	13.0
No degree %	0.8	-0-	-0-	9.1	-0-
Schools					
Women's prestigious %	34.0	26.2	17.6	60.0	47.8
Prestigious %	26.4	28.6	17.6	20.0	39.1
Private %	9.4	7.1	29.4	-0-	4.3
Public %	30.2	38.1	35.3	30.0	8.7
Married %	76.2	69.2	70.6	100.0	87.0
Children, % with	61.0	57.7	52.9	90.9	61.0

We were able to identify only three black women out of our total of 318 top female leaders in 1980. One, of course, was Patricia Roberts Harris, former secretary of health and human services; another was former congresswoman Barbara C. Jordan, who sat on the board of Texas Commerce Bancshares; and the third was Margaret Bush Wilson, a civil rights lawyer who sat on the board of Monsanto, the Committee on Economic Development, the American Red Cross, and Washington University.

Finally, it is interesting to observe that three-quarters of the nation's top women leaders were married and over 60 percent of them were mothers. Most of the women at the top today have combined marriage and family with careers that have taken them to the nation's highest institutional positions. Of course, these are extraordinary women. They compose less than 5 percent of the nation's top leadership. Most were born in the 1920s and 1930s and reached adulthood in a period of history when marriage and family were seemingly more central to American culture.

WHY WOMEN AREN'T GETTING TO THE TOP

Despite the impressive progress of women in leadership positions in the last decade, women still have not achieved the top rung—chairperson or chief executive officer. Only one woman, Katherine Graham of the Washington Post Company, chairs a major corporate institution in America. (Liz Claiborne, founder of the clothing company that bears her name, was the only other woman CEO in the top 1,000 corporations in 1987; Catherine B. Cleary of First Wisconsin Bank was the only female president of a large bank in 1980.) A *Fortune* survey asking executive recruiters to identify women who *might* become chief executive officers drew a complete blank; even the few companies with women in senior management positions conceded that these women were not going to win the top job.[29]

Serious explanations are not easy to develop. Blatant sexism—dirty jokes, references to "girls," or overt hostility toward women—is seldom encountered in high corporate and banking circles. The barriers women confront are very subtle and often not recognized by men. Women frequently fail to get "fast-track" assignments or especially sensitive posts. Yet these are the jobs that lead to the top. The reasons are difficult to pinpoint. One observer was quoted:

> At senior management levels competence is assumed. What you're looking for is someone who fits, someone who gets along, someone you trust. Now that's subtle stuff. How does a group of men feel that a woman is going to fit? I think it's very hard.[30]

A woman bank executive says, "The men just don't feel comfortable."

There are many other explanations and all of them are controversial: Men are reluctant to openly criticize a woman, and therefore women executives do not receive constructive feedback. Government affirmative-action efforts are directed primarily at entry-level positions rather than senior management posts. Women choose staff assignments rather than fast-track, operating-head assignments; they are cautious and unaggressive in corporate politics. Women have lower expectations about peak earnings and positions, and these expectations become self-fulfilling. Women bear children, and even during relatively short maternity absences they fall behind their male counterparts. Women are less likely to want to change locations than men, and immobile executives

---

[29]Susan Fraker, "Why Women Aren't Getting to the Top," *Fortune*, April 16, 1984, pp. 40–45.

[30]Ibid., p. 40.

are worth less to a corporation than mobile ones. Women executives in sensitive positions come under even more pressure than men in similar posts; women executives believe that they get much more scrutiny than men and must work harder to succeed.

Cross-national elite studies confirm these patterns of women in elite positions. Results of a systematic study of institutional elites in the United States, West Germany, and Australia by sociologist Gwen Moore indicate that: (a) few women have achieved elite positions in major national institutions; (b) women elites are concentrated in the political and the voluntary association sectors; (c) women elites have fewer inter-sectoral ties; (d) marriage and parenthood is less common among women elites than their male counterparts; (e) most women elites are recruited from very high-status social backgrounds; and (f) women elite participation, while still very low, has increased significantly over the last two decades.[31]

SANDRA DAY O'CONNOR: A CONSERVATIVE ON THE COURT

For nearly 200 years the U.S. Supreme Court was America's most exclusive male club. After 101 male justices, Sandra Day O'Connor was named to the Supreme Court by President Reagan in 1981. At the time of her appointment, O'Connor was a fifty-one-year-old state appellate court judge in Arizona. Justice O'Connor had no previous experience as a federal court judge, but she had the active support of Arizona's senior U.S. senator and Republican warhorse, Barry Goldwater. More importantly, she was a "she." Reagan was anxious to deflect attacks on his opposition to the Equal Rights Amendment and his failure to appoint many women in his own administration. As one Reagan aide put it: "This is worth twenty-five assistant secretaries, maybe more!" Feminist groups were forced to support the appointment, even though O'Connor's record in Arizona was moderately conservative.

Sandra Day grew up on her family's large Arizona ranch, graduated from Stanford with honors, and then went on to Stanford Law School. She finished near the top of her class, along with Chief Justice of the Supreme Court William Rehnquist (who was first in the class). She married John Jay O'Connor, a Phoenix attorney, and raised three sons. She entered Arizona politics about the time her youngest son entered school. She was appointed to the Arizona State Senate in 1969 and was later elected twice to that body. She rose to majority leader in

---

[31]Gwen Moore, "Women in Elite Positions," *Sociological Forum* Vol. 3 (December, 1988), 566–585.

1973. She left the Arizona legislature in 1975 to become a Phoenix trial judge. In 1979, she was appointed by a Democratic governor to the Arizona Court of Appeals. Work on this state intermediate court, however, does not involve major constitutional questions.

O'Connor had some business experience: She was formerly a director of the First National Bank of Arizona and Blue Cross/Blue Shield of Arizona. But until her appointment to the U.S. Supreme Court, she was an obscure state court judge. Her service as a Republican leader in the Arizona State Senate qualified her as a moderately conservative party loyalist. However, it appears that her professional and political friendships had more to do with bringing her to President Reagan's attention than her record as a jurist. She had known Justice William Rehnquist since her law school days. She had known former Chief Justice Warren Burger for a long time. And Barry Goldwater had been her mentor in Arizona Republican politics. When Reagan's political advisors told him during the presidential campaign that he was not doing well among women voters, the candidate responded by pledging to appoint a woman to the Supreme Court. Reagan's fulfillment of his campaign pledge was a politically popular decision.

In Supreme Court deliberations, Justice O'Connor has generally reflected the moderate conservatism of recent Republican appointees to the court. She frequently votes with Justices Rehnquist, Scalia, and White.[32] On gender questions she has taken an independent role.

MULTIPLE PATHS TO THE TOP

How do people at the top get there? Certainly, we cannot provide a complete picture of the recruitment process. But we can learn whether the top leadership in government is recruited from the corporate world, or whether there are separate and distinct channels of recruitment.

Biographical information on individuals occupying positions of authority in top institutions in each sector of society reveals that there are multiple recruitment paths to top institutional positions. Table 7–4 shows the principal lifetime occupational activity of individuals at the top of each sector of society. (This categorizing of people according to their lifework depends largely on their own designation of principal occupation in *Who's Who.*)

As we might expect, the corporate sector supplies most of the occupants of top positions in the corporate sector (82.3 percent). The corporate sector also supplies a majority of the top leadership in civic

[32]See Lawrence Baum, *The Supreme Court*, 3rd Ed. Washington: Congressional Quarterly Inc., 1989.

TABLE 7-4 Recruitment to Top Institutional Positions

SECTOR FROM WHICH TOP ELITES RECRUITED*	CORPORATE					PUBLIC INTEREST					GOVERNMENT		ALL
	INDUS-TRY	BANK-ING	UTILITIES	INSUR-ANCE	INVEST-MENT	MEDIA	LAW	FOUNDA-TIONS	EDUCA-TION	CIVIC	GOVERN-MENT	MILITARY	
Corporate %													
Industry	67.5	52.6	28.1	32.7	4.4	24.4	0	27.9	42.9	56.7	4.0	2.3	43.4
Banking	6.7	22.3	12.5	8.4	12.4	3.1	0	10.2	10.0	7.1	1.3	0	9.9
Utilities	3.8	7.6	36.2	6.7	0	1.2	0	3.0	6.1	4.8	0	0	7.3
Insurance	1.7	2.2	4.1	32.3	0	1.2	1.1	3.0	2.6	2.7	0	0	5.2
Investments	2.6	2.1	3.0	1.6	77.0	3.1	0	3.6	4.9	2.9	.4	0	4.6
Total	82.3	86.8	83.9	81.7	93.8	33.0	1.1	47.7	66.5	74.2	5.7	2.3	70.4
Public Interest %													
Media	.7	0.9	1.9	.9	.9	55.6	0	6.6	5.5	3.6	3.1	2.3	4.2
Law	7.7	6.3	6.3	5.3	1.8	5.6	96.8	9.6	11.6	5.5	61.5	7.0	9.4
Foundations	.6	0.3	.5	.9	0	0	0	6.6	1.8	1.1	.4	0	1.0
Education	7.7	4.0	6.5	9.5	1.8	4.4	2.1	23.4	12.0	8.2	10.1	7.0	8.2
Civic	.1	0.1	0	.2	0	0	0	2.0	.4	2.1	.4	0	0.5
Total	16.8	11.6	15.2	16.8	4.5	65.6	98.9	48.2	31.3	20.5	25.5	16.3	23.4
Governmental %													
Government	.6	1.2	.3	.4	1.8	1.2	0	4.1	2.2	5.3	15.7	9.3	5.1
Military	.1	0	.5	.9	0	0	0	0	0	0	3.1	72.1	1.1
Total	.7	1.2	.8	1.3	1.8	1.2	0	4.1	2.2	5.3	18.8	81.4	6.2

*Columns may not total 100.0 because of rounding.

and cultural organizations (74.2 percent), a majority of the trustees of private and renowned educational institutions (66.5 percent), and about half of the trustees of the major foundations (47.7 percent). However, the corporate world provides less than 10 percent of governmental elites.

Top leaders in government are recruited primarily from the legal profession (61.5 percent); some have based their careers in government itself (15.7 percent) or in education (10.1 percent). This finding is important. Government and law apparently provide independent channels of recruitment to high public office. Thus, high position in the corporate world is not a prerequisite to high public office.

The mass media provide another separate path to elite membership. A majority of presidents and directors of television networks, wire services, and the influential press have been associated throughout their lives with the mass media. Of course, the nation's top lawyers have spent most of their lives in the legal profession.

Educators supply only a small fraction of the top leadership of the nation. Of the top governmental leaders, only 10.1 percent were educators, and educators compose about 8 percent of the trustees of civic and cultural associations and about 23 percent of the trustees of foundations. Indeed, educators do not even supply a majority of the membership of university boards of trustees. Only 12 percent of our educational elites were drawn from the ranks of educators. Corporations only occasionally call upon educators to join corporate boards; less than 10 percent of corporate directors are educators.

LIFE AT THE TOP: COMPENSATION, TRAVEL, WORK

"All societies offer rewards to men assuming leadership positions," writes sociologist Suzanne Keller.

> Some rewards are tangible material benefits such as money, land, cattle, or slaves, while others are intangible such as social honor and influence. . . . Rewards play a two-fold role in the recruitment of elites: they motivate individuals to assume the responsibilities of elite positions; and they maintain the values of hierarchical social position.[33]

Institutional leaders receive compensation in many forms. Corporate executives usually receive a bonus based on company performance, in addition to their salary. Then there are stock options, low-interest loans, and deferred compensation paid out over future years to reduce the current tax bite. There are indirect forms of compensation too, the

[33]Keller, *Beyond the Ruling Class*, pp. 183–84.

so-called perquisites of office, or "perks," which may include personal aides and assistants, plush offices and equipment, paid club memberships, expense accounts, and the use of company cars and planes.

Top corporate salaries provide further evidence that most corporations are run by managers not stockholders. In recent years the average compensation—salaries plus bonuses—of CEOs of the nation's corporations have jumped to approximately $1 million per year. In 1988, *Business Week* reported that Walt Disney Company Chairman Michael D. Eisner received about $31 million; Jim P. Manzi, the 36-year-old chairman of Lotus Corp. (computer software) took home $26 million; and Chrysler Chairman Lee Iacocca settled for about $18 million.[34] These multimillion-dollar packages include the exercise of stock options, which allow executives to purchase company stock at lower-than-market price. These options provide still another incentive for executive performance and may be the most important contribution to long-term executive commitment to the company. "Golden parachutes" (compensation packages designed to protect top managers if they are ousted) are also becoming very common. These may provide severance pay of many millions of dollars to CEOs and lesser amounts to hundreds of other managers in the event of a corporate takeover.

The salaries of governmental leaders are considerably lower than those of corporate executives, although the perks are roughly equivalent. The President of the United States receives a salary of $350,000, plus additional funds for expenses, travel, and official entertainment. Expenses of the White House staff—which includes salaries, office expenses, and travel for special assistants, aides, and secretaries—run $10 million or more per year. The Vice-President receives $115,000 in salary plus expenses. All Cabinet members receive $99,500 in salary. The Chief Justice of the Supreme Court receives $115,000; the other Justices receive $110,000. Members of Congress—both senators and representatives—receive an annual salary of $89,500, but they are each supplied another $200,000 or more to hire staff assistants and run their offices. Committee chairpeople may spend over $2 million per year running their committees.

Life at the top is not all business (see Table 7–5). A survey of the nation's top corporate executives by *Fortune* magazine, which included responses from half of the presidents of the nation's 500 largest corporations, reports many interesting tidbits about life at the top of the corporate world:

> Over 60 percent of these corporate executives own or rent second "getaway" homes.

[34]*Business Week*, May 2, 1988, pp. 50–51.

TABLE 7–5 Superpower Dinner: The White House Guest List

Life at the top includes a full social calendar. Indeed, elites often complain about their manifold social duties and commitments. Seeing and being seen at prestigious social events is a time-consuming responsibility.

Who is invited to the White House to dine with the leadership of the Soviet Union? One of the most sought-after social invitations of recent years was the guest list at the White House state dinner for Mikhail and Raisa Gorbachev and other Russian leaders during the 1987 summit meeting. At no other single social occasion in the world has so much power been assembled in a single room.

The White House guest list for the Gorbachev dinner include not only the top political leadership of the Soviet Union and the United States but also many key corporate and banking elites. Protocol also requires a generous sprinkling of artists, athletes, and celebrities, to lighten the conversation.

WHITE HOUSE DINNER GUEST LIST, DECEMBER 8, 1987

The President and Mrs. Reagan

Mikhail S. Gorbachev, General Secretary of the Central Committee of the Communist Party of the Soviet Union, and his wife, Raisa

Eduard A. Shevardnadze, Soviet Minister of Foreign Affairs

Aleksandr N. Yakovlev, member of the Politburo and Secretary of the Central Committee

Anatoly F. Dobrynin, Secretary of the Central Committee

Vladimir M. Kamentsev, Deputy Prime Minister

Sergei F. Akhromeyev, First Deputy Defense Minister and chief of the General Staff

Anatoly Chernyayev, senior assistant to the General Secretary of the Central Committee

Valery Boldin, head of the General Department of the Central Committee

Nikolai Kruchina, chief administrator of the Central Committee

Aleksandr A. Bessmertnykh, Deputy Foreign Minister

Yuri V. Dubinin, Soviet Ambassador to the United States, and his wife, Liana

Georgi A. Arbatov, director of the U.S.A. and Canada Institute of the Soviet Academy of the Sciences

Dwayne O. Andreas, chairman, Archer-Daniels-Midland Company, and his wife, Inez

Pearl Bailey, singer, and her husband, Louis Bellson, musician

Howard H. Baker Jr., chief of staff to the President, and his daughter, Cissy Baker

James A. Baker 3d, Secretary of the Treasury, and his wife, Susan

Saul Bellow, author, and Janis Freedman

Kenneth Bialkin, lawyer, and his wife, Ann

Dr. James H. Billington, Librarian of Congress, and his wife, Marjorie

J. Carter Brown, Director, National Gallery of Art

Dave Brubeck, musician, and his wife, Iola

Zbigniew Brzezinski, counselor, Center for Strategic and International Studies, and his wife, Emilie

Vice President Bush

Ruth Bunche, widow of Dr. Ralph Bunche

Senator Robert C. Byrd, Democrat of West Virginia, and his wife, Erma

Secretary of Defense Frank C. Carlucci and his wife, Marcia

Representative Dick Cheney, Republican of Wyoming, and his wife, Lynne V. Cheney, chairman, National Endowment for the Humanities

Van Cliburn, concert pianist, and his mother, Rildia Bee Cliburn

Claudette Colbert, actress

Adm. William J. Crowe Jr., Chairman, Joint Chiefs of Staff, and his wife, Shirley

Joe DiMaggio, retired baseball player

(Continued)

TABLE 7–5   Superpower Dinner: The White House Guest List (Continued)

Senator Robert J. Dole, Republican of Kansas, and his wife, Elizabeth H. Dole, former Secretary of Transportation

Kenneth M. Duberstein, deputy chief of staff to the President, and his wife, Sydney

Chris Evert, tennis professional

Ted Graber, interior designer

The Rev. Billy Graham, evangelist, and his wife, Ruth

Dr. Armand Hammer, chairman, Occidental Petroleum Corporation, and his wife, Frances

Richard M. Helms, president, Safeer Company, and former Director of Central Intelligence, and his wife, Cynthia

John H. Johnson, president and publisher, Johnson Publishing company, and his wife, Eunice

Robert G. Kaiser, assistant managing editor for national news, The Washington Post, and his wife, Hannah

Max M. Kampelman, counselor, State Department

Dr. Jeane J. Kirkpatrick, senior fellow, American Enterprise Institute, and former delegate to the United Nations, and her husband, Dr. Evron M. Kirkpatrick, president, Heldref Publications

Henry A. Kissinger, chairman, Kissinger and Associates, and former Secretary of State

Meadowlark Lemon, Shooting Stars basketball team, and his wife, Lorelei

Susanne Massie, author and historian, Harvard Russian Research Center

Jack F. Matlock Jr., American Ambassador to the Soviet Union, and his wife, Rebecca

Zubin Mehta, conductor, New York Philharmonic, and his wife, Nancy

Representative Robert H. Michel, Republican of Illinois, and his wife, Corinne

Paul H. Nitze, Ambassador at Large

Richard N. Perle, resident scholar, American Enterprise Institute, and former Assistant Secretary of Defense, and his wife, Leslie

Donald E. Peterson, chairman, Ford Motor Company, and his wife, Jody

Gen. Colin L. Powell, assistant to the President for national security affairs, and his wife, Alma

Maureen E. Reagan and Dennis Revell, co-chairmen, Republican National Committee

Chief Justice William H. Rehnquist and his wife, Natalie

Mary Lou Retton, former Olympic gymnast

Rozanne L. Ridgway, Assistant Secretary of State for European and Canadian Affairs, and Capt. Theodore Deming, United States Coast Guard

James D. Robinson 3d, chairman, American Express Company, and his wife, Linda

David Rockefeller, chairman, International Advisory Committee, Chase Manhattan Bank, and his wife, Margaret

Selwa Roosevelt, Chief of Protocol, and her husband, Archibald B. Roosevelt Jr.

Mstislav Rostropovich, music director, National Symphony Orchestra, and his wife, Galina Vishnevskaya

Secretary of State George P. Shultz, and his wife, Helena

Dimitri K. Simes, Carnegie Endowment for International Peace, and his wife, Natasha

Hedrick Smith, correspondent, The New York Times, and his wife, Susan

Roger B. Smith, chairman, General Motors Corporation, and his wife, Barbara

Senator Ted Stevens, Republican of Alaska, and his wife, Catherine

James Stewart, actor, and his wife, Gloria

Robert S. Strauss, attorney, Akin, Gump, Strauss, Hauer & Feld, and his wife, Helen

Kathleen Sullivan, CBS News anchor, and Michael Kiner, architect and developer

Dr. Edward Teller, associate director emeritus, Lawrence Livermore National Laboratory

Vernon A. Walters, United States representative to the United Nations

TABLE 7–5 Superpower Dinner: The White House Guest List (Continued)

Caspar W. Weinberger, former Secretary of Defense, and his wife, Jane Charles Z. Wick, Director, United States Information Agency, and his wife, Mary Jane	George Will, columnist Representative Jim Wright, Democrat of Texas and House Speaker, and his wife, Betty

A surprisingly large number (48 percent) collect original works of art.

The most popular leisure activity is golfing (56 percent), followed by boating, hunting, tennis, and running. Few attend theaters, go to movies, or watch TV (other than the news).

A majority do not smoke, and contrary to popular impressions, most top executives live longer than the average American.[35]

Most people at the top are well traveled: four out of five travel outside the United States each year. Europe is the leading destination, but 20 percent travel to South America each year and 40 percent to Asia.

However, it is important to note that most top leaders in corporations and government work long and hard. The norm is sixty to seventy hours per week, traveling six to ten days per month, and spending many weekends devoted to business.[36] Most top elites put their jobs before their families or themselves. On their way to the top, most have relocated six or more times. Most top leaders express the belief that their families' lives have suffered because of their careers. Because they have worked so hard all their lives, retirement is often difficult.

SOCIAL CLUBS: ELITES AT PLAY

Institutional leaders are "joiners." The overwhelming majority of those who hold top positions in America belong to one or more social clubs. More importantly, over one third of the people at the top belong to just a few very prestigious private clubs. Corporate directors, network moguls, Cabinet members, foundation presidents, and superlawyers rub shoulders at places such as the Links and the Knickerbocker in New York, and the Metropolitan and the Burning Tree in Washington. They relax together on a summer outing under California redwoods at the

[35]Robert S. Diamond, "Self-Portrait of the Chief Executive," *Fortune*, May 1970, pp. 181, 320–23.

[36]Based on a *Wall Street Journal*–Gallup Poll survey of chief executives of 1,300 large U.S. companies. *Wall Street Journal*, August 19, 1980, p. 31.

Bohemian Grove. These private clubs provide an opportunity for informal interaction among elites in different segments of society. The importance of these clubs in developing elite consensus and cohesion is the subject of a great deal of speculation. E. Digby Baltzell writes: "At the upper class level in America . . . the club lies at the very core of the social organization of the access to power and authority.[37] Ferdinand Lundberg says: "The private clubs are the most 'in' thing about the . . . elite. These clubs constitute the societal control centers of the elite."[38]

Perhaps the most persuasive case for the importance of such private social clubs is set forth by sociologist G. William Domhoff:

> The Bohemian Grove [a luxury retreat on 2,700 acres of giant redwoods maintained by the Bohemian Club of San Francisco], as well as other watering holes and social clubs, are relevant to the problem of class cohesiveness in two ways. First, the very fact that rich men from all over the country gather in such close circumstances as the Bohemian Grove is evidence of the existence of a socially cohesive upper class. It demonstrates that many of these men do know each other, that they have face-to-face communications, and that they are a social network. In this sense we are looking at [clubs] as a *result* of social processes that lead to class cohesion. But such institutions also can be viewed as facilitators of social ties. Once formed, these groups became another avenue by which the cohesiveness of the upper class is maintained.[39]

The Bohemian Grove, seventy-five miles north of San Francisco, resembles a plush summer camp for older and influential Boy Scouts. Ronald Reagan is a Bohemian, as is George Bush. Here top government officials can relax comfortably with Leonard Firestone (tires), Alden Clausen (BankAmerica), Walter Wriston (Citicorp), Willard C. Butcher (Chase Manhattan), former President Gerald R. Ford, and others of similar status. They may invite guests such as Henry Kissinger, Howard Baker, or Richard Nixon. The Grove itself is divided into a number of camps: the "Owls," "Mandalay," the "Hillbillies," "Cave Men," and so on (Ronald Reagan is an "Owl"). During an encampment, Bohemians try to forget their cares, listen to distinguished speakers, engage in games and skits, drink, and enjoy "good fellowship." Bohemians accept no women as members or as guests or even as employees.

It is our judgment, however, that club membership is a result of

[37]E. Digby Baltzell, *The Protestant Establishment* (New York: Random House, 1964), p. 354.

[38]Ferdinand Lundberg, *The Rich and the Super-Rich* (New York: Bantam Books, 1968), p. 339.

[39]G. William Domhoff, *The Bohemian Grove and Other Retreats* (New York: Harper & Row, 1974), p. 88.

TABLE 7–6 Club Memberships of Top Leaders

	CORPORATE					PUBLIC INTEREST					GOVERNMENT		ALL
	INDUS-TRY	BANK-ING	UTILITIES	INSUR-ANCE	INVEST-MENT	MEDIA	LAW	FOUNDA-TIONS	EDUCA-TION	CIVIC	GOVERN-MENT	MILITARY	
Club Membership %													
None	34.9	30.3	34.6	37.9	16.8	36.1	30.5	30.6	35.8	33.8	76.3	85.9	36.2
One to four	33.3	37.1	39.8	40.2	51.3	39.3	48.4	43.3	29.0	32.8	20.7	11.8	35.4
Five or more	31.8	32.6	25.6	21.9	31.9	24.6	21.1	26.1	35.2	33.4	3.0	2.3	28.4
Exclusive Clubs* %													
None	64	57.4	65.4	70.9	57.5	65.8	65.3	65.8	56.3	63.0	95.7	95.1	64.7
One or more	36	42.6	34.6	29.1	42.5	34.2	34.7	34.2	43.7	37.0	5.3	4.9	35.3

*Links (N.Y.), Century (N.Y.), Knickerbocker (N.Y.), Piping Rock (N.Y.), River (N.Y.), Metropolitan (D.C.), Pacific Union-Bohemian (S.F.), Brook (N.Y.), Burlington (S.F.), California (L.A.), Casino (Chi.), Chagrin Valley (Clev.), Chicago (Chi.), Denver (Den.), Detroit (Det.), Eagle Lake (Hous.), Everglades (Fla.), Hartford (Conn.), Hope (R.I.), Idlewild (Dallas), Maryland (Md.), Milwaukee (Mil.), Minneapolis (Minn.), New Haven Town (Conn.), Philadelphia (Phil.), Rittenhouse (Phil.), Racquet (St. L.), Rainier (Seattle), Richmond (Va.), Cuyamuca (San Diego), Charleston (S.C.), Rolling Rock (Pitts.), Saturn (Buf.), St. Louis (St. L.), Somerset (Bos.), Union (Clev.), Woodhill (Minn.). Listing courtesy of G. William Domhoff.

top position-holding in the institutional structure of society rather than an important independent source of power. An individual is selected for club membership *after* he has acquired an important position in society; he seldom acquires position and power because of club memberships. Personal interaction, consensus-building, and friendship networks all develop in the club milieu, but the clubs merely help facilitate processes that occur anyway. Nonetheless, the club memberships of persons at the top are worthy of attention.

Corporate leaders are more likely to be members of private social clubs than are governmental leaders. Table 7–6 shows that over two thirds of our corporate elites held private club memberships; nearly a third of them held five or more memberships. In contrast, only 23.7 percent of top governmental leaders held such memberships, and even fewer military chiefs were club members. Doubtless this differential reflects the greater importance of social interaction in the corporate world (and perhaps the fact that businesspersons can shift the exorbitant costs of such memberships to their corporations while government officials cannot). The fact that a majority of top governmental and military elites are *not* club members undercuts the importance attributed to club membership by many "power elite" writers. If a majority of top governmental elites do *not* sip cocktails at the Metropolitan Club, it is difficult to argue that the real decision-making in Washington takes place in that club's lounge.

Nonetheless, the fact that nearly half of the top elites in the corporate, legal, educational, foundation, and mass media sectors of society belong to one of *forty* selected clubs is impressive testimony to the prestige of these clubs.

SUMMARY

The elitist literature on power stresses the disproportionate numbers of top leaders drawn from the upper and upper-middle strata of society. But even classical elite theorists acknowledge the necessity of some opportunities for upward mobility in society, if only to strengthen support for the political system among the masses. The pluralist literature on power describes a more open leadership system where individuals from all social backgrounds can rise to the top if they have the necessary skills, information, and talents. However, pluralists acknowledge that opportunities to acquire such qualities are unequally distributed among classes in society. Pluralists also argue that social class is a poor predictor of decision-making behavior. We have not resolved this debate, but perhaps we have added some more factual information about the social composition of top institutional leaders.

On the whole, those at the top are well-educated, older, affluent, urban, WASP, and male. Although a few blacks have recently been appointed to top corporate boards, in 1980 there were hardly more than 20 blacks among the more than 7,000 top position-holders in our study.

Blacks are noticeably absent from corporate boardrooms, and there are few blacks in government, although they represent 12 percent of the U.S. population. Likewise, there are very few women at the top of the nation's institutional structure. Overall, less than 5 percent of top leaders are women. Only recently have women gained entrance into the boardrooms of large corporations. Even in government, despite a vice-presidential nomination and a Supreme Court seat, women still occupy only about 8 percent of the key posts. Women are more likely to be found as trustees of universities, foundations, and cultural organizations, but even in these sectors women leaders are far outnumbered by men. Top women leaders are upper and upper-middle class in origin, like their male counterparts. However, women leaders tend to have more education and they are younger. Women leaders are more likely to have been recruited from education, the mass media, or law, than from the (mostly male) ranks of corporate management.

There is a slight tendency for corporate elites to be more urban and "upper class" than governmental elites. There are more Ivy Leaguers in corporate boardrooms than in government, and there appear to be more private prep school types in corporate management than in government. Governmental leaders tend to have more advanced degrees, not only in law, but also in academic and professional fields.

There are multiple recruitment paths to the top of the nation's institutional structure. The corporate world, however, supplies a majority of the top leaders in the corporate sector itself, as well as in civic and cultural organizations, foundations, and universities. However, top governmental leaders are recruited primarily from the law, and to a lesser extent from government itself and education. The mass media, the law, and education all provide separate recruitment channels. In short, the corporate world, while an important recruitment channel, is not the exclusive road to the top.

CHAPTER 8
CONFLICT AND CONSENSUS AMONG INSTITUTIONAL LEADERS

CONFLICT OR CONSENSUS AMONG ELITES?

How much agreement exists among people at the top about the fundamental values and future directions of American society? Do America's top leaders agree on the *ends* of policies and programs and disagree merely on the *means* of achieving those ends? Or are there significant differences among American elites over the goals and purposes of our society?

Social scientists frequently give conflicting answers to these questions— not because of differences in the results of their research, but because of differences in the interpretation of these results. Although it is sometimes difficult to survey elite attitudes and opinions (individuals at the top do not have much time to spend with pollsters), nonetheless, social scientists have produced a number of good studies of the values of corporate executives, governmental officials, political party leaders, university intellectuals, and even newspersons.

Pluralists contend that these studies reveal significant conflicts between Democrats and Republicans, liberals and conservatives, corporate directors and labor leaders, intellectuals and bankers, and other leadership groups, over a wide range of policy issues. They cite studies showing significant differences between various segments of the nation's elite over tax policy, welfare programs, government regulation of business and labor, energy and environmental questions, alternative approaches to national health care, and the appropriate measures to deal with inflation and recession. The nation's leadership also appears divided over some foreign and defense policy issues: whether or not to build up new manned bombers or new missile systems, the appropriate posture of the United States in strategic arms limitation talks with the Soviets, and how to deal with Soviet-supported insurgencies in the Third World.

By contrast, elitists contend that despite these differences over *specific* policy questions, all segments of American leadership share a broad consensus about the *fundamental* values of private property, limited government, separation of church and state, individual liberty, equality of opportunity, advancement based on merit, and due process of law. Moreover, since the Roosevelt era, American elites have generally supported liberal social welfare programs including social security, fair labor standards, unemployment compensation, a federally aided welfare system, government regulation of public utilities, and countercyclical fiscal and monetary policies. Today, elite consensus also includes a commitment to equality of opportunity for women and blacks and a desire to end direct discrimination. Finally, elite consensus includes a desire to exercise influence in world affairs and to oppose Soviet expansionism.

We contend that there is, indeed, a broad consensus among America's leaders on fundamental values and future directions of the nation. Disagreement among various segments of the nation's elite occurs *within* a framework of consensus on underlying values. The range of disagreement is relatively narrow, and disagreement is generally confined to *means* rather than ends. It is doubtful that any elite, however hierarchical, is ever free of competing ambitions or contending ideas. Indeed, some conflict may be essential to the health of an elite system. Sociologist Suzanne Keller writes:

> The point need not be labored that doubt and conflicts are necessary: societies advance both as a result of achievements and as a result of disagreements and struggles over the ways to attain them. This is where power struggles play a major indispensable role. Loyalty to common goals does not preclude conflict over how they are to be realized.[1]

So we expect to find conventional "liberal" and "conservative" arguments occurring within a broad and unifying consensus.

---

[1]Suzanne Keller, *Beyond the Ruling Class: Strategic Elites in Modern Society* (New York: Random House, 1968), p. 146.

THE LIBERAL ESTABLISHMENT

The traditional philosophy of America's elite has been liberal and public-regarding. By this we mean that institutional leaders have shown a willingness to take the welfare of others into account as an aspect of their own sense of well-being: They have been willing to use governmental power, to correct perceived wrongs done to others. This is a familiar philosophy—elite responsibility for the welfare of the poor and downtrodden, particularly minority populations. The liberal establishment believes that it can change people's lives through the exercise of governmental power: end discrimination, abolish poverty, eliminate slums, ensure employment, uplift the poor, eliminate sickness, educate the masses, and instill dominant culture values in all citizens. The prevailing liberal impulse is to *do good,* to perform public services, and to assist the poorest in society.

Historically, upper-class values in America have been liberal, public-regarding, and service-oriented. Society's elites are confident that with sufficient effort they can improve people's lives. They feel a strong obligation to improve not only themselves but also everyone else, whether they want to be improved or not.

Leadership for liberal reform has always come from America's upper social classes. This leadership is more likely to come from established "old families" rather than "new rich," self-made people. Before the Civil War, abolitionist leaders were "descended from old and socially dominant Northeastern families" and were clearly distinguished from the emerging "robber barons"—the new leaders of the Industrial Revolution. Later, when the children and grandchildren of the robber barons inherited positions of power, they turned away from the Darwinist philosophy of their parents and toward the social welfarism of the New Deal. Liberalism was championed not by the working class, but by men such as Franklin D. Roosevelt (Groton and Harvard), Adlai Stevenson (Choate School and Princeton), Averill Harriman (Groton and Yale), and John F. Kennedy (Choate School and Harvard).

The "elite consensus" defies simplistic Marxian interpretations of American politics; wealth, education, sophistication, and upper-class cultural values do *not* foster attitudes of exploitation, but rather of public service and do-goodism. Liberal elites are frequently paternalistic toward segments of the masses they define as "underprivileged," "culturally deprived," "disadvantaged," and so on, but they are seldom hostile toward them.

Today's upper-class liberalism was shaped in the era of Franklin Delano Roosevelt. Roosevelt came to power as a descendant of two of America's oldest families, the Roosevelts and the Delanos, original Dutch patrician families of New York whose landed wealth predates the English capture of New Amsterdam. The Roosevelts and other patrician families whose wealth was gained well before the Industrial Revolution never fully accepted the Social Darwinism "public be damned," rugged individualism of the industrial capitalists. They were not schooled in the scrambling competition of the upwardly mobile nouveau riche, but instead in the altruism and idealism of comfortable and secure wealth and assured social status. In describing FDR, historian Richard Hofstadter summarizes upper-class liberalism:

> At the beginning of his career he took to the patrician reform thought of the progressive era and accepted a social outlook that can best be summed up in the phrase "noblesse oblige." He had a penchant for public service, personal philanthropy, and harmless manifestos against dishonesty in government; he displayed a broad easy-going tolerance, a genuine liking for all sorts of people; he loved to exercise his charm in political and social situations.[2]

This liberal consensus, of course, is not strictly or necessarily altruistic. *The values of welfare and reform are functional for the preservation of the American political and economic system.* A radical criticism of the liberal establishment is that its paternalism toward the poor and minorities is in reality self-serving; it is designed to end poverty and discrimination while preserving the free enterprise system and the existing class structure.

THE NEOCONSERVATIVES

While American politics continues in the liberal tradition, that tradition is broad enough to encompass critics of "excessive" government interference in society. The war in Vietnam, the Great Society, urban rioting, campus unrest, Watergate, and inflation all combined in the 1960s and 1970s to raise doubts about the size and scope of governmental power. Elite interest in liberal reforms was tempered by the failures and costs of well-meaning yet ineffective (and sometimes harmful) public programs. Elites learned that society's problems cannot be solved simply by passing a law, creating a new bureaucracy, and spending a few billion dollars. War, poverty, ill-health, discrimination, joblessness, inflation, crime, ignorance, pollution, and unhappiness have afflicted society for a long time. Elites no longer assume that these problems can be erased from society by finding and implementing the "right" public policies.

The "neoconservatives" among America's elite continue to be re-

[2]Richard Hofstadter, *The American Political Tradition* (New York: Knopf, 1948), pp. 323–24.

formist and public-regarding, but they no longer have the confidence and ambition (bordering on arrogance) of the liberals of the 1960s. They have more respect for the free market system and less confidence that government regulations will achieve their desired effects. They are more respectful of traditional values and institutions, including religion, family, and the community. They believe in equality of opportunity where everyone is free to strive for whatever they wish, but they do not believe in absolute equality, where the government ensures that everyone gets equal shares of everything. Finally, neoconservatives believe that the United States must maintain a strong national defense if democracy is to survive in a world that is overwhelmingly hostile to American values.[3]

The neoconservatives disapprove of unequal treatment suffered by racial minorities but generally oppose affirmative-action and busing programs that involve racial quotas. Neoconservatives are skeptical that laws, bureaucracies, regulations, and public spending can improve the nation's health or guarantee employment or protect the environment. Government is being "overloaded" with tasks, many of which should be left to the individual, the family, the church, or the free-market system. Government has attempted to do too much for its citizens, and by failing to meet its promises, government has lost respect and legitimacy. The war in Vietnam was not a national "crime," but instead a "tragic error." The United States must regain its military power and remain a force for good in the world.[4]

In its beginning, the neoconservative position was a reaction of a few intellectuals to the turbulence of the 1960s. The early movement included sociologists Nathan Glazer, Irving Kristol, and Daniel Bell; political scientists James Q. Wilson, Aaron Wildavsky, and Daniel Patrick Moynihan (now a U.S. senator from New York); and political sociologist Seymour Martin Lipset. They captured control of an established liberal journal, *Commentary,* and created a new journal of their own *The Public Interest.* A neoconservative base emerged in the American Enterprise Institute, a Washington policy-planning organization that grew to challenge the liberalism of the more prestigious Brookings Institution. (See Chapter 9.)

The message of these neoconservative intellectuals may not have been heard in elite circles if the nation had not faced rampaging inflation and declining productivity. But by 1980, the United States had experienced a decade-long inflation—the worst in its history. Personal savings were disappearing rapidly. The incentive to invest was crippled by high taxes. Factories and machines became outmoded. U.S. products

[3]Irving Kristol, "What Is a Neoconservative?" *Newsweek,* January 19, 1976, p. 87.
[4]Peter Steinfels, *The Neoconservatives* (New York: Simon & Schuster, 1979).

could no longer compete with products from Europe and Japan in the world (and even the U.S.) market. Americans as a whole spent too much and saved too little. Federal tax and budget policies promoted immediate consumption instead of investment in the future. A large segment of the federal government's budget (up to three quarters of it) was declared "uncontrollable"—notably the social insurance, welfare, and pension programs. Heavy taxes discouraged work, investment, and productivity.

The trend toward neoconservatism in elite thinking did not alter the underlying commitment to liberal, reformist values. But it represented a more realistic view of what can be achieved by government, and a more traditional view about the importance of personal initiative, enterprise, work, and family. These views were not limited to the Reagan administration. They enjoyed wide acceptance among the nation's top leaders in every sector of society.

The Reagan administration came to Washington with a well-developed policy agenda. Government, Reagan argued, was the problem, not the solution. Government taxing, spending, and monetary policies promoted immediate consumption, instead of investment and economic growth. Government taxing and spending had to be lowered and inflation brought under control. And indeed in his first term, President Reagan succeeded in reducing *the rate of growth* of nondefense spending, even though social welfare spending continued to grow. Double-digit inflation was cured with a stiff dose of high interest rates, and later both inflation and interest rates declined dramatically. In the Economic Recovery Tax Cut Act of 1981, personal income taxes were reduced on the average by 25 percent. More importantly, in this act and later in the Tax Reform Act of 1986, top marginal tax rates were reduced from 70 percent to 28 percent and many loopholes were closed. Unemployment fell to historically low levels; the numbers *and percentages* of Americans with jobs reached unprecedented high levels. The United States enjoyed the longest continuous expansion of the gross national product in its history. For five years Reagan pursued the rebuilding of America's defense which had begun in the Carter administration. By 1986 the Soviets were sufficiently impressed to begin serious arms negotiations. In 1987 the United States and USSR signed the first arms agreement in history to actually eliminate an entire class of nuclear weapons.

But the combination of lower taxes, increased defense spending, and continued high levels of social welfare spending, produced unprecedented federal deficits. Indeed, the national debt more than doubled during the Reagan administration. Trade imbalances mushroomed and American industry continued to stagnate in world markets. Huge government deficits kept real interest rates high; the United States became the world's largest debtor nation; and future generations were burdened with heavy interest payments. Elites worried that America's prosperity was based on shaky debt foundations, that the nation had mortgaged its future, that a future economic crisis might rival the worst in history.

THE NEOLIBERALS

Today many liberals retain their faith in the power of government to "do good" and to solve society's problems, yet they reject many traditional liberal programs as unworkable. Neoliberalism "is an attempt to combine the traditional Democratic compassion for the downtrodden and outcast elements of society with different vehicles than the categorical aid programs or quota systems or new federal bureaucracies."[5] More than anything else, neoliberalism is a search for *new ideas* for government programs to restore the nation's economic health, uplift the poor, end discrimination, distribute income more equally, and provide education and medical care to all.

Chief among the neoliberal concerns is the nation's economy, which they recognize was inflationary and unproductive under previous liberal administrations. Unlike old liberals who placed social issues first on their agenda, the neoliberals are aware that little progress on social problems can be expected unless the economy is healthy. Instead of the "no growth" attitudes of liberals in the 1970s with their hostility toward industry, science, and technology, the neoliberals argue that government must take an active role in promoting and directing the nation's industrial growth.

Neoliberals propose a national "industrial policy" in which the government would promote and direct investments in order to make the United States more competitive in international markets. Instead of the traditional liberal confrontations between government and business, the neoliberals propose direct government-business cooperation to bolster productivity, encourage investment, promote innovation, and boost international sales. Government might direct grants and loans to stimulate new economic development and industrial revitalization; it might also help to arrange labor settlements that improve productivity and keep down prices. The problem, of course, is whether a government industrial policy would act primarily to encourage new high-tech industries (as many neoliberals suggest) or try to revive the older smokestack industries (as traditional liberals and union leaders wish). Since the neoliberal proposals will encourage shifts in the labor force, they usually

---

[5]Randall Rothenberg, *The Neoliberals* (New York: Simon & Schuster, 1984).

add government "human capital" programs to retrain and relocate workers.

Who are the neoliberals? Among scholars and writers, one might list Lester Thurow, economist and author of *The Zero Sum Society;* Charles Peters, editor of the *Washington Monthly;* James Fallows, author of *National Defense;* and Robert Reich, author of a book on industrial policy, *The Next American Frontier.* These neoliberals are generally critical of the traditional "interest group" liberals who would sacrifice America's growth, productivity, and competitive edge in world markets in order to satisfy the selfish demands of union leaders, protectionist-seeking industries, and other special interests. The struggle between the neoliberals and traditional liberals is being fought mainly *within* the Democratic party.

CONSENSUS ON EQUALITY

Perhaps no issue has been so much at the heart of American political life since the nation's founding than that of equality. Today, voting rights, school busing, feminism, affirmative action, and income redistribution are all essentially questions of equality—what it is, how much we want, and how best to achieve it.

American elites, from the Founding Fathers to the current national leadership, have defined equality as *equality of opportunity*—the elimination of artificial barriers to success, fame, and wealth. *Absolute equality*—the equal division of income and wealth among people—was referred to as "leveling" by our Founding Fathers, and it has always been denounced by the nation's leadership. In 1816, Thomas Jefferson wrote:

> To take from one, because it is thought his own industry and that of his fathers has acquired too much, in order to spare to others, who, or whose fathers have not, exercised equal industry and skill, is to violate arbitrarily the first principle of association, the guarantee to everyone the free exercise of his industry and the fruits acquired by it.[6]

Elites have traditionally defended the principle of merit. At the same time, elites (more than masses) have supported efforts to eliminate artificial barriers to advancement such as race, religion, class, and sex. But support for equality of opportunity has not meant support for equality of results. Despite occasional demagogic rhetoric, redistributional ideas wither and die among national leaders when given specific contextual meanings.

[6]Quoted in Hofstadter, *The American Political Tradition*, p. 45.

Consider a *Washington Post*—Harvard University survey of 2,500 recognized national leaders.[7] These leaders were selected from nine groups: businesspersons, farm leaders, intellectuals, news media executives, Republican officials, Democratic officials, blacks, feminists, and youth. (Of course, these leaders include many individuals who would *not* be considered institutional elites according to our more rigid definition in Chapter 1.) The first question was designed to ascertain the meaning of "equality"—specifically, to learn whether American leaders idealized *equality of opportunity* in the fashion of traditional liberal thought, or *equality of results* in the fashion of modern equalitarianism. The question was: "Which do you prefer: equality of opportunity—giving each person an opportunity for an education to develop his or her ability—or equality of results—giving each person a relatively equal income regardless of his or her education and ability?"

The striking outcome was that *all* of the leadership groups chose *equality of opportunity* by overwhelming margins. Even black, feminist, and youth leaders chose equality of opportunity and rejected equality of results by margins of twelve to one. Businesspersons, farm leaders, and media executives chose equality of opportunity by ninety to one.

The next question was how much inequality was thought to be "fair." Leaders were asked how much a "fair salary" would be for different occupations. The figures shown in Table 8-1 were those produced for "semiskilled workers in an auto assembly plant" and "a president of one of the top 100 corporations."

The most important finding of this inquiry was the belief among *all* types of leaders that inequalities ranging from six to one to thirteen to one were considered fair. Predictably, black and feminist leaders

TABLE 8-1   How Elites Believe Incomes Should Be Distributed

LEADERSHIP GROUPS	AUTO WORKER	CORPORATE EXECUTIVE	EXECUTIVE/WORKER RATIO
Businesspersons	$16,000	$206,000	13 to 1
Farm leaders	12,000	111,000	9 to 1
Intellectuals	17,000	119,000	7 to 1
News media executives	16,000	131,000	8 to 1
Republican officials	13,000	146,000	11 to 1
Democratic officials	16,000	128,000	8 to 1
Blacks	18,000	114,000	6 to 1
Feminists	15,000	88,000	6 to 1
Youth	13,000	105,000	8 to 1

Source: *Washington Post*, September 26, 1976, p. A8.

[7]*Washington Post*, September 26, 1976.

thought business executives deserved somewhat less pay relative to workers than did business executives themselves. But the really striking conclusion is that *all* elites, even minority group leaders, believed large inequalities in income to be fair.

POLITICAL ELITES: DEMOCRATS AND REPUBLICANS

Yet within the national consensus on behalf of private property, free enterprise, rewards according to merit, individual liberty, and due process of law, there are identifiable differences of opinion over specific policies and programs. Conventional politics in the United States center on *party leaders:* Democratic and Republican party leaders differ over "liberal" and "conservative" dimensions. Interestingly, Democratic and Republican rank-and-file *voters* show less disagreement over the issues than party leaders. For example Democratic and Republican party *leaders* can be clearly differentiated as liberals and conservatives. The mass public is more conservative than liberal in self-identification; Democratic voters are evenly split between these labels, while Republican voters tend to describe themselves as conservative. But Republican voters are not as conservative as Republican leaders, and Democratic voters are not as liberal as Democratic leaders.

The same pattern—Democratic and Republican party elites differing with each other, with the mass public somewhere in the middle— occurs on many domestic and foreign policy issues. Democratic leaders want to expand the size and services of government; Republican leaders want smaller government and fewer services; the mass public is evenly divided. Democratic leaders say the government is doing too little for blacks; Republican leaders disagree and so does the mass public, although not as strongly as Republican leaders. Democratic leaders are prepared to cut defense spending; Republican leaders favor keeping it at least at current levels and so does the mass public. Republican leaders are more worried about Communist takeovers in Central American than U.S. involvement in war; Democratic leaders are more worried about war and so is the mass public. In short, political elites have substantial policy disagreements on specific domestic and foreign policy issues.

FACTIONALISM AMONG ELITES

How much conflict exists among America's elites? Are American elites generally cohesive, with only traditional Democratic and Republican affiliations and conventionally liberal and conservative attachments dividing them? Or are there serious conflicts among elites—serious splits that

TABLE 8-2 Democratic and Republican Party Elites Differ with Each Other and the Mass Public over "Liberal" and "Conservative" Labels and Specific Issues

	DEMOCRATIC LEADERS*	MASS PUBLIC			REPUBLICAN LEADERS*
		DEMOCRATS	TOTAL	REPUBLICAN	
Describe self as:					
"Conservative"	5	22	30	43	60
"Liberal"	39	25	20	12	1
Prefer:					
small government, fewer sewers	16	33	43	59	87
bigger government, more sewers	58	56	44	30	3
Agree that government is paying too little attention to needs of blacks	68	45	34	19	14
Favor keeping military and defense spending at least at current levels	32	59	66	73	84
Are more worried about Communist takeover in Central America than about U.S. involvement in war there	12	25	37	55	80

*Republican and Democratic delegates to presidential nominating convention in 1988.

Source: Results reported in New York Times, August 14, 1988.

threaten the national consensus and the stability of the system itself? Are political conflicts in America merely petty squabbles among ambitious individuals, competing interest groups, or competing institutions—all of which agree on the underlying "rules of the game"? Or is American leadership seriously divided—so much so that the very framework of the political system is being shaken?

The pluralist view is that competition is a driving force in the American political system. Yet the very purpose of this system, according to pluralist political theory, is to manage competition, to channel it through the institutional structure, to modify its intensity, to arrange compromises and balance conflicting interests. In short, pluralism recognizes and encourages competition as a system of checks and balances within American society.

In general, pluralists contend that competition will be limited by several forces that act to maintain an "equilibrium" in the political system. First of all, there is supposed to be a large, nearly universal *latent group* in American society that supports the constitutional system and the prevailing rules of the game. This group is not always visible, but it can be activated to administer overwhelming rebuke to any faction that resorts to unfair means, violence, or terrorism. Secondly, *overlapping group membership* is also supposed to maintain the system in equilibrium: Many individuals belong to a number of groups so that group leaderships must moderate their goals and philosophies to avoid offending members who have other group affiliations. Finally, pluralists offer the notion of *checks and balances* that arise from competition itself. No single segment of society—no single group of powerful leaders—could ever command a majority. Thus, the power of corporations is checked by government, government by parties and civic groups, the mass media by government and advertisers, and so on. These "countervailing" centers of power function to check the influence of any single segment of the nation's elite.

Elitists, of course, see a much greater cohesion and unity among various segments of the nation's leadership. Yet elitism does not imply a single, monolithic body of power-holders. Elitism does not pretend that power in society does not shift over time, or that new elites cannot emerge to compete with old elites. Indeed, it is unlikely that there ever was a society in which various individuals and factions did not compete for power and preeminence. A "circulation of elites" is clearly necessary to ensure a renewal of elite leadership through the contribution of slightly different interests and experiences that new members bring to their roles.

Elite theory contends, however, that serious splits among elites—disagreements over the fundamental values and future directions of American society—are rare. Indeed, perhaps the only really serious split in the nation's elite led to the Civil War—the split between Southern planters, landowners, exporters, and slave owners; and Northern manufacturers, merchants, and immigrant employees; over whether the nation's future, particularly its Western land, was to be devoted to a plantation, exporting, slave economy or to a free, small farmer, market economy for domestic manufactured goods. This conflict led to the nation's bloodiest war. However serious we believe our present internal conflicts to be, they do not match the passions that engulfed this nation over a century ago.

THE RISE AND FALL OF THE SUNBELT COWBOYS

Elite factionalism occurs along a number of fault lines. But in our judgment, the most important factional division occurs between the newly rich, entrepreneurial Southern and Western *cowboys* and the established, managerial Eastern *yankees*. We believe this factionalism transcends partisan squabbling among Democrats and Republicans, or traditional riffs between Congress and the President, or petty strife among organized interest groups. The conflicts between *cowboys* and *yankees* derives from differences in their sources of wealth and the newness of the elite status of the *cowboys*.

New opportunities to acquire wealth and power develop as a result of technological changes and adjustments in the economy. In recent decades, major new areas of opportunity have developed in independent oil drilling operations; the aerospace industry; computer technology and business machines; real estate development, particularly in the "Sunbelt" from southern California and Arizona through Texas to Florida; and discount drugs and merchandising, fast foods, and low-cost insurance.

The new wealth of the *cowboys* is frequently unstable. Wealth that is institutionalized in giant corporations—corporations that form the basis of an industrialized economy, such as autos, steel, oil, and chemicals—is likely to remain intact over generations with only minor fluctuations in value. But many of today's *new* rich have acquired their wealth in relatively new and unstable industries. Independent oil operations and the aerospace industry are highly cyclical businesses. The computer industry has shown remarkable change over time. And fortunes in real estate, drugstores, discount merchandising, and low-cost insurance can fluctuate dramatically.

By contrast, the power of established *yankees* is institutionalized and stable. The *Yankees* include the descendants of the great entrepreneurial families of the Industrial Revolution (the familiar Rockefellers, Fords, Mellons, du Ponts, Kennedys, Harrimans, and so forth). Other *yankees* have been recruited through established corporate institutions, Wall Street and Washington law firms, Eastern banking and investment firms, well-known foundations, and Ivy League universities.

The *cowboys* do not fully share in the liberal, social welfarism of the dominant Eastern Establishment. The *cowboys* are "self-made" individuals who have acquired wealth and power in an intense competitive struggle that continues to shape their outlook on life. Their upward mobility, their individualism, and their competitive spirit shape their view of society and the way they perceive their new elite responsibilities. In contrast, the *yankees* have either inherited great wealth or have attached themselves to established institutions of great wealth, power, and prestige. The *yankees* are socialized, sometimes from earliest childhood, in the responsibilities of wealth and power. They are secure in their upper-class membership, highly principled in their relationships with others, and public-regarding in their exercise of elite responsibilities.

The *cowboys* are new to their position; they lack old-school ties, and they are not particularly concerned with the refinements of ethical conduct. The *yankees* frequently regard the *cowboys* with disdain—as uncouth and opportunistic gamblers and speculators, shady wheeler-dealers and influence-peddlers, and uncultured and selfish bores.

The *cowboys* are newly risen from the masses—many had very humble beginnings. But it is their experience in *rising* from the masses that shapes their philosophy, rather than their mass origins. As we would expect, they are less public-regarding and social welfare-oriented than the *yankees,* and tend to think of solutions to social problems in individualistic terms—they place primary responsibility for solving life's problems on the individual. *Cowboys* believe that they "made it" themselves through initiative and hard work and advise anyone who wants to get more out of life to follow the same path. The *cowboys* do not feel guilty about poverty or discrimination—clearly neither they nor their ancestors had any responsibility for these conditions. Their wealth and position was not given to them—they earned it themselves and they have no apologies for what they have accomplished in life. They are supportive of the political and economic system that provided them the opportunity to rise to the top; they are very patriotic—sometimes vocally anti-Communist—and moderate to conservative on most national policy issues.

THE BILLIONAIRE COWBOYS

The personal wealth of the *cowboys* places them at the top of lists of America's wealthiest individuals (Table 2–12). But their wealth is not yet institutionalized in the fashion of the great Establishment families—the

Rockefellers, Mellons, du Ponts. The billionaire *cowboys* do *not* control the nation's largest corporations, banks, utilities, insurance companies, foundations, and policy-planning organizations. Nonetheless, they represent a potential challenge to the Establishment as they consolidate and institutionalize their wealth over time.

A few prominent examples of the operations of the Sunbelt *cowboys* illustrate their freewheeling independence and the instability of their wealth.

THE BECHTELS. Representative of the swashbuckling style of the true Sunbelt *cowboys* is the father and son construction team that heads the Bechtel Corporation. Steven D. Bechtel and his son Steven D. Bechtel, Jr. control a little-known, family-held, corporate colossus, which is the *world's* largest construction company. The senior Bechtel never obtained a college degree, but he acquired engineering know-how as a builder of the Hoover Dam. Bechtel conceived of and built the San Francisco Bay Area Rapid Transit, and he and his son built the Washington, D.C., METRO subway system.

Steven D. Bechtel, Jr. received an engineering degree from Purdue University in 1946 after service in the U.S. Marine Corps during World War II. He worked in many positions in the Bechtel Corporation before replacing his father as chairman.

The Bechtel Corporation has built an entire industrial city—Jubayl in Saudi Arabia; a copper industry including mines, railroads, and smelters in Indonesia; and the world's largest hydroelectric system in Ontario, Canada. Bechtel was fired as the contractor for the Trans-Alaska pipeline when cost overruns first occurred; but the final price of $8 billion turned out to be eight times higher than the original estimate, and it seems in retrospect that Bechtel would have done a more cost-effective job if it had been allowed to complete the work. The Bechtel Corporation remains family-owned, and therefore refuses to divulge to the SEC or other prying bureaucracies its real worth.

The Bechtels have recruited established leaders to direct their far-flung enterprises. Before he became secretary of state, George Shultz was serving as president of the Bechtel Corporation. Before he became secretary of defense, Casper Weinberger was serving as vice-president of Bechtel. Both men had gone to Bechtel after serving in President Nixon's Cabinet, and both men have excellent Eastern Establishment connections. So even though the Bechtels themselves remain independent, their personal wealth and the colossal size of their privately owned corporation allow them to hire the top leadership in the nation.

THE HUNTS. The late billionaire H.L. Hunt was once asked by reporters whether he was worried about his son's extravagance (Lamar Hunt had lost over $1 million in one year as the owner of the new

American League football team, the Kansas City Chiefs). "Certainly it worries me," replied the legendary oil magnate. "At that rate he'll be broke in 250 years."

The senior Hunt began drilling for oil in Smackover, Arkansas, in 1920. His very first well (which he won in a poker game) produced a gusher. By 1937, the independent Hunt Oil Company of Dallas, Texas, was worth millions, and at his death in 1974, H.L. Hunt was believed to be one of the richest men in America. His sons, Nelson Bunker, William Herbert, and Lamar, have continued to amass vast personal wealth. "Bunky" Hunt, who regularly refuses interviews and declines publicity, admitted to a congressional committee that he was probably worth over a billion dollars, but he added, "A billion dollars isn't what it used to be." He refused to say how much he was worth: "Senator, it's been my experience that anyone who knows how much they're worth, ain't worth very much."

Operating out of the First National Bank of Dallas, the Hunts manage a vast array of businesses, including the Hunt Energy Corporation and Placid Oil; 3.5 million acres of real estate, including prime downtown Dallas properties; 100,000 head of cattle; and 700 thoroughbred horses. But in 1979, Bunky Hunt and his brother William Herbert decided on an even more ambitious scheme—to corner the world market in silver.

The Hunts began to buy silver at $6 an ounce. Their purchases were so vast that they decided to buy a leading Wall Street investment firm, Bache Halsey Stuart Shields, to facilitate their operations. When silver jumped to $11 an ounce, they contacted their oil-rich Arab friends and recommended more heavy buying. By early 1980, the Hunts had forced the price of silver to $50 an ounce and their holdings were worth an estimated $7.5 billion. However, much of their holdings were in the form of "futures contracts"—guarantees to pay a set price for silver at a certain date in the future. Rising interest rates in the United States attracted many investors away from silver (and gold) and into high-interest-paying bank certificates and money market funds. Increasingly the Hunts were called upon to pay cash for the unpaid portions of their futures contracts. Finally, on March 27, 1980, "Silver Thursday," the Hunts and their Bache brokers were unable to meet their debts. Panic ensued on Wall Street, as well as in the Federal Reserve System, the U.S. Treasury, and the Commodities Future Trading Commission. The price of silver tumbled to $10 an ounce. Bache was barely saved from bankruptcy, and many investors lost millions. A $1.1 billion loan was made to the Hunts to keep them from dumping their silver on the market and further depressing the price. Their scheme to corner the silver market failed.

The wealth of the Hunts and many other *cowboys* is unstable; it is not tied to large institutions. At one time Bunky Hunt was the world's wealthiest man, worth an estimated $16 billion. Today, the Hunt empire is bankrupt and its assets tied up in bankruptcy court. Other Texas oilmen have also fallen: Clint Murchison, Jr. was forced to sell the Dallas Cowboys and later to file bankruptcy; John Connally, former Texas governor, secretary of the treasury, and oil and real estate entrepreneur, was also forced into bankruptcy. The problems of these new-wealth *cowboys* have been attributed to declining worldwide oil prices and deflation in land and real estate values. Many of them had borrowed heavily to expand their empires only to find interest rates rise and their revenues decline.

THE BASS BROTHERS.   The original Bass fortune was created in typical *cowboy* fashion. Sid Richardson was a Texas oil wildcatter who had worked the fields for many years before finding his gusher. He borrowed, traded, and financed oil leases, and bought out the New York Central railroad, winning and losing fortunes over his lifetime. He backed winners in politics including former Texas Governor John B. Connally and President Lyndon B. Johnson. He never married, but he took in his only nephew, Perry Bass, as a partner. When Sid Richardson died in 1959, he left his Texas oil wells to Perry Bass's four sons.

Today the four Bass brothers control a vast empire in oil and gas (Texaco, Northwest Energy, Consolidated Oil and Gas, Charter Co.); high tech (GTECH, Prime Computers); real estate (downtown Ft. Worth; Americana Hotels; Pier 39, San Francisco; Punta Gorda, Florida); clothing (Munsingwear, Nike); fast foods (Church's Fried Chicken); manufacturing (LTC, Fairchild, Champion Parts, Allis Chalmers); banking (InterFirst); and entertainment (Walt Disney). And their personally owned oil wells keep flowing.

The rapid expansion of the Bass fortune is generally attributed to the skills of the oldest Bass brother—Sid Richardson Bass, named after the family's founder. All of the brothers—Sid, Edward, Robert, and Lee—were schooled at Andover and Yale. Sid Richardson Bass is also a Stanford M.B.A., a trustee of the Yale Corporation, a trustee of New York's Museum of Modern Art, and head of Bass Brothers Enterprises, the umbrella group for the many Bass companies and corporations.

The Basses may not have invented "greenmail," but they have been one of its leading practitioners. "Greenmail" is the profit made by a corporate raider who begins buying up a company's stock, threatens a takeover and ouster of the current management, and then sells his stock back to the worried management at a large profit. The Basses were involved in major threats to the management of Texaco and Walt Disney Productions. The Basses have adopted Ft. Worth as their family project, turning the "cowtown" with its stockyards and familiar scents into a complex of gleaming new towers with fashionable shops and restaurants.

The Basses are deeply involved in Texas politics through their Good Government Fund and the Bass Brothers Political Action Committee. They support both Democrats (U.S. Senator Lloyd Bentsen, former Speaker of the House Jim Wright) and Republicans (U.S. Senator Phil Gramm).

To date, the Bass family has displayed considerable unity, even though each brother is associated with different projects. They are described as simply "the boys" in Ft. Worth.

H. ROSS PEROT. No one better fits the *cowboy* image than the diminutive billionaire Ross Perot. His individualism, patriotism, and hostility toward large bureaucracies—both governmental and corporate— are legendary in Texas and the nation. *Newsweek* refers to him as the "Last Take-Charge Guy in America."[8]

Perot made his fortune in the computer industry, turning an initial investment of $1,000 into a multibillion-dollar business, Electronic Data Systems (EDS). EDS fluctuated violently on the stock market, first rising from $17 a share to $162 and then crashing back to $29. At one point in his career, Perot had the dubious distinction of being the only man ever to *lose* $1 billion.[9] Apparently these stock market fluctuations fascinated Perot, so he purchased du Pont, Walston Inc., one of the largest brokerage firms on the New York Stock Exchange. But Perot failed as a broker; du Pont Walston collapsed and Perot temporarily disappeared from the list of wealthiest Americans. But EDS gradually recovered and Perot's interests in oil, gas, and real estate prospered. In 1984 he sold EDS to General Motors for $2.5 billion and a seat on the GM board.

Perhaps Perot hoped to use his GM post to reform corporate America, to bring to the nation's largest industrial corporation the same initiative, energy, and competitiveness that drove the *cowboy* entrepreneur. But GM was not ready for Perot; his public attacks on GM's "archaic" management style were not appreciated in the boardroom. GM chairman Roger Smith won approval from the board to buy out Perot. Perot left GM, reportedly bitter and vengeful. He went back into the computer business, creating Perot Systems to compete with EDS, now a GM subsidiary.

In the meantime Perot's swashbuckling style was not limited to business. In 1979 Perot solved his own Iranian hostage crisis in typical *cowboy* fashion: by flying to Iran, breaking some of his employees out of jail, and smuggling them to the Turkish border. The exploit inspired a TV miniseries, *On Wings of Angels*. Perot also undertook to reform the Texas school system; he forced Texans to reevaluate traditional priorities by successfully sponsoring a law to require high school football

[8]*Newsweek*, January 9, 1989, p. 38.
[9]"The Man Who Lost a Billion," *Fortune*, September, 1973.

players to pass courses. Perot is a major force in the Vietnam MIA movement.

It is important to note that despite Perot's personal wealth and reputation for power, when he went up against the management of the nation's largest industrial corporation, he lost the big prize—control of the corporation itself.

THE NEW TYCOONS: DONALD TRUMP

Established corporate management has long professed a concern for the public interest and a devotion to the "corporate conscience." Indeed, the Business Roundtable[10] issued a formal *Statement on Corporate Responsibility,* which asserted that "the long-term viability of the business sector is linked to its responsibility to the society of which it is a part."[11] It quotes its own former chairman and the former chairman of General Electric, Reginald Jones:

> A corporation's responsibilities include how the whole business is conducted every day. It must be a thoughtful institution which rises above the bottom line to consider the impact of all of its actions on all, from stockholders to the society at large. *Its business activity must make social sense just as its social activities must make business sense.*[12]

But these sentiments are encountered more often among established corporate managers than among self-made entrepreneurs. They are sentiments more likely to be expressed by *yankees* in New York corporate boardrooms than by *cowboys* lunching at the Dallas Petroleum Club. New tycoons, whether they make their home in Manhattan or Houston, are more likely to believe that they best serve society by serving their own economic interests. They share with a few "classical" economists—most notably Nobel Prize–winner Milton Friedman—the belief that entrepreneurs best serve the nation by pursuing profit, increasing productivity, and striving for optimum efficiency.

Perhaps no one better exemplifies the energy, vision, and daring of America's new generation of self-made tycoons than Donald Trump. The most innovative and celebrated real estate baron of our time, Donald Trump has literally changed the face of our world—from Manhattan's dazzling Trump Tower and Grand Hyatt to the glitzy new

---

[10]The Business Roundtable is discussed in "The Civic Associations" in Chapter 5, and in "The Policy-Planning Establishment" in Chapter 9.

[11]Business Roundtable, *Statement on Corporate Responsibility,* New York, October 1981.

[12]Ibid, p. 14. Italics in original.

casinos of Atlantic City. And Trump's rise to wealth and power, at a very young age, testify to the extraordinary opportunities in America.

Donald Trump started with a mere $50 million—a stake derived from his father's modest yet successful New York building and real estate business. He turned this stake into $1 billion before reaching age thirty. "I gave Donald free rein," said his father. "He has great vision and everything he touches seems to turn to gold. Donald is the smartest person I know."[13]

Young Donald attended private schools in New York City and graduated from New York Military Academy as an honor cadet. As a boy he reportedly hung around his father's construction sites. He started college at Fordham University in New York, but at his father's urging, transferred to the Wharton School at the University of Pennsylvania. Bored with classes, he renovated property in his spare time, worked in his father's office during summers, and absorbed the real estate business. At twenty-two, with his Wharton School degree in hand, he was ready to rebuild New York City. He convinced his father to remortgage apartment buildings to generate cash for expansion; Donald Trump wanted to leave the "outer boroughs"—Queens, the Bronx, Brooklyn—to invade Manhattan.

Trump had already developed a reputation as the boy wonder of New York real estate when the opportunity arose to become a true real estate mogul. In 1974 New York City was on the verge of bankruptcy, and one of tha nation's oldest corporate institutions—the Penn Central railroad—was already bankrupt. Other Manhattan real estate owners were liquidating their holdings or lying low waiting for more promising times. Then Donald Trump appeared, in his early trademark burgundy-colored suits and matching shoes, his initials "DLT" on his shirts, cuff links, and chauffeur-driven Cadillac limousines, offering to buy Penn Central's Manhattan properties. These he purchased for Depression-era prices, and he proceeded to develop, in a deal with the Hyatt Corporation, his first major hotel, the Grand Hyatt. Trump was twenty-eight years old when he negotiated these deals and then pushed a major tax abatement for his new buildings through City Hall. Construction of the magnificent Trump Tower in Manhattan quickly followed, and then Trump turned his sights on Atlantic City. The voters of New Jersey passed a referendum permitting casino gambling in the dilapidated old resort city. Trump moved in quickly, obtained the necessary casino license from the state, and built the dazzling casino-hotel Harrah's. He purchased Resorts International, retained its Taj Mahal property in Atlantic City, and sold its remaining casinos to game-show mogul Merv Griffith. In one of his few failures, he created the USFL to challenge the

[13]Jerome Tuccille, *Trump* (New York: Jove, 1985), p. 57.

NFL for the allegiance of the nation's professional football fans; his team, the New Jersey Generals, prospered but the league floundered.

Typical of many new wealth entrepreneurs, Trump does not hide his assets. Indeed he believes that using his own name on a property increases its value. Currently Trump owns: in Manhattan, the Trump Tower, the Trump Plaza, and the Trump Parc Hotel; in Atlantic City, casinos Trump Plaza and Trump's Castle and the new Taj Mahal; in Palm Beach Florida, Trump Towers and the Mar-a-Lago private mansion, golf course, and beach; as well as the Trump Princess, reportedly the world's greatest private yacht, a ghostwritten book *Trump: The Art of the Deal,* and even a bicycle race—the "Tour de Trump."

Trump has demonstrated that the entrepreneurial spirit can prevail over the bureaucratic repression of government. Trump is politically shrewd and media smart. He regularly succeeds in overcoming the obstacles to development thrown up by armies of bureaucrats in New York City, New York State, and New Jersey. His empire is largely private, operating under a maze of corporate enterprises, most of which bear his own name. He has reportedly attempted to buy control of several of the nation's corporate institutions but has not succeeded in doing so so far.

THE NEW CLASS: AN EMERGING ELITE?

The creation and dissemination of ideas and information has become a central function in advanced industrial societies. Indeed, the importance of this function in modern society has led to the argument that professions in the mass media and entertainment industries, the foundations and think tanks, government bureaucracies and public interest groups, compose the vanguard of an ascendant "New Class" that will eventually displace the old economic leaders as society's ruling elite.[14]

The power of the New Class in a "post-industrial" society is based upon its mastery of knowledge and information, creative ideas, and technical expertise. However, it is generally recognized that the New Class is not yet a cohesive group, nor does it directly control the institutions and resources that are needed to support its work. The New Class is dependent upon governmental and corporate support—research, contracts, grants. Government bureaucracies expand in part because of the demands of these increasingly powerful policy entrepreneurs, program administrators, and public-interest lobbyists. Political scientist Aaron Wildavsky writes about the New Class:

[14]Daniel Bell, *The Coming of Post-Industrial Society* (New York: Basic Books, 1973); B. Bruce-Briggs, ed., *The New Class* (New Brunswick: Transaction Books, 1979); Irving Kristol, *Two Cheers for Capitalism* (New York: Basic Books, 1978).

Its defining existential condition is that high income and professional standing alone do not enable its members to maintain the status and privilege to which they aspire. Their money cannot buy them what they want, so their task, as they define it, is to convince others to pay collectively for what they cannot obtain individually. Thus government lies at the center of their aspirations and operations.[15]

The New Class is *not* an institutional elite; it does *not* exercise formal authority over any significant segment of the nation's material resources; and it is *not* included in our definition of the nation's elite. But we do not dismiss the arguments of the New Class theorists: that ideas, information, and expertise may become "a new form of property" in a "post-industrial" society; that power, wealth, and celebrity may eventually transfer to the holders of this intangible form of property; and that this new elite may hold "significantly different values" than existing elites.

According to sociologist Daniel Bell, the New Class is critical of American business, government, the military, and organized religion; the New Class has contributed to a decline in public confidence in these institutions, as well as a loss of popular faith in traditional values.

However, there is only very limited empirical evidence that the New Class espouses any different values than traditional economic elites. Political scientists Stanley Rothman and S. Robert Lichter surveyed various segments of the New Class—reporters, journalists, and television news producers, in the most influential outlets;[16] top Hollywood movie writers, directors, and producers;[17] and public-interest-group lobbyists and lawyers.[18] If anything, these New Class members came from even *more* privileged social-class backgrounds than traditional economic elites, and they benefited even more from educations at private prep schools and prestigious universities. And the New Class is overwhelmingly white and male.

The New Class generally agrees with traditional elites about the value of the private enterprise system (see Table 8–3). And the New Class certainly supports the notion of unequal incomes based on merit. Socialist ideas about equality in the distribution of wealth are poorly received among these highly competitive and achievement-oriented peo-

[15]Aaron Wildavsky, "Using Public Funds to Serve Private Interests," in *The New Class,* ed. Bruce-Briggs, p. 79.

[16]Stanley Rothman and S. Robert Lichter, "Media and Business Elites," *Public Opinion,* (October—November 1981), pp.42—46.

[17]Stanley Rothman and S. Robert Lichter, "What Are Movie-Makers Made of?" *Public Opinion* (December–January 1984), pp. 14–18.

[18]Stanley Rothman and S. Robert Lichter, "What Interests the Public Interests," *Public Opinion* (April–May 1983), pp. 44–48.

TABLE 8–3 New Class and Traditional Elite Attitudes

PRECENT AGREEING	TRADITIONAL ELITE BUSINESS EXECS	NEW CLASS		
		MEDIA[1]	HOLLYWOOD[2]	PIGs[3]
Private enterprise				
·Big corporations should be publicly owned.	6%	13%	15%	37%
Private enterprise is fair to workers.	89	70	67	NA
Less regulation of business would be good.	86	63	49	18
Meritocracy				
People with more ability should earn more.	90	86	94	71
Role of government				
Government should guarantee jobs.	29	48	38	80
Government should reduce gap between rich and poor.	23	68	59	94
Social-cultural values				
Homosexuality is wrong.	60	25	28	12
Homosexuals should not teach in public schools.	51	15	13	8
Adultery is wrong.	76	47	42	55
Women have a right to decide on abortion.	80	90	96	95

[1]Composed of 240 journalists and broadcasters at "the most influential media outlets." See *Public Opinion* (October–November 1981), pp. 42–46.
[2]Composed of 149 writers, producers, and directors of the 50 top-grossing films from 1965 through 1982. See *Public Opinion* (December–January 1984), pp. 14–18.
[3]Composed of 157 leaders or top staffers of 74 public interest groups ("PIGs") and public interest law firms. See *Public Opinion* (April–May 1983), pp. 44–48.

ple. But it is true that the New Class supports a larger role for government in society than traditional elites.

Perhaps the most obvious distinction between the New Class and traditional elites is found in moral and cultural values. As anyone who has observed the positive portrayal of homosexuality, abortion, and adultery in television, movies, and books would suspect, the New Class is significantly more cosmopolitan than traditional elites.

The New Class theory might be summarized as follows:[19]

1. In a complex and highly technical society, knowledge and expertise are functionally important, and those who have it can challenge traditional institutional elites for control of policy-making.

[19]This summary parallels Clarence N. Stone, "The New Class or the Old Convergence," *Power and Elites*, 1 (September 1984), 1—22.

2. The New Class can develop constituencies for its services and can capture key governmental programs and agencies.
3. The New Class is attitudinally different from traditional economic elites, and working through government and the mass media it can develop its own agenda for social reform and a new ethos for a post-industrial society.

Our reasons for rejecting this New Class notion, in favor of our own institutional elite theory, can be organized along similar lines:

1. The complexity of society actually makes technocratic solutions very uncertain and unreliable.[20] Decision-makers prefer pragmatic, fragmented, sequential decision-making; they are disillusioned with expert advice and frequently skeptical of highly abstract or theoretical solutions to social problems. The technocrats are not on top, but merely on tap, for call by institutional leaders when and if they decide to use them.
2. The New Class has little "common consciousness." Its members are divided between "professional estates" (scientific, technological, scholarly, administrative, legal, cultural) and between various institutional locations (business, media, government, universities, lobbying organizations, law firms, and so on). Moreover, their presumed access to government power is certainly no greater than that of economic elites. Government may have need of expertise, but it also has need of economic resources and the cooperation of those who control those resources.
3. The New Class is deeply committed to the values of individualism and personal merit and supportive of a society in which the most talented, hard-working, creative, and enterprising individuals receive disproportionate rewards. These are the same values that have always inspired America's traditional elites. The New Class has the same social advantages and educational credentials as traditional elites. Its support of the "new morality" in television, films, and books does not threaten the institutional positions or economic interests of traditional elites.

SUMMARY

Elitist and pluralist scholars disagree over the extent and significance of conflict among the nation's leaders. Pluralists observe disagreements over specific programs and policies; they contend that this competition is a significant aspect of democracy. Competition among elites makes policies and programs more responsive to mass demands, because competing elites will try to mobilize mass support for their views. Masses will have a voice in public policy by choosing among competing elites with

---

[20]See David Braybrock and Charles E. Lindblom, *A Strategy for Decision* (New York: Free Press, 1970).

different policy positions. Moreover, competitive elites will check and balance each other and help prevent abuses of power. In contrast, elitist scholars observe a fairly broad consensus among the nation's leaders on behalf of fundamental values and national goals. Elitists contend that the range of disagreement among elites is relatively narrow and generally confined to means rather than ends.

It is our own judgment, based on our examination of available surveys of leadership opinion as well as public statements of top corporate and governmental executives, that consensus rather than competition characterizes elite opinion. Despite disagreements over specific policies and programs, most top leaders agree on the basic values and future directions of American society.

The established liberal values of the nation's leadership include a willingness to take the welfare of others into account as a part of one's own sense of moral well-being, and a willingness to use governmental power to correct the perceived wrongs done to others—particularly the poor, blacks, and other minorities. Popular notions of corporate and financial leaders as exploitative, reactionary robber barons are based on nineteenth-century stereotypes.

Contemporary "neoconservative" and "neoliberal" political statements are merely variations on the underlying liberal consensus of the nation's top leadership. Neoconservatives express less confidence that government bureaucracies and spending programs can achieve liberal values. Neoliberals also express doubts about traditional taxing, spending, and regulatory programs; they call for "new ideas" to achieve the liberal values shared by all top leaders. Disagreement among various sectors of national leadership—businesspersons, Democratic and Republican politicians, bureaucrats, mass media executives, and labor leaders—is confined to a relatively narrow set of issues—the size of government budgets, specific details of tax reform, and the adequacy of current defense spending. There is widespread agreement on the essential components of welfare-state capitalism.

Nonetheless, there is evidence of elite factionalism. In recent years, a major fault line among the nation's leaders is the division between the newly rich Southern and Western *cowboys* and the established Eastern *yankees*. The *cowboys* have acquired their wealth since World War II in independent oil operations, the aerospace and computer industries, Sunbelt real estate from California through Texas to Florida, and discount stores. These *cowboys* do not fully share the liberal values of the established *yankees*. They are self-made persons of wealth and power—individualistic, highly competitive, and politically conservative. The *yankees* have enjoyed wealth for generations or have slowly climbed the rungs of the nation's largest corporations, law firms, banks, and foundations. They have acquired a sense of civic responsibility, and they look upon the *cowboys* as unprincipled gamblers, shady wheeler-dealers, and uncultured influence-peddlers.

Established corporate management generally professes a devotion to "corporate responsibility." They wish to exercise power in public affairs, to be respected in Washington, to cultivate a favorable media image. In contrast, many of new self-made tycoons believe that they best serve the nation by making their enterprises profitable.

Despite the personal wealth and celebrity which many self-made new rich have achieved, they have made few inroads into established institutional power positions. New wealth is often unstable; fluctuations in the prices of oil or real estate can have a drastic effect on the futures of these new tycoons. Established institutional management enjoys a more stable power base. While occasionally threatened by wealthy independent corporate raiders, on the whole, the nation's established corporate leadership has generally succeeded in maintaining its dominant power position.

CHAPTER 9
HOW INSTITUTIONAL LEADERS MAKE PUBLIC POLICY

POLICY AS ELITE PREFERENCE OR GROUP INTERACTION?

Are the major directions of public policy in America determined by a relatively small group of like-minded individuals interacting among themselves and reflecting their own values and preferences in policy-making? Or are the major directions of American policy a product of competition, bargaining, and compromise among a large number of diverse groups in society? Does public policy reflect the demands of "the people" as demonstrated in elections, opinion polls, and interest-group activity? Or are the views of "the people" easily influenced by communications flowing downward from elites?

The elitist model of the policy process would portray policy as the preferences and values of the dominant elite. According to elitist political theory, public policy does not reflect demands of "the people," but rather the interests, sentiments, and values of the very few who participate in the policy-making process. Changes or innovations in public policy come about when elites redefine their own interests or modify their own values. Of course, elite policy need not be oppressive or exploitative of the masses. Elites may be very public-regarding, and the welfare of the masses may be an important consideration in elite decision-making. Yet the central feature of the model is that the *elites* make policy, not the masses. The elite model views the masses as largely passive, apathetic, and ill-informed about policy. Public opinion is easily manipulated by the elite-dominated mass media, so that communication between elites and masses flows downward. The "proximate policy-makers"—the President, Congress, the courts, and bureaucracy—knowingly or unknowingly respond primarily to the opinions of elites.

No serious scholar today claims that the masses make policy—that each individual can directly participate in all of the decisions that shape his or her life. The ideal of the New England town meeting where the citizenry convenes itself periodically as a legislature to make decisions for the whole community is irrelevant in today's large, complex industrial society. Pure democracy is and always has been, a romantic fiction. Social scientists acknowledge that all societies, even democratic societies, are governed by elites.

By contrast, the pluralist model of the policy process portrays public policy as the product of competition, bargaining, and compromise among many diverse *groups* in society. Few individuals can participate directly in policy-making, but they can join groups that will press their demands upon government. Interest groups are viewed as the principal actors in the policy-making process—the essential bridges between individuals and government. Public policy at any time reflects an equilibrium of the relative influence of interest groups. Political scientist Earl Latham describes public policy from the pluralist viewpoint as follows:

> What may be called public policy is actually the equilibrium reached in the group struggle at any given moment, and it represents a balance which the contending factions or groups constantly strive to tip in their favor. . . . The legislature referees the group struggle, ratifies the victories of the successful coalition, and records the terms of the surrenders, compromises, and conquests in the form of statutes.[1]

The individual can play an indirect role in policy-making by voting, joining interest groups, and working in political parties. Parties themselves are viewed as coalitions of groups: the Democratic party, a coalition of labor; ethnic groups, blacks, Catholics, central-city residents, black intellectuals, and southerners; the Republican party, a coalition of middle-class, white-collar workers, rural and small-town residents, suburbanites, and Protestants. According to this model, mass demands flow upward through the interest groups, parties, and elections to the proximate policy-makers.

---

[1]Earl Latham, "The Group Basis of Politics," in *Political Behavior*, eds. Heinz Eulau, Samuel J. Eldersveld, and Morris Janowitz (New York: Free Press, 1956), p. 239.

AN OLIGARCHICAL MODEL OF NATIONAL POLICY-MAKING

Any model of the policy-making process is an oversimplification. The very purpose of a model is to order and simplify our thinking about the complexities of the real world. Yet too much simplification can lead to inaccuracies in our thinking about reality. Some models are too simplistic to be helpful; others are too complex. A model is required that *simplifies,* yet at the same time *identifies,* the really significant aspects of the policy process.

Let us try to set forth a model of the policy-making process derived from the literature on national elites—an "oligarchical model of the national policy-making process." Our model will be an abstraction from reality—not every major policy decision will conform to our model. But we think the processes described by the model will strike many knowledgeable readers as familiar, that the model indeed actually describes the way in which a great many national policies are decided, and that the model at least deserves consideration by students of the policy-making process.

Our "oligarchical model" of national public policy-making is presented in Figure 9–1. The model assumes that the initial resources for research, study, planning, and formulation of national policy *are* derived from corporate and personal wealth. This wealth is channeled into foundations, universities, and policy-planning groups in the form of endowments, grants, and contracts. Moreover, corporate presidents, directors, and top wealth-holders also sit on the governing boards of the foundations, universities, and policy-planning groups to oversee the spending of their funds. In short, corporate and personal wealth provide both the financial resources and the overall direction of policy research, planning, and development.

The foundations are essential linkages between wealth and the intellectual community. The foundations determine broad policy objectives—strategic arms limitations, relations with the Soviet Union and China, defense strategies, urban renaissance, the quieting of racial violence in cities, population control, improved public health care systems, and so forth. The foundations provide the initial "seed money" to analyze social problems, to determine national priorities, and to investigate new policy directions. At a later period in the policy-making process, massive government research funds will be spent to fill in the details in areas already explored by these initial studies.

Universities necessarily respond to the policy interests of foundations, although of course they also try to convince foundations of new and promising policy directions. Nonetheless, research proposals originating from universities that do *not* fit the previously defined "emphasis" of foundation interests are usually lost in the shuffle of papers.

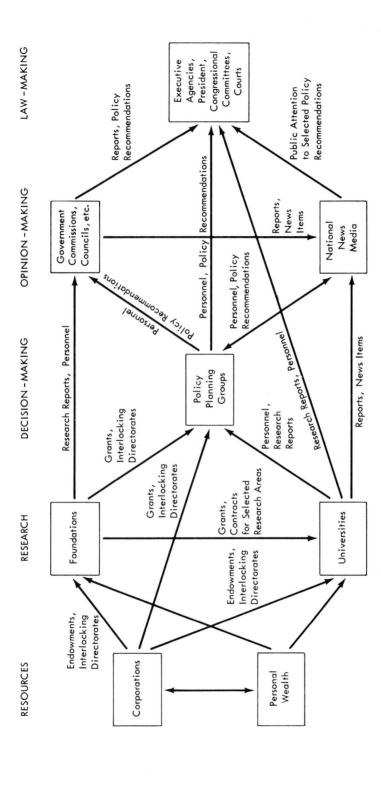

RESOURCES   RESEARCH   DECISION-MAKING   OPINION-MAKING   LAW-MAKING

Executive Agencies, President, Congressional Committees, Courts

Reports, Policy Recommendations

Public Attention to Selected Policy Recommendations

Government Commissions, Councils, etc.

National News Media

Reports, News Items

Personnel, Policy Recommendations

Research Reports, Personnel

Personnel Policy Recommendations

Personnel, Policy Recommendations

Policy Planning Groups

Grants, Interlocking Directorates

Grants, Interlocking Directorates

Personnel, Research Reports

Research Reports, Personnel

Reports, News Items

Foundations

Grants, Contracts for Selected Research Areas

Universities

Endowments, Interlocking Directorates

Endowments, Interlocking Directorates

Corporations

Personal Wealth

FIGURE 9–1   The Policy Process: The View from the Top

251

While university intellectuals working independently occasionally have an impact on the policy-making process, on the whole intellectuals who would be heard must respond to policy directions set by the foundations, corporations, and government agencies that underwrite the costs of research.

The *policy-planning groups* are the central coordinating points in the policy-making process. They bring together people at the top of the corporate and financial institutions, the universities, the foundations, the mass media, the powerful law firms, the top intellectuals, and influential figures in the government. They review the relevant university- and foundation-supported research on topics of interest, and more importantly they try to reach a consensus about what action should be taken on national problems under study. Their goal is to develop *action recommendations*—explicit policies or programs designed to resolve or ameliorate national problems. At the same time, they endeavor to build consensus among corporate, financial, media, civic, intellectual, and government leaders around major policy directions.

Certain policy-planning groups—notably the Council on Foreign Relations, the Business Roundtable, the American Enterprise Institute, and the Brookings Institution—are influential in a wide range of key policy areas. Other policy-planning groups—the Population Council (world population control), Resources for the Future (environmental concerns), and the Urban Institute (urban problems), for example—specialize in certain policy issues.

Corporate representatives—company presidents, directors, or other high officials—sit on the boards of trustees of the foundations, universities, and policy-planning groups. The personnel interlocking between corporation boards, university trustees, foundation boards, and policy-planning boards is extensive. (We have described interlocking among the Rockefeller and Ford foundations, and the Council on Foreign Relations, the Business Roundtable, and the Brookings Institution in Chapter 5.)

Policy recommendations of the key policy-planning groups are then distributed to the mass media, federal executive agencies, and the Congress. The mass media play a vital role in preparing public opinion for policy change. The media define the "problem" as a problem and thus set the agenda for policy-making. They also encourage political personalities to assume new policy stances by allocating valuable network broadcast time to those who will speak out in favor of new policy directions.

The White House staff, congressional committee staffs, and top executive administrators usually maintain close contact with policy-planning groups. Frequently before the results of government-sponsored research are available, federal executive agencies, with the assistance of policy-planning groups, will prepare legislation for the Congress to implement policy decisions. Particular versions of bills will pass between executive agencies, the White House, policy-planning groups, and the professional staffs of the congressional committees that will eventually consider the bills. The groundwork is laid for making policy into law. Soon the work of the people at the top will be reflected in the actions of the "proximate policy-makers."

THE POLICY-PLANNING ESTABLISHMENT

The policy-planning organizations are at the center of this "oligarchic" model of national policy-making. We have already documented their financial support and interlocking directorships with the nation's largest industries, banks, utilities, insurance companies, and the mass media (see Chapter 5).

Now let us turn to some of the policy decisions in which the leading policy-planning organizations—the Council on Foreign Relations and Trilateral Commission, the Business Roundtable, the Brookings Institution, the American Enterprise Institute, and the Heritage Foundation—have been influential.

THE COUNCIL ON FOREIGN RELATIONS. Political scientist Lester Milbraith observes that the influence of the CFR throughout government is so pervasive that it is difficult to distinguish the CFR from government programs: "The Council on Foreign Relations, while not financed by government, works so closely with it that it is difficult to distinguish Council actions stimulated by government from autonomous actions."[2] The CFR itself, of course, denies that it exercises any control over U.S. foreign policy. Indeed its by-laws declare that "The Council shall not take any position on questions of foreign policy and no person is authorized to speak or purport to speak for the Council on such matters."[3] But policy initiation and consensus-building do not require the CFR to officially adopt policy positions.

In the Kennedy and Johnson administrations, the Council took the lead in formulating U.S. policy in Southeast Asia—including both the initial decision to intervene militarily in Vietnam and the later decision to withdraw. Council members in the Kennedy-Johnson administration included Secretary of State Dean Rusk, National Security Adviser

[2]Lester Milbraith, "Interest Groups in Foreign Policy,"in *Domestic Sources of Foreign Policy*, ed. James Rosenau (New York: Free Press, 1967), p. 247.

[3]Council on Foreign Relations, *Annual Report*, 1988, p. 160.

McGeorge Bundy, Assistant Secretary of State for Far Eastern Affairs William P. Bundy, CIA Director John McCone, and Undersecretary of State George Ball. The Council consensus up to November 1967 was clearly in support of the U.S. military commitment to South Vietnam. (Of all top establishment leaders, only George Ball dissented from the war as early as 1965.) Following the Tonkin Gulf Resolution and the introduction of U.S. ground combat troops in February 1965, President Lyndon Johnson created a private, informal group of CFR advisers, with the assistance of CFR chairman John J. McCloy, which later became known as the "Senior Advisory Group on Vietnam." The group was not an official governmental body and it included more private elites than public officeholders. Twelve of the fourteen members of the Senior Advisory Group were CFR members; only Johnson's close personal friend Abe Fortas and General Omar Bradley were *not* CFR members. As the war continued unabated through 1967, the Council, at the urging of George Ball, recruited Professor Hans Morganthau of the University of Chicago to conduct a new private study, "A Reexamination of American Foreign Policy." Following the Tet offensive in February 1968, President Johnson called a special meeting of his Senior Advisory Group. The Group met for two days, March 25 and 26, during which time key members Douglas Dillon, Cyrus Vance, Arthur Dean, Dean Acheson, and McGeorge Bundy switched from "hawks" to "doves." They presented their new consensus to the President. Five days later, on March 31, 1968, President Johnson announced a de-escalation of the war and his personal decision to retire from public office.

At this point, the CFR, which was doubtlessly relieved that Johnson and his immediate advisers were left as the scapegoats of the Vietnam disaster, immediately launched a new group, the "Vietnam Settlement Group," headed by Robert V. Roosa and Cyrus Vance. The group devised a peace proposal allowing for the return of prisoners and a standstill ceasefire, with the Viet Cong and Saigon dividing the territory under their respective controls. Secretary of State Kissinger avoided directly attributing U.S. policy to the CFR plan, but the plan itself eventually became the basis of the January 1973 Paris Peace Agreement.

Following Vietnam, the CFR, under David Rockefeller's tenure as chairman, began its "1980s Project." This was an ambitious program even for so powerful a group as the CFR. But money from the Ford, Lilly, Mellon, and Rockefeller foundations provided the necessary resources. The project officially began in 1975 and lasted until 1980, and it included an international campaign on behalf of "human rights"; an effort to restrict international arms sales; and a study of "North-South global relations"—relations between richer and poorer countries. Upon taking office in 1977, the Carter administration set all of these policies in motion. It restricted international arms sales; it encouraged private and World Bank loans to less developed countries; and, most importantly, it initiated a worldwide "human rights" campaign in which U.S. trade and aid were curtailed in countries that did not live up to human rights standards. Not only did the Carter Administration adopt the CFR program in full, but it also brought CFR members into the government to administer these programs, including Cyrus Vance (secretary of state), Harold Brown (secretary of defense), Walter Mondale (Vice-President), Zbigniew Brzezinski (national security adviser), W. Michael Blumenthal (secretary of the treasury), Sol Linowitz (negotiator of the Panama Canal Treaty), Andrew Young (U.N. ambassador), and Paul Warnke (negotiator of the SALT II Agreement).

But the CFR itself, still under Rockefeller's direction, gradually became aware of the crumbling foreign and military policies of the United States during the Carter administration. In 1980, the CFR issued a stern report citing "sharp anguish over Americans held hostage by international outlaws" (Iran) and "the brutal invasion of a strategic nation" (Afghanistan).[4] It described U.S. defenses as "a troubling question." More importantly, the CFR announced the end of the "1980s Project," with its concern for "human rights," and initiated a new study program—on Soviet Union and U.S.–Soviet relations. Even before Carter left office, leading CFR members had decided that the "human rights" policy was crippling U.S. relations with its allies but was not affecting policies in Communist countries. Moreover, the CFR recognized "the relentless Soviet military build-up and extension of power by invasion, opportunism, and proxy," and recommended that the U.S–Soviet relationship "occupy center stage in the coming decade."[5] Thus, elite support for a harder line in foreign policy and a rebuilding of America's defenses had been developed through the CFR even before Ronald Reagan took office.

The CFR announced its new hard line toward the Soviet Union in a 1981 report, *The Soviet Challenge: A Policy Framework for the 1980s.* It recommended a comprehensive, long-term military build-up by the United States, and it even argued that arms control should no longer be the "centerpiece" of U.S. policy toward the Soviets. It also recommended that the United States be prepared to use force in unstable areas of the world such as the Persian Gulf.

The Reagan administration, like those that preceded it, relied heavily on CFR advice. However, because of some conservative objections to the "internationalism" of the Council on Foreign Relations, CFR members on the Reagan team did not publicize their membership. Indeed, during the 1980 campaign, CFR and Trilateral Commission mem-

[4]Council on Foreign Relations, *Annual Report,* 1979–80, p. 11.
[5]Ibid., p. 12.

ber George Bush was forced to resign from both organizations to deflect right-wing attacks that he was part of the CFR "conspiracy" to subvert U.S. interests to an "international government." Nonetheless, Secretary of State Alexander Haig, Secretary of State George P. Shultz, Defense Secretary Caspar Weinberger, Treasury Secretary Donald Regan, and CIA Director William Casey were CFR members.

When David Rockefeller stepped down as CFR chairman in 1985, his place was taken by Peter G. Peterson, chairman of the board of the Wall Street investment firm, Lehman Brothers Kuhn Loeb, and a director of RCA, General Foods, 3M, Black and Decker, and Cities Services.

The CFR strongly supported the new thaw in U.S.–Soviet relations "spurred by the atmosphere of *glasnost,* the summit, and the Intermediate-range Nuclear Force treaty."[6] It welcomed a number of high Soviet officials to its meetings. NBC anchorman Tom Brokaw introduced Soviet Information Chief Gennadi Gerasimov, and arms negotiator Paul C. Warnke introduced chief Soviet negotiator Victor Karpov. The CFR remains intensely interested in *perestroika* and the future of the U.S.–Soviet nuclear and conventional arms negotiations.

In the controversial area of Central American policy, the CFR urged a policy "obviously at variance" with the Reagan administration's. The CFR wanted "power sharing and a military truce" between the Sandinistas and the democratic resistance within Nicaragua. President Reagan pressed for military aid to the "Contra" guerilla forces. In the end CFR prevailed over the President; Congress abandoned the Contras and ended U.S. efforts to oust the Communist regime from Managua.

The CFR strongly influenced the accession of the Aquino government in the Philippines and the ouster of the Marcos regime. Thus, it now confronts a problem partly of its own making—how to resolve the dispute between the United States and Aquino over U.S. bases in the Philippines.

CFR meetings are secret. The remarks of government officials who speak at CFR meetings are held in confidence. A CFR rule states:

> Full freedom of expression is encouraged at Council meetings. Participants are assured that they may speak openly, as it is the tradition of the Council that others will not later attribute their statements to them in public media or forums or knowingly transmit them to persons who will. All participants are expected to honor that commitment.[7]

The CFR strongly opposes any tendency toward identifiable Re-

---

[6]Council on Foreign Relations, *Annual Report,* 1988, p. 22.
[7]Council on Foreign Relations, *Annual Report,* 1982–83, p. 158.

publican or Democratic party stands on foreign policy. The CFR blamed President Reagan: "There has been a dismaying tendency in recent years for candidates and administrations to denigrate their predecessors and to suggest that truth and virtue are being rediscovered. The fact is that our permanent interests do not change every four years."[8] CFR commissioned its lead article in its journal *Foreign Affairs* in 1988 to reinforce non-partisanship: Henry Kissinger and Cyrus Vance, former Republican and Democractic secretaries of state on "Bipartisan Objectives for American Foreign Policy."[9]

THE TRILATERAL COMMISSION. A discussion of the CFR would be incomplete without some reference to its multinational arm, the Trilateral Commission. The Trilateral Commission was established by CFR Board Chairman David Rockefeller in 1972, with the backing of the Council and the Rockefeller Foundation. The Trilateral Commission is a small group of top officials of multinational corporations and governmental leaders of industrialized nations, who meet periodically to coordinate economic policy between the United States, Western Europe, and Japan. According to David Rockefeller, a small, private group of international bankers, business leaders, and political figures—about 290 in all—can assist governments in a wide variety of decisions. "Governments don't have time to think about the broader, longer-range issues," says Rockefeller, in typically elitist fashion. "It seemed to make sense to persuade a group of private, qualified citizens to get together to identify the key issues affecting the world and possible solutions."[10] Perhaps the most important contribution of the Trilateral Commission was the initiation of regular summit meetings between the heads of Western European nations, the United States, and Japan to discuss economic policy.

In early 1989 Soviet General Secretary Mikhail Gorbachev met with the Trilateral Commission to discuss his proposals for European troop reductions. Former Secretary of State Henry Kissinger represented the United States; former Prime Minister Yasuhiro Nakasone represented Japan; and former French President Valery Giscard d'Estaing represented Europe.[11]

THE BUSINESS ROUNDTABLE. The Business Roundtable was established in 1972 "in the belief that business executives should take an increased role in the continuing debates about public policy." The organization is composed of the chief executives of the 200 largest corpora-

[8]Ibid., p. 24.
[9]Council on Foreign Relations, *Foreign Affairs*, Vol. 66 (Summer 1988).
[10]*Newsweek*, March 24, 1980, p. 38.
[11]*New York Times*, January 19, 1989, p. 4.

tions in America, and is financed through corporate membership fees. Former Du Pont chairman Irving Shapiro summarized the purposes of the Roundtable: "We wanted to demonstrate that there are sensible human beings running big companies, people who think beyond their own interests."[12]

The real impetus to the formation of the Business Roundtable, however, was the worsening inflation of the 1970s, a series of oil crises and resulting public criticism of the oil companies, and the growing consumer and environmental movements that threatened big business with costly regulations. The Roundtable came together from three existing business organizations: (1) the "March Group" of chief executive officers of large corporations, led by John Harper of Alcoa and Fred Borch of General Electric, which was fighting the creation of a federal consumer protection agency; (2) the Construction Users Anti-Inflation Roundtable, headed by Roger Blough of U.S. Steel, which was devoted to combating rising construction costs, especially the cost of labor; and (3) the Labor Law Study Committee, which was fighting changes in labor laws which permit common-site picketing.

Why did corporate America feel that it needed a central policy-planning organization? For many years, the U.S. Chamber of Commerce, the National Association of Manufacturers, the Business Council, and hundreds of industry associations such as the powerful American Petroleum Institute had represented business in traditional pluralist interest-group fashion. Why did business create this super organization? The Business Roundtable itself says:

> The answer is that business leaders believed there was a need that was not being filled, and they invented the Roundtable to fill it. They wanted an organization in which the chief executive officers of leading enterprises would get together, study issues, try to come to a consensus, develop positions and advocate those positions. The executives who created the Roundtable believed that the U.S. economy would be healthier, there would be less unwarranted intrusion by government into business affairs, and the interests of the public would be better served if there were more cooperation and less antagonism. It was decided that one way business could be a more constructive force, and have more impact on government policymaking, was to bring the chief executives directly into the picture. The Roundtable therefore was formed with two major goals:
> —to enable chief executives from different corporations to work together to analyze specific issues affecting the economy and business, and
> —to present government and the public with knowledgeable, timely information, and with practical, positive suggestions for action.[13]

[12]*Times*, April 13, 1981, p. 76.

[13]Business Roundtable public statement, "What the Roundtable Is," dated January 1988—201 Park Avenue, New York, New York, 10166.

In brief, traditional interest-group representation was inadequate for the nation's top corporate leadership. It wished to come together *itself* to decide upon public policy.

The power of the Business Roundtable stems in part from its "firm rule" that a corporate chief executive officer cannot send a substitute to meetings. Congress members were impressed when Frank T. Cary, chairman of IBM, appeared at a congressional hearing on business regulation; or when Theodore F. Brophy, chairman of GTE, spoke to a congressional committee about taxation; or when Robert A. Beck, chairman of Prudential, talked to Congress members about social security; or when John D. Ong of BF Goodrich testified before the Senate Judiciary Committee about antitrust policy. In the Reagan inner circle of friends, Justin Dart, chairman of Dart and Kraft, and Joseph Coors, the Colorado brewer, presented the Roundtable views directly to the President. Irving Shapiro of Du Pont served as Roundtable chairman during its early years. Now the chairman serves a two-year term; recent chairmen have included Clifford Garvin of Exxon, Ruben Mettler of TRW, and Edmund T. Pratt of Pfizer.

The Roundtable was at the forefront of "deregulation," tax cutting, and budget cutting in the Reagan years. One of Reagan's personal friends (Holmes Tuttle) reported: "The morning after the Inauguration, Justin Dart and I sat down with the President and gave him our impression of the budget. We kept saying the same thing: cut, cut, and then cut some more."[14] The Roundtable argued successfully that proposed environmental regulations should undergo economic impact analysis in order to learn what the cost of compliance really is and whether this cost is worth whatever improvement the regulations bring.

The Roundtable perceives current federal deficits as a problem of excessive federal spending, requiring significant reductions in entitlement programs. Tax increases, particularly taxes on business, would harm the United States in international business competition. Robert Kilpatrick of the CIGNA Corporation chaired the Roundtable's Federal Budget Task Force, "reasserting the Roundtable position that the major thrust of deficit reduction must be addressed at the spending side of the budget." The Roundtable favors "de-indexing" of all entitlement programs, including social security, so that Congress would be forced to vote any increases each year.

The Roundtable opposed the plant-closing notification law, and persuaded President Reagan to veto it in 1988. It successfully opposed expansion of the Clean Air Act in 1988, which would have "placed excessive burdens on business based on inadequate environmental analysis." And the Roundtable has taken the lead in opposing federally

[14]*Time*, April 13, 1981, p. 77.

mandated worker health insurance. The Roundtable supported the
U.S.–Canada Free Trade Agreement.

The Roundtable's most pressing current concern is "the abuse of
capital markets" by hostile corporate raiders. The Roundtable represents
managerial opposition to corporate takeovers, and the Roundtable does
not hesitate to ask Congress for protection from the dreaded raiders.
Roundtable member H.B. Atwater, chairman and chief executive officer
of General Mills, testified before Congress in 1987 against "the few
manipulators who put companies into play for short-term financial
gain." He decried the adverse effects of leveraged buyouts on employees, communities, bond markets, and governments. (He tactfully avoided
mentioning the adverse effects of hostile takeovers on ousted top managers.) He named Carl Ichan and T. Boone Pickens as examples of
"manipulators" who sought short-term profits at the expense of corporations and their employees.[15]

THE BROOKINGS INSTITUTION. The Brookings Institution remains
the dominant policy-planning group for American domestic policy. This
is true despite the growing influence of competing think tanks over the
years. Brookings staffers dislike its reputation as a "liberal think tank,"
and they deny that Brookings tries to set national priorities. Yet the
Brookings Institution has been very influential in planning the war on
poverty, welfare reform, national defense, and taxing and spending policies. The *New York Times* columnist and Harvard historian writing team,
Leonard and Mark Silk, describe Brookings as the central locus of the
Washington "policy network," where it does "its communicating: over
lunch, whether informally in the Brookings cafeteria or at the regular
Friday lunch around a great oval table at which the staff and their
guests keen over the events of the week like the chorus of an ancient
Greek tragedy; through consulting, paid or unpaid, for government or
business at conferences, in the advanced studies program; and, over
time, by means of the revolving door of government employment."[16]

The Brookings Institution began as a modest component of the
progressive movement of the early twentieth century. A wealthy St.
Louis merchant, Robert Brookings,[17] established an Institute of Government Research in 1916 to promote "good government," fight "bossism,"
assist in municipal reform, and press for economy and efficiency in

[15]Testimony of H.B. Atwater, Chairman of the Business Roundtable Task Force on
Corporate Responsibility, before the House Committee on Telecommunications and Finance, June 11, 1987.

[16]Leonard Silk and Mark Silk, *The American Establishment* (New York: Basic Books,
1980), p. 160.

[17]Brookings also served as chairman of the board of trustees of Washington University in St. Louis for twenty years, building a small college into a major university.

government. It worked closely with the National Civic Federation and other reformist, progressive organizations of that era. Brookings himself was appointed to the War Production Board by President Woodrow Wilson.

The original trustees of Brookings included Frederic H. Delano (wealthy banker and railroad executive, a member of the first Federal Reserve Board, and an uncle of President Franklin Delano Roosevelt), James F. Curtis (banker and assistant secretary of the treasury under President Taft), Arthur T. Hadley (president of Yale University), Herbert Hoover (then a self-made millionaire engineer and later secretary of commerce and President of the United States), and Felix Frankfurter (Harvard law professor, later to become Supreme Court Justice).

The first major policy decision of the Brookings Institution was the establishment of an annual federal budget. Before 1921, the Congress considered appropriation requests individually as they came from various departments and agencies. But the Brookings Institution proposed, and the Congress passed, the Budget and Accounting Act of 1921, which created for the first time an integrated federal budget prepared in the executive office of the President and presented to the Congress in a single budget message. This notable achievement was consistent with the early interests of the Brookings trustees in improving economy and efficiency in government.

The Brookings Institution assumed its present name in 1927, with another large gift from Robert Brookings as well as donations from Carnegie, Rockefeller, and Eastman (Kodak). It also added Wall Street lawyer Dean Acheson to its trustees; he remained until his appointment as secretary of state in 1947. For many years, the full-time president and executive officer of Brookings was Robert D. Calkins, former dean of the School of Business at Columbia University.

Under the leadership of Robert Calkins, the Institution broke away from being "a sanctuary for conservatives" and recruited a staff of in-house liberal intellectuals. The funds for this effort came mainly from the Ford Foundation; later a Ford Foundation staff worker, Kermit Gordon, was named Brookings Institution president. (He served until his death in 1977.) First under Calkins and later under Gordon, Brookings fashioned itself as a policy-planning organization and rapidly gained prestige and prominence in elite circles. When Republicans captured the presidency in 1968, Brookings became a haven for unemployed liberal Democratic intellectuals and bureaucrats. "In the late sixties and early seventies, Brookings took on the appearance of a government-in-exile as refugees from the Johnson Administration found new offices in the Brookings edifice. . . ."[18] Charles L. Schultze, former chairman of the

---

[18]Silk and Silk, *The American Establishment*, p. 154.

Council of Economic Advisers, began the publication of an annual "counter-budget" as a critique of the Nixon budgets. These are published each year under the title "Setting National Priorities." President Kermit Gordon, drawing on his experience as budget director under President Johnson, pressed forward with the notion of an alternative to the presidential budget. Gordon persuaded Charles Schultze and Alice Rivlin at Brookings to develop a proposal for a new congressional budget and a Congressional Budget Office. In 1974, Congress obligingly established new budgetary procedures, and created new and powerful House and Senate Budget Committees, and a new joint Congressional Budget Office headed, of course, by Brookings staffer Alice Rivlin.

The Brookings Defense Analysis Project was begun in 1969 and resulted in a series of studies which, in the words of a Brookings report, "informed and stimulated debate in the Congress, the executive branch and the press." Perhaps the most important recommendation to emerge from the Defense Analysis Project was the recommendation to drop the B-1 bomber from the U.S. arsenal. Brookings made its B-1 report in February 1976; President Carter announced the cancellation of the bomber in July 1977 despite strong recommendations of military advisers to retain the bomber. But Brookings clearly overpowered the "military-industrial complex." The B-1 bomber was revived by the Reagan administration.

Brookings, however, is clearly part of the larger Washington establishment:

> Above all, Brookings is part of the Washington system. Its purpose is to influence public policy, and to be influential it must have a highly developed sense of the possible and accept the status quo in its essentials. [19]

Brookings people are encouraged to move in and out of top government posts. The current Brookings president, Bruce MacLaury, has said:

> In principle it is good to have people moving in and out of the government. This is the advantage which Brookings has over a place like Yale: that people have gotten their hands dirty.[20]

Louis W. Cabot, chairman of the board of trustees of the Brookings Institution, declares that "The top challenge for Brookings is to anticipate the major policy issues of the future. . . . Thanks to Brookings'

[19]Ibid., p. 157.
[20]Ibid., p. 158.

modest endowment, we are able to set our own agenda and focus on what we believe to be the most important public policy issues."[21] Economic issues have dominated the Brookings agenda: slow growth of American productivity, international trade imbalances, and federal deficits.

Do the trustees determine research directions at Brookings? This is a very sensitive topic. In a heated letter to the *Journal of Politics* in 1979, Brookings Governmental Studies director Gilbert Y. Steiner asserted that "the trustees have precious little authority over anything and none at all over the findings and conclusions that are presented in Brookings books."[22]

However, President MacLaury has acknowledged that the trustees are deeply engaged in the activities of Brookings to the point of vetoing proposed research projects and that interventions by the trustees have caused controversy within the institution. Brookings scholars, with their university backgrounds, expect academic freedom. But MacLaury was quoted in the *New York Times* as saying: "There is always the question about the role of the trustees, particularly with regard to academic freedom. But we are a think tank. We are not a university."[23] Chairman Louis W. Cabot states that "Our trustees enrich our research planning with pragmatic insights gained from experience in business and finance, government, the law, and academe. They provide the direction and commitment needed to keep Brookings and its work up to the standards we have set for ourselves."[24]

Brookings scholars are recruited for their potential contributions to policy-making, not for their teaching or even their scholarship per se. They are recruited to work on areas of interest to Brookings. They do not enjoy tenure. They need not obtain project grants or contracts in order to undertake a study, as scholars in most other think tanks must do. The power of the president, trestees, and benefactors does not extend to the management of policy research.

Yet according to the Brookings bylaws, the board of trustees "is responsible for general supervision of the Institution, approval of fields of investigation, and safeguarding the independence of the Institution's work." The president is given the resposibility for recommending policy research projects and selecting the staff; the board of trustees selects the president. These structural arrangements ensure that the trustees,

[21]The Brookings Institution, *Annual Report*, 1988 p. 3.

[22]Gilbert Y. Steiner, "On Dye's Presidential Address," *Journal of Politics*, 41 (February 1979), 315–16.

[23]Quoted in *New York Times*, December 14, 1983, p. 8.

[24]The Brookings Institution, *Annual Report*, 1988, p. 4.

and implicitly the financial contributors, maintain overall institutional control.

THE AMERICAN ENTERPRISE INSTITUTE.   For many years, Republicans dreamed of a "Brookings Institution for Republicans" which would help offset the liberal bias of Brookings itself. In the late 1970s, that role was assumed by the American Enterprise Institute (AEI). The American Enterprise Association, as it was first called, was founded in 1943 by Lewis H. Brown, chairman of the Johns-Manville Corporation, to promote free enterprise. William J. Baroody, Sr., a staffer at the U.S. Chamber of Commerce, became executive director in 1962 and adopted the name American Enterprise Institute. William J. Baroody, Jr. assumed the presidency of AEI after his father. In 1976, the AEI provided a temporary haven for many Ford administration refugees, including Treasruy Secretary William E. Simon, Transportation Secretary Carla Hills, and AEI's "Distinguished Fellow," former President Gerald R. Ford. More importantly, however, the AEI began to attract distinguished "neoconservative" scholars, including sociologist Irving Kristol, economist Murray Weidenbaum (later chairman of the Council of Economic Advisers), and political scientists Seymour Martin Lipset, Austin Ranney, and Jeanne Kirkpatrick (former U.N. ambassador). The AEI appealed to both Democrats and Republicans who were beginning to have doubts about big government. The AEI began the publication of two excellent journals—*Public Opinion* and *Regulation.* President William Baroody, Jr. distinguished the AEI from Brookings:

> In confronting societal problems those who tend to gravitate to the AEI orbit would be inclined to look first for a market solution . . . while the other orbit people have a tendency to look for a government solution.[25]

But Robert V. Roosa, former chairman of the Brookings Institution, and senior partner in the Wall Street investment firm of Brown Brothers, Harriman & Co., resented the implications that Brookings is "liberal," while the AEI is "conservative":

> AEI is selling against Brookings. They don't have to do that—they have a role to fill. . . . We do some things on the conservative side—and more now. . . . We say to corporations "We're on your side too."[26]

THE HERITAGE FOUNDATION.   Conservative ideologues have never been welcome in the Washington establishment. Yet influential conservative businessmen gradually came to understand that without an institu-

---

[25]Silk and Silk, *The American Establishment,* p. 179.
[26]Ibid.

tional base in Washington they could never establish a strong and continuing influence in the policy network. Their estrangement from the centers of power were captured in a statement from the Heritage Foundation:

> In those days (1975) we jokingly used to say a phone booth was just about big enough to hold a meeting of conservative intellectuals in Washington . . . we were considered irrelevant by the "opinion-makers" in the media and the power-brokers in the Congress ignored us . . . A conservative "think tank," they said, was a contradiction in terms; conservatives had no ideas. History, of course, has proven them wrong.[27]

So they set about the task of "building a solid institutional base" and "establishing a reputation for reliable scholarship and creative problem-solving." The result of their efforts was the Heritage Foundation.

The Heritage Foundation was the brainchild of several congressional staffers and conservative publicists, including the direct-mail wizard Paul Weyrich. The funding came from Colorado businessman-brewer Joseph Coors, who was later joined by two drugstore magnates, Jack Eckerd of Florida and Lewis I. Lehrman of New York. Heritage boasts that it accepts no government grants or contracts and that it has a larger number of individual contributors than any other think tank. Prominent among its trustees are Frank Shakespeare, chairman of the board of RKO; Robert F. Dee, chairman of the board of SmithKline Beckman; William E. Simon, former secretary of the treasury; and Coors, Eckerd, and Lehrman. Prominent among its contributors are the Richard Mellon Scaife and the John M. Olin foundations.

Unquestionably, competition among think tanks is affected by the outcome of national elections. The Heritage Foundation would have been unlikely to win much influence in Washington had Ronald Reagan not been elected President. Heritage prides itself on being "on the top of the news" with quick *Backgrounders*—reports and memoranda ready at the drop of a press release. Scholarly books and monographs are not in style at Heritage. "Marketing is an integral part of Heritage's product," explains President Edwin Feulner. Despite the emphasis on current, topical, and brief analyses, the Heritage Foundation's flagship publication, *Policy Review*, has gained respect in academic circles.

Heritage is "unabashedly conservative." Resident scholars at Heritage are not particularly distinguished. President Feulner explains, "AEI has the big names—the Herb Steins, the Arthur Burnses. We have young Ph.D.s just out of graduate school on their first or second job."[28] But

[27]Heritage Foundation, *Annual Report*, 1985, p. 1.

[28]Charles Holden, "Heritage Foundation: Court Philosophers" *Science*, 211 (1981), 1019–20.

there is very little direct evidence of Heritage influence in public policy. The Reagan administration came to Washington with the most conservative agenda in fifty years. The Heritage Foundation helped publicize that agenda, but there are no specific policy initiatives that can be traced to Heritage. At its tenth anniversary banquet in 1984, Reagan hailed the foundation as changing "the intellectual history of the West" and testified to its "enormous influence on Capitol Hill and—believe me, I know—at the White House." George Bush was even more extravagant, telling Heritage, "You have been real world movers." But these plaudits were designed more to polish the conservative images of the President and Vice-President than to describe the real influence of Heritage. Heritage inflates its own image by taking credit for policies that would have been enacted anyway. Liberals unintentionally cooperate in this image-making by attributing sinister power to this conservative think tank.

THE POLICY-PLANNING DIRECTORS

A collective portrait of the trustees of CFR, the Business Roundtable, and the Brookings Institution confirms the impressions derived from the brief biographies presented in Chapter 5. Those biographies "flesh out" the statistics in Table 9–1; "naming names" reminds us that the leaders of the policy-planning organizations are real people. But the aggregate figures on corporate, governmental, university, and civic organization interlocking, as well as the education and social character of these individuals, also deserve attention.

First of all, it is clear that the policy-planning organizations do in fact provide structured linkages with the corporate world. The directors of these policy-planning organizations averaged over four corporate directorships each; only 6 percent of the policy-planning directors were *not* members of corporate boards. In the CFR, only Graham T. Allison, J.F. Kennedy School dean at Harvard, and Lane Kirkland, AFL–CIO president, reported holding *no* corporate directorships. *All* Roundtable directors are corporate directors; indeed, one must be a corporate chief executive officer as a condition of membership. On the Brookings board, only one college professor, together with Lane Kirkland, reported holding *no* corporate directorships.

Second, the directors of the policy-planning organizations have considerable government experience. They averaged 1.2 government posts during their careers; about half of all of the directors reported some governmental experience. Almost all of the CFR directors held governmental posts at one time or another in their careers. Half of the Brookings directors had served in government. This is an important comment of the four organizations: Clearly the CFR and Brookings

TABLE 9-1   The Policy-Planning Directors: A Collective Portrait

	CFR N = 22	BROOKINGS N = 18	ROUNDTABLE N = 44	TOTAL N = 84
POSITIONS EVER HELD				
Corporate directorships				
Average number	3.2	5.0	4.3	4.1
(% with none)	(18.2%)	(11.1%)	(0%)	(6.0%)
Government offices				
Average number	3.0	1.2	0.4	1.2
(% with none)	(4.5%)	(50.0%)	(75.0%)	(51.2%)
University trusteeships				
Average number	1.0	1.0	1.3	1.2
(% with none)	(31.8%)	(38.9%)	(27.3%)	(32.1%)
Civic association offices				
Average number	5.2	5.7	5.3	5.1
(% with none)	(0%)	(0%)	(6.8%)	(2.4%)
Total institutional affiliations				
(average)	12.4	12.4	11.3	11.6
EDUCATION				
Percent college education	100.0%	100.0%	100.0%	100.0%
Percent prestigious university*	81.8%	77.7%	52.3%	69.0%
Percent law degree	22.7%	11.1%	11.4%	17.9%
Percent graduate degree				
(including law)	90.9%	66.7%	47.7%	58.3%
SOCIAL CHARACTER				
Percent female (number)	9.0%(2)	11.1%(2)	0	2.3%
Percent black (number)	4.5%(1)	5.5%(1)	0	1.2%
Average age	57.5	57.7	58.9	59.9
Private club membership				
Average number	2.8	3.4	3.0	2.9
(% with none)	(36.4%)	(27.8%)	(34.1%)	(31.0%)

*Harvard, Yale, Chicago, Stanford, Columbia, M.I.T., Cornell, Northwestern, Princeton, Johns Hopkins, Pennsylvania, and Dartmouth.

Source: Marquis, *Who's Who in America*, 1980–81. Data on eight directors were not available.

directors are more experienced in governmental affairs than the directors of the Business Roundtable.

Third, the policy-planning directors maintain an active interest in education. The average director held 1.2 university trusteeships; only 32 percent of our directors had *not* held a university trusteeship.

Fourth, it is clear that the policy-planning directors also form a bridge between their organizations and a wide range of civic and cultural organizations. The average director held five reported posts (not merely memberships) in civic and cultural associations. These included, for example, the Metropolitan Museum of Art; the Rockefeller, Ford, and Carnegie foundations; and other policy-planning groups such as the Urban Institute, American Assembly, and Resources for the Future. Only 3 percent did *not* report holding official posts in civic or cultural organizations.

The coordinating function of the policy-planning directors is made strikingly clear when we observe that the directors averaged over eleven institutional positions each! Certainly, the policy-planning organizations provide extensive linkages with the corporate, governmental, university, and civic and cultural institutions.

If we investigate their educational backgrounds, we find that the policy-planning directors are distinctively "Ivy League." Over two thirds of the directors of the CFR, the Business Roundtable, and the Brookings Institution graduated from just twelve prestigious universities. Nearly 20 percent of the policy-planning directors are lawyers. More importantly, perhaps, is the prevalence of postgraduate degrees among the policy-planning directors, including law degrees and an impressive number of M.B.A.s and Ph.D.s from prestigious universities. Over half of the directors held advanced degrees, and this figure does *not* include the numerous honorary degrees that are regularly bestowed upon them. This finding supports speculations by other writers of the growing importance of expertise in policy-planning.

In addition to their impressive educational credentials, and a great deal of experience in corporate, governmental, university, and civic affairs, the policy-planning directors bring considerable experience in life itself to their jobs—their average age is sixty. However youthful the *staffs* of the policy-planning organizations may be, overall direction of these organizations is secure in the hands of experienced individuals of public affairs. Membership in private clubs (emphasized as a coordinating device by some writers) was common: The average director reported 2.8 club memberships. Only about one third did *not* report any club memberships.

In brief, the policy planners have a great deal of experience in directing affairs in the corporate, governmental, university, and civic worlds. They are extraordinarily well educated, with the majority holding advanced degrees and most of these obtained from prestigious Ivy League universities. And, of course, the policy-planning directors are overwhelmingly white, male, and middle-aged.

THE ROLE OF THE "PROXIMATE POLICY-MAKERS"

The activities of the "proximate policy-makers"—the President, Congress, federal agencies, congressional committees, White House staff, and interest groups—in the policy-making process have been described in countless books and articles. The term *proximate policy-maker* is derived from political scientist Charles E. Lindblom, who uses it merely to distinguish between citizens and elected officials: "Except in small political systems that can be run by something like a New England town meeting, not all citizens can be the immediate, or *proximate*, makers of policy. They yield the immediate (or proximate) task of decision to a small minority."[29] In typically pluralist fashion, Lindblom views the activities of the proximate policy-makers as the *whole* of the policy-making process. But our oligarchic model of public policy-making views the activities of the proximate policy-makers as only the *final phase* of a much more complex process. This is the open, public stage of policy-making, and it attracts the attention of the mass media and most political scientists. This public phase of policy-making is much easier to study than the private actions of corporations, foundations, universities, policy-planning groups, and mass media executives. Most pluralists concentrate their attention on this phase of public policy-making and conclude that it is simply a process of bargaining, competition, and compromise among governmental officials.

Undoubtedly, bargaining, competition, persuasion, and compromises over policy issues continue throughout this final law-making phase of policy-making. This is particularly true in the formulation of domestic policy; by contrast, the President is much freer to pursue elite recommendations in foreign and military policy areas without extensive accommodation of congressional and interest-group pressures. Of course, many elite recommendations fail to win the approval of Congress or even of the President in the first year or two they are proposed. Conflict between the President and Congress, or between Democrats and Republican, or liberals and conservatives, and so forth, may delay or alter somewhat the final actions of the proximate policy-makers.

But the agenda for policy consideration has been set by other elites *before* the "proximate policy-makers" become actively involved in the policy-making process. The major directions of policy change have been determined, and the mass media have prepared the public for new policies and programs. The formal law-making process concerns itself with details of implementation: Who gets the "political" credit, what agencies get control of the program, and exactly how much money will be spent? These are not unimportant questions, but they are raised and decided within the context of policy goals and directions that have already been determined. These decisions of the "proximate policy-makers" tend to center about the *means* rather than the *ends* of public policy.

[29]Charles E. Lindblom, *The Policy-Making Process* (Englewood Cliffs, N.J.: Prentice-Hall, 1968), p. 30.

SUMMARY

Pluralist scholars focus their attention on the activities of "the proximate policy-makers"—the President, Congress, the courts, and bureaucracy. They observe competition, bargaining, and compromise among and within these public bodies over specific policies and programs. They observe the role of parties, interest groups, and constituents in shaping the decision-making behavior of these proximate policy-makers. But it is quite possible that the activities of the proximate policy-makers are merely the final phase of a much more complex structure of national policy formation.

Our oligarchical model of national policy-making attempts to trace elite interaction in determining the major directions of national policy. It portrays the role of the proximate policy-makers as one of implementing through law the policies that have been formulated by a network of elite-financed and elite-directed policy-planning groups, foundations, and universities. The proximate policy-makers act only after the agenda for policy-making has already been set, the major directions of policy changes have been decided, and all that remains is the determination of programmatic specifics.

The initial resources for research, study, planning, and formulation of policy come from donations of corporate and personal wealth. These resources are channeled into foundations, universities, and policy-planning groups. Moreover, top corporate elites also sit on the governing boards of these institutions to help determine how their money will be spent. The policy-planning groups—such as the Council on Foreign Relations, the Business Roundtable, the American Enterprise Institute, and the Brookings Institution—play a central role in bringing together individuals at the top of the corporate and governmental worlds, the foundations, the law firms, and the mass media, in order to reach a consensus about policy direction.

CHAPTER 10
INSTITUTIONAL ELITES
IN AMERICA

Power in America is organized into large institutions, private as well as public—corporations, banks, investment firms, governmental bureaucracies, media empires, law firms, universities, foundations, cultural and civic organizations. The nation's resources are concentrated in a relatively few large institutions, and control over these institutional resources is the major source of power in society. The people at the top of these institutions—those who are in a position to direct, manage, and guide institutional programs, policies, and activities—compose the nation's elite.

The *systematic* study of the nation's institutional elite is still in an exploratory stage. Although a great deal has been written about "the power elite," much of it has been speculative, impressionistic, and polemical. Serious difficulties confront the social scientist who wishes to move away from anecdote and ideology to serious scientific research on national elites—research that "names names," attempts operational definitions, develops testable hypotheses, and produces some reliable information about national leadership.

The first task confronting social science is to develop an opera-

271

tional definition of national elite. Such a definition must be consistent with the notion that great power resides in the institutional structure of society; it must also enable us to identify by name and position those individuals who possess great power in America. Our own definition of a national institutional elite produced 7,314 elite positions. Taken collectively, individuals in these positions controlled more than one half of the nation's industrial assets; more than one half of all the assets in communications and utilities; two thirds of all banking assets; more than three quarters of all insurance assets; and they directed the nation's largest investment firms. They commanded nearly half of all assets of private foundations and universities, and they controlled the television networks, the national press, and major newspaper chains. They dominated the nation's top law firms and the most prestigious civic and cultural associations and occupied key federal government posts in the executive, legislative, and judicial branches and the top military commands.

Our selection of positions of institutional power involved many subjective judgments, but it provided a starting place for a systematic inquiry into the character of America's elite structure. It allowed us to begin investigation into a number of important questions: Who are the people at the top of the institutional structure of America? How did they get there? What are their backgrounds, attitudes, and values? How concentrated or dispersed is their power? Do they agree or disagree on the fundamental goals of society? How much cohesion or competition characterizes their interrelationships? How do they go about making important policy decisions or undertaking new policy directions?

HIERARCHY AND POLYARCHY
AMONG INSTITUTIONAL ELITES

Before summarizing our data on institutional elites, it might be helpful to gain some theoretical perspectives on our findings by suggesting *why* we might expect to find evidence of either hierarchy or polyarchy in our results.

European social theorists—notably Weber and Durkheim—provide theoretical explanations of why social structures become specialized in advanced societies, and why coordination mechanisms are required. These theorists suggest that increasing functional *differentiation* of elites occurs with increasing socioeconomic development. In a primitive society, it is difficult to speak of separate economic, political, military, or administrative power roles; in primitive life, these power roles are merged together with other roles, including kinship, religion, and magical roles. But as separate economic, political, bureaucratic, and military institutions develop, and specialized power roles are created within these institutions, separate elite groups emerge at the top of separate institutional structures. The increased division of labor, the scale and complexity of modern social organizations, and specialization in knowledge, all combine to create functional differentiation among institutional elites. This suggests polyarchy among elites in an advanced society such as the United States.

Yet even though specialized elite groups are required to direct relatively autonomous institutional sectors, there must also be some social mechanisms to coordinate the exercise of power by various elites in society. This requirement of *coordination* limits the autonomy of various institutional elites. Thus, specialization acts to bring elites together, as well as to force them apart. Social theory does not necessarily specify *how* coordination of power is to be achieved in modern society. Nor does it specify *how much* unity is required to maintain a relatively stable social system or, conversely, how much competition can be permitted. Certainly there must be *some* coordination if society is to function as a whole. The amount of coordination can vary a great deal, however, and the mechanisms for coordination among elites differ from one society to another.

One means of coordination is to keep the relative size of elite groups small. This smallness itself facilitates communication. If there are relatively few people who actually direct institutional activity, then these people can have extraordinary influence on national policy. What's more, the small size of these groups means that institutional leaders are known and accessible to each other. Of course, policy-planning groups, governmental commissions, and advisory councils, or informal meetings and conferences, are instrumental in bringing "specialists" together. But how small *is* America's elite? C. Wright Mills, wisely perhaps, avoids any estimate of the size of "the power elite"; he says only that it is "a handful of men."[1] Floyd Hunter estimates the size of "top leadership" to be "between one hundred and two hundred men."[2] We have already indicated that our definition of the elite produces an estimated size of 7,314 positions occupied by 5,778 individuals—considerably more than implied in the power elite literature, but still few enough to permit a great deal of personal interaction.

Another coordinating mechanism is to be found in the methods by which elites are recruited. The fact that elites who are recruited to different institutional roles share the same social class and educational backgrounds should provide a basis for understanding and communica-

[1] C. Wright Mills, *The Power Elite* (New York: Oxford University Press, 1956), p. 7
[2] Floyd Hunter, *Top Leadership, U.S.A.* (Chapel Hill: University of North Carolina Press, 1959), p. 176.

tion. Social homogeneity, kinship links, similarity of educational experience, common membership in clubs, common religious and ethnic affiliations, all help to promote unity of outlook. Yet at the same time we know that a certain amount of "circulation of elites" (upward mobility) is essential for the stability of a social system. This means that some heterogeneity in social background must be tolerated. But again social theory fails to quantify the amount of heterogeneity that can be expected.

A related mechanism for coordination is common career experiences. If elite members were drawn disproportionately from one career field—let us say industry or finance—there would be greater potential for unity. But again, social theory does not tell us how much, if any, commonality in career lines is functionally requisite for coordination of specialized elites.

Still another form of coordination is a general consensus among elites on the rules to resolve conflicts and to preserve the stability of the social system itself. Common values serve to unify the elites of various institutional systems. Moreover, agreement among elites to abide by the rule of law and to minimize violence has a strong utilitarian motive, namely to preserve stable working arrangements among elite groups. Finally, unifying values also legitimize the exercise of power by elites over masses, so the preservation of the value system performs the dual function of providing the basis of elite unity, while at the same time rationalizing and justifying for the masses the exercise of elite power. Unfortunately, social theory does not tell us *how much* consensus is required among elites to facilitate coordination and preserve a stable social system. Social theory tells us that elites must agree on more matters than they disagree, but it fails to specify how broad or narrow the range of issues can be.

Because social theory suggests *both* convergence and differentiation among institutional elites, it is possible to develop competing theoretical models of the social system—models which emphasize either hierarchy or polyarchy. For example, the notion of the "power elite" developed by C. Wright Mills implies *hierarchy* among economic, political, and military power-holders. The idea suggests unity and coordination among leaders of functionally differentiated social institutions. Mills speculates that a large-scale, centralized, complex, industrial society *necessitates* coordination:

> At the pinnacle of each of the three enlarged and centralized domains, there have arisen those higher circles which make up the economic, the political, and the military elites. At the top of the economy, among the corporate rich, there are the chief executives; at the top of the political order, the members of the political directorate; at the top of the military establishment, the elite of soldier-statesmen clustered in and around the

Joint Chiefs of Staff in the upper echelon. . . . Each of these domains of power—the warlords, the corporation chieftains, the political directorate— tend to come together, to form the power elite of America.[3]

Thus, the hierarchical or elitist model rests upon the theoretical proposition that increasing complexity requires a high degree of coordination and consequently a great concentration of power.

In contrast, the polyarchical or pluralist model emphasizes differentiation in institutional structures and leadership positions—with different sets of leaders and different institutional sectors of society and with little or no overlap, except perhaps by elected officials responsible to the general public. According to this view, elites are largely specialists, and leadership roles are confined to a narrow range of institutional decisions. These specialists are recruited through separate institutional channels—they are not drawn exclusively from business or finance. Further, the functional specialization of institutional elites results in competition for power, a struggle in which competing elites represent and draw their strength from functionally separate systems of society. How do pluralists assume coordination is achieved among elites? The argument is that functionally differentiated power structures produce an equilibrium of competing elites. Resulting checks and balances of competition are considered desirable to prevent the concentration of power and assure the responsibility of elites.

In short, social theory postulates both hierarchy *and* polyarchy among elites in the social system. It is the task of systematic social science research to determine just *how much* convergence or differentiation exists among elites in the national system.

WHO'S RUNNING AMERICA? SUMMARY OF FINDINGS

Our findings do not all fit neatly into either an hierarchical, elitist model of power, or a polyarchical, pluralist model of power. We find evidence of both hierarchy and polyarchy in the nation's institutional elite structure. Let us try to summarize our principle findings regarding the questions posed at the beginning of this volume.

1. CONCENTRATION OF INSTITUTIONAL RESOURCES. The nation's resources are concentrated in a relatively small number of large institutions. More than one half of the nation's industrial assets are concentrated in 100 industrial corporations; two thirds of U.S. banking assets are concentrated in the fifty largest banks; and one half of our assets in communications and utilities are concentrated in fifty corporations.

[3]Mills, *The Power Elite*, pp. 8–9.

More than three quarters of the nation's insurance assets are concentrated in just fifty companies; fifty foundations control 40 percent of all foundation assets; twenty-five universities control two-thirds of all private endowment funds in higher education; three network broadcasting companies control 70 percent of the television news and entertainment; and fifteen newspaper empires account for more than one half of the nation's daily newspaper circulation. It is highly probable that thirty Wall Street and Washington law firms exercise comparable dominance in the legal field; that fifteen Wall Street investment firms dominate decision-making in securities; and that a dozen cultural and civic organizations dominate music, drama, the arts, and civic affairs. Federal government alone now accounts for 22 percent of the gross national product and two thirds of all government spending. More importantly, concentration of resources in the nation's largest institutions is increasing over time.

2. INDIVIDUAL VERSUS INSTITUTIONAL RESOURCES. The resources available to individuals in America are infinitesimal in comparison with the resources available to the nation's largest institutions. Personal wealth in itself provides little power; it is only when wealth is associated with top institutional position that it provides the wealth-holder with any significant degree of power.

Managerial elites are gradually replacing owners and stockholders as the dominant influence in American corporations. Most capital investment comes from retained earnings of corporations and bank loans, rather than from individual investors.

Nonetheless, personal wealth in America is unequally distributed: The top fifth of income recipients receives over 40 percent of all income, while the bottom fifth receives less than 5 percent. This inequality is lessening very slowly over time, if at all.

3. THE SIZE OF THE NATION'S ELITE. Approximately 6,000 individuals in 7,000 positions exercise formal authority over institutions that control roughly half of the nation's resources in industry, finance, utilities, insurance, mass media, foundations, education, law, and civic and cultural affairs. This definition of the elite is fairly large numerically, yet these individuals constitute an extremely small percentage of the nation's total population—less than three-thousandths of 1 percent. However, this figure is considerably larger than that implied in the "power elite" literature.

Perhaps the question of hierarchy or polyarchy depends on whether one wants to emphasize numbers or percentages. To emphasize hierarchy, one can comment on the tiny *percentage* of the population that possesses such great authority. To emphasize polyarchy, one can comment on the fairly large *number* of individuals at the top of the nation's institutional structure; certainly there is room for competition within so large a group.

4. INTERLOCKING VERSUS SPECIALIZATION. Despite concentration of institutional resources, there is clear evidence of specialization among institutional leaders. Eighty-five percent of the institutional elites identified in our study were specialists, holding only one post of the 7,314 "top" posts. Of course, many of these individuals held other institutional positions in a wide variety of corporate, civic, and cultural organizations, but these were not "top" positions as we defined them. Only 15 percent of our institutional elites were interlockers holding more than one top post at the same time.

However, the multiple interlockers—individuals with six or more top posts—not surprisingly turned out to be giants in the industrial and financial world. Another finding is that there was a good deal of vertical overlap—top position-holders who have had previous experience in other top corporate, governmental, and legal positions—more so than there is horizontal (concurrent) interlocking. Only one quarter of governmental elites have held high corporate positions, and nearly 40 percent of the corporate elites have held governmental jobs. Yet even this vertical overlapping must be qualified, for most of the leadership experience of corporate elites was derived from *corporate* positions, and most of the leadership experience of governmental elites was derived from *government and law.*

There are, however, important concentrations of combined corporate, governmental, and social power in America. Large corporations such as AT&T have many interlocking director relationships with industrial corporations, banks, utilities, and insurance companies. There are identifiable groupings of corporations by interlocking directorships; these groupings tend to center around major banks and regions of the country. In addition, there is concentration of power among the great, wealthy, entrepreneurial families—the Rockefellers, Mellons, duPonts, Fords. One of the most important of these concentrations over the years has been the Rockefeller family group, which has had an extensive network in industrial, financial, political, civic, educational, and cultural institutions.

5. INHERITORS VERSUS CLIMBERS. There is a great deal of upward mobility in American society, as well as "circulation of elites." We estimate that less than 10 percent of the top corporate elites studied inherited their position and power; the vast majority climbed the rungs of the corporate ladder. Most governmental elites—whether in the executive bureaucracy, Congress, or the courts—also rose from fairly obscure positions. Elected political leaders frequently come from parochial backgrounds and continue to maintain ties with local clubs and groups.

Military leaders tend to have the largest percentage of rural, southern, and lower-social-origin members of any leadership group.

6. SEPARATE CHANNELS OF RECRUITMENT. There are multiple paths to the top. Our top elites were recruited through a variety of channels. Governmental leaders were recruited mainly from law and government; fewer than one in six was recruited from the corporate world. Military leaders were recruited exclusively through the military ranks. Most top lawyers rose through the ranks of the large, well-known law firms, and mass media executives were recruited primarily from newspaper and television. Only in the foundations, universities, and cultural and civic associations was the formal leadership drawn from other sectors of society.

7. SOCIAL CLASS AND ELITE RECRUITMENT. Individuals at the top are overwhelmingly upper- and upper-middle-class in social origin. Even those who climbed the institutional ladder to high position generally started with the advantages of a middle-class upbringing. Nearly all top institutional elites are college-educated, and half hold advanced degrees. Elites are notably "Ivy League": 54 percent of top corporate leaders and 42 percent of top governmental leaders are alumni of just twelve well-known private universities. Moreover, a substantial proportion of corporate and government leaders attended one of just thirty-three private "name" prep schools.

Very few top corporate or governmental elites are women, although more women are now being appointed to top corporate boards. A greater number of women serve in top positions in the cultural world, but many of these women do so because of their family affiliation.

It is clear that very few blacks occupy any positions of authority in the institutional structure of American society. We estimated that in 1980 only about ten blacks served as directors of the nation's corporations, banks, or utilities.

Corporate elites are somewhat more "upper-class" in origin than are governmental elites. Governmental elites had slightly lower proportions of private prep school types and Ivy Leaguers than corporate elites, and governmental elites were less eastern and urban in their origins than corporate elites. Governmental leaders in our study had more advanced professional degrees (generally law degrees) than did corporate elites.

8. CONFLICT AND CONSENSUS AMONG ELITES. Elites in all sectors of American society share a consensus about the fundamental values of private enterprise, limited government, and due process of law. Moreover, since the Roosevelt era, elites have generally supported liberal, public-regarding, social welfare programs—including social security, fair labor standards, unemployment compensation, a federally aided welfare system, government regulation of public utilities, and countercyclical fiscal and monetary policies. Elite consensus also includes a desire to end minority discrimination—and to bring minority Americans into the mainstream of the political and economic system. Today's liberal elite believes that it can change people's lives through the exercise of governmental power—eliminate racism, abolish poverty, uplift the poor, overcome sickness and disease, educate the masses, and generally *do good.*

While American politics continue in this liberal tradition, there has been a growing disillusionment among elites with government interventions in society, and a reaffirmation of the role of the home, the community, and the free market in shaping society. The neoconservatives are still liberal and public-regarding in their values, but inflation, Watergate, civil unrest, and Vietnam combined to dampen their enthusiasm for large, costly government programs. Even among neoliberals there is a realization that many old liberal programs and policies are inadequate to society's needs today, and they are committed to a search for "new ideas" to foster economic growth and cure society's ills.

Elites from all sectors of society (even leaders of blacks, women, and youth) believe in equality of opportunity rather than absolute equality. Elites throughout American history have defended the principle of merit. Absolute equality, or "leveling," has never been part of the nation's elite consensus.

Elite disagreement does occur *within* this consensus over fundamental values. However, the range of disagreement is relatively narrow and tends to be confined to means rather than ends. Specific policy disagreements among various elite groups occur over questions such as the oil depletion allowance, federal versus state and local control of social programs, tax reform, specific energy and environmental protection proposals, and specific measures for dealing with inflation and recession.

9. FACTIONALISM AMONG ELITES. Traditional pluralist theory emphasizes competition between Democrats and Republicans, liberals and conservatives, labor and management, and other conventional struggles among interest groups. Elitist theory, on the other hand, emphasizes underlying cohesion among elite groups, but still admits of some factionalism. A recognized source of factionalism is the emergence of new sources of wealth and new "self-made" individuals who do not fully share the prevailing values of established elites. Since the eve of World War II, new bases of wealth and power have developed in independent oil-drilling operations, the aerospace industry, computer technology, real estate development in the Sunbelt (from southern California to Florida), discount drugs and merchandising, fast foods, and low-cost insurance. We have labeled these new elites "the Sunbelt *cowboys.*"

The *cowboys* are not liberal or public-regarding, or as social welfare–oriented as are the *yankees*, our label for the established institutional elites. The *cowboys* tend to think of solutions to social problems in much more individualistic terms, and they are generally moderate to conservative on most national policy issues.

Despite the self-importance of many new persons of wealth, established eastern institutional wealth and power continue to dominate national life. New wealth is frequently unstable and highly sensitive to economic fluctuations.

10. AN OLIGARCHIC MODEL OF NATIONAL POLICY-MAKING. Traditional pluralist theory focuses attention on the activities of the proximate policy-makers in the policy-making process, and the interaction of parties, interest groups, President and Congress, and other public actors in the determination of national policy. In contrast, our oligarchic model of national policy-making views the role of the proximate policy-makers as one of deciding specific means of implementing major policy goals and directions which have *already been determined* by elite interaction.

Our oligarchic model assumes that the initial resources for research, study, planning, organization, and implementation of national policies are derived from corporate and personal wealth. This wealth is channeled into foundations, universities, and policy-planning institutions, where corporate representatives and top wealth-holders exercise ultimate power on the governing boards. Thus, the foundations provide the initial seed money to analyze social problems, to determine national priorities, and to investigate new policy directions. Universities and intellectuals respond to the research emphases *determined by the foundations* and produce studies that conform to these predetermined emphases. Influential policy-planning groups—notably the Council on Foreign Relations, the Business Roundtable, the American Enterprise Institute, and the Brookings Institution—may also employ university research teams to analyze national problems. But their more important function is consensus-building among elites—bringing together individuals at the top of corporate and financial institutions, the universities, the foundations, and the top law firms, as well as the leading intellectuals, the mass media, and influential figures in government. Their goal is to develop action recommendations—explicit policy recommendations having general elite support. These are then communicated to the proximate policy-makers directly and through the mass media. At this point federal executive agencies begin their research into the policy alternatives suggested by the foundations and policy-planning groups. The role of the various public agencies is thus primarily to fill in the details of the policy directions determined earlier. Eventually, the federal executive agencies, in conjunction with the intellectuals, foundation executives, and policy-planning-group representatives, prepare specific legislative proposals, which then begin to circulate among "the proximate policy-makers," notably White House and congressional committee staffs.

The federal law-making process involves bargaining, competition, persuasion, and compromise, as generally set forth in pluralist political theory. But this interaction occurs *after* the agenda for policy-making has been established and the major directions of policy changes have already been determined. The decisions of proximate policy-makers are not unimportant, but they tend to center about the *means* rather than the *ends* of national policy.

POWER: INSIDER AND OUTSIDER VIEWS

Powerful people seldom acknowledge their own power. David Rockefeller was once asked to analyze his own power. He responded in a fashion typical of many elites:

> If you are interested in the analysis of power, I would think this is somewhat relevant: I'm not sure it is the power of an individual or even an institution, but more the power of cooperation and ideas.[4]

Washington insiders—top government officials and influential staffers, consultants and scholars in the foundation and think tanks, columnists and reporters—see their environment as pluralistic, competitive, and constantly changing. They do not see themselves as "elites"; they are acutely aware of their defeats, frustrations, and limitations. They view "ruling-class" theorists as hopelessly naïve, unschooled, and inexperienced. Leading scholars who come to Washington to the Brookings Institution or the American Enterprise Institute or government itself, compare their own influence with that of competing policy-planning scholars, not with the thousands of scholars outside of the network. They rarely write about their own power, and when they do it is usually in self-deprecatory terms.

From an insider's perspective, then, the policy "process" appears highly competitive, constantly changing, and occasionally chaotic, in the way that Polsby and other pluralists describe it.[5] Winning in the power "game" is the goal. Players in the game, both institutions and individuals, strive to influence policy in order to win prestige, celebrity, and a reputation for power. Economic resources are a means to power, not the

---

[4]Quoted in *Forbes*, May 15, 1972, p. 250.
[5]See Nelson Polsby, "Tanks but No Tanks," *Public Opinion* (April–May 1983), pp. 14–16.

end of power. The competition is fierce. No one wins every battle; defeats, frustrations, and standoffs are experienced by even the most powerful players. Winners today are losers tomorrow. Insiders describe the Washington policy process from this individualistic viewpoint. There is no central direction to the process. Issues change almost daily; no one regularly controls the agenda.

To outsiders, however, the policy network appears highly structured. If there are hundreds of academics who have acquired the status of Washington insiders, there are tens of thousands who have not. Students of the policy network who are themselves outside of that network tend to see a highly structured set of relationships among corporations, foundations, think tanks, and government. They attribute little importance to the petty jostling for prestige, status, and influence among individuals—politicians, bureaucrats, businessmen, or intellectuals. They perceive this competition to be narrow in scope and bounded by institutional constraints. They perceive a consensus on behalf of economic growth, a stable business cycle, incentives for investment, economy and efficiency in government, a stable two-party system, and maintaining popular support for political institutions. Disagreement occurs over the means to achieve these ends, not over the ends themselves. Outsiders describe the policy network from an organizational and societal perspective, rather than from an individual perspective.

WHO'S RUNNING AMERICA? THEORY AND RESEARCH

Systematic research on national leadership is no easy task. Most of the serious social science research on elites in America has concentrated on local communities. Frequently, analysts have extrapolated the knowledge derived from *community* power studies to *national* power structures. As a result, much of our theorizing about power in America rests on inferences derived from the study of community life. Yet to assume that national elites are comparable to community elites not only violates the laws of statistical sampling but also runs contrary to common-sensical understanding of the size and complexity of institutions at the national level.

We do not yet have sufficient evidence to confirm or deny the major tenets of elitist or pluralist models of national power. Our research on institutional elites produces evidence of both hierarchy and polyarchy in the nation's elite structure. If we were forced to summarize our views of the elitist-pluralist debate in the light of our findings, we could do no better than to draw upon a brief statement that appears near the end of G. William Domhoff's book, *The Higher Circles:*

If it is true, as I believe, that the power elite consist of many thousands of people rather than several dozen; that they do not meet as a committee of the whole; that there are differences of opinion between them; that their motives are not well known to us beyond such obvious inferences as stability and power; and that they are not nearly so clever or powerful as the ultraconservatives think—it is nonetheless also true, I believe, that the power elite are more unified, more conscious, and more manipulative than the pluralists would have us believe, and certainly more so than any social group with the potential to contradict them. If pluralists ask just how unified, how conscious, and how manipulative, I reply that they have asked a tough empirical question to which they have contributed virtually no data.[6]

But we shall avoid elaborate theorizing about pluralism, polyarchy, elitism, and hierarchy in American society. Unfortunately, theory and conceptualization about power and elites have traditionally been so infected with ideological disputation that it is presently impossible to speculate about the theoretical relevance of our data on institutional leadership without generating endless, unproductive debate.

Our purpose has been to present what we believe to be interesting data on national institutional elites. We will leave it to our readers to relate this data to their own theory or theories of power in society. We do believe, however, that systematic understanding of power and elites must begin with operational definitions, testable hypotheses, and reliable data if we ever expect to rise above the level of speculation, anecdote, or polemics in this field of study.

---

[6]William Domhoff, *The Higher Circles* (New York: Random House, 1970), p. 299.

INDEX

Lankforth, Philip M., 183
Lapp, Ralph E., 102
Lasky, Victor, 46
Lasswell, Harold, 3, 17
Latham, Earl, 249
law, 10, 138–47
Lerner, Daniel, 3
"liberal establishment," 161–63, 224–25
Lichter, Linda, 135
Lichter, S. Robert, 135, 243
Lincoln Center, 152–53
Lindblom, Charles E., 15, 16, 245, 269
Lipset, Seymour Martin, 226
Lundberg, Ferdinand, 218
Lynd, Robert, 3

MacRae, Duncan, 183
managers, 33–43, 50–52
Mann, Dean E., 99, 100, 191
Matthews, Donald R., 191
McCoombs, Maxwell F., 118
media, 10, 116–37
mergers, 36–41
Metropolitan Museum of Art, 151–52, 163
Michels, Robert, 4
Milbraith, Lester, 253
military, 11, 101–04
Mills, C. Wright, 4, 5, 6, 60, 103, 139, 166, 174, 273, 274, 275
Mintz, Beth, 167
Moore, Gwen, 168, 193, 210
Mosca, Gaetano, 3
multi-nationals, 25–27
Museum of Modern Art, 152, 163

neoconservatives, 225–28
neoliberals, 228–29
"new class," 242–45
Nielsen, A. C., 134

Ostrander, Susan A., 195
ownership, 43–48, 52–56

Panitt, Merritt, 131
Pareto, Vilfedo, 2
Peters, Charles, 229
Phillips, Kevin, 126
pluralism, 6–9
politicians, 66–88

policy-making, 248–70, 280
Polsby, Nelson, 8, 165, 281
power
  bureaucratic, 11, 93–101
  congressional, 11, 104–11
  corporate, 10, 15–63
  definition, 4–9
  economic, 15–63
  foundations, 11, 117–51
  governmental, 11, 64–115
  institutional, 4–6, 271–83
  interlocking, 165–86, 272–77
  judicial, 111–13
  media, 10, 116–37
  military, 11, 101–04
  policy-making, 248–70
  positions, 9–13
"preppy," 193–94
president, 66–88

"raiders," 36–41
recruitment, 187–221
Reich, Robert, 229
Ricci, David, 165
Robinson, Michael, 128, 130, 135
Rockefeller Foundation, 150, 162
Rose, Arnold M., 165
Rothenberg, Randall, 228
Rothman, Stanley, 135, 243

Schmidhauser, John R., 112
Schultz, Robert O., 4, 5
Segal, Michael, 82
Shaw, Donald I., 118
Sheehan, Robert, 45
Sherrill, Robert, 73
Silk, Leonard, 162, 163, 260, 264
Silk, Mark, 162, 163, 260, 264
Smart, Reginald G., 188
Smigel, Erwin O., 139
Smith, David N., 161
Smith, Diane K., 135
Smith, Robert Rutherford, 119
Smithsonian Institution, 153–54
Stanley, David T., 99, 100, 191
Steiner, Gilbert Y., 263
Steinfels, Peter, 226
Stewart, James B., 140
Stone, Clarence N., 244
Supreme Court, 111–13
Swartz, Michael, 167
Sweezy, Paul M., 29

LEADERSHIP INDEX